THE
DECLINE
of
NATIONS

The DECLINE *of* NATIONS

FIRST EDITION

Copyright 2020 Joseph F. Johnston

ISBN: 9781645720072 (Hardcover)

ISBN: 9781645720089 (ebook)

For inquiries about volume orders, please contact:

Republic Book Publishers

501 Slaters Lane #206

Alexandria VA 22314

editor@republicbookpublishers.com

Published in the United States by Republic Book Publishers

Distributed by Independent Publishers Group

www.ipgbook.com

Book designed by Mark Karis

Printed in the United States of America

THE
DECLINE
of
NATIONS

JOSEPH F. JOHNSTON, JR.

REPUBLIC

BOOK PUBLISHERS

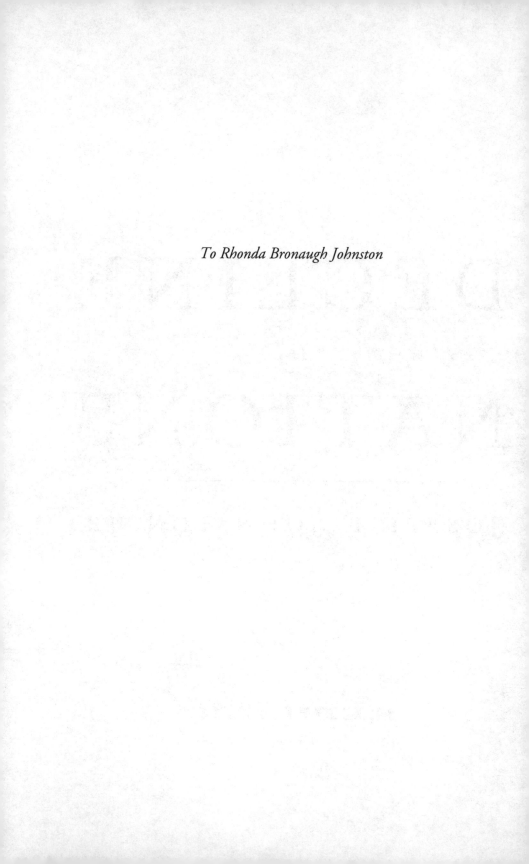

To Rhonda Bronaugh Johnston

CONTENTS

ACKNOWLEGMENTS

I WANT TO GIVE SPECIAL THANKS to Ben Koons, a graduate of Princeton and Oxford and a graduate student in philosophy at Yale, for his skillful and thorough research assistance and editorial advice on this project. I am also grateful to Nick Capaldi and Don Rumsfeld for their very helpful comments. Thanks also to John Vella for his assistance on early drafts of this book. In addition, many thanks for their advice and comments to Al Regnery, Eric Kampmann, Megan Trank, Dane Starbuck, Bill Greene, Sam Holt, Lauren Mann and Aymerique d'Alton. I want to acknowledge the invaluable assistance of my wife, Rhonda Johnston—a scholar, astute historian and wise counselor.

Finally, I want to express my gratitude to Liberty Fund, and to all of my former colleagues there, who provided me with an incomparable continuing education in the ideas which really matter.

INTRODUCTION

"If Sparta and Rome perished, what State can hope to endure forever?"
—JEAN-JACQUES ROUSSEAU, *THE SOCIAL CONTRACT*, BOOK III, CHAP. XI.

BASED ON EXPERIENCE, we know that all living things, including human societies, grow and decline. The historical record shows that nations, as well as the civilizations of which they are a part, rise and fall in accordance with what Edward Gibbon, in *The Decline and Fall of the Roman Empire*, called "the vicissitudes of fortune, which spares neither man nor the proudest of his works."[1] Institutions that appear to be stable and permanent are subject to the shocks of war and revolution, and to the imperceptible erosion of time, obsolescence, indiscipline, and neglect.

Over the centuries, there have been a great many published theories purporting to explain the rise and fall of nations—too many to summarize in one book. I want to begin with one thesis that I find particularly imaginative and compelling: the narrative of decline written by

---

1   Edward Gibbon, *The Decline and Fall of the Roman Empire*, Bury ed., IV (London: Methuen, 1909), Chapter LXXI, Vol 7, p. 313.

the fourteenth-century Arab philosopher and historian Ibn Khaldun. His masterwork on the philosophy of history, the *Muqaddimah*, sets forth a model of decline that has been widely influential among serious students of history.

According to Ibn Khaldun's trenchant analysis, the cycle of a civilization begins with the founding of a tribe or dynasty by hardy people who live simply and defend themselves vigorously. The frugality of their lives promotes discipline, toughness of spirit, enterprise, and courage. These are the qualities needed for a society to become commercially successful and prosperous. The tribe is bound together by a strong sense of social cohesion and solidarity (a translator uses the term "group feeling;" we could use other terms such as "patriotism" or "public spirit"). A successful society produces cities, which are the seats of all civilized arts and sciences. The wealth of urban populations comes from their business and commercial activities. Eventually, however, the successful society becomes addicted to abundance, leisure, and luxury. Members of the tribe lose their vigor and hardiness. Military discipline evaporates, and "group feeling" wanes. The population works less and demands increased benefits from the rulers, who impose higher taxes and incur more debt. "Finally," says Ibn Khaldun, "civilization is destroyed because the incentive for cultural activity is gone."[2] Sooner or later, the feeble and undisciplined society will collapse and will be swallowed up by a hardier, more vigorous tribe. The applicability of Ibn Khaldun's analysis is obvious enough. During the course of this book, we will occasionally refer to Ibn Khaldun's thesis as a model against which to test the interlocking forces that threaten our own country's future.

The test of great societies and their institutions is whether they have the will and the flexibility to adapt to drastic changes and novel circumstances, as Rome did in the early empire and Britain did during the industrial revolution and the Napoleonic wars. The United States

---

2   Ibn Khaldun, *The Muqaddimah* (Princeton: Princeton University Press, 1974), p. 231. Ibn Khaldun recommends that governments maintain low tax rates to help forestall this economic disintegration.

today confronts a terrorist threat of unknown dimensions, as well as more traditional adversaries and, in addition, the destabilizing challenges of globalization. All of this is occurring in a social context of economic instability, civic apathy, extreme divisiveness, and moral and cultural decline. The patriotism and civic awareness of Americans were initially stimulated by the terrorist attacks of 2001, but this temporary restoration of "civic virtue" seems now to be ebbing away. Nevertheless, the nation still has the good fortune to enjoy a largely free society, creative scientific and business communities, and many patriotic citizens who are willing to risk their lives to defend liberty. These are significant blessings.

The United States began with a successful revolt against Britain in the late eighteenth century, followed by the implementation of a novel constitutional structure that proved to be one of the outstanding accomplishments in the political history of Western civilization. The nation expanded rapidly during the nineteenth century, reaching the Pacific Ocean as a result of the Mexican War of 1846–48. Following the American Civil War, the United States began its rise to great power status, based upon dynamic economic growth and a rising, industrious population. As economic historian Robert J. Gordon has written, "The century of revolution in the United States after the Civil War was economic, not political, freeing households from an unremitting daily grind of painful manual labor, household drudgery, darkness, isolation, and early death."[3] The development of electricity, the internal combustion engine, new medical techniques, and many revolutionary scientific discoveries led to dramatic improvements in the standard of living of the American people. The period between 1870 and 1970 featured not only America's impressive economic rise but also outstanding military victories, the successful absorption of millions of immigrants, significant cultural achievements, and the beginning of a process of healing America's tragic racial divide. The United States appeared to be at the

---

3   Robert J. Gordon, *The Rise and Fall of American Growth* (Princeton: Princeton University Press, 2016), p. 1.

pinnacle of its success as a nation in the years following World War II, when it held a position of extraordinary economic and military strength as well as political stability. As we will see, however, other less auspicious trends were becoming manifest during this period, including increasingly centralized government, welfare dependency, and the weakening of traditional standards of education and individual responsibility.

"Decadence" is usually defined as a process of falling away or declining from a prior state of health or excellence toward a deteriorated or impaired condition. It is a degeneration of vital signs, of energy, of fitness. For societies, decline is seen in the loss of historic vitality, discipline, self-confidence, and capacity for hard action and sacrifice. In part, as Ibn Khaldun recognized, decadence may be the natural result of a surfeit of prosperity. As a character in Shakespeare's *Cymbeline* notes, "Plenty and peace breeds cowards: hardness ever of hardiness is mother."[4] In the late Roman Empire, as in much of Europe during the 1930s, decadence was evidenced by the failure to respond to external and internal menaces, the absence of internal cohesion, a weakening of religious feeling, and the lack of strong, agreed-upon convictions and powerful social bonds.

There is no reason why the United States should be immune from the detrimental forces that have affected other societies. In 1987, the historian Paul Kennedy published *The Rise and Fall of the Great Powers,* in which he argued that America's economic and military strength was likely to decline relative to that of its principal competitors. At first glance, this conclusion appears to have been wrong. The position of the United States as the world's leading power was strengthened after the collapse of the Soviet Union. In the second decade of the twenty-first century, America's technological and conventional military supremacy is without precedent in the modern world, and its corporations continue to dominate the global economy. With less than 5 percent of the world's population, the United States produces nearly one-quarter of the world's

---

4   Shakespeare, *Cymbeline,* III, vi.

output.[5] But was Kennedy's prediction really wrong, or just premature?

Even on the superficial level of economic statistics, the western European nations, China, and Japan are in the same league as the US technologically and industrially, and it is likely that India and perhaps others will close the gap in the near future. Meanwhile, the US government has committed the nation to a level of deficit spending and debt that will severely burden future generations of taxpayers. Excessive deficits and national indebtedness endanger national defense and economic productivity. The United States faces a vicious terrorist insurgency of uncertain duration, as well as rival military powers, with few dependable allies. Over the long run, deep and unpredictable forces will determine the nation's relative power and vitality. Military and economic factors are undeniably important; but they, in turn, are dependent on demographic, social, moral, and cultural trends that are vital determinants of national strength.

There is a considerable body of evidence to support the conclusion that American society is subject to stresses that may ultimately prove critically damaging. Some of our cities are torn by crime, drugs, family breakdown, unemployment, and poverty. Our public educational system works poorly: large numbers of adolescents graduate from school each year without marketable skills, producing a two-tier society consisting of those who have managed to acquire useful knowledge and those who have not. American college students are shockingly ignorant of the basic facts about our nation's heritage. There are large disparities in income and wealth that could lead to a potentially explosive class conflict similar to violent revolutions throughout history. The strength of American capitalism has been badly damaged by a tidal wave of greed and managerial default, aided by reckless government policies, culminating in a brutal economic downturn in 2007–08 followed by an agonizingly slow recovery. High divorce rates and illegitimacy have weakened the family. Traditional religion—a vital adhesive force in any

---

5   World Bank, World Development Indicators, 2015.

society—has been under attack for a century by skeptics and socialist utopians.

The United States is flooded with millions of immigrants who drive down wage rates and place serious burdens on public services; many of these immigrants are not being effectively educated or assimilated into our civic culture and constitute a ready source of recruits for the divisive voices of demagoguery and resentment. Too many of America's elites, especially in the universities, have adopted a hostile attitude toward America's Western cultural traditions, promoting instead a "multicultural" agenda that encourages the division of our society into ethnic groups fighting for subsidies and privileges. This is a sign of weakness: citizens will fight for a nation but not for multicultural diversity.

Political leadership has become "followership," relying upon public opinion polls rather than upon principle. Honor and character have been replaced by personality and celebrity. Cultural, religious, and moral values are not communicated from generation to generation. As a young Los Angeles gang leader said in a public interview, "They give us sex education and condoms, but they don't teach us any rules." In foreign affairs, we have imprudently expanded our commitments, while allowing our defenses to weaken.

On the other hand, American society retains considerable vitality and capacity to adapt to new circumstances. We still have time-tested institutions which, if sustained, can provide the basis for renewal of civic life. Our model of constitutional government, even though weakened, has furnished an example for other societies emerging from tyranny into freedom.

The purpose of this book is to investigate the conditions of national strength as well as the forces associated with national decline and to apply the results of this analysis to the United States as it exists in the early part of the twenty-first century. In the course of the investigation, we will seek to go beneath the common indicia of economic and military strength and to consider the tangible and intangible qualities that constitute a strong, civilized society.

FORCES FOR NATIONAL COHESION

The emphasis of this study is on what is called the "nation" or the "nation-state." A nation is more than just a political state or government. A nation is a people associated in a common territory and united by a common history, language, customs, and institutions, and often by a common religion. Its inhabitants are called citizens, and they are held together by common bonds of national solidarity.[6] While "empires," like those of Rome and Britain, differed in important respects from nations as we know them today, they originated as cohesive states and manifested the characteristic features of national vitality. Some observers have speculated that the nation-state is destined to be replaced by some form of international political order, but there is no persuasive evidence that this will occur in the foreseeable future.

The forces that contribute to national cohesion include:

Linguistic Homogeneity
A nation's traditions and values originate from, and are conveyed through, a common language. Linguistic identity reinforces a sense of ethnic kinship that is often absent in multi-ethnic states, such as the Ottoman Empire and the Soviet Union, which maintained national unity largely through force.

A Feeling of National and Cultural Identity
Nations are held together by emotion, not reason. The sentiment of national solidarity is based on a felt cultural continuity, represented by common traditions, language, religious beliefs, literature, heroes, and symbols. It is the intangible essence of a nation: what Ibn Khaldun called "group feeling." The elements of cultural continuity must be effectively transmitted from one generation to the next. If they are not, the unifying emotion will wither.

---

6   See Roger Scruton, *A Political Philosophy* (London: Bloomsbury, 2014), Chapter 1, "Conserving Nations;" and Pierre Manent, *Democracy without Nations? The Fate of Self-Government in Europe* (Wilmington, NC: ISI Books, 2013).

Military Power

National defense is a universally recognized obligation of the state; and in a healthy society, the citizens will play the leading part in supporting the state's obligation. When the people have lost the will to fight, defeat is inevitable.

Economic Strength

Experience has shown that prolonged economic stagnation or decline leads to demagoguery, class conflict, and often tyranny or collapse. A proper civic and vocational education must be provided to ensure that no significant group is deprived of the opportunity to participate in the nation's economic success.

Social Stability and Leadership

In successful societies, leadership is exercised through a self-confident, continuing group variously referred to, depending on the national culture or historical setting, as an aristocracy, an establishment, an elite, or a dominant minority. This group must have a lively sense of duty and must also be flexible and open to new talent so that it does not degenerate into an oligarchy or plutocracy.

Effective Government Based on the Rule of Law

A unified nation needs a government that can effectively keep the peace, protect liberty and property, support those who are too weak or old to support themselves, and adjudicate disputes in accordance with known rules and fair procedures. If the government becomes ineffective, corrupt, or oppressive, the mutual trust between rulers and ruled that sustains any society will disappear.

These features of national cohesion arise over long periods of time and are realized in varying degrees in different societies. In mature nations, they are mutually interlocking and supporting. When one aspect of cohesion strengthens or declines, others are likely to follow. This mutual interrelationship—analogous to the interactions of a complex physical system or a symphony orchestra—is a point that will be emphasized throughout this book.

The major themes of decline to be developed include the following: (1) The inability or unwillingness of a nation to defend its people against external or internal enemies; (2) excessive foreign commitments that cannot be met without undue expenditure of money and manpower; (3) long-term economic decline that impairs national defense and standards of living; (4) the destructive impact of excessive government spending, taxation, and regulation; (5) educational decline, which contributes to the coarsening and deterioration of the culture and adversely affects the nation's ability to meet challenges and inspire its people to higher attainments; (6) a decline in self-reliance, discipline, and civic awareness that adversely affects the citizens' willingness to accept responsibility and undergo hardship; (7) a decline of religion and morality; and (8) the deterioration or abdication of a nation's leadership group—its "elite."

In the United States, many of the cohesive forces have weakened for reasons that will be explored; others are apparently strong, especially military and economic power. But is this strength real or illusory? The terrorist attack of 2001 seemed to reinvigorate national cohesion, but can this attitude survive a series of long, costly, and possibly inconclusive conflicts? The basic question is straightforward: has the wide expansion of luxury, hedonism, overexpansion, and the omnicompetent therapeutic state imperiled the vigor and cohesion of our society and its capacity for action?

SOME UNDERLYING ASSUMPTIONS

In the present study, the underlying assumptions are simple: there is such a thing as "civilization," whose characteristics include urban life, economic vigor, art and literature, a reasonably stable and predictable legal system, and a recognized code of morality and civility. Some societies are more civilized than others: contemporary France is more civilized than Iran under the Ayatollahs. A society in which good literature flourishes is more likely to be gratefully remembered than a society of barbarians. A nation in which private property and freedom of speech are protected by the rule of law is happier than a nation ruled by the whim of an autocrat. No apology is made here for the "Eurocentric" character of these assumptions. As we will see, the failure of the West to resist a powerful attack on European civilization may itself signify declining self-confidence and loss of nerve at the heart of our culture.

The plan of the book is as follows: First, we will examine two case studies—ancient Rome and modern Britain. These case studies will reveal certain persistent and related themes of decline. Finally, we will apply these interrelated themes to the United States and offer some general observations on the subject of decadence. The concluding chapter will offer an analysis of the indicators and suggestions for addressing some of the manifestations of national weakness.

I

ROME

FOR ANY STUDY OF THE DECLINE AND FALL OF NATIONS, Rome is the paradigm case. The story of Rome was the core historical event that inspired Gibbon, Spengler, Toynbee, and many other prominent historians. No historian of decline can avoid it.

The history of Rome has been interpreted and re-interpreted for 2,000 years. The fall of Rome has had an intrinsic fascination for literate people over the centuries. Rome is important to us because every aspect of Roman civilization—law, politics, literature, culture, and religion—is inextricably bound up with the culture of Western Europe and European America. So close is this union that much of the history of the West could be described as a series of footnotes to the history of Rome. Even the Christian Church in the West was so thoroughly Romanized that its principal branch is aptly called the "Roman Catholic Church." The political history of Rome has directly or indirectly inspired every important development in the theory and practice of politics, including the American and French Revolutions.

THE ROMAN REPUBLIC

Early Rome

The origins of Rome can be traced to a group of small villages on the Tiber that came together during the eighth century BC (the traditional date is 753 BC). By about 600 BC, Rome had become a relatively prosperous town governed by kings who were probably Etruscan in origin. In about 500 BC, the monarchy was overthrown, and a republic was established. After a long period of continuous warfare with neighboring tribes, Rome came to dominate central Italy and establish firm control over the entire Italian peninsula south of the Arno by about 270 BC.

The early Roman state has been described as "a republic in arms." Every citizen was required to perform military service, and no man could hold political office until he had served in the army for a substantial period. In their military operations, the Romans showed courage, tenacity, intense discipline, and considerable imagination. The principal industries of the Roman state were war and agriculture. Commercial affairs began to assume increasing prominence as Rome expanded its colonies throughout the Mediterranean basin. These settlements provided the basis for Romanization of the entire Mediterranean world and provided notable commercial and military advantages to the mother country.

Constitution and Society in the Roman Republic

The institutions of the Roman Republic provided later theorists and statesmen with the model of a working constitution. There were two consuls, elected for one-year terms, who shared the full "imperium"— that is, the power of military command and the executive power of government. Either consul could veto the other's proposals. This elementary system of checks to executive power was, at the time and for long afterward, a unique creation in the history of government. The Romans did occasionally replace the consuls with a dictator in times of emergency, but his term was limited to six months, and he could not hold successive terms. Because of the Romans' respect for tradition, the rules of limited tenure for consuls and dictators were generally observed.

The consuls were nominated by the Senate and were elected by an assembly of freeholders called the Centuriate Assembly (*comitia centuriata*) that was based upon standard army units (centuries). All freeholders served in the army, and citizens fought and voted together in the same units. The basic political structure was therefore closely identified with military life, with the consequence that military discipline and order were an integral part of the political system—a point of fundamental importance. The Centuriate Assembly was not a democratic body in the modern sense. The centuries, for purposes of voting, were divided into five classes based on wealth, of which the two wealthiest classes possessed a majority of the votes. The Centuriate Assembly not only elected the consuls but enacted laws, judged criminal appeals, and declared war and peace.[1]

Roman society recognized a fundamental distinction between patricians and plebeians. Individual patricians and their plebeian supporters were linked by a patron-client relationship called *clientela*, a form of moral and legal obligation in which the client promised obedience to the patron in return for the patron's support in lawsuits and other difficulties. Following a long series of conflicts between patricians and plebs, the patricians were forced to grant the plebs' demand for the creation of "tribunes of the people," another unique Roman constitutional balancing device whose function was to protect the plebs from oppression by the patrician officials. The institution of the tribunate was highly significant in Roman history because it gave the leaders of the plebeians a major share in the power structure of the republic, and thus served as a useful balancing element which helped to preserve civil order for an extended period.[2] The tribunes had the power to veto the

---

1   For a summary of the customs and institutions that led to Rome's early success, see Mary Beard, *SPQR: A History of Ancient Rome* (New York: Liveright, 2015), Chapters 3 and 4.

2   See the interesting essay by Jose Ortega y Gasset, *Del Imperio Romano*, translated into English as *Concord and Liberty* (New York: W. W. Norton, 1946). Ortega says: "Assuming the year 471 BC to be the approximate date of its establishment, we may observe that for three centuries and a half the tribunate kept Rome from sliding down the *montagne Russe* of revolution." *Id.* p. 43.

acts of other magistrates and were charged with convening assemblies of the plebeians (*concilia plebis,* or popular assemblies), constitutionally separate from the comitia centuriata, for the purpose of passing resolutions on questions of interest to the common people.

The most renowned of the Roman Republic's political institutions was the Senate, composed of the top families of the state. Originally all members of the Senate were members of the Roman nobility, but by the fourth century BC, plebeians were able to become senators. Strictly speaking, the Senate did not have executive or legislative powers, but it served as the principal advisory body to the elected magistrates, and it asserted special competence in foreign policy and public finance. The vast influence of the senatorial families was such that their advice was usually heeded by the consuls, who were generally tied to the great families through marriage or obligation. The Senate's prestige, moreover, enabled it to control the vote in the Centuriate Assembly on most occasions during the early years of the Republic. Nevertheless, the real power of the popular assembly gradually increased until it became a dangerous force in the hands of skilled demagogues.

The classic summary of the Roman constitution was written in the second century BC by the Greek historian Polybius, whose writings have influenced many political theorists, including the framers of the United States Constitution. Polybius presented the Roman constitution as an ideal system of checks and balances designed to combine the best features of monarchy, aristocracy, and democracy and to forestall the evils (tyranny, oligarchy, and mob rule) that naturally emerged from the corruption of each of these forms of government. The proper equilibrium of government, Polybius declared, "is maintained by the impulsiveness of the one part being checked by its fear of the other."[3] Polybius presented an idealized model, but his description was accurate enough in its general outline, and it is easy to see why it influenced later theorists. This model was undoubtedly in the minds of the framers of the US Constitution.

---

3   *Polybius on Roman Imperialism* (Washington, DC: Regnery Gateway, 1987), p. 192.

Underlying the success of the republican constitution was the Romans' deep respect for community, tradition, and the rule of law. Republican Romans had a highly developed sense of duty to the family, the military unit, the laws, and the state. This sense of civic obligation, and the military discipline that accompanied it, amounted to a form of civil religion and was transmitted to Rome's colonies, providing essential support both for Rome's military victories and its legal system. The tradition of civic obligation and patriotism (analogous to Ibn Khaldun's "group feeling") is an important feature of successful nations, and its breakdown is a common characteristic of societies in decline.

The Breakdown of the Roman Republic

The Punic Wars between Rome and Carthage (which began in 263 BC and ended in 146 BC) established Rome's domination of the Mediterranean, but the conflict had serious adverse consequences for the domestic economy. Many of Italy's most fertile lands were devastated as a result of Hannibal's campaigns. The requirement of sixteen years of military service, although a source of strength and social cohesion in the Roman republic, imposed serious burdens on small landholders in times of sustained warfare. As a result, many independent farmers lost their land to large landowners or to the Roman state. The growing predominance of large estates, owned by absentee landlords and operated by slaves, had a disastrous effect on the free rural poor. Many farmers were forced to leave the land and flocked into the cities, where they became a serious burden on the state. Importations of foreign grain from conquered provinces hastened the ruin of small farmers, and the influx of slaves also tended to depress rural and urban wage rates.[4] The system of slavery and the contempt of the upper classes for trade and commerce hindered the emergence of a viable middle class. These conditions created the potential for civil unrest and manipulation by

---

4   Tenney Frank, ed., *An Economic Survey of Rome,* I (New York: Octagon Books, 1975), pp. 376–86; Theodor Mommsen, *The History of Rome,* II (New York: C. Scribner, 1870), p. 444.

ambitious politicians. The shift from an agrarian society of independent farmers to an urban civilization of rootless jobseekers increasingly dependent on government patronage was a perilous transition for Rome. Adequate economic conditions and institutions for urban job formation were never developed in the ancient world.

The newly arrived urban masses did not own property and, under Roman tradition, were therefore deemed unfit for military service. But many of them were entitled to vote in the popular assemblies. When the "people" came increasingly to resemble an urban mob instead of a community of independent freeholders, the theoretical sovereignty of the popular assembly became a practical danger to the stability of the state. To forestall this danger, politicians felt compelled to spend growing sums of money to bribe the populace. This practice fostered dependency and irresponsibility. The carefully balanced Roman constitution began to slip out of gear.

The critical period for the Roman Republic began when Tiberius Gracchus became tribune in 133 BC. Although descended from a noble family, T. Gracchus cultivated popular support by proposing to revive the Licinian law of 367 BC, which limited the amount of public land that could be leased by one person, thus threatening to dispossess many prominent and wealthy landowners of part of their land. The Senate, however, adamantly opposed the land-reform proposal. When Gracchus's reform bill was vetoed by one of his fellow tribunes, Gracchus made a momentous and fatal decision: he induced the assembly to depose the recalcitrant tribune. This action was wholly without precedent in Roman history. If the Senate could be ignored and the tribunes arbitrarily deposed, the constitutional system of checks and balances would be nullified and total power would be vested in the hands of the popular assembly and its populist leaders. T. Gracchus then offered himself as a candidate for immediate reelection to the tribunate—another violation of custom. Opposition by the nobility to these developments, as might be expected, was violent. The election turned into an armed brawl, and T. Gracchus was killed on the street by a group of senatorial partisans. Tiberius's brother, Gaius, as tribune, continued the revolution by using the popular assembly to enhance his own powers and by increasing the distribution of grain to a growing urban proletariat. Several decades later, Marcus Tullius Cicero spelled out the consequences of the Gracchus brothers' grain distribution law: "Gaius Gracchus moved his grain law: a delightful business for the plebs, for it generously provided sustenance free of toil; patriots, by contrast, fought back, because they reckoned that the plebs would be seduced from the ways of hard work and become slothful, and they saw that the treasury would be drained dry."[5] Cicero's admonition may be relevant to the public policies of today's welfare states.

The polarization of Roman society continued under the popular general Marius (155–86 BC), who was the first military leader to gain and hold power through the personal allegiance of his army, thus setting another unfortunate precedent in Roman history. Once the legions ceased to be the servants of the Roman state (acting through the Senate and the elected consuls) and instead bestowed their loyalty on their own commanders, republican government was no longer possible. A permanent gap developed between soldiers and civilians. Such a cleavage always poses dangers for republican government. The evil of unchecked armies led by military adventurers was to plague Rome for centuries and would play a prominent part in its ultimate collapse.

Following the death of Marius in 86 BC, the senatorial party was revived under the leadership of another general, Sulla, whose bloody reprisals against his political opponents were even worse than the excesses of Marius. Another disastrous precedent had been set: if laws could be made by force, they could be unmade by force. After Sulla's death in 78 BC, the Senate once more caved in to the threat of armed violence when Pompey in 70 BC forced his way into the consulship and assumed what amounted to unlimited power. By this time, the Senate was dead as an

---

5   Marcus Tullius Cicero, *Speech on Behalf of Publius Sestius,* tr. Robert A. Kaster (Oxford: Clarendon Press, 2006), p. 86.

effective force, and some form of autocracy was inevitable. What remained of the history of the republic was a dismal tale of civil war and despotism.

The Roman territorial empire began to expand widely in the late Republic. By the early first century BC, the rule of Rome had been extended to Spain, southern Gaul, Macedonia, and Asia Minor, and Rome's colonies brought enormous riches to the capital. Retired soldiers were granted land throughout the empire, which furthered the Romanization of the colonies. The republican military and administrative system was not designed to manage a far-flung empire; military force had to be made available from Spain to Syria. As still more provinces were added, the burden became costly. Small farmers could not be away on distant military assignments for long periods of time, so professional armies had to be hired. The citizen republic in arms was no longer viable. The very existence of the colonial empire, therefore, offered a strong incentive to the development of a centralized military autocracy. These developments provide us with another historical lesson: the maintenance of an extensive, permanent empire and its accompanying foreign commitments require military and fiscal and administrative measures that eventually become irreconcilable with the preservation of free republican institutions at home.

After the constitutional balance of the Roman republic had been effectively destroyed by the cataclysmic events of the half-century from T. Gracchus to Sulla, the final half-century of the republic witnessed a succession of struggles for power between military commanders. The first triumvirate of Pompey, Caesar, and Crassus in 60 BC was merely a temporary step on the road to full autocracy. Subsequently, Caesar caused the adoption of a bill providing for distribution of grain in Rome without any charge whatever. This measure completed the pauperization of the Roman proletariat by making it dependent on state subsidies—another valuable historical lesson. Caesar violated the Roman constitution by refusing to give up his army command at the demand of the Senate even though his term as commander had expired. Next, he sought and obtained the dictatorship for life, putting the final nail in the coffin of the republic. The assassination of Caesar by Brutus and Cassius was not accompanied by any plan for resolving the constitutional crisis. The Roman mob, a beneficiary under Caesar's will, had no sympathy for his killers, as Shakespeare reminded us in *Julius Caesar*. Corrupted by decades of handouts and subject to no effective discipline, the Roman people were ready for autocracy, bread, and circuses.[6] After a short civil war, control of the state was seized by a triumvirate consisting of Marc Antony, Lepidus, and Octavian (Caesar's adopted son). The triumvirs ruthlessly liquidated their political enemies. Finally, after another brief period of civil war, Octavian defeated Antony at Actium in 31 BC and became the sole ruler of Rome under the name of "Augustus." A new era in Roman history had begun.

To summarize, the republic was destroyed by the following forces:

1. The decline of the independent peasantry and the rise of class warfare
The movement of large numbers of independent farmers from the country to the cities swelled the ranks of rootless urbanites. The land question was never successfully resolved, and the senatorial party was too shortsighted to understand that this issue could be used against the Senate with devastating effect by demagogues manipulating the growing urban mob of unemployed peasants. Because of their implacable hostility to trade, the senatorial aristocrats could not contemplate a policy of encouraging commerce and industry, which might have provided jobs for some of the unemployed and moderated the hostility between classes. The gap between rich and poor became much greater. The urban poor were kept in a state of helpless subservience, dependent upon the beneficence of government and the indulgence of generals. Throughout history, an underemployed population has been an easy target for populist demagogues.

---

6   The term "bread and circuses" was used by the Roman author Juvenal (c. 100 AD) to describe the political strategy of the government to keep the masses fed, entertained, and compliant. The phrase has resonance for today's welfare-consumer societies.

2. The expansion of empire and the breakdown of political institutions

A far-flung empire requires large standing armies, centralized administration, a permanent civil service, and a great deal of revenue. These needs overwhelmed the carefully balanced constitutional framework of the Roman republic. The popular assembly, swelled by an influx of ex-soldiers, immigrants, and landless peasants, could no longer be controlled by the traditional Roman relationship of *clientela*. The mob was easily swayed by grain distributions and other forms of bribery. The Senate made no effort to modify the traditional institutions to meet these threats—for example, by lengthening the terms of the consuls or making the Senate itself more representative. Factionalism and violence were rampant. As Cicero argued in *The Republic*, written about 54 BC, once the Roman republic had broken up into quarreling groups, it was no longer a "commonwealth" at all because each faction sought only its own interest and disregarded the common weal. The sense of civic obligation eroded, and autocracy became inevitable.

3. Inability to control the army

The depredations of Marius and Sulla showed that the Roman legions could be induced to follow their own generals, who were no longer subject to effective civilian control. Upper-class youths avoided military service; the "citizen-soldier" was replaced by professionals. This created a serious gap between the citizens and the army. The danger could perhaps have been mitigated by more effective policies of rotation or continued insistence upon civilian service in the military, but such measures would have been politically unpopular, and the Senate, once more, took no action. The result was a century of civil war that ruined most of the prosperous families of Rome and led to a military dictatorship. The incompatibility between civilian and military cultures is a potential source of trouble in any society.

4. Immorality, indiscipline, and irreligion

The influence of "moral causes" upon historical events is always difficult to assess. The evidence is largely literary, and the literature is often written by traditionalists who deplore the present and urge a return to a mythical golden age. Nevertheless, the sources are virtually unanimous in concluding that a serious decline in religious sentiment in public as well as private morality took place in the final decades of the republic. The sanctity of the family began to disintegrate. Divorce became common, and family ties were loosened.[7] The conquest of the eastern provinces had produced enormous wealth that could not be profitably invested in trade or industry because of the prevailing hostility among the upper classes to such occupations. Much of this wealth was accordingly spent on personal luxury, influence-peddling, and corruption. Under the influence of massive immigration and cultural fragmentation (the condition that is known today as "multicultural diversity"), the customary Roman restraints on conduct began to disappear. Celebrity, power, and self-indulgence were more important than character and honor—a recurrent theme in wealthy societies. The deterioration of morality made it more difficult to sustain the tradition of a republic of virtue ruled by austere and disciplined custodians of the public weal. The sense of civic obligation and respect for law, which undergirded the republican constitution, began to erode. Meanwhile, the traditional religion began to lose its hold on the educated classes, while Romans of all classes began to search for other sources of spiritual solace, principally from the Near Eastern "mystery religions."

These forces were closely interrelated: each contributed to the others. The result was the collapse of the republic and the inauguration of imperial rule. One fact stands out: in the words of the great historian Theodor Mommsen, the republic was "brought to ruin in politics and morals, religion and literature, not through outward violence but through inner decay ... thereby making room for the new monarchy of Caesar."[8]

---

7   Edward Gibbon, *The Decline and Fall of the Roman Empire*, Bury ed., IV (London: Methuen, 1909), pp. 509–10.

8   Mommsen, *The History of Rome*, IV, p. 737.

THE ROMAN EMPIRE

Following the collapse of the republic, the Roman state experienced a revival, due primarily to the pacification imposed by the Emperor Augustus. For more than two centuries, peace and prosperity prevailed under a series of competent emperors (interspersed with a few notorious degenerates). But this age of expansion and prosperity was purchased at a heavy price, and in the third century AD, the costs to the average citizen began to outweigh the benefits. The story of the decline of the empire has often been told but bears repeating.

Augustus and the Julio-Claudian Dynasty

The civil wars following the death of Caesar were exceptionally brutal. The Roman people were subjected to looting, heavy taxation, and outright confiscation by the various protagonists in the conflict. The Romans, like most people faced with chronic social upheaval, were ready to accept any kind of order in preference to the chaos of perpetual civil war. Octavian, following his defeat of Mark Antony in 31 BC, brought peace to Rome and was rewarded by the Senate with the titles of "Augustus" and "Princeps." In the words of Tacitus, "he found the whole state exhausted by internal dissensions, and established over it a personal regime known as the Principate."[9]

Augustus put a stop to the widespread killing and confiscation, repatriated treasure from abroad, expanded the coinage, repaired roads, and inaugurated a public works program that gave employment to many of the urban poor. In the provinces, administration was vastly improved, and the benefits of Roman civilization were extended around the entire Mediterranean basin. Augustus also assumed total control over the army and to a large extent removed the Roman legions from politics. (This salutary feature of Augustus's reign did not long survive his death.)

The Roman principate under Augustus continued to be called a *res publica*, and the early emperors paid lip service to republican

---

9   Tacitus, *The Annals of Imperial Rome*, I (Dorset Press, 1984), p. 31.

traditions, but in practice they created a new structure of government. Power was increasingly centralized in the hands of the emperor and his appointees. Gradually, over time, the imperial throne looked eastward and surrounded itself with the trappings of oriental monarchy: titles, courtiers, ceremonies, and deification of the emperor (beginning with the deification of Augustus after his death). While Rome enjoyed great prosperity during the next two centuries, it gave up its free institutions. As Gibbon observed, "The Romans had aspired to be equal; they were leveled by the equality of servitude."[10] In other words, we should not be misled by the political rhetoric of security and prosperity, which can easily become a justification for tyranny.

Under Augustus, the persistence of republican institutions was a legal fiction. The real government, both in Italy and in the provinces, soon passed into the hands of imperial bureaucrats, while the old republican magistracies became empty honors. Edicts of the *princeps* became the principal source of law. The Senate retained some influence because of the wealth and social position of its members. In practical fact, however, it was wholly subordinate to the emperors, who controlled admission to the Senate and could enrich or ruin its members financially. These developments, which took place over a long period, signaled the decline of the Roman aristocracy as an effective ruling class and its replacement by a military and bureaucratic elite whose positions were based on patronage, money, and the instinct for power. The collapse of the aristocracy deprived Rome of its natural social and cultural leadership, a process whose adverse consequences became increasingly apparent.

Augustus was the first of the so-called Julio-Claudian dynasty, which held the imperial throne for a half-century following his death in AD 14. No constitutional provision had been made for a successor to the *princeps*. Toward the end of his life, Augustus associated his adopted son Tiberius as co-ruler and conferred upon him both the *imperium*

---

10   Gibbon, *op. cit.*, IV, p. 477.

and the tribunician power. It was therefore natural that Tiberius should become the successor upon Augustus's death. Tiberius was succeeded in 37 AD by Gaius, nicknamed "Caligula," a great-grandson of Augustus who was mentally unbalanced if not wholly insane. Suetonius accuses him of incest with all three of his sisters, as well as torture and murder and demanding to be treated as a god.[11] Finally, the commanders of the Praetorian guard concluded that Caligula's instability had become a danger to the state, and they murdered him in 41 AD together with his wife and daughter. Caligula thus became the first emperor to be both made and destroyed by the praetorians.

There is no need to repeat the sorry chronicle of the rest of the Julio-Claudian emperors, which is easily accessible to us through the writings of Tacitus, Suetonius, Petronius, and other Roman authors. The histories of the time are packed with examples of the sycophancy of the Senate to the emperors, the increasingly undisciplined behavior of the Roman legions, the swarms of paid informers and professional slanderers, widespread corruption and bribery, and the instability of a state in which rulers could so easily be assassinated and replaced at the whim of their own military guards. Lacking confidence in the future, the better families stopped having children, a trend so disturbing to Augustus that he enacted legislation to encourage childbearing. Extravagance and gluttony were rampant. As the emperor Tiberius noted, "Frugality used to prevail because people had self-control and because we were citizens of one city ... But victories abroad taught us to spend other people's money."[12] In this lapidary pronouncement, Tiberius captured one of the principal themes of national decline: the erosion of discipline and frugality by the easy access of political leaders to "other peoples' money," whether through conquest or taxation.

Rome's success, as Tacitus observed, was in part based upon the

---

11   Suetonius, *The Twelve Caesars* (New York: Penguin, 1979), pp. 167–68.

12   Tacitus, *Annals,* p. 144.

austere morality of the early republic. A famous phrase by the poet Ennius is *moribus antiquis res stat Romana virisque* (Rome abides through the morals and men of old). The characteristic virtues of Romans were adherence to tradition, courage, dignity, "gravitas" (seriousness), fortitude, and simplicity of manners. While the evidence of poets and satirists is not always empirically accurate, the overwhelming weight of the literary evidence in the first century AD supports the conclusion that morality among the leading classes had seriously deteriorated. The Roman writers have given us numerous examples of corruption, lust, vulgar display of wealth, and viciousness of every kind. A significant segment of the lower classes, meanwhile, was permanently corrupted by the dole.[13]

The Flavian and Antonine Period
The disastrous reign of Nero was followed by the "year of the four emperors" (AD 68–69), culminating in the seizure of the throne by Vespasian, who was the founder of the short-lived "Flavian" line, consisting of Vespasian and his two sons, Titus and Domitian. Domitian, who succeeded to the throne in AD 81, inaugurated a new period of tyranny, proscriptions, and executions. The praetorian guard once again stepped in and murdered Domitian in AD 96, replacing him with Nerva, who returned to the precedent set by Augustus and adopted Trajan, a capable and distinguished soldier, as his colleague and successor. This act of statesmanship inaugurated a period of stable government and internal peace.

For nearly a century following Nerva's selection of Trajan, the constitutional problem of succession seemed to have been resolved. Trajan adopted Hadrian as his successor, and Hadrian in turn chose Antoninus Pius, who selected Marcus Aurelius. All were competent and dedicated leaders. From the accession of Trajan in AD 98 to the death of Marcus Aurelius in 180, the empire flourished as never before. This was the

---

13   Hadas, *A History of Latin Literature* (New York: Columbia University Press, 1952), pp. 97–100 (citing Sallust).

century described by Gibbon as the happiest in human history. The frontiers were fortified, Roman law and citizenship were spread into the provinces, commerce was promoted, and the tax system was regularized.

Despite the appearance of political stability, however, the Roman constitutional structure was inherently shaky. The adoption of one man by another is subject to all the frailties of human choice and is unlikely to be successfully repeated over a long period in the absence of solidly based institutional support. The system broke down with disastrous results after Marcus Aurelius selected his debased son, Commodus, as his successor. Commodus, after a brief period of indolence, reacted to an assassination plot by embarking upon a reign of terror. Many members of the nobility, suspected of disloyalty or disliked by the emperor and his advisors, were executed and their property confiscated. The emperor depleted the treasury by lavish expenditures and spent his time engaging in sexual orgies and gladiatorial combat. As might have been expected, Commodus made numerous enemies in the course of his ruthless proscriptions, and he was murdered in 192.

The Decline of the Empire
In AD 197, after a fierce civil war, Septimius Severus, a native of North Africa and commander of the Roman army on the Danube, defeated various rivals and seized the imperial throne. The principal object of Severus's policy was to expand the army and increase its pay and perquisites: a program that was continued by many of his successors and proved to be ruinous to the empire's taxpayers. Severus is reported to have advised his sons to "be generous to the soldiers and don't care about anyone else." The inevitable result of this policy was to make the army more dangerous than ever. Severus inaugurated a reign of terror more vicious than any that had preceded it and concentrated the judicial as

well as the administrative power in his own hands.[14] The Roman government, from this time on, was in theory as well as in fact an arbitrary despotism. The emperor took on the additional title of "dominus," signifying divine authority; he and his wife were represented as sun and moon deities on the imperial coinage.

The result of Septimius Severus's confiscations, unprecedented in scale, was a substantial increase in the number of large estates under direct imperial control. The destruction of private property rights and the centralization of property in the hands of the state had a number of disastrous consequences. The immense wealth of the imperial treasury was a standing invitation to ambitious generals to try their luck at seizing the throne by force. In addition, management of these huge estates by government bureaucrats rather than by private owners damaged agricultural productivity. The military regimentation of the empire was now applied to fiscal affairs: local city officials and merchant guilds became personally responsible for the tax obligations of communities, while peasant households were forced to supply recruits for the army as well as requisitions in kind from the land. This was the beginning of a process of militarization and bureaucratization whose consequences were damaging to the Roman economy. Taxes rose relentlessly, while soldiers and bureaucrats oppressed the population.[15]

Meanwhile, serious incursions were made by barbarian tribes in Germany and the Danube region. By the end of the third century, the ravages of civil and foreign war, plague, inflation, and taxation had badly damaged the Roman Empire. Nevertheless, the Empire continued to show considerable resilience. The imperial frontiers were by and large preserved. In AD 212, the famous edict of the emperor Caracalla made

---

14   At or about the time of Severus's reign, the jurists Ulpian and Papinian propounded the doctrine that all decisions of the emperor had the force of law. *Cambridge Ancient History*, XII (Cambridge University Press, 1961), pp. 29, 35.

15   Frank, *An Economic Survey of Ancient Rome*, V, p. 85; *Cambridge Ancient History*, XII, pp. 30–31; Ramsey MacMullen, *Corruption and the Decline of Rome* (New Haven, CT: Yale University Press, 1988), pp. 14, 42–48.

every free inhabitant of the Empire a full Roman citizen—a dramatic development in the ancient world, which created many new Roman citizens and also increased the tax revenues of the imperial treasury.[16] A succession of good generals at the end of the third century (most of them from the Balkan provinces) reinvigorated the Roman army and won a series of important victories over the barbarians. The work of fortifying the empire was continued by the Emperor Diocletian, a soldier from Dalmatia (present-day Croatia), who had risen through the ranks to assume the throne in 284. For administrative and military purposes, Diocletian divided the empire into four geographical parts, each with its own ruler (but all subordinate to himself). Because of Diocletian's reorganization, the Roman Empire survived its third-century problems, but at a heavy cost. The empire had now become a despotism that exercised a high degree of compulsion over private economic activity and individual freedom.

Diocletian's peaceful abdication of the throne in 305 was followed by nineteen years of civil war. By 324, Constantine had prevailed over his rivals and had united the empire under his own personal rule. Constantine's major innovations were the movement of the capital to Byzantium, subsequently known as Constantinople, and the recognition of Christianity as the state religion. Constantine believed, probably correctly, that the defense of the vulnerable Danube frontier on the north and the Euphrates to the east could be more successfully conducted from the Bosphorus. He may also have wished to separate the seat of government from the traditional paganism of Rome in order to advance the Christian religion. Whatever the reason, relocating the capital was a fateful step because it destroyed the geographical and psychological centrality of Rome, enhanced the influence of "easternizing" trends to the detriment of Roman institutions, and set the stage for the final split of the empire and the birth of a new Byzantine civilization in the east.

In the middle-to-late fourth century, large numbers of Goths began to

---

16   Mary Beard, *SPQR*, p. 527.

appear on the north shore of the Danube, seeking entrance to the eastern Roman Empire. These barbarian migrants were threatened by pressure from militant Huns originating from the Russian steppes. Seeking refuge from the Hunnic invaders, the Goths crossed the Danube and conducted armed raids against the Roman Baltic provinces in the 370s. The eastern Emperor Valens decided to attack the Gothic invaders at Adrianople in 378. Valens, however, had at the same time committed a substantial part of his army to defending against a Persian attack in the Middle East. He launched his attack with an inadequate force and suffered a disastrous defeat. Valens was killed, and his army was virtually wiped out. The Goths proceeded to rampage through much of the Balkans before the Romans were able to counterattack and stabilize the area.[17]

The Adrianople disaster was important because it demonstrates a prominent tendency of all empires: overstretch. When, during the late fourth centuries, the various barbarian tribes began to put serious pressure on the eastern and western frontiers, the Roman army was simply unable to sustain an all-points defense over such a vast territory. After Adrianople, Rome's military weakness became more evident. Most Roman citizens were unwilling to serve in the army: draft resistance and desertion were common. Constantine was compelled to admit large numbers of Germans into the army, resulting in what some historians have called the "barbarization" of the army.[18] As always in human history, the deterioration of the military forces weakened the society's resistance to attack from foreign and domestic enemies.

In the empire of the "New Rome," every trace of the former simplicity of Roman manners disappeared, and the government was conducted in the style of an oriental despotism. The symbol of oriental autocracy was Constantine's introduction of the diadem, a jeweled

---

17   For a comprehensive treatment of this episode and other major events in the history of the late Roman Empire, see Peter Heather, *The Fall of the Roman Empire: A New History of Rome and the Barbarians,* (New York: Oxford University Press, 2006), Chapter 4.

18   J.B. Bury, *History of the Later Roman Empire,* I (Dover ed., 1958), pp. 2–3.

crown of Persian origin. There was no longer any pretense of separation of powers; the emperor was responsible for all appointments and ruled by personal decree. The empire was wrapped in an impenetrable web of contradictory laws and unenforceable decrees, enforced by a vast administrative apparatus. The complex rules and procedures of this bureaucracy spawned a horde of lawyers who engaged in their natural talent for fomenting lawsuits. In the far-flung caravans of the Middle East, as Gibbon caustically noted, many camels must have been laden with law books.

Corruption was endemic throughout the empire. Official positions and judicial decisions were procured by bribery. Army units were withdrawn from the frontiers and quartered in the towns, where the soldiers supported themselves by extorting money and produce from a helpless population. The army, now predominantly stationed in urban areas and swollen with luxury and corruption, was increasingly reluctant to fight. Ramsey MacMullen's study, *Corruption and the Decline of Rome,* makes a strong case for the conclusion that corruption was a significant factor in the army's failure to provide adequate security against barbarians and brigands.[19] Since protection of lives and property against violence is the most basic function of government, the Roman Empire of the fourth and fifth centuries could hardly have retained the loyalty of its citizens for long. In addition, the population of the empire declined, due in part to a series of plagues.

Following the death of Constantine in 337, the military situation deteriorated as a major invasion of Huns from the east forced large numbers of Goths across the Danube into Roman territory. In about 405, a horde of barbarians from various tribes crossed the Rhine and ravaged Gaul without effective opposition. The Visigoths under Alaric invaded Italy and sacked Rome in 410. A succession of Roman emperors continued to rule, but their control over the western provinces was only nominal. The invasion of North Africa by the Vandals in the 430s was

---

19   MacMullen, *Corruption and the Decline of Rome,* pp. 171–79.

a particularly serious blow to the western empire because North Africa provided the grain supply that supported Italy. The last Roman emperor was deposed in 476 by the German general Odovacer, who took the title of king of Italy. Italy, Gaul, Spain, and Africa became largely barbarian kingdoms. The Western Roman Empire was no more. The western kingdoms were gradually, over several centuries, transformed into separate, unique European nations. Yet they continued to be strongly influenced by the Roman language, law, and culture. Indeed, the resulting civilization of western Europe would not have been possible but for the powerful and enduring influence of Rome. The eastern or Byzantine Empire continued to exist for almost 1,000 years; it retained much of the Roman law but was linguistically and culturally a quite distinct society.

Before attempting to reach any general conclusions respecting the decline and fall of Rome, we will briefly review certain critical aspects of Roman life: Rome's economy, its religion, and its system of law.

THE ROMAN ECONOMY

In spite of the problems of imperial succession, the commercial life of the early empire benefited from the relative stability of the state. Tax collection in the provinces was regularized, and interest rates were relatively stable.[20] Yet there were serious flaws in the Roman economic structure. Wealthy men of all classes spent their money on land, slaves, and luxuries. The social stigma attached to commerce inhibited the development of new forms of production, while the concentration of land ownership deepened the gulf between classes. There was no reason for an industrial system to emerge since every large estate could use slave labor to satisfy local needs, while most production in the cities took place in small, specialized shops. Although trade was important to the vitality of the empire, the Romans made little effort to invent

---

20 Frank, *An Economic Survey of Ancient Rome*, V, 36–40; Michael Grant, *History of Rome* (New York: Scribner's, 1978), pp. 261–64.

new products or to open up new markets. Business practices under the empire remained rudimentary, and capital formation was primitive. It has been estimated that the entire commerce and industry of the Roman Empire never produced more than 10 percent of total revenues, public and private.[21] Economic growth was largely limited to booty from war, whatever yields could be extracted from the soil, and a relatively modest amount of trade with the provinces. Since the number of adjacent territories available for looting was limited and the provincial tax base was relatively static, it is obvious that the costs of defense and administration could not continue to rise forever without eventually leading to serious economic problems. In short, the Romans never developed an economic base adequate to support their extensive empire.

This was a classic example of what historian Paul Kennedy has called "overstretch"—the assumption by a nation of military or other obligations that exceed its capacity to pay for them. As the costs of empire grew, greater burdens were placed on a static economy. Taxes, which were levied principally on the value of land, cattle, and slaves, were raised relentlessly to levels which the ancient farm economy could not sustain. The Roman sources of the late third and fourth centuries are unanimous in representing the tax burden as "the intolerable and increasing grievance of their own times."[22]

In addition to confiscation and taxation, the emperors resorted to the favorite manipulative device of unscrupulous rulers: inflation of the money supply. Beginning with Marcus Aurelius, they progressively debased the silver content of the denarius until, by the middle of the third century, it was virtually worthless and traders had to resort to barter. As always, inflation had serious adverse effects on commerce and on public confidence. Although Diocletian and his successors in the fourth century managed to stabilize the economy temporarily,

21   Grant, *History of Rome,* p. 266.

22   Gibbon, *op. cit.,* I, pp. 414–15; II, p. 210; M. I. Finley, *The Ancient Economy* (Berkeley: University of California Press, 1973), p. 90.

barbarian attacks, oppressive taxation, the fall in population, and stagnant productivity combined to produce a fiscal crisis by the end of that century. Food supplies were forcibly requisitioned, and citizens were required to maintain roads and fortifications by a system of compulsory labor. Many of the free tenants (*coloni*), because they could not afford the rent for their land after paying the heavy taxes imposed upon them, abandoned their farms and left the land uncultivated. As a result, tax revenues were further diminished. To ameliorate this problem, the Roman rulers turned the *coloni* and their children into compulsory tenants, legally attached to the land. Employees in some professions were forbidden to abandon their jobs and compelled to perform whatever services the state required. The municipalities, having lost both their liberties and their sources of revenues, gradually decayed. The temptation of all central governments is to expand their power at the expense of regions and localities; and Rome provides a clear instance of the threat to liberty posed by excessive centralization, burdensome taxation, and oppressive government.

It is no exaggeration to conclude that the prosperous classes in the Roman Empire were taxed and regulated out of existence. Since this group provided much of the demand and capital for works of architecture, sculpture, and books, cultural standards also deteriorated. Those who were economically destroyed by taxation and confiscation simply dropped out of the productive economy or turned to vandalism. Farms and businesses were deserted, and whole cities were abandoned. The population of the empire fell sharply.[23] These trends are manifestations of decadence in the strict sense of the term.

The Roman system in the late empire was a form of state authoritarianism in which the central authority dictated economic decisions. The Hellenic ideal of a body of free citizens speaking and acting in the

---

23 See *Cambridge Ancient History*, XII, p. 274. It has been estimated that the population of the late empire fell by one-third from 70 million to 50 million. Id., p. 267. Plagues and barbarian inroads certainly contributed, but the economic collapse played a major part.

public forum had degenerated into a form of tyranny whose only goal was to feed the bureaucracy and to hold the empire together at all cost, regardless of the consequences to the citizens. A kind of social passivity had infected the Roman people. No aspiring group of entrepreneurs, dissidents, or upwardly mobile professionals existed to break the chains of bureaucratic control. The aristocracy was dormant, the middle class submissive, and the slaves quiescent. The creativity of the ancient world had been transferred from the realm of political economy to the spiritual world of religion, where there was still room for freedom.

ROMAN RELIGION

From the beginning, Roman religion and law were closely connected. Contracts had religious sanction, and religious rituals were regarded as contractual. This connection is important to an understanding of the extraordinary depth of the Romans' attachment to formality and tradition both in religion and in law. The very word *religion* (re + ligio, from "ligare," to bind) conveys the sense of tying the present to the past through acts of piety. The priest was the public's representative to the gods and the repository of sacred tradition. As in most traditional societies, religion and the family were linked. The head of the household, or *paterfamilias,* was the priest for family worship of the household gods, and his legal status was enhanced by this function. As Rome expanded, its household and agricultural gods took the form of state deities. Rome's expansion by means of war and commerce in the third and second centuries BC introduced Etruscan and Greek religious ideas, along with temples, images of the gods, and the whole panoply of classical mythology.

By the late republican period, many educated Romans had turned either to Epicureanism, Stoicism, or skepticism. The historian Polybius, reflecting the view of the educated classes, argued that the principal utility of the traditional religion was to keep the common people in check "by mysterious terrors and scenic effects."[24] Cicero, in the *Laws*, makes the political function of religion quite explicit: "We must persuade our citizens that the gods are the lords and rulers of all things … For surely minds which are imbued with such ideas will not fail to form true and useful opinions."[25] To assert the social utility of religion, however, is not enough to preserve it. Ordinary people will not be fooled indefinitely by "mysterious terrors and scenic effects." Religious beliefs must be nourished by an active faith working through living social institutions. Just as an army cannot survive without competent officers, a religion cannot survive without spiritual leadership. If society's elites do not believe in the essential doctrines of the religion, their skepticism will infect the public sooner or later. The decline of religion, moreover, is usually associated with the erosion of public morality and civic virtue.

By the middle of the third century AD, traditional polytheism was in full retreat, and ordinary Romans turned in increasing numbers to Eastern "mystery religions." These cults varied widely but shared certain common features: (1) rituals of penance and purification; (2) direct communion with the god; and (3) a redeemer or redemptive process leading to personal salvation or immortality.[26] Many Roman emperors favored the cult of the sun-god, perhaps because of the propaganda advantages of identifying the imperial throne with the solar deity. The cult of the emperor was also promoted in order to stimulate Romanization in the far-flung outposts of the empire. By the end of the third century AD, the divinity of the emperor had become well established. Aurelian (270–75) identified himself with the sun god and was honored as "*dominus et deus*." The Roman government, by this time, was close to becoming a full-fledged theocracy.

Christianity, of course, was ultimately the most powerful of the

---

24   Polybius on Roman Imperialism, Book VI, p. 217.

25   Cicero, *Laws,* II (Loeb ed., 1961), p. 389.

26   See John Ferguson, *The Religions of the Roman Empire* (Ithaca, NY, Cornell University Press, 1985).

new spiritual forces and won an astonishing victory over its rivals in spite of repeated persecutions. The strength of Christianity lay, first of all, in the extraordinary cohesion and discipline of the early Christian communities, which combined fidelity and moral purity with unusual courage. Second, the promise of personal immortality must have been a powerful spiritual force. The inclusive nature of the Christian sect was also important: the growing ranks of persons who had little or nothing left in the world were welcomed into the faith. Christianity also gained a great deal from its admission of women as members of the church; Mithraism, its principal rival, excluded them. Finally, and most important, the historical personality of Christ as personal Redeemer was of incalculable value. His actual appearance on earth and his personal sacrifice for the benefit of all men made concrete what was only theoretical or implicit in other religions.

The first systematic persecutions of Christians occurred under Decius in 249 and again under Valerian in 257. A major persecution was conducted under Diocletian from 303 to 311. The legal basis for the persecution of Christians was their refusal to offer to the emperor the sacrifice required of all citizens. More substantial, perhaps, was their unwillingness to perform military service. Such lack of patriotism might legitimately have been viewed as criminal during the republic when the obligation of military service was universal among free men of property. By the end of the third century AD, however, large segments of the population, especially in Italy, were able to avoid military service altogether, and the legions were staffed with barbarians from the frontiers. It seems gratuitously harsh to blame Christians for conduct that others engaged in with impunity. A more enlightened government would have devised a punishment for nonviolent civil disobedience short of feeding the dissenters to wild animals. Yet the Roman authorities had cause to be concerned. Christianity was a threat because it undermined the Roman Empire at its most vulnerable point: the sanctification of the state. Although willing to render unto Caesar those secular benefits that were properly his, Christianity claimed exclusive spiritual authority in matters of faith and morals, overriding the claims of the state.

The emperor Constantine in the early fourth century played a critical role in the advancement of Christianity. Constantine credited the Christian God with divine intervention to assure his victory over his rival at the battle of the Milvian Bridge in 312 and thereafter actively promoted the Christian faith. He convened the Council of Nicea in 325, which formulated a creed that helped to unify discordant Christian doctrines. Under Constantine, Christianity began to displace the old Roman ideological foundations. The Christian emperors of the fourth and fifth centuries defended the empire because they had to. But Christianity was by its very nature incompatible with the total sovereignty claimed by the Roman state and its autocratic rulers. The balance of forces had changed; Christianity survived, but the Roman empire did not. The death knell of classical civilization was pronounced by St. Augustine, the most influential of all the Western church fathers. In *The City of God*, Augustine argued that the sack of Rome by the Goths in 410 should not disturb Christians, whose true home does not lie in the earthly city. The true explanation for the destruction of Rome, he argued, lay in the debasement of Roman morals and the accompanying collapse of civic virtue.

Christianity was not the sole or even primary cause of the empire's collapse, but it certainly played its part, along with the other forces discussed in this chapter, in applying the *coup de grace* to a decadent society. The eternal was now understood to be irrevocably different from and superior to every earthly power, including Rome's. This recognition shattered what remained of the spiritual justification for the Roman state. The beliefs introduced into the Roman world by the victorious Christians became the basis of a new civilization, which eventually incorporated some of the best features of classical culture. In the meantime, Christianity released the individual from the constraints of the classical view that man was wholly subordinate to the state and gave him a spiritual freedom that was entirely new in the world.

ROMAN LAW

The body of Roman law, developed over the course of hundreds of years, is one of the great achievements of any civilization. While prior societies had laws and even codes of law, Rome was the first to develop a science of law. The Greeks, despite their creative genius, never showed any real interest in jurisprudence; it took the practical common sense of Romans to give an organized body of law to the Western world. The importance of Roman law for the extension and preservation of classical civilization can scarcely be exaggerated. It was essential to the spread of commerce, the preservation of order, the maintenance of the family, and the inheritance of property.

From the beginning of their history, the Romans had a deep regard for law and justice. The early Roman law, like the English common law centuries later, was based on longstanding custom, expressed by the motto *leges sine moribus vanae* (laws without customs are vain). The renowned Twelve Tables, adopted around 450 BC, established basic legal principles binding all Romans and codified the forms of legal actions by which citizens could enforce their rights. Our knowledge of the Tables is only fragmentary; it appears that they did not purport to codify all of Roman law or even much of it. But the citizen could at least point to a recognized source of authority in order to limit the discretion of the magistrates. Law was rendered orderly rather than arbitrarily and was made ascertainable by the ordinary citizen. These were major advances toward the rule of law in contrast to rule by priests or tyrants. The Romans also developed the idea of a "natural law," applicable not only to Roman citizens but to all mankind—one of the most enduring creations of Roman thought.

Legal concepts were continually debated in Rome. Every citizen was expected to share in the burdens of the law, whether as judge, witness, juror, guardian, or merely spectator. "Who is the good man?" asks Horace: "He who observes the decrees of the senate, the statutes and the rules of law; by whose judgment many important cases are decided; by whose surety affairs are safe; and by whose testimony causes are upheld."

Juvenal's model citizen is a good soldier, faithful guardian, trustworthy arbiter and unperjured witness.[27] Traditional legal rules and institutions were an integral part of the fabric of the Roman people. They could not simply be altered or replaced at will. This conservative attitude, also reflected in the Roman tradition of religious and familial piety, was one of the forces that held the Roman *res publica* together for so long in the face of fearful challenges. The Roman assembly could and did legislate, but such legislation was rare. Because of the Romans' cautious attitude toward lawmaking, legislation was not favored during the period of the republic and was adopted only to cope with particular crises. As Hans Julius Wolff has observed concerning Roman law, legislation "served the purpose of adapting the structure of state and law to changed conditions, but never that of radically altering it."[28] The result was a degree of certainty and stability in the legal system that contributed significantly to the cohesiveness of Roman society.

Principal credit for the systematic structure of Roman law must be given to the *jurists* (or jurisconsults), private legal experts who gave opinions to parties and to magistrates. The jurists, in rendering their opinions, were not legally bound to follow precedents. But the force of tradition was such that they were reluctant to vary from established principles; instead, they attempted to adapt those principles to changed circumstances. This conservative tendency is at the heart of any great system of law since without it, the citizens cannot plan their transactions but are at the mercy of official discretion and private oppression. The status of the independent jurists did not survive the destruction of the Roman aristocracy at the hands of the soldiers competing for the imperial throne. Under the Empire, the creation of new law now occurred, not as a result of private opinions of the jurisconsults in individual cases but through the issuance of imperial edicts. This development meant the

---

27   Horace, *Epistles,*I, xvi; Juvenal, *Satires,* VIII, pp. 71–86.

28   Wolff, *Roman Law* (Norman, OK: University of Oklahoma Press, 1976), p. 67.

end of a "common-law" system based on private case law and the beginning of a bureaucratic system of law by official decree. "Thus," according
to Wolff, "the Roman jurist was gradually being transformed from a
member of the ruling class in an aristocratic republic into a servant of
authoritarian government."[29] The changed role of the jurist paralleled
the overall decline of the senatorial aristocracy and the disintegration
of those republican institutions based upon it.

By the third century AD, the imperial bureaucracy monopolized
the making of new law down to the smallest detail and discouraged any
original interpretation. Decrees poured forth from the imperial government. The crushing weight of bureaucracy was as fatal to the further
development of law as it was to other forms of commercial and cultural
activity. Legal science no longer served the needs of the litigants but
advanced the desire of the rulers for more power, more revenues, and
more administration. This legal overload in the late Roman Empire is in
many ways comparable to today's vast outpouring of laws from the US
Congress and the thousands upon thousands of regulations that emerge
every year from the American administrative state. (See the discussion
in Chapters 8 and 9.)

The study of Roman law continued in the eastern empire, but the
principal focus of this work was classification and codification. Little
original scholarship was produced, while the complexity and sheer
volume of legal enactments continued to increase, as imperial decrees
were piled atop one another in an attempt to solve the complex problems of a multicultural society that had become increasingly dependent
on government. The more instability there was, the more decrees were
issued. This condition of *hyperlexis* illustrates a basic political truth: the
need to legislate and regulate constantly and excessively is a sign of constitutional malfunction and tyranny. One inevitable result of excessive
lawmaking was a swelling volume of time-consuming and expensive
litigation initiated by a growing horde of lawyers. The codification

---

29   Wolff, p. 110.

of Roman law in the sixth century AD under Justinian was a mighty work of compilation; but it reflected the unfortunate fate of a people, in Gibbon's words, "oppressed at the same time by the multiplicity of their laws and the arbitrary will of their master."[30]

The lesson from Roman history seems clear enough: the rule of law is essential, but too much law can be burdensome and oppressive.

CONCLUSION

By the fifth century AD, the ancient Roman aristocracy had been wiped out, and the free political institutions of republican Rome had been replaced by a despotism on the oriental model. The population of Italy had sharply declined, and the middle classes had been badly hurt by inflation, taxation, and civil war. The level of education in the western empire had deteriorated drastically. The western empire was gradually "barbarized" by primitive peoples scarcely touched by the civilization they admired and envied; their loyalty was to their own tribes, not to Rome. The final collapse following the barbarian victories of the fifth century was merely the completion of a process long in the making.

The bare facts of decline and collapse are clear enough. The Goths, fleeing from the Huns, crossed the Danube in large numbers in AD 376, and the Roman army suffered a crushing defeat at Adrianople in 378. During the following 100 years, barbarian assaults continued, and Rome's military position, especially on the western front, deteriorated. In addition, the instability of the Roman political system worsened with a series of assassinations and usurpations of the imperial throne. These weaknesses allowed various barbarian armies to make major inroads into Gaul, Spain, and North Africa. The loss of territories and revenues, particularly in the "bread basket" provinces of North Africa, greatly reduced the western empire's ability to maintain its armed forces, giving the barbarians virtually free reign. Romulus Augustulus, the last Roman emperor in the west, was deposed by Ostrogoth forces under

---

30   Gibbon, *op. cit.*, IV, p. 542.

Odovacar in 476, and the Roman state in the west came to an end. The territories of the western empire were then occupied and ruled by a succession of independent Gothic and other Germanic kingdoms.[31] Roman cultural and legal customs persisted in some areas for a time, but by about AD 600, what some historians later disparaged as the "dark ages" had begun. The infrastructure of Roman civilization in the west was virtually destroyed. Standards of quality of pottery, construction materials, and other consumer goods deteriorated drastically. Coinage almost completely disappeared in western Europe. Trade collapsed. Some areas, such as Britain, sank to a level of complexity "well below that of the pre-Roman Iron Age."[32] After the fall of Rome, it took centuries for Europeans to restore the standards of living they had enjoyed under Roman rule. Literacy largely disappeared, except among the clergy. Architectural skills were lost. Food production and population declined sharply. Classical historian Bryan Ward-Perkins concludes: "The post-Roman centuries saw a dramatic decline in economic sophistication and prosperity, with an impact on the whole of society, from agricultural production to high culture, and from peasants to kings."[33] This represented, without doubt, the end of classical civilization in the West. No one living in Italy, Gaul, or Spain in AD 300 could have predicted it. Given the erratic course of human history, there is no assurance that it could not happen again.

CAUSES OF THE FALL

The great historian of Rome, Edward Gibbon, placed principal blame on the decay of the military spirit and the loss of the zeal for liberty among the senate and people of Rome, who, in the end, trusted their

---

31 For a thorough and readable treatment of these events, see Peter Heather, *The Fall of the Roman Empire,* Chapter 10.

32 Bryan Ward-Perkins, *The Fall of Rome and the End of Civilization* (Oxford: Oxford University Press, 2005), p. 118.

33 Id., p. 183.

defense to mercenary armies and abandoned their freedom to tyrants. Gibbon drew from his analysis of Roman history the following political principle: "A martial nobility and stubborn commons, possessed of arms, tenacious of property and collected into constitutional assemblies, form the only balance capable of preserving a free constitution against enterprises of an aspiring prince."[34] Gibbon's analysis featured civil war, barbarian inroads, intolerable taxation, and the inability to control Rome's rapacious legions. The luxury and corruption of the age played a prominent part. In the pursuit of present enjoyment, Romans of the late empire were unwilling to invest in the future or to fight for their freedom. Finally, Gibbon believed that Christianity contributed to the military and civic weakness that undermined the empire. "The clergy successfully preached the doctrines of patience and pusillanimity: the active virtues of society were discouraged; and the last remains of military spirit were buried in the cloister."[35] Gibbon's description was generally consistent with the evidence and with common sense, although he exaggerated the role of Christianity in the fall of the empire. Christianity gained real strength only during and after the destructive civil wars of the third century AD; by this time the republican constitution admired by Gibbon had long disappeared, and the empire itself was in disarray.

In the two-and-a-half centuries since Gibbon wrote, additional material has come to light, and many other historians have taken their turn at explaining Rome's decline. The conditions responsible for the downfall of Rome are summarized here separately for purposes of analysis but are, in fact, closely interrelated and mutually reinforcing.

1. Barbarian invasions and the weakening of national defenses
The one institution over which the emperors, after the second century AD, never succeeded in establishing adequate control was the most

---

34   Gibbon, *op. cit.*, I, p. 65.

35   Gibbon, IV, p. 175.

dangerous of all: the army. In the early republic, the army was identical with the citizen body because all free, propertied men were also soldiers. By the time of the late republic, citizen armies had been largely replaced by professional armies. The early emperors established the disastrous precedent of making large gifts of money to the troops at each change of rulers in order to secure their loyalty. The greatest emperors were able to keep the soldiers in harness, but the legions were hopelessly out of control for much of the post-Antonine period. The troops plundered at will, extorted money and produce from the townspeople, and in general behaved more like occupying armies than guardians of public order. Since the citizens were reluctant to serve in the army, most of the empire was disarmed and thus wholly vulnerable to the depredations of corrupt and licentious troops. In the end, the erosion of military readiness meant that the army could not protect the frontiers against barbarian invasions, especially when the invading tribes became more numerous and active in the fourth and fifth centuries. Due to the inability to tap new resources quickly in an already overtaxed agricultural economy, the Empire was not capable of raising enough troops in time to fend off the multiple invasions. The consequences of military deterioration have been summarized by a military historian: "the western Empire relapsed into a cycle—ultimately fatal—of shrinking revenues and declining power during the fifth century ... the inability of the imperial government to repel groups such as the Visigoths led to their settlement, with official agreement, in productive provinces: southwestern Gaul, much of Spain and finally, and most crucially, North Africa, passed out of Roman control."[36]

The military history of the late Empire teaches an important and enduring truth: both the origins and the realities of war are unpredictable, and it is dangerous to rely on the memory of past triumphs. As the ancient Roman saying has it, *"Si vis pacem, para bellum."* If you want peace, prepare for war—meaning the next war, not the last one.

---

36   Michael Whitby, *Rome at War: AD 293–696* (Oxford: Osprey, 2002), p. 69.

2. Constitutional instability and the breakdown of the social order

Between AD 193 and 293 , there were more than seventy emperors.[37] Of these, only a few died a natural death. Most were chosen and destroyed by the army or the praetorian guard. Under the circumstances, it was a near-miracle that the empire survived as long as it did. The failure to solve the problem of succession to the imperial power was a leading cause of Rome's eventual collapse. There was no legal process, such as impeachment, for the removal of an emperor, so political opponents had to resort to assassination or war. Once the republican constitution with its traditional checks and balances had been destroyed, there were no limits, either in theory or practice, to the power of the state. The Roman republic had developed ingenious devices for bifurcating power, such as the balance between consuls, senate, assembly, and tribunes, but after these devices had been rendered impotent by the centralization of authority, there was no longer any institutional means of limiting the power of the imperial government over its citizens. In this respect, the Romans' reverence for law deserted them when it was most needed. This decline of constitutional law has its counterpart in the United States today as judges and administrators increasingly assume the authority properly vested in the people and their elected representatives.

In the case of Rome, the origins of this political and legal failure are connected with the decline of the Roman aristocracy. Every successful nation depends upon a diligent, loyal, and effective sociopolitical elite or establishment. The institutions of the Roman republic, at their best, worked because of a strong senate based on an independent aristocracy which, while burdened with the rigidities of all aristocracies, was reasonably open to access through talent and marriage. The collapse of the aristocracy deprived Rome of its natural leadership and undermined the delicate constitutional balance among senate, popular assembly, and tribunes. The aristocracy contributed to its own downfall by abject cowardice and loss of nerve. In return for wealth, dignity, and meaningless honors, the senators accepted a position of helpless subservience to

---

37   Mary Beard, *SPQR*, p. 530.

the emperor and the generals. The commercial middle class might have developed into a counterweight to imperial misrule. But the newly rich merchants were too eager to ape the nobility by pouring their wealth into landed estates and nonproductive opulence. The more industrious among the equestrian class were co-opted into the imperial bureaucracy, where they served willingly as the hired hands of despotism. The passivity of the middle classes in the face of bureaucratic tyranny was a sign of social decay as well as a cause of constitutional weakness.

It is possible that the development of representative government might have broadened the constitutional structure and provided greater political stability, as well as more balance between Rome and the provinces. The idea of representative government, however, never developed in the ancient world, with the possible exception of the Roman tribunate, which was disastrously weakened by civil war at the end of the republic and then effectively destroyed by the emperors. The Romans were familiar with the Greek experiment in direct democracy, in which all eligible citizens participated directly in the assembly, but this example was generally regarded with disfavor in the Roman world. By the time of Caesar, moreover, Roman assemblies were so easily manipulated by demagogues that they could not be converted into effective instruments of government. Eventually, the constitutional system evolved into a top-heavy behemoth that could tax and spend but could not defend the lives and property of Romans against the harm from corrupt insiders and external barbarians. Citizens have little reason to remain loyal to such a government, either then or now.

The massive influx of unassimilable immigrants, described previously, further damaged social cohesion. By the fourth century, the cultural identity of Roman citizens began to fragment as foreign customs and cults proliferated. The cities were no longer able to "Romanize" the masses. Lawlessness was pervasive. Social disarray and disintegration proceeded relentlessly as increasing numbers of barbarians pressed against the frontiers. In sum, this experience provides one of history's best examples of the dangers of uncontrolled immigration.

3. *Economic Decline and "Overstretch"*

The erosion of discipline and the influx of barbarians were not the only factors contributing to the breakdown of the fabled Roman military machine. The economic resources simply did not exist in the late empire to support an "all-points" frontier defense on such a vast scale. By the third century, defending a frontier from Britain to the Black Sea and the Middle East required an army of at least 400,000 men, a huge number for that time. Raising money to support the defense effort required increasingly burdensome taxation and requisitions in kind from landholders. Revenue shortfalls and tax evasion were constant problems. The government forced property owners to furnish soldiers from the peasants who worked their fields, as well as to supply grain, clothing, and utensils to the army. In an early confirmation of supply-side tax theory, the tax revenues fell as tax rates rose. Countless people, especially those in the productive middle classes, were financially ruined and the vitality of cities destroyed. With the decay of urban life, self-sustaining rural estates became the chief centers of activity, and the free peasantry sank into serfdom. The Roman authorities tried to remedy matters by binding workers to their professions and enacting other coercive regulations. As with modern varieties of state coercion, the heavy hand of Roman bureaucracy succeeded only in further depressing the level of economic activity.

A more resilient and diversified economy might have provided Rome with a better chance of survival. The Roman aristocracy and upper middle class, however, took little interest in trade and industry, which were considered to be occupations for freedmen and slaves. Tradesmen made little effort to expand markets, and available funds were sunk into land rather than capital investment. New products, new machines, and new jobs were neither sought nor created; the economy remained largely dependent on agricultural production. When farm productivity was threatened by civil war, confiscation, and excessive taxation, there was no industrial-commercial sector to fall back on. There is an important correlation between economic and military power.[38] A more productive economy might have compensated for Rome's imperial "overstretch" by enabling the empire to support armies on the frontier while it gave its citizens a better and freer life back home. As it was, deprived of any real hope of peace and material well-being, the average Roman in this period had little reason to support the imperial state.

4. *Moral and Spiritual Collapse*

The collapse of the Roman Empire has often been associated with moral corruption. As Ibn Khaldun argued, it is a universal truth, from which no civilization is exempt, that excessive wealth tends to breed indolence and corruption. Many of Rome's intellectual leaders were well aware of the decline in values. Cicero, Horace, Tacitus, and others warned of the fatal consequences of luxury and self-indulgence, which were the natural result of the enormous unearned riches brought to Rome from the conquered provinces. It would be foolish to assert that moral decline *caused* the fall of Rome—just as it would be wrong to argue that any other single factor was responsible. Historical causation is a seamless web with no outer limits and no clear divisions. On the other hand, it is hard to deny that there was a significant shift in Roman moral values after the republican period and during the empire. As historian and classicist Victor Davis Hanson has noted, the enormous accretion of wealth produced luxury and license. "The new empire also diluted a noble and unique Roman agrarianism. It eroded nationalism and patriotism. The empire's wealth, size and lack of cohesion ultimately diminished Roman unity, as well as traditional marriage, child-bearing and autonomy."[39] This insight is consistent with Ibn Khaldun's thesis of moral decline discussed in the Introduction.

The qualities of austerity, discipline, frugality, patriotism and

---

38   See Paul Kennedy, *The Rise and Fall of the Great Powers* (New York: Random House, 1987).

39   Victor Davis Hanson, "Our modern 'Satyricon': The fall of Rome must remind today's profligates what keeps civilization alive," *Washington Times* (May 16, 2019).

pietas—the hallmarks of the Roman republican temperament—were scarcely to be found by the fourth century AD. These are the moral characteristics of the citizen-soldier. Lacking such values, the subjects of the late empire refused to serve as soldiers, and "civic virtue" in the traditional sense disappeared. The defense of the state was turned over to a professional army increasingly staffed by barbarians and its government to military tyrants and bureaucrats. When the basic values of the society can no longer be successfully transmitted, that society's very existence is imperiled.

In all civilizations, moral values are identified with the religious culture. The character of the classical polity was shaped by allegiance to the institutions of the *civitas,* the most important of which were the religious rites that propitiated the gods and acknowledged the limitations on human conduct. These religious rites undergirded the civic rectitude, piety, and austerity that distinguished Roman society at its best. Without this "public orthodoxy," respect for the polity could not survive.[40] When traditional pagan civic practices disappeared, municipal communities lost a great deal of their social cohesion. As the historian J. B. Bury noted, "With the passing of paganism something went out of the vitality of ancient town life which could never be restored."[41] The Christian communities, of course, had an intense cohesiveness of their own; but the thrust of Christianity was diametrically opposed to the civic and religious framework of the Roman state and ultimately subversive to it. Christianity attacked the Roman Empire at its very core—the sanctification of imperial authority.

The Christian faith was inconsistent with the theory and practice of the late Roman Empire, which had imposed upon its subjects an oppressive and hopeless tyranny. Under these circumstances, once the artificial religious sanction of paganism was removed, there was little

---

40   Frederick Wilhelmsen, "Cicero and the Politics of Public Orthodoxy," in *Christianity and Political Philosophy* (Athens, GA: The University of Georgia Press, 1978).

41   Bury, *History of the Later Roman Empire,* I, p. 61.

inducement for the subjects to remain loyal to the empire. In this sense, the victory of Christianity was a victory for human freedom, even though it was achieved at the cost of further weakening what was left of the cultural foundation of classical civilization. That foundation was not destroyed but went underground, to be partially revived in western Europe centuries later.

5. A Failure of Will

The collapse of Rome's traditional religion and ancient values was accompanied by still another characteristic feature of decadent civilizations: the loss of self-confidence. The Romans gradually abandoned the sense of divine mission portrayed in Virgil's *Aeneid* and their belief in the fundamental rightness of Rome's place in the world. A civilization has meaning for its citizens insofar as they acknowledge and respect the traditions and ideals that constitute the essence of that civilization. The Roman's reverence for his ancestors, for the land, and for the native deities; his self-discipline and willingness to fight at a moment's notice; his allegiance to traditional political institutions; the fundamental virtues of *dignitas, gravitas,* and *pietas*; and the love of rhetoric, drama, and beautiful buildings; these were what gave meaning to Rome. Once Rome's leading classes had abdicated, there was no longer any group of men with the means, independence, courage, and will to keep the ideals of Rome alive. By the fifth century, most Roman citizens were unwilling to fight, and the army consisted increasingly of the kinsmen of the very barbarians who threatened the empire. A civilized nation without ideals it is willing to fight for is a nation that is unlikely to defeat ruthless and determined adversaries: this is a lesson that modern Western nations, addicted to consumerism and self-indulgence, ignore at their peril.

The Roman Empire began in an atmosphere of hope when Augustus assumed the principate and brought an end to the bloody civil wars of the first century BC. It then endured for nearly five centuries, much of this period occupied with foreign wars and internal dissension. Although Augustus paid homage to the balanced institutions of republican Rome, he began the process of concentrating the powers of the several institutions in his own hands. This process was zealously continued by his successors, with the willing or unwilling acquiescence of most of the traditional sources of power in Rome, such as the Roman aristocracy. By the third century AD, the emperors had assumed virtually unlimited power and were being treated as deities. By the end of the fourth century, the imperial government had become a brutal tyranny enforced by military rule, a predatory bureaucracy, confiscatory taxation, and the virtual serfdom of the agricultural work force. These measures were not sufficient to stem the tide of the barbarian invasions. Through neglect and weakness, the Roman citizens had permitted the gradual but permanent loss of their liberty, accompanied by the decline and fall of their society.

2

BRITAIN

"IN THE SECOND CENTURY OF THE CHRISTIAN ERA," according to Gibbon, "the empire of Rome comprehended the fairest part of the earth, and the most civilized portion of mankind."[1] Fifteen centuries later, the island nation of Britain began its remarkable march toward imperial power, and by the nineteenth century, it dominated an even vaster part of the earth. Just prior to World War I, the British Empire embraced one-fourth of the earth's inhabited surface and 400 million people, a greater variety of races and cultures than had inhabited the Roman Empire. Unlike the citizens of the late Roman Empire, moreover, Britain's subjects were not governed by a dismal and oppressive tyranny. Britain bestowed upon most of its colonies the benefits of its own unique system of government, under which rights of liberty,

---

1   Edward Gibbon, *The History of the Decline and Fall of the Roman Empire,* ed. J. B. Bury (London: Methuen & Co., 1909).

property, and self-government were protected by the common law and established institutions.

During the eighteenth and early nineteenth centuries, Britain single-handedly created the industrial revolution. In the 1850s, Britain produced two-thirds of the world's coal, at least one-half of its cotton textiles and iron, more than one-half of its steel, and virtually all of its machine tools. Britain remained the world's major industrial power throughout the nineteenth century and into the twentieth. London was the financial center of the globe; and English ideas, institutions, fashions, and attitudes dominated the civilized world.

Three-quarters of a century later, Britain's empire and its industrial supremacy had collapsed. By the 1970s, Britain was among the weakest of the industrialized nations. Its share of the world export market for manufactured products had fallen from 29 percent to 8 percent. The British economy was the butt of jokes, and English labor practices had given rise to a new term of derision: the "British disease." This economic decline forced Britain to divest its empire and its citizens to liquidate most of their foreign assets. Inflation and unemployment increased. Economic deterioration was accompanied by political weakness. Overseas military commitments were drastically reduced; for its security, Britain became increasingly dependent on its former American colony. Evidence of social malaise appeared as rates of divorce, illegitimacy, and crime began to rise. Educational as well as esthetic standards deteriorated, and funding for the arts and sciences dropped sharply. The nation succumbed to the dreary cheapness of pre-fabricated modernism. In brief, decline brought with it a blurring and weakening of those features of society that define a high civilization. Nevertheless, just as Rome recovered in the early principate, so Britain has managed to recapture, if not its empire, at least a part of its entrepreneurial vitality and some of the self-assurance, creativity, and common sense for which it was once renowned. The story of Britain's rise, decline, and recovery is certainly not complete, but it has important lessons for today.

THE RISE OF THE EMPIRE

The foundations of the British Empire were laid in the early seventeenth century when Britain's sailing fleet took control of the North Atlantic. As in the case of all powerful states, national greatness and military strength were inseparably linked. Contemporaries understood that naval power was the basis for colonial commerce. As Lord Halifax wrote in 1694, a strong navy to defend overseas trade was "the life and soul of Government."[2] While territory as such was not initially a principal object of British policy, eighteenth-century wars did place extensive territories under the control of the British crown. Admiral Hawke's destruction of the French fleet at Quiberon Bay in 1759 made it impossible for France to support its colony of Quebec; the result was the incorporation of French Canada into the British Empire in the Treaty of Paris of 1763. The predominance of British sea power, together with the legendary daring and resourcefulness of British leaders, made possible England's conquest of India. At the battle of Plassey in 1757, Robert Clive, with about 1,000 European soldiers and 2,000 Indian auxiliaries, defeated 50,000 troops of the Nawab of Bengal. This astonishing victory was followed by the conquest of the Indian subcontinent over the following century, which in turn led to British domination of vast territories in Southeast Asia.

Britain's imperial expansion suffered a setback when the thirteen American colonies successfully rebelled with the assistance of France, but the British navy quickly reasserted itself during the Napoleonic wars. The British naval victories of the Nile and Trafalgar made England essentially invulnerable to attack from the continent and led to Britain's worldwide naval supremacy. Naval power, in turn, was dependent upon financial power. Britain and its allies achieved victory in the Napoleonic wars largely because of Britain's superior capacity to raise money for the support of military forces. Although Britain's population was far smaller than France's, by 1800 England had outpaced the rest of the world

---

2   Gerald S. Graham, *Tides of Empire* (Montreal: McGill-Queens University Press, 1972), p. 26.

in commercial and industrial expansion and had developed through the Bank of England a workable system of public finance as well as a stable money supply and a dependable supply of credit. This economic and financial base (unique in the world at that time) allowed Britain to finance its own war effort and to subsidize half a million troops in the allied coalition against Napoleon. The British people also had the benefit of a Parliament, which, though far from representative in the modern sense, was constitutionally empowered to levy taxes and enact legislation. France, by contrast, lacked a reliable system of public finance, and its tax system was corrupt and highly arbitrary. Britain emerged from the Napoleonic wars in 1815 with the world's most powerful economy, a relatively stable society based on the rule of law, and a commercial empire extending through the Indian ocean and into the Pacific.

The nineteenth-century evangelical movement, with its emotional call to the fulfillment of Christian duty, played an important role in the growth of the British Empire. The spread of the faith was a sacred obligation for many Britons. The religious impulse led to the abolition of slavery in the British colonies and the spread of Christian missions throughout the world. In India, the application of Christian principles inspired the British governors to suppress such abhorrent native practices as infanticide and suttee (the burning of widows).

The British Empire was, to a significant extent, a product of the discipline imposed by a successful aristocracy. The exercise of administrative powers, whether in India, Uganda or Jamaica—often under dangerous conditions, backed only by a few hundred reliable troops, exposed to virulent diseases, and remote from the comforts of European life—required self-discipline, loyalty to one's calling, the ability to operate under a system of delegated responsibility, and the willingness to face pain and danger without giving up. These were precisely the characteristics inculcated by the public school system, as depicted in *Tom Brown's School Days* and a host of other books. Anecdotes of the empire reflect the cult of stoicism and endurance beaten into English boys from early childhood. Tom Brown is the youthful counterpart of "Chinese"

Gordon, who neglected opportunities to escape in order to meet his death at the hands of a band of murderous fanatics in the Sudan. The paradigm was repeated time and again throughout the empire.

One of the secrets of Britain's success was holding the cost of empire to manageable levels. In general, the British did not seek to hold large land areas but preferred strategically located naval bases. (India was an exception.) The naval bases did not require large garrisons. By today's criteria, Britain's military expenditures were surprisingly low: it has been estimated that, from the 1830s until the end of the nineteenth century, the entire annual cost of the army and navy in peacetime was between 2 percent and 3 percent of annual national income. Moreover, Britain's governing classes recognized the need to use military power with great caution. The British navy existed as a stabilizing force to protect trade and to serve the interests of the European balance of power, not to conquer more territory or to intervene in disputes where Britain's vital interests were not affected. In Lord Rosebery's words, "We cannot afford to be Knight Errant of the World, careening about to redress grievances and help the weak."[3]

For the most part, Britain ruled its colonies with a light hand. By the time Victoria assumed the throne, most Englishmen assumed that the predominantly white colonies, and perhaps others as well, would eventually manage their own affairs. At the beginning of Victoria's reign in 1837, *imperialism* had been little more than an unpremeditated series of commercial and military enterprises with no expansionist purpose and no fixed goal of building an empire. But all human institutions develop their own internal and expansive logic as well as their self-interested constituencies. (The twentieth-century welfare state is an example.) The logic of empire, and the interest of merchants, seemed to call for expansion. By the 1870s, the British public had become obsessed with empire. From the aristocratic viewpoint of the British upper classes (like the Roman aristocracy), a business career was unthinkable; to expand

---

3   Graham, *op. cit.* p. 82.

the empire by military force, on the other hand, was a suitable occupation for a young gentleman. The imperial appeal proved highly popular. Ironically, the new imperialism encouraged the scramble for markets and profits that the aristocrats and professors deplored.

At about the same time, Benjamin Disraeli, the romantic novelist and Tory leader whose political instincts seldom failed him, sensed the growing popularity of imperialism (particularly among the newly enfranchised lower middle classes) and adopted it as Conservative party policy. In a speech in 1872, Disraeli told his audience that they could choose to be subjects of a comfortable, insular, ordinary country or of "a great country, an imperial country, a country where your sons ... command the respect of the world."[4] Other intellectual and political leaders joined Disraeli in urging the British people to engage in open, unadorned expansionism. Britain joined the great nineteenth-century imperialist adventure partly out of a presumed need to expand its markets. According to England's leading imperialist, Cecil Rhodes, "Great Britain's position depends upon her trade, and if we do not open up the dependencies of the world which are at present devoted to barbarism we shall shut out the world's trade."[5]

The symbolic zenith of the British Empire was Queen Victoria's Diamond Jubilee in 1897. Representatives of the Queen's subjects from all over the empire came to London for the Jubilee, and the occasion was celebrated in British colonies around the world. The empire appeared to be unassailable, and British prestige had never been greater. A vast array of steamship lines, telegraph cables, and railroads united the Empire. British emigrants were scattered in key positions throughout the colonies. The English language and English customs had spread among native peoples, who were eager to learn the proper modes of dress, the ritual of high tea, and the rules of cricket, in addition to the

---

4   James Morris, *Heaven's Command: an Imperial Progress* (New York: Harcourt Brace Jovanovich, 1973), p. 382.

5   James Morris, *Pax Brittanica* (New York: Harcourt Brace Jovanovich, 1968), p. 109.

basic principles of government and the rule of law.

It is undeniable that Britain's imperial record was marred by blunders and crimes, of which perhaps the most notorious instance was the oppression of Ireland. On balance, though, given the generally dismal performance of human beings in ruling over others, the British record was a good one. The suppression of violence was part of the job and was normally conducted within the bounds of civilized behavior. General Charles Napier summed up the prevailing British philosophy: "a good thrashing first and great kindness afterwards"—a viewpoint similar to that of the great military leaders of republican Rome. The British, like the Romans, were willing to tolerate most local customs, but there were limits. When a local potentate argued that the practice of suttee was customary in India and therefore should be tolerated, Napier is said to have responded: "My nation also has a custom. When men burn women alive, we hang them."[6] Britain's achievements in India included reconstituting the coinage; stamping out the "Thugs" and other bandits; building schools, roads, irrigation systems and railways; improving public health; and creating a system for the impartial administration of justice. The same accomplishments were repeated throughout the empire.

Much of the debate over imperialism has centered on the issue of "exploitation" of the colonies. In some cases, no doubt, the colonies were exploited. India was required to buy equipment in Britain, and the prohibition on Indian tariffs meant that Indian cotton manufacturers were hurt by competition from the Lancashire mills. There were, however, some compensations for the Indian people. Withdrawal of British authority would have meant anarchy for much of the country under the arbitrary rule of local princes. British rule brought with it the beginnings of public health, transportation, education, and the regular administration of justice. Many of these civilized practices were also introduced into Africa, although with less success. Cultural relativists sometimes argue that roads, literacy, and systems of law represent Western values

---

6   Morris, *Heaven's Command*, p. 180.

that should not be forced upon non-Western societies. This argument is usually made by intellectuals in Western universities and not by the people who are faced with starvation or whose daughters are burned alive by their in-laws or killed by witch doctors. A century ago, educated people assumed that there was a distinction between civilization and barbarism and that it would be a good thing if savages could be persuaded to adopt civilized rules of behavior and Christian values. Not everyone favored imperialism; but at least there were standards for distinguishing savagery from rationality. Today, under the onslaught of relativism and anti-Western propaganda, the standards have been weakened. It is not at all clear that this devaluation of values is a net gain for the world.

THE ECONOMIC BASE

The Industrial Revolution
Britain's domination of the oceans of the world, as well as its remarkable prosperity at home, depended upon an expanding economic base. The industrial revolution made this possible; and it is important to understand why it happened and how it made Britain the leading global power.

Historians have rightly celebrated the industrial revolution, which began in Britain, as a watershed in human history. It brought an end to the Middle Ages and, for better or worse, ushered in the modern world of technology, mobility, and mass democracy. The word *revolution*, however, implies a more sudden change than actually occurred. The economic transformation of Western Europe did not take place overnight. It was the result of a long historical trend toward increased trade and urbanization that began in the eleventh century. A feudal, agricultural society led by military chiefs was gradually transformed by merchants and artisans into a market economy; serfdom and the feudal nobility disappeared over time partly because they were impediments to the new ways of doing business. Economic relations came to be based on contract rather than status, and property became more freely transferable. The rule of law was of critical importance: the British courts developed a system of law that protected private property and private transactions. The society that emerged from this process was characterized by a relatively high degree of freedom, individualism, and mobility.

During the late-seventeenth and early-eighteenth centuries, new scientific techniques were used to enhance agricultural productivity. The increase in food supplies made it possible to feed a growing population. Ultimately, the proportion of the population required to produce food dropped from the medieval level of 80 to 90 percent to less than 5 percent. This displacement of agricultural workers was a tragedy for many of those who were uprooted, but it changed the nature of modern society by providing labor for factories and giving rise to the urbanization of society. Urbanization, in turn, provided a critical mass of consumers of "civilized" commodities, from silver tea services to drama, music, poetry, painting, and buildings.[7] This long-running social drama was an example of a basic theme in the history of civilization: important and lasting changes in modes of living and in the civilized arts do not occur without painful adjustments. All of these developments, in conjunction, provided the necessary conditions for the industrial revolution. What made it revolutionary was a series of technological inventions that permitted the substitution of mechanical power for manpower. By the 1820s, one person operating a power loom could produce twenty times the output of a manual worker. The industrial revolution also produced a new form of economic organization—the factory system—which led to an extraordinary increase in production. This productivity provided the wealth without which neither the British Empire nor Britain's growing population could have been sustained.

The development of commercial law was an important contributing factor in Britain's success as a trading and manufacturing nation. Through a process of common-law adjudication, the British courts

---

7   For the evidence, see *The Economic History of Britain Since 1700*, ed. Floud and McCloskey, I (New York: Cambridge University Press, 1983) (hereinafter "Economic History") pp. 21, 68; Rosenberg and Birdzell, *How the West Grew Rich* (New York: Basic Books, 1986), p. 168.

developed rules for mercantile transactions that were fair, objective, and certain. Commercial contracts and negotiable instruments were more secure and predictable under British law than in other countries—an important benefit for British trade. Finally, the Bank of England provided a consistent source of sound credit, a benefit that most other nations did not enjoy.

Nineteenth-Century Economic Miracle
The statistics tell a remarkable story. Economic historians have estimated that between 1780 and 1860, along with a three-fold increase in population, British gross national product quintupled, annual per capita income more than trebled, and real wages rose by 44 percent. This growth was sustained by a ten-fold increase in capital investment, which in turn led to a significant increase in annual output per worker. Ordinary people received real benefits from these changes. A piece of cloth that sold for seventy or eighty shillings in the 1780s could be purchased for five shillings in the 1850s. It has been estimated that real consumption per person more than doubled between the 1760s and the 1850s. Consumer goods, pharmacies, and grocery stores proliferated. Nutrition and sanitary standards improved dramatically. Even for the lower income groups, standards of living improved.[8]

Britain's spectacular economic success in the nineteenth century can be explained in part by the conversion of its political leaders to the doctrines of Adam Smith: free trade, low taxes, sound money, and minimal government regulation. Beginning in the 1820s, tariffs were steadily lowered. In the 1840s, Robert Peel greatly reduced or abolished most duties on imports and exports. The "corn laws" (protective tariffs on grain) were repealed in 1846. Gladstone completed the liberal program of economic reform in the 1860s, removing many additional items from tariff and reducing others to minimal levels. These policies

8   See *Economic History,* I, pp. 136, 159, 174 and Table 7.5; Asa Briggs, *A Social History of England* (New York: Penguin, 1985), p. 189.

stimulated an impressive rise in British trade. Meanwhile, income tax rates were steadily lowered during the first two-thirds of the nineteenth century. As the tax rate was lowered, tax revenues actually increased as the economy grew.[9] Income taxes remained relatively low until World War I; then rates were steadily raised until they reached 50 percent and even higher after World War II. It is no coincidence that the period of Britain's economic rise coincided with decreases in tax rates, while the subsequent economic decline was accompanied by tax increases.

Excessive government spending was anathema to Adam Smith, who argued that the proper role of government was limited to defense, preservation of order, education, and certain public works that could not be built without government assistance. The Victorian governments in Britain implemented Smith's ideas; government spending as a percent of national income fell substantially during the nineteenth century. Gladstone's famous political principle—that money should be allowed "to fructify in the pockets of the people"—stands as a monument to British classical liberalism. To anticipate subsequent developments, we will see that the Smithian minimal state was turned on its head in the twentieth century. By the 1970s, one out of every three employees worked for the government or government-controlled entities.

While giving appropriate recognition to the economic doctrines of Adam Smith, we should not overlook the well-known Victorian moral values. Smith himself was a moral philosopher, and he knew that moral principles were not irrelevant to the creation of wealth. The growth of the British economy was supported by solid Victorian virtues: thrift, self-help, discipline, and hard work. The religious revival of the nineteenth century gave added strength to bourgeois morality; but even agnostics shared the earnestness, sense of duty, and capacity for work of their religious contemporaries. When Margaret Thatcher looked for principles to support the restoration of economic freedom in the 1980s,

---

9   Alvin Rabushka, *From Adam Smith to the Wealth of America* (New Brunswick, NJ: Transaction, 1985), p. 66. Under Gladstone, income tax rates were reduced to less than 2 percent.

she instinctively reached back to "Victorian values."

Spurred by low taxes, free trade, sound money, a ready labor force, and the bourgeois virtues of thrift and hard work, economic growth continued unabated in the second half of the nineteenth century. Per capita national income more than doubled between 1860 and 1914, during a period when the population grew from 29 million to 45 million. For the century between 1815 and 1914, per capita real income rose by 400 percent: a truly impressive rate of growth. Output of industrial goods rose dramatically. Victorian Britain had become the "workshop of the world."[10]

The Impact of the Industrial Revolution on the Working Classes

In assessing the industrial revolution, it is important to remember that in pre-industrial times, mass poverty existed all over Europe and throughout the world. Fernand Braudel has assembled the evidence for the existence in all pre-industrial societies of an enormous sub-proletariat living at the level of bare subsistence. Between a quarter and half of the population in Stuart England lived in abject poverty. The factory system, with all its faults, at least provided an alternative to starvation and beggary.[11]

It must nevertheless be conceded that the manner in which the industrial revolution proceeded was a great tragedy for many people and, in some respects, for the "English way of life." There was real hardship for displaced "cottage weavers" when machine-produced textiles replaced home-produced goods. By permitting wretched conditions in factories, the early industrialists forgot that power and wealth entail social obligations. This was a lesson that the aristocracy failed to teach and the rising middle-class businessmen failed to learn. Most sensitive

---

10   See *Economic History*, II, pp. 122–23, 133–34, 174, 199 and Table 6.1; Rabushka, pp. 111–12; Havighurst, *Britain in Transition* (Chicago: University of Chicago Press, 1985), p. 43.

11   Fernand Braudel, *The Wheels of Commerce* (New York: Harper & Row, 1982), pp. 506–7; Braudel, *Capitalism and Material Life 1400–1800* (New York: Harper & Row, 1973), pp. 52–53.

observers were horrified by the new conditions. The old system was bad for the poor, yet tolerable because it was sanctified by antiquity. The new system seemed both brutal and vulgar. The consequences of the social shock induced by industrialization included widespread embitterment, environmental devastation, class conflict, a socialist political movement, the destruction of the British aristocracy, and the rise of "mass culture." As is so often the case, part of the price of "progress" was pain and upheaval.

The worst features of the industrial revolution could have been mitigated. The factory owners should have recognized their responsibility to improve the working conditions of the laborers who made prosperity possible. They should have seen that poor education, deplorable housing, and inhuman working conditions would have detrimental effects on the work force and on society as a whole. Their attitude was short-sighted since it led to a growing belief among reformers that better conditions and fair compensation could be achieved only through socialist measures enforced by the coercive power of the state. The capitalists' myopia inspired several generations of social critics who were able to portray businessmen as satanic monsters exploiting the poor. As always, the abdication of leadership by the existing elite created a gap that was filled by other leaders and different philosophies. The British aristocracy played little part in the new industrialism, and the capitalists were morally unprepared for leadership. As a result, capitalism gradually gave way to Fabian socialism, and leadership was stripped away from the natural guardians of society.

As is so often the case with historical investigations, there are mixed and even contradictory messages. Industrialization disrupted traditional customs and may have accelerated the acceptance of a materialistic and relativistic worldview. On the other hand, the industrial revolution was a remarkable achievement of mind and imagination, combining scientific theory, experimentation, engineering, ambition, hard work, discipline, and the spirit of adventure. Capitalism, moreover, turned men's inherent aggressiveness into channels that, while not wholly benign, were less harmful than the alternatives. As Samuel Johnson said, "There are few ways in which a man can be more innocently employed than in getting money."[12] Such contradictions are inherent in the human experience and can never be resolved through historical analysis or through the historical process itself. We can only conclude that, with better leadership, the evil could have been mitigated and more of the good preserved.

THE CULTURAL COUNTER-REVOLUTION

While Britain was creating the most powerful industrial and commercial economy in the world, an unusual cultural phenomenon occurred: Britain's intellectual leaders, together with much of the religious, educational, and social establishment, rejected the technological and economic premises on which Britain's prosperity was based. Instead of seeking to understand and shape the industrial revolution, English writers, clerics, and aristocrats outdid one another in heaping scorn upon the industrialists and condemning the evils of capitalism.

In this respect, the social history of the Victorian period resembles that of Augustan Rome. Successful British businessmen wanted their children to become members of the upper classes. But the social position of the nobility and squirearchy was based on the ownership of land and the values associated with landowning. The rising entrepreneurs, in order to gain social respectability, consented to an implicit trade-off in which their children were admitted to the upper classes at the price of rejecting the entrepreneurial culture that was responsible for their families' success. The boys were sent to Eton, Rugby, and other "public schools," where they were taught that the only suitable occupations for gentlemen were agriculture, military service, the church, or governmental office. Marrying money was acceptable; making it "in trade" was not. The young scholars, steeped in the classics, imbibed the same

---

12   James Boswell, *The Life of Samuel Johnson* (London: Penguin Books, 2008), p. 435 (first published 1791).

anticommercial sentiments in Cicero, Horace, and other classical writers that had inspired their Roman counterparts nineteen centuries earlier. At the very moment of its historical triumph, in short, the rising British business class repudiated the values that had created it and devoted its energies to aping the manners of the dying aristocracy.[13] As a result of the cultural counter-revolution, too many intelligent Englishmen spent too much time trying to promote illusory utopian solutions rather than making the difficult but constructive effort to merge the capitalist system into the Western moral tradition.

Beginning in the 1820s, Britain produced a series of writers whose collective talents were prodigious and whose influence was vast. They included Sir Walter Scott, George Eliot, Charles Dickens, Thomas Carlyle, John Ruskin, Matthew Arnold, William Morris, the "Christian Socialists" and many others. These writers shared a common dislike (often verging on hatred) for industrial capitalism and laissez-faire economic theory. Some of the critics, like Scott and Ruskin, were nostalgic medievalists, while others, like the Christian Socialists, were influenced by the rising tide of socialist doctrine. Looking toward a renewed period of organic community and spiritual harmony, they could not accept the triumph of the capitalist system and the crude materialist values of the rising industrial class. The social critics succeeded all too well in making free market principles appear inhumane but without putting anything in their place other than a vague preference for socialism, which lacked any practical basis.

Most of the Victorian social critics had little understanding of economic principles. John Ruskin, for example, attacked free-market principles on the ground that employers became rich only by impoverishing their employees and customers. "The force of the guinea you have in your pocket depends wholly on the default of a guinea in your neighbor's pocket," wrote Ruskin. "The art of making yourself rich

---

13   See Martin Wiener, *English Culture and the Decline of the Industrial Spirit, 1850–1980,* Chap. 2 (New York: Cambridge University Press, 1986).

in the ordinary mercantile economist's sense, is therefore equally and necessarily the art of keeping your neighbor poor."[14] The assertion that the economy is a zero-sum game, so that one person can gain only if another person loses a like amount, was a favorite theme of Ruskin and later socialists. But this view ignored the growing evidence that the entire society (including the average worker) was becoming richer. Ruskin's view was nevertheless accepted by many, then and later, who were looking for ammunition against capitalism and competition.[15] The solution urged by Ruskin, Arnold, and many of the other social critics was a strong central government that would have authority to direct the economy. This advice fit in nicely with the socialist ideas that were beginning to spread across Europe.

Similar attitudes pervaded the books of Charles Dickens and other nineteenth-century novelists. English poetry and fiction, like the odes of Augustan Rome, were filled with rural nostalgia and sighs of discontent over the oppressions of the present. The distaste for commercial enterprise was omnipresent. In novels as in elevated social circles, the nobility and its camp-followers sneered at those who were "in trade:" barristers looked down on solicitors because they took money directly from clients; and men who wrote books or gave sermons scorned those who demeaned themselves by producing goods.

One of the most powerful of the nineteenth century social critics, Thomas Carlyle, did propose a vision of a new social contract that, if implemented, might have contributed to a more intelligent and civilized social order while sparing Britain the destructive practices of socialism. The nation's hereditary landowning aristocracy was the traditional source of leadership, and Carlyle originally assumed that this elite would continue to furnish guidance and governance to Britain. By the middle

---

14   John Ruskin, *Unto This Last* (London: Cassell's Little Classics, 1909), p. 130.

15   One of Ruskin's biographers speaks of "the well-attested influence of the book [*Unto This Last*] on Tolstoy, Ghandi and the British Labour movement." Patrick Conner, *Savage Ruskin* (Detroit: Wayne State University Press, 1979), p. 136.

of the nineteenth century, however, Carlyle's hope that the landed aristocracy would retain political leadership was no longer a practical possibility. Parliamentary reform had eroded the political control of the landowners and repeal of the "corn laws" had reduced their economic power. The creation of wealth had passed into the hands of the commercial and industrial middle classes. Late in life, Carlyle concluded that authority and stability could be preserved only if the "industrial heroes" and "captains of industry" became the new aristocracy.[16] Their vigorous work ethic, which Carlyle shared, would provide the moral sanction for the new industrial order. The burden of leadership would require the industrialists to develop a sense of social responsibility and to achieve a deeper relationship with the workers. Carlyle called for a new "chivalry of labor" and a "permanent contract" between employer and employee. The workers should be given a permanent interest in the enterprise. Society would recognize a new hierarchy in which superiority would be based on merit and willing acquiescence. Carlyle urged the captains of industry to unite with the old aristocracy to form the "Noble of the Future," who would civilize the world of industry by annihilating the dirt and squalor defacing Britain and return to the honest production of well-made goods.

Carlyle's proposed solution to the social problem offered some hope of preserving important features of the British social tradition while taking advantage of the creative energy of the new industrial order. The aristocracy would supply the values of honor and decency, while the entrepreneurs offered the talent and energy. Together, they could govern Britain in the interest of values higher than mere profitability, but without impairing the dynamism of industrial capitalism. By improving the lot of the workers through a new social contract to replace the old feudal one, the realization of Carlyle's inspiration might have spared Britain a century of class warfare.

---

16 Carlyle, *Past and Present* (London: Chapman and Hall, 1843) in *Collected Works*, XIII (London), p. 335; and *Shooting Niagara* (London: Chapman and Hall, 1867).

As it turned out, Carlyle's wish for a union of the old aristocracy and the rising capitalists was partly realized but not in the way he had hoped. The two groups combined in a marriage of convenience. The landed aristocrats needed money, and the entrepreneurs needed social respectability; therefore, the aristocrats encouraged their daughters to marry businessmen, while the businessmen acquired titles, moved into country houses, and sent their children to schools in which they were taught to despise trade and favor socialism. This took the British elite down a path that led eventually to collectivization and mediocrity. Lord Macauley captured the essence of the matter in 1833:

> The curse of England is the obstinate determination of the middle classes to make their sons what they call gentlemen. So we are overrun by clergymen without livings; lawyers without briefs; physicians without patients; authors without readers; clerks soliciting employment, who might have thriven, and been above the world, as bakers, watchmakers, or innkeepers.[17]

Victorian Education

During the course of the Victorian era, the cultural hostility to capitalism became deeply embedded in the British educational system, whose acknowledged purpose was to fit upper-class boys into the proper aristocratic mold. Education in the leading schools consisted largely of the Greek and Roman classics. These works conveyed the social doctrines of the ancient aristocracy and the Roman *literati,* whose contempt for commerce and non-agricultural enterprise was legendary. Science was badly neglected in the curricula of British schools. The universities conveyed similar attitudes, actively discouraging undergraduates from pursuing business careers. The neglect of science and engineering soon placed Britain at a competitive disadvantage. As early as the 1820s and 1830s, German states established polytechnic institutes for training

---

17   Quoted in Paul Johnson, *A History of the English People* (New York: Harper & Row, 1985), p. 290.

engineers. In the United States, business leaders promoted engineering studies, and state governments financed extensive programs of technical education in public universities. British educators, on the other hand, deemphasized science and, where science was taught at all, favored theoretical or "pure" science over applied science. Engineering was scarcely taught at all in the schools; British engineers continued to receive most of their training on the shop floor.[18]

The results of Britain's neglect of scientific and technical education soon became apparent. As early as the 1860s, British visitors to Germany began to warn that the Germans were moving ahead of Britain in the newer technologies. By World War I, Germany was producing far more graduate engineers per year then Britain.[19] The British school system was, for the most part, nationalized in the 1890s, but (as in the case of the nationalization of industry much later) state control did more harm than good. Tory governments early in the twentieth century, consistent with their cultural attitudes, installed a curriculum that virtually ignored science and technology. Subsequently, under Labour governments, egalitarian ideologues debased academic standards across the board. The weakness of Britain's state school system was an important factor in its economic decline.

Tories and Fabians

The most important conservative political figure in the nineteenth century was Benjamin Disraeli. Disraeli believed that Britain had become divided into "two nations"—rich and poor—a division which he blamed principally on industrial capitalism. Disraeli correctly perceived that the exclusive worship of material progress was false and superficial. The contemporary European, he argued, can speak of progress only because "by an ingenious application of some scientific acquirements he

---

18   Elbaum and Lazonick, *The Decline of the British Economy* (Oxford: Oxford University Press, 1987), pp. 173–79.

19   Paul Johnson, *op. cit.*, p. 337; *Economic History*, II, p. 224.

has established a society which has mistaken comfort for civilization."[20] Disraeli was right to resist the equation of comfort and civilization. Like the romantic idealists and the literary critics, however, he neglected a basic point: both comfort and civilization are made possible by economic resources, which, in the modern world, can *only* be produced by "scientific acquirements." Instead of trying to understand science and technology and to make them part of a single cultural milieu accessible to all educated people, the Victorian romantics ignored science and scorned its practical applications. Because of this rejectionist attitude, Britain not only continued to suffer from Disraeli's "two nations," it also developed two cultures, each increasingly remote from the other.

By the early 1890s, three different versions of socialism had emerged—Marxism, Fabianism, and "ethical socialism." Marx's ideas were important in helping Fabians and other socialists to formulate their thinking, but Marxist doctrines of class struggle and violent revolution never made much headway in England. Far more important was ethical socialism, which took its inspiration from the writings of Carlyle, Ruskin, Morris, and a group of religious activists known as "Christian Socialists."[21] The quasi-religious tone of the ethical socialists gave English socialism a sense of moral righteousness suitable for a sacred crusade—in this case, a crusade to establish a perfect society on earth. The aura of sanctimonious utopianism permeated socialist propaganda for decades and made socialistic doctrines essentially impervious to empirical evidence, a characteristic that has persisted among socialists to the present day.

In spite of the crusading tone of the ethical socialists, the British, true to their social habits, did not choose to impose socialism by revolution but instead moved toward it by incremental steps. The principal vehicle for the gradual realization of the socialist utopia was the Fabian

---

20   Blake, *Disraeli* (New York: St. Martin's Press, 1967) p. 765.

21   Edward Norman, *The Victorian Socialists* (Cambridge, UK: Cambridge University Press, 1987).

Society, an organization founded in the 1880s. Among its most important members were Sidney and Beatrice Webb, George Bernard Shaw, H. G. Wells, and Clement Attlee. The Fabians accepted such basic socialist doctrines as the injustice of capitalism and the necessity for collective ownership of the means of production. Most Fabians, however, did not favor starting a new socialist party; instead, they hoped to work within the existing political structure. But socialist doctrines were incompatible with both the Liberal Party and the Conservative Party. Accordingly, the Fabians joined a new Independent Labour Party (predecessor of the Labour Party), founded in 1893. Sidney Webb also founded the London School of Economics that spread the doctrines of socialist economics around the world. The most influential of the literary Fabians was George Bernard Shaw, who wielded his pen in the service of socialism for more than half a century. The popular "Fabian Essays," edited by Shaw and first published in 1889, passed through numerous editions. In his plays and articles, Shaw attacked the foundations of capitalism and private property. Shaw's solution to the "social question" was the compulsory redistribution of income and property by the state—a practice that became increasingly popular among European governments in the twentieth century.

By World War II, the critics of capitalism had won the battle of ideas. Defenders of free enterprise were as rare in England as sunny days in March. As a result, there was little articulate opposition to the great postwar leap into government ownership and confiscatory taxation that accelerated the decline of the already-troubled British economy.

Killing the Golden Goose

In retrospect, we can now see that the antipathy to trade, shared by upper-class Britons and most of the Victorian *literati*, was based on a misconception. Let us grant the Victorian critics' premise that a nation's greatness is measured by its culture (in the broadest sense) and not by the amount of coal and iron that it produces. The relationship between culture and productivity, however, is more complex than the Victorian social critics supposed. Any culture worth having is supported by a material base. Greek and Roman civilization depended upon trade and commerce as well as upon agricultural production. (As noted in Chapter 1, the Romans never developed fully their commercial and industrial potential, but commerce was essential to the spread of Roman culture throughout the Empire.) Without the material resources provided by commerce, the Greeks would have remained in the Bronze Age. Temples, statues, drama, and philosophy were possible only because commercial enterprise produced the surplus necessary to support craftsmen, poets, lawmakers, and philosophers, as well as soldiers. The British intelligentsia failed to recognize that commercial activity was not the enemy of culture, but rather a necessary condition of it. Classical Greece and Rome, the Renaissance city states, seventeenth-century Holland, and eighteenth-century England provide examples of this truth. Even the high Gothic culture of the European Middle Ages depended on the wealth produced by towns and trade. The Victorian social critics, overcome by their anticommercial bias, lost track of this essential point.

The social reformers were right to be worried about the social effects of the industrial revolution. But they failed to see that there were two sides to the balance sheet. Every society has its characteristic strengths, and every strong society is marked by a certain aggressiveness. For instance, armed knights and militant clerics led Medieval Christian society. Later, the strength of Western society burst forth in successive waves of commercial and technological energy. The industrial revolution spread the language and culture of Britain to the corners of the globe and offered to millions the hope that they might someday be relieved from destitution.

The industrial society created a moral hazard, in part, because it enriched people who had not been trained in the proper uses of wealth. The solution, however, was not to make the rich poorer but to make more people wiser and better. To this end, the critics and the aristocrats should have joined with Carlyle's "captains of industry" rather than isolating them; the moral and social guardians might then have persuaded the newly rich that their wealth gave them special obligations. Instead, the critics fostered a negative and hostile climate that contributed to the social split that Disraeli had feared and to the erosion of the material base on which Britain's prosperity rested. When the Fabian socialists and Tory paternalists finally succeeded in impairing Britain's industrial economy, the nation did not become morally or culturally better; it merely became shabbier and weaker.

Underlying all of the critics' broadsides against capitalism was an abhorrence of competition, which they declared to be brutal and degrading and which they feared would lead to social anarchy. A laissez-faire economy in a civilized country, however, is not anarchic if restrained by customary social institutions such as family and church, by principles of fair dealing, and by traditional legal rules that encourage honest bargains while penalizing fraud, duress, and breach of fiduciary duty. Additional rules, such as factory legislation, can be made by the legislature when needed. Such a system is the precise opposite of anarchy; it is the embodiment of the rule of law. It is a system, however, that is easily broken if subjected to excessive tinkering. The interventionist, paternal state advocated by Ruskin, Arnold, and the Fabians is not necessarily favorable to "sweetness and light" (to use Arnold's phrase), as the twentieth century abundantly demonstrated.

Perhaps the most serious intellectual error of the Victorian social critics—an error the more unpardonable in view of their wide learning—was their denigration of science and technology as inferior, materialistic pursuits. They should have recognized the enterprise of Western science for what it was: an astonishing intellectual achievement. Science is based in large part on mathematics, which, as philosophers from Plato to Whitehead have understood, is a conceptual discipline only tangentially related to the material world. The actual *doing* of science requires a combination of rigorous analytical objectivity, discipline, and creativity: qualities that flourished in western Europe and especially in Britain. The industrial revolution, for which the scientific revolution was a necessary predicate, did produce certain social consequences that were far from benign. But Britain's inability to cope with those consequences without succumbing to the temptations of socialist envy was a sign of decadence. The squeamish cultural reaction against capitalism deprived British society of the fullest energies of its most dynamic men by giving them the cold choice of remaining social outsiders or conforming to a social code that had lost its vitality. Instead of following Carlyle's vision, the critics of capitalism attacked what was strongest and most vital in their nation and thereby contributed to its decline.

THE DECLINE OF THE BRITISH ECONOMY

In the last decades of the nineteenth century, Britain began to decline economically relative to its major industrial competitors. In 1870, Britain produced 50 percent of the world's pig iron and 43 percent of the steel. By 1913, these percentages had fallen to 14 percent and 10 percent respectively. Statistics from other industries are equally dramatic. By 1914, the leading industrial powers were the United States and Germany. Paul Kennedy has constructed a set of composite statistics showing the "total industrial potential" of the great powers between 1880 and 1938. Kennedy's figures show that, between 1880 and 1938, Britain's index of industrial potential moved from 73.3 to 181, but that of the United States moved from 46.9 to 528 and Germany's from 27.4 to 214. In terms of industrial strength, in other words, America and Germany were growing much faster than Britain. This relative economic decline had serious consequences for Britain's position as a great power.[22]

Why did Britain's economy fare so poorly compared to the economies of its commercial rivals? The short answer is that beginning around 1860, Britain invested too little, consumed too much, and lost its technological lead. It is true, of course, that Britain had a head start,

---

22 See Paul Kennedy, *The Rise and Fall of the Great Powers* (New York: Random House, 1987), pp. 201–2 and Tables 17 and 18; Economic History, II, p. 107 et seq. and Tables 1.2 and 1.3; Elbaum and Lazonick, pp. 51, 57; Aaron Friedberg, *The Weary Titan: Britain and the Experience of Relative Decline 1895–1905* (Princeton: Princeton University Press, 1988), pp. 24–25 and Table 2–1.

but its lead was to some extent artificial; there was no possible way that Britain could have held on to its overwhelming market share in the face of determined competition. But the inevitability of some reduction in the industrial disparity does not explain the extraordinary difference in growth patterns.

One of Britain's problems was its failure to develop new technologies and new products. Britain's exports were concentrated in the basic industries of the industrial revolution—in particular, textiles, iron, steel, and coal. In the period between 1900 and World War I, Britain's competitors began to apply advanced techniques to those industries and to protect them with high tariffs. British manufacturers either had to reduce per unit costs through labor-saving technology, develop new products, or open up new markets for existing products. In general, they chose the last option by shifting their sales efforts to colonial and other undeveloped markets rather than by attempting to develop new industries and products.[23] Britain lagged far behind, for example, in the emerging technologies of electrical goods, automobiles, and aircraft, and in industrial productivity generally—mainly due to the failure to modernize plant and equipment. This left the huge markets of Europe and America increasingly open to Britain's competitors. Meanwhile, enormous amounts of capital were being exported from Britain for investment abroad. These capital exports drained funds from the domestic economy, resulting in the under-capitalization of British industry and a serious shortage of risk capital.

Deteriorating labor relations further weakened Britain's productivity. Strikes, slowdowns, and other manifestations of industrial strife proliferated. The owners were certainly not blameless. Lacking the sense of responsibility that they ought to have learned, they moved slowly and grudgingly to correct indefensible conditions in their factories. By the end of the nineteenth century, class antagonisms had already hardened,

---

23   Corelli Barnett, *The Pride and the Fall: The Dream and Illusion of Britain as a Great Nation* (New York: Free Press, 1987), pp. 94, 105.

and a divisive, ideological labor movement was well-established. Early in the twentieth century, trade unions took effective control of the shop floors in many British industries. Union resistance provided an additional excuse for timid managers to avoid innovation. Rigid work rules and union insistence upon preserving jobs at any cost constituted a virtually insurmountable barrier to efficiency.

The spread of socialism in the late nineteenth and early twentieth centuries is a classic example of the importance of ideas in history. When the Independent Labour Party was established in 1893, the delegates, meeting at Bedford in the heart of Britain's industrial region, voted overwhelmingly to support the central goal of socialism: "to secure the collective ownership of all the means of production, distribution and exchange."[24] It is difficult to imagine a more radical departure from the classical liberal ideal of individual freedom to own property and to trade freely with others. The founding of the ILP was a decisive turning point. For much of the following century, Britain would move, gradually but steadily, in the direction of state collectivism.

Lloyd George's "People's Budget" of 1909 signaled the beginning of the undisguised political battle to redistribute wealth. The result was what Jacques Barzun has called "the Great Switch:" the transformation of classical liberalism into its political opposite—the regulatory welfare state. The budget included 25 percent inheritance taxes on estates of one million pounds and over and a 20 percent tax on the unearned increment in value when land changed hands, as well as large increases in income tax rates. The assumption underlying the People's Budget was that incomes, as well as increases in the value of property at death or upon transfer, should be partially confiscated by the state for the purpose of subsidizing groups chosen by the legislature. This principle has had a long and destructive life ever since.

World War I, in addition to depleting the ranks of the aristocracy

---

24   Pierson, *Marxism and the Origins of British Socialism* (Ithaca, NY: Cornell University Press, 1973), pp. 187, 206.

on the battlefield, diminished the patrimony of the landowning classes in a less honorable way. Lloyd George's punitive estate taxes applied to each transfer of land. When more than one heir to a single piece of property was killed in the war, the property was subject to successive death duties. Many families could not sustain the burden and were forced to sell their land. It has been estimated that six to eight million acres changed hands in England between 1918 and 1921.[25] A transfer of land on this scale was unequalled at least since the time of Henry VIII and possibly since the Norman Conquest. Hundreds of country homes were demolished and their contents sold at auction. The destruction of their patrimony was evidence enough that the British aristocracy and squirearchy had been nullified as an effective political force. As in the case of Rome, the collapse of the aristocracy produced a vacuum in the society's political, cultural, and moral leadership. The upper class was moribund and despoiled, and the middle class was politically unskilled and not yet entirely trusted.

A further consequence of the World War was to accelerate the growth of government by means of the extensive controls imposed upon industry, trade, food, and natural resources. The apparent success of government controls during wartime led many to argue that they would be equally successful in peacetime. This conclusion did not follow, of course, since the emotional cohesion of all-out war is never repeated in peacetime. Freedom-loving people, in any event, should have been suspicious of forced regimentation to achieve political goals. But reformers accepted the assumption that wartime coercion provided a model for peacetime policies. By the 1920s, a basic political change had occurred in Britain. The Liberal Party began to disintegrate, along with the principles of laissez-faire and minimal government on which the party had been founded. The left, now identified with Labour, advocated a program of nationalization and collectivist social reform. Now that it had become fashionable to believe that government could "solve" social problems, the political demand for

---

25   F.M.L. Thompson, *English Landed Society* (London: Routledge & Kegan Paul, 1963), pp. 332–33.

government intervention was irresistible. Numerous ill-considered interventionist measures were adopted in the 1930s, including government-sponsored cartels to regulate production and prices. These corporatist, anticompetitive policies increased structural rigidities and caused a further decline in efficiency.[26]

Centralized government control of the economy was widely supported by writers and intellectuals, who were virtually unanimous in condemning economic liberalism and calling for a "planned society." George Bernard Shaw and the Webbs visited Russia and enthusiastically recommended Soviet communism as a model for the future.[27] Communist cells were formed in universities. Members of the "Apostles" at Cambridge, an old and respected secret society, dedicated themselves to the communist cause. It became fashionably progressive to argue that economic freedom was meaningless, that equality through redistribution was a desirable goal, and that the economy could be scientifically planned by civil servants. These assumptions were directly contrary to the values on which Britain's prosperity and empire had been founded. The social planners, unfortunately, did not give serious consideration to the possibility that excessive regulation and redistribution of wealth through high progressive tax rates might impair the economy's ability to produce. This turned out to be a damaging oversight.

THE RETREAT FROM EMPIRE

Even if its economy had not been weakened by socialist policies at home, Britain's control over dozens of countries around the world could not last. How could a military force of two hundred thousand men and a navy of a few hundred ships, no matter how competently led, hold together a polyglot empire containing millions of people? Yet the retreat

---

26   J.R. Hay, *The Development of the British Welfare State, 1880–1975* (London: E. Arnold, 1978), p. 93; T.O. Lloyd, *Empire and Welfare State* (Oxford, Oxford University Press, 1984); Elbaum and Lazonick, *op. cit.,* pp. 277–78.

27   S. and B. Webb, *Soviet Communism: A New Civilization?* (New York: C. Scribner's Sons, 1936).

from empire was unduly precipitous and could have been managed with less damaging consequences for Britain and its colonies. The essential element in Britain's control over its vast imperial holdings was a majestic self-confidence, usually described by non-Britons as arrogance. The Boer War (1899–1902) shattered the social consensus on which this national self-confidence depended. While Britain eventually won the war, it did so with considerable difficulty. British war measures—including the establishment of concentration camps for Boer families—unleashed a torrent of criticism. Casualties were heavy, resources were strained, and morale deteriorated. By the time the war ended, some of the bravado of invulnerability had been lost. A parallel can be drawn between the Boer War and the Vietnam War of the 1960s and 1970s.

The aristocratic social structure that had supported the empire was eroding. The Liberal Party victory in the election of 1906 ended a long period of Conservative rule, diminishing permanently the power of the landowning interests in Parliament. The Parliament Act of 1911 drastically curtailed the powers of the House of Lords. Radical changes in taxation, previously described, weakened the economic position of the ruling elite. The focus of England's political energy had shifted from empire to social reform.

Even Britain's dominance of the seas began to erode. The loss of worldwide naval supremacy further weakened Britain's international position and its ability to maintain its imperial commitments. Meanwhile, on the European continent, the nineteenth-century balance of power began unraveling as the military power of Germany grew. Unlike the European powers, Britain lacked a trained army reserve; thus, the German military strategists who devised the Schlieffen plan in the run-up to World War I plausibly believed that Germany could win quickly without having to face a British army. Britain had become strategically overextended: its commitments exceeded its resources. Britain's relative economic decline left it without the financial ability to sustain a worldwide empire and fight a continental war. Predominance in most industrial sectors had passed to other nations. Imperial decline began when Britain tried to play the part of the world's leading power without the necessary resources. It was a classic example of "overstretch"—a recurring theme in the decline of nations.

The century of the "Pax Britannica" ended in 1914. World War I killed off 10 percent of British men under forty-five and left Britain with a huge national debt. Overseas assets had been sold *en masse* to finance the war effort. Increased taxes and government controls had become a permanent feature of British life. There was a reaction after the war against everything Victorian. Victoria's empire, along with chastity, temperance, and thrift, became a subject of ridicule rather than veneration. Soon after the war, Britain signaled its acceptance of a reduced role in the world by its concurrence in the naval restrictions imposed by the Washington Naval Conference of 1922. As a consequence, Britain scrapped over 600 ships. The mere idea of such an agreement would have seemed raving lunacy to any Victorian statesman. Obviously, Britain's 200-year command of the seas was over. The colonies, meanwhile, began to separate from Britain, some by consent and others by revolt.

The trumpets of war were temporarily replaced by the siren song of disarmament. In the Kellogg-Briand Pact of 1928, the contracting powers agreed to renounce war as an instrument of national policy and to resolve all disputes by pacific means. Sixty-two nations, including Germany, Japan, and Italy, signed this document, which has been aptly described as "an attempt to keep the peace by incantation."[28] In spite of a series of ominous events, including the Japanese invasion of Manchuria in 1931, Italy's aggression against Abyssinia in 1935, and Germany's occupation of the Rhineland in violation of the Versailles Treaty, appeasement was the order of the day. Politicians, newspapers, and the public displayed a naive faith in the League of Nations in spite of the inability of that body to take action against aggression. The peace proposals of Hitler were accepted

---

28 Samuel Eliot Morison, *The Oxford History of the American People* (New York: Oxford University Press, 1965), p. 922.

at face value by British leaders of both parties, who outdid each other in their eagerness to "understand" the German dictator. This passivity in the face of aggression was shared by most of the Western democracies. "The democracies wrongly believed," as Victor Davis Hanson has observed, "that their laxity would be seen as magnanimity."[29]

The unwillingness on the part of politicians and the public to recognize unpleasant facts had a disastrous effect on Britain's military forces. By the mid-1930s, Britain had fallen well behind Germany and Japan in nearly every category of arms. The United Kingdom was not willing to pay for the technology required to preserve its position as a leading military power, just as it was unwilling to meet the challenge of its rivals in industrial technology. Spending priorities had shifted: social welfare expenditures now absorbed a much higher proportion of the budget.

Britain's near-disastrous lack of preparedness for both of its major twentieth century wars reveals a weakness at the core of nations governed by liberal principles, which emphasize, inter alia, the peaceful resolution of disputes and the avoidance of armed force. Liberal democratic societies respond promptly to the desires of their electorates. Especially when deprived of the leadership of a militarily trained elite (Gibbon's term is "martial nobility"), most voters do not want to think about war and are reluctant to pay taxes to support military establishments. As a result, liberal democracies are seldom prepared for a serious war. They assume that international organizations and "international law" are real forces capable of preventing violence, whereas at best they are useful instruments for maintaining a peace that already exists. While rules of international law can help resolve boundary disputes, they are effective in serious matters only if backed by the military power of real nations. The reluctance to face the reality of international behavior led British politicians to encourage their constituents' naive hope that good intentions alone could avoid war.

In World War II, Britain again fought bravely and successfully

---

29   Victor Davis Hanson, *The Second World Wars* (New York: Basic Books, 2017), p. 32.

with a great deal of help from its allies. But the war marked the end of Britain's position as a major world power and dealt the final blow to its empire. Several factors were at work. Britain's economic decline, exacerbated by the debts of World War II, meant that the costs of empire were intolerably burdensome. Instead of economic revival, Britain's immediate goal after the war was to establish a welfare state. Private resources were heavily taxed and redistributed to provide domestic subsidies for health, housing, and inefficient industries. These policies impaired economic productivity and deprived England of the surplus revenues needed to support an overseas role.

The result was the "policy of scuttle." After more than 200 years of British rule in India, Lord Mountbatten in 1947 ended it in less than ninety days. The subcontinent was partitioned between India and Pakistan; the British abandoned their charge and walked away. The country slipped into chaos as Muslims, Hindus, and Sikhs engaged in mutual slaughter. Whole communities were massacred. At least 200,000 died, and millions were left homeless. The remaining colonies dropped away one by one: Burma and Ceylon in the 1940s, Nigeria, Kenya, and other African colonies in the 1950s and 1960s. The former colonies were abandoned to their own devices without adequate preparation. Many of them, especially in Africa, quickly fell victim to military brutality, corruption, oppression, and economic mismanagement. In retrospect, these colonies would have been better off if the British had persevered until the infrastructure of democracy under law had been more carefully developed; but Britain lacked the finances and the willpower to continue its imperial role, even temporarily.

The Suez crisis of 1956 signaled the final collapse of British imperialism. Following Egyptian president Nasser's nationalization of the Suez Canal, an act that threatened oil supplies and other commercial interests, Britain joined France in military support of Israel's attack on Egypt in late October 1956. Promptly thereafter, Britain and France caved in to pressure from their allies, especially the United States, and agreed to a ceasefire, followed by a hasty withdrawal, giving Nasser and his Soviet backers an unexpectedly easy victory. The Suez debacle ended any pretense that Britain was still a great power. A few years later, Prime Minister Harold Wilson announced that Britain would withdraw its armed forces east of Suez, reflecting the belated recognition that its foreign commitments were in excess of its economic and military capabilities. Henceforth, Britain's former role as the protector of commercial freedom would be assumed by the new, rising Western power—the United States.

Britain, of course, was not alone in losing its empire. In 1900 there were several major territorial empires, including the British, French, German, Austro-Hungarian, Ottoman, Dutch, Japanese, and Portuguese. With the exception of the United States (which had some imperial features), only the Soviet empire remained by 1980, and it subsequently disintegrated. It would have been difficult for any of the European powers to have retained its empire in the face of the damaging impact of two European wars, the rise of nationalism, and the active sponsorship of "national liberation movements" by the Soviet Union and its satellites. Britain was in the best position to effect an orderly, long-term liquidation but failed to do so for the reasons already discussed.

What can we learn from the British experience? A basic lesson is that over-expansion is risky. A nation should not undertake global defense commitments unless it has both the resources and the will to maintain them. Britain had the resources and the will in the nineteenth century but lost both in the twentieth. Why did Britain's power decline as rapidly as it did? First, as noted, it was overextended and could not afford to defend its empire. Second, Britain chose to emphasize the redistribution of wealth rather than its creation. Third, it fell behind its competitors in industrial technology. And, finally, in an age of relativism, Western values were deemed to be no better than those of any other society; therefore, the burdens of empire were morally pointless. Loss of confidence by Western elites in the values of Western civilization had done more than undermine colonial empires; it called into question the very foundations of Western culture.

SOCIETY, VALUES, AND CULTURE

The Victorians took moral values seriously. Indeed, the word *Victorian*, somewhat unfairly, has come to stand for puritanical moralism. In reading Victorian literature, one is impressed with the extraordinary emphasis on work and self-discipline. Carlyle's celebration of the sanctity of work was repeated by hundreds of less-talented scribes. The opposite of work, idleness, was fiercely condemned. Thrift, or living within one's income, was another basic virtue for the Victorians. Samuel Smiles wrote a book called *Thrift* (1875), in which he argued that "every thrifty person may be regarded as a public benefactor, and every thriftless person as a public enemy." The Victorians also promoted the virtues of *respectability* and *self-respect*. These were important attitudes in fostering a culture of freedom and responsibility.

Religion was enormously important in nineteenth-century Britain. The influence of the evangelical movement made moralizing respectable and popular. The decline of religious faith in the latter part of the century weakened the most important conventional support for morality. The impact of Darwinism upon Christianity was exacerbated by the unfortunate attempt by many clergymen to characterize evolution as an infernal lie instead of recognizing it as simply another way of looking at the divine order of nature. By insisting upon a literal interpretation of the Bible, including biblical chronology, the churchmen were fighting a battle they could not win. Christians should have welcomed any new insights into the majesty of God's creation. Instead, the literalists' insistence that the biblical account was the only way of accounting for the physical world presented the opponents of religion with an irresistible opportunity to make the clergymen look foolish. The spread of the Darwinian model also tended to challenge conventional notions of morality. If life was merely a struggle for the "survival of the fittest," it could be argued that moral principles were no more valid for humans than they were for tigers. The growing influence of rationalism, positivism, and the "new criticism" of the Bible further undermined the moral authority of the church. Churchgoing dropped off sharply in the last decades of the nineteenth century. By 1903, only two persons out of eleven regularly attended church services in London.[30] (By the end of the twentieth century, the percentage of churchgoers had dropped to 10 percent and is probably less today.) If one assumes that religion provides a principal sanction for morality, the social consequences of this de-Christianization are potentially harmful.

The dramatic cultural change was reflected in the English literature of the 1920s. The postwar spirit of despair and disillusion was captured in T.S. Eliot's 1922 poem "The Wasteland" ("What are the roots that clutch, what branches grow/Out of this stony rubbish ... A heap of broken images, where the sun beats,/And the dead tree gives no shelter, the cricket no relief,/And the dry stone no sound of water"); and in fiction such as Aldous Huxley's brutally satirical novel *Point Counterpoint* (1928), describing a hopeless culture in which vindictive and pretentious pseudo-intellectuals ruthlessly destroy each other.

This decline of values in early twentieth-century Britain led to two important consequences. First, the abandonment of traditional moral principles by the "leading classes" eventually spread downward through the society, a process that historian Arnold Toynbee called "mimesis." Second, the decay of Victorian values under the combined assault of Darwinism, Freudianism, and relativism led to the deterioration in self-reliance and civic virtue, qualities that are essential to a free and successful society. The Victorian values were not just bourgeois values; they were also civic values. Thrift, prudence, and hard work were precisely those qualities that enabled people to improve their condition, support their families, and participate in community life. The destruction of common-sense values also contributed to the outbreak of crime and violence that further undermined the stable communities on which successful civic life depends.

---

30   Havighurst, *op. cit.*, p. 23.

POST-WORLD WAR II: THE CONSTRUCTION
OF THE WELFARE STATE

At the end of World War II in 1945, Britain was still considered a great power, with a victorious army of nearly three million men in Europe, as well as a reasonably effective navy and air force. Between 1939 and 1944, Britain's factories had produced enormous quantities of aircraft, artillery pieces, tanks, and vehicles. The statistics, however, are misleading. The productivity of British industry had been declining relative to that of Britain's competitors for many years. Much of Britain's war effort had been financed by loans from the United States. British industry was plagued by low morale and bad labor relations. During the war, the government purchased an uneasy harmony in the workplace through uneconomic subsidies and wage increases, which could not easily be reversed.[31]

On the political front, prominent leaders in government, church, and academia agreed that a "new Britain" would have to be established through central planning. The focal point of this effort was the Beveridge Commission on Social Insurance and Allied Services, headed by William Beveridge, which in December 1942 issued its report calling for a national crusade to reform society and abolish privilege. The Commission recommended a universal system of compulsory social insurance embracing all persons, with the goal of providing a guaranteed minimum income for everyone. In the years immediately after the war, Parliament pursued this utopian goal and created a full-fledged welfare state. The National Insurance Act (1946) established a government insurance program covering sickness, old age, and unemployment. The National Health Service Act created a free and universal health service, financed by taxation. Hospitals were nationalized. The National Assistance Act replaced the Poor Laws—relief was to be paid through a National Assistance Board and financed out of national taxation rather than out of local taxes. Local communities were thus stripped of their

---

31 Correlli Barnett, *op. cit.,* pp. 5–6, 73–84, 153–54.

traditional responsibility for the poor, who now became wards of the central government.

The Labour Party, following its electoral victory in 1945, moved rapidly to implement the Fabian goal of government ownership of major industries. The coal industry was nationalized in 1946, followed later by overseas communication, electricity, railroads, trucking, airlines, and steel. For industries that were not nationalized, "development councils" were established to implement state control. The result was a form of the corporate state in which government bureaucracies and planning commissions replaced individual enterprise. The result could be seen in giant, overstaffed, unprofitable companies and huge, dreary housing projects.

A number of assumed premises underlay the creation of the welfare state. The first premise was that most of the British people were incapable of providing for their own basic needs. This assumption inspired a series of welfare programs that made the people increasingly dependent upon the state. Benefits were given not only to the poor but also to the nonpoor in order to secure the political support of the middle class. Thus, taxpayers were compelled to subsidize needy and nonneedy alike rather than to limit subsidies to the poor and thereby allow productive workers to keep more of their own earnings. A second assumption was that the grant of social benefits through government was a manifestation of generosity, charity, or "caring." The benefits in question were financed by forcing some people, under penalty of law, to pay taxes (up to 90 percent of their income in post-war Britain) to support others. Whatever this practice may be called, it is not charity, and it has nothing to do with "caring." Instead, it reflected the political reality that the recipients of state subsidies had more votes than those who were subject to high tax rates. That many of the recipients were also taxpayers merely reflected the willingness of the middle classes to be bribed with their own money. This was not an adequate moral basis for the construction of a genuinely charitable society. The third premise was that the benefits were somehow free, or at least could be paid without serious inconvenience to the nation as a whole. This assumption is endemic in modern Western societies, in which the public is attached to government healthcare, retirement, and welfare systems provided by government in the misguided belief that they provide free benefits.

The growth of the welfare state created new groups of demanding claimants (or "rent-seekers" as they are called by economists). These included nationalized industries, unions, students, educators, local councils, public housing tenants, community workers, the national health service, needy urbanites, farmers, and, eventually, almost every segment of society that was capable of organizing. The combined effect of the political pressure from these groups was a proliferation of government subsidies, which in turn required higher taxes. Since the claimants outnumber the producers, the welfare state is a political juggernaut that is very difficult to restrain.

The Growth of Government

By the 1960s, the British citizen, whether he liked it or not, was the beneficiary of compulsory education, comprehensive health service, public housing, state pensions, and government-enforced union work rules, all supported by heavy taxation. There was virtually no activity that was not regulated or subsidized by government. The size and power of the government bureaucracy spread throughout every sector of the economy, suppressing innovation and initiative. By 1977, nearly 30 percent of the entire workforce was employed by the public sector, in contrast to 5.8 percent in 1901. The rise of government expenditure was even more dramatic. Between 1870 and 1970, government spending rose from 9 percent of national income to 43 percent. Most of this increase was for social welfare programs, including social security, health, housing, and education.[32]

As the British welfare state grew, the age-old priorities of government were reversed. The traditional role of the central government in England had been to maintain an army and navy and to perform

---

32   P. J. Madgwick, *Britain since 1945* (London: Hutchinson, 1983), pp. 60, 151.

functions that private citizens could not efficiently perform for themselves—for example, administering justice, regulating commerce, running the empire, and building roads and bridges. After World War II, the priorities changed rapidly. Defense expenditure accounted for half of total government expenditure in 1952 but for less than one-fourth by 1975. Essentially the same shift in priorities occurred in most of the Western democracies. Defense had become politically unfashionable and social welfare irresistible.

Economic Stagnation and the "British Disease"

In the immediate post-war years, industrial construction was cut back to a minimum in order to funnel resources into government-subsidized residential housing programs ("parlours before plant," as the slogan went) and other welfare state programs. Companies were simultaneously choked with subsidies and stifled with burdensome regulations. Inflation continued to rise, and productivity remained unresponsive to government stimulation. The combination of high inflation and low productivity gave rise to a new economic term: *stagflation*—a term that was also applied to the US economy in the 1970s. Meanwhile, the juggernaut of collectivism rolled on, under Tories as well as Labourites. Public spending by 1972 had increased to a staggering 52 percent of national income.[33] Low levels of investment were accompanied by declining production and rising unemployment.

The resulting economic stagnation was known as the "British disease," characterized by virtually unrestrained union power, crippling strikes, poor quality of goods, and failure to compete effectively in international markets. By the end of the 1970s, Britain's relative economic position had reached its lowest point in a century. In 1950, Britain had a higher standard of living than any other comparable European country; by the mid-1970s, Britain's standard of living had fallen below that of all European Economic Community (EEC) countries except Italy. The

---

33   T. O. Lloyd, *op. cit.,* p. 434.

core of the problem was simple: too many resources were being taken away from productive investment by government taxation and applied to nonproductive uses. At the same time, Britain's "safety net" programs provided a disincentive to work. Nigel Lawson, who became chancellor of the Exchequer in 1983, spoke an unpalatable truth when he said that many people made a rational decision to live on unemployment benefits rather than take a job.[34]

In short, the British experience showed that, particularly in a modern economy, excessive dependence on government leads to stagnation, weakness, and decline. John Stuart Mill summarized the dangers of mass society and the collective state in the last lines of his essay, "On Liberty."

"The mischief begins when, instead of calling forth the activity and powers of individuals and bodies, [the State] substitutes its own activity for theirs ... a State which dwarfs its men, in order that they may be more docile instruments in its hands even for beneficial purposes—will find that with small men no great thing can really be accomplished; and that the perfection of machinery to which it has sacrificed everything will in the end avail it nothing, for want of the vital power which, in order that the machine might work more smoothly, it has preferred to banish."[35]

Education

Another significant factor in the decline of Britain was its educational system, which Paul Johnson has called "the great failure of both nineteenth- and twentieth-century England."[36] As previously noted, much of the English hostility to technical and vocational training is traceable

---

34   For the economic evidence, see Economic History, II, pp. 375–76, 388, 391–95; Barnett, *op. cit.,* p. 304; Kennedy, *op. cit.,* p. 481; Briggs, *op. cit.,* p. 296.

35   John Stuart Mill, "On Liberty," in Mill, *Utilitarianism, Liberty and Representative Government* (New York: E.P. Dutton, 1951), p. 229.

36   Paul Johnson, "The English Disease," *Wilson Quarterly* (Autumn 1987), p. 117. See also Michael Porter, *The Competitive Advantage of Nations* (New York: Macmillan, The Free Press, 1990), p .497. Porter places the primary blame for Britain's economic decline on its weak educational system.

to the nineteenth-century gentlemanly ideal of a "liberal education." Overall, expenditures on scientific and technical education were *de minimis*. This was remarkably short-sighted, since Britain's prosperity and, indeed, the very survival of its universities and other cultural institutions were dependent on the resources produced by commerce and industry, which in turn depended on matching the technological progress being made by Britain's competitors.

In the meantime, the quality of secondary education was seriously impaired by the egalitarian attack on "elitism." The essential objective of socialism was the abolition of social and economic privilege, which, Labourites believed, required the elimination of educational privilege. As a step toward this goal, the Labour government attacked the state-supported "grammar schools," which were academically selective and served as a training ground for talented children whose parents could not afford independent private schools. (Many British politicians, including Margaret Thatcher, were products of the grammar schools, which provided excellent training in math and science as well as in classical subjects.) The Labour Government in 1976 forced the grammar schools to become either "comprehensives" (large, state-supported schools equivalent to US high schools) or independent, fee-paying schools. The net result of the "comprehensive revolution" was to reduce standards and lower the quality of secondary education. As a consequence, many children left school with no useful academic qualifications, and millions were functionally illiterate. A study at the end of the twentieth century showed that "decades of educational complacency and neglect have led to astonishingly high levels of illiteracy and innumeracy."[37]

The revolution in values described earlier in this chapter accelerated

---

37 "Education: The Uses of Literacy," *The Economist*, June 17, 2000; "Brittannia Redux," Special Report, *The Economist*, Feb. 3, 2007, p. 9: "More than one-third of British adults have left school with no formal qualifications. About one-sixth are functionally illiterate and one-fifth innumerate, meaning they cannot read and write or deal with numbers as well as an average 11-year old." See also John Merks, *The Betrayed Generations: Standards in British Schools 1950–2000* (London: Centre for Policy Studies, 2001); and Roger Scruton, *Where We Are: The State of Britain Now* (London: Bloomsbury, 2017), pp. 216–17.

during the decade of the 1960s, in which a drastic erosion of traditional social restraints took place throughout the Western world. Adolescents were "liberated" from conventions of speech, clothing, and behavior as well as from parental control. Drug consumption, juvenile delinquency, and violent crime increased. Serious offenses recorded by the police in Britain rose by more than 300 percent between 1951 and 1977, and violence against persons increased by more than 1,000 percent. Aggressiveness and hostility to authority were evident in the drug culture, rock music, "punk" behavior, and rowdy soccer mobs. The decline of traditional sexual morality accelerated. Abortion became a commonly accepted practice. Divorces increased by 300 percent between 1951 and 1976, and the number of illegitimate births rose by 80 percent during the same period.[38]

One foreseeable consequence of the welfare state was to weaken the family. Since the state provided healthcare, old age pensions, unemployment protection, and housing subsidies, there was less need to rely on families for care and comfort. This process was self-perpetuating: as family structures weakened, people who suffered reversals became still more dependent on the state. The proportion of British families headed by one parent began to rise rapidly during the 1960s, trebling between 1963 and 1978. These families were usually poor and headed by women. State payments to single parents provided, in effect, a subsidy for teenage pregnancy. Similar trends were evident in other European countries and in the United States.

A more basic and perhaps more ominous indicator of social change was the declining birth rate. In the late-nineteenth century, each British marriage produced an average of four children. By the 1950s, the average had fallen to less than two-and-one-half births per family—a drop of more than one-third in two generations. In subsequent decades, the number of children per woman fell still further.[39] This was a troubling

---

38 Madgwick, *op. cit.,* pp. 58, 61.

39 Madgwick, *op. cit.,* p. 58.

sign because it meant that a smaller number of young people would have to pay the growing healthcare and welfare costs of a much larger number of old people. While the birth rate among native-born Britons began to decline, beginning in the 1950s, large numbers of Asian and Caribbean immigrants arrived in England and settled in urban "ghettoes." The wave of immigration contributed further to social unrest. As we will see, the consequences of large-scale immigration would soon become even more serious.

The physical beauty of England's heritage also began to deteriorate. Since most personal fortunes had been destroyed by taxation, families could not preserve their ancient homes, many of which were sold to developers, demolished, or taken over by the National Trust. Much of the new construction was planned and financed by government agencies—an unlikely source of architectural excellence. New buildings, especially in the cities, were drab concrete-and-glass structures of no artistic merit. The stylistic vacuum can be explained in part by the dominance of modernistic theories of architecture, inspired by the Bauhaus movement, which dictated the elimination of decoration and other "useless" accessories. In any event, Britain in the aftermath of World War II could not afford to build beautiful buildings because its economy was badly impaired. It is hardly a coincidence that the people who wrecked the economy were, by and large, the same people who supported the most dismal forms of proletarian architecture. Government housing policies contributed to the destruction of lower-class communities by building bleak, high-rise "council housing estates" that became breeding grounds for vandalism and crime.

Many English writers and intellectuals had assumed that socialism would bring about the promised land. These illusions were quickly shattered. Socialism turned out to be just another basket of unfulfilled promises, stitched together by a jumble of onerous regulations. Critics, poets, and artists complained that British culture was being "starved" of resources by government stinginess. But a better explanation for the decline of culture was that its natural market had been decimated by taxation. This left the state as the principal remaining customer for the arts. Politicians, however, preferred spending money on welfare, health, and housing because these programs bought more votes than subsidizing opera. Even when the politicians were willing to spend money on culture, it did not follow that decisions made by bureaucrats subject to political pressures would produce good art. Government may have kept some cultural activities alive, but the general condition of the arts was not healthy.

By the end of the 1970s, there was irrefutable evidence that Britain's economy had declined precipitously, dragging the living standards of Britons down with it. The central planners had managed to do what two world wars had not done: they had turned Britain into a third-class economic power. The economic decline was accompanied by the emergence of serious social problems: family break-up, violence, pornography, drugs, idleness, illegitimacy, educational decline, and a collapse of traditional values. Corelli Barnett, a prominent writer and social critic, glumly summarized thirty years of the welfare state: "a dream turned into a dank reality of a segregated, subliterate, unskilled, unhealthy and institutionalized proletariat hanging on the nipple of state maternalism."[40]

By the late 1970s, political observers began to speculate that a more dynamic economy might reduce the adverse social effects of welfare dependency. If taxes were lowered, the monopoly power of trade unions reduced, and industry freed from the dead hand of government, Britons might once more display to the world their skill and energy. With the restoration of economic discipline, it might even be possible to talk about the restoration of other traditional values. This was the ambitious program that Margaret Thatcher set out to achieve in 1979.

In her 1979 election campaign, Margaret Thatcher, the Tory candidate for prime minister, presented herself as the champion of freedom against the forces of socialism and bureaucracy. A graduate of Oxford

---

40   Barnett, *op. cit.,* p. 304.

and a lawyer, Thatcher had been influenced by the writings of Adam Smith, Friedrich von Hayek, Milton Friedman, and other free-market thinkers. The choice before the electorate, as Mrs. Thatcher said, was "to take further strides in the direction of the corporatist all-powerful state or to restore the balance in favor of the individual."[41] The outcome of the 1979 election was a clear victory for Thatcher and the Conservative Party. (Thatcher was reelected as prime minister in 1983 and again in 1987.)

An early achievement of the Thatcher government was to reduce substantially the top rate of income tax. She attacked inflation with tight monetary policies. Exchange controls and credit restrictions were progressively eliminated. The basis of her economic policy was the conviction (subsequently borne out) that lower taxes, sound money, and less regulation would increase productivity and restore confidence. Another accomplishment of the Thatcher government, perhaps the most difficult politically, was to reduce the power of Britain's labor unions by limiting their right to strike, restraining wage increases in the public sector, and forcing lay-offs in the nationalized industries. A number of large government-owned companies were successfully privatized, leading to a more competitive Britain and greater prosperity. The government encouraged private ownership in housing by selling over a million government-owned housing units to their tenants. Margaret Thatcher's economic and political program, popularly labeled as "Thatcherism," was summarized by her biographer, Charles Moore, as follows: "It was opposed to big government, high taxes and high deficits, the political power of trade unions and Communism. It was in favor of individual opportunity and choice, free markets, strict monetary control, nuclear weapons and a vigorous NATO alliance.... Thatcherism set out to prove that the modern world could be shaped in the interests of greater liberty."[42]

The favorable economic effects of Thatcher's policies soon began to appear. The proportion of unionized workers in the labor force fell sharply and days lost to strikes were cut in half. Manufacturing

---

41   Havighurst, *op. cit.*, p. 588.

42   Charles Moore, *Margaret Thatcher*, Vol. II, (Allen Lane: UK, 2015), p. 91.

productivity during the 1980s rose rapidly. The inflation rate fell from a high of 27 percent in 1975 to 2.4 percent in 1986. The top rate of income tax fell from 83 percent to 40 percent, and the deficit was substantially reduced.[43] Business confidence was restored, investment and exports rose, and the credit markets boomed. The City of London strengthened its position as the leading financial center of Europe. By the end of the century, Britain's economy was the fourth largest in the world, behind the United States, Japan, and Germany.[44]

Margaret Thatcher resigned in November 1990 after eleven years in office and was succeeded as prime minister by John Major, who served until 1997. His tenure in office was relatively uncontroversial, but the Conservative Party suffered a major electoral defeat in May 1997, and a revived (and more moderate) Labour Party took power under its dynamic young leader, Tony Blair.

Under Blair, Labour made a historic break from its left-wing past, symbolized by repeal of the longstanding "Clause IV" in the party's constitution that had supported the public ownership of the means of production and exchange. As a result of the movement away from traditional socialist principles, the party was now referred to as "New Labour." Blair preserved Thatcher's trade union reforms and introduced moderate reforms in welfare, education, and healthcare. His foreign policy was interventionist, featuring a close alliance with the United States under President George Bush. This policy was unpopular with much of the British public, and in 2007, Blair resigned and was replaced as prime minister by Gordon Brown, who had been chancellor of the Exchequer. In the 2010 general election the Conservatives won a majority, and David Cameron became prime minister as the head of a coalition with the Liberal Democrat party. In the 2015 election the Conservative Party

---

43   See "Freedom Fighter," *The Economist,* April 13, 2013, p. 13; Charles Moore, *Margaret Thatcher,* II, p. 676.

44   Geoffrey Owen, *From Empire to Europe: The Decline and Revival of British Industry Since the Second World War* (London 1999).

won the largest number of votes but less than a majority, and Cameron continued as prime minister. Cameron's domestic policy was characterized as "progressive conservatism" (roughly comparable to George Bush's "compassionate conservatism"). Cameron had campaigned on a promise to reduce public spending, and the coalition did reduce government spending to some extent. The budget deficit was slightly reduced, but hopes of eliminating the budget deficit have never been realized. The welfare state continued to roll on, in Britain as elsewhere in Europe. Cameron's six years in power saw a significant decline in Britain's military power. This trend toward demilitarization was even more evident on the continent, where defense spending shrank to dangerously low levels. Defense spending in Britain dropped from 7 percent of GDP in 1959 to 2.1 per cent of GDP in 2015. (Britain, however, continues to spend more on defense than other European countries.)

Immigration

Beginning around the turn of the twenty-first century, net migration into Britain increased significantly. According to the UK Office of National Statistics (ONS), net migration into the UK since 2004 has averaged between 200,000 and 300,000 immigrants per year.[45] This number would be higher if illegal immigrants were included. Based on the UK population of about 65.6 million as of 2017, this level of migration would mean an increase of at least five million people in twenty years, which would be unsustainable as a practical matter. Mass immigration has contributed to overcrowding and social unrest. As British author Roger Scruton has written, "[W]hole sections of our cities seem to belong to some other country, while housing, healthcare and education are all in crisis from the pressure of incoming numbers."[46] While reliable statistics on countries of origin are difficult to find, we know

---

45 www.migrationwatchuk.org

46 Roger Scruton, *Where We Are: The State of Britain Now* (London: Bloomsbury, 2017), p. 202.

that many of these immigrants are and will be culturally difficult to assimilate, as evidenced by outbreaks of terrorist violence by immigrant groups throughout Europe. Europeans have learned the hard way that many of those who have recently arrived do not share basic European values, such as Western views about equality between the sexes, individual liberty, tolerance, religious freedom, or the rule of law.[47]

Withdrawal from the European Union

Perhaps the most contentious issue in British politics in the early years of the twenty-first century involves the relationship between Britain and the European Union. While many educated Britons consider themselves as Europeans in a cultural sense, Britain has for centuries remained politically aloof and relatively independent from the continent. This was due not only to its geographical position as an island but also to its ethnic history, from the original Neolithic inhabitants to various invaders including Celts, Gaels, Angles, Saxons, Danes, and Normans, as well as its unique language, customs, and legal institutions.

After the two disastrous wars of the twentieth century, European leaders favored increasing economic integration as a means of moderating the internecine hatreds that had devastated the continent. The first step was the creation of the European Coal and Steel Community in 1952, followed by the Treaty of Rome in 1957 that created the European Economic Community, a customs union at its inception. A number of European nations joined, including Britain (with some domestic opposition) in 1973. Over time, additional common institutions were created, including a European parliament, and the EEC became the "European Union." In 1985 the Schengen Agreement was signed, giving rise to open borders without passport controls among the

---

47   See Douglas Murray, *The Strange Death of Europe: Immigration, Identity, Islam* (London: Bloomsbury, 2017), p. 261. For fictional depictions of the predicted demise of Europe, see Jean Raspail, *The Camp of the Saints* (1973) and Michel Houellebecq, *Submission* (2015). On the impact on housing, see Lionel Shriver, "Mass immigration drives the housing crisis," *The Spectator,* March 17, 2018, p. 24.

member states. In 2002 a number of member countries, not including Britain, created a "Eurozone" with a common currency.

The growing degree of political integration in the EU moved the member nations in the direction of a federation, which was consistent with the policy of most continental members but was viewed with increasing skepticism in Britain. Membership in the EU required Britain to accept limitations on its freedom of action, including an external source of legislation in Brussels with the power to enact regulations with full effect in Britain. Margaret Thatcher had recognized what was happening in 1988: "We have not successfully rolled back the frontiers of the state in Britain only to see them reimposed as a European superstate exercising a new dominance from Brussels."[48] By the end of the twentieth century, continental Europe was in a state of economic and demographic decline. Yet the European push for more integration continued apace under Britain's Labour government and the Conservative-Liberal Democrat coalition that took office in 2010. EU regulations became increasingly burdensome and costly. The continental economies, with the exception of Germany, were not sufficiently productive to sustain the enormous costs of the socialist welfare states their populations demanded, and they were burdened by heavy indebtedness and high unemployment. European governments began to accept large numbers of immigrants, many of whom were culturally unassimilable. In the first two decades of the twenty-first century, outbreaks of radical Islamic violence deepened the public's concern. Indeed, the prospect of the Islamization of Europe has led some observers to question whether Europe's traditional civilization can survive.[49]

British voters eventually recognized the plain truth that the British people's right to govern themselves was in jeopardy and that the danger was exacerbated by the threat of open immigration under the Schengen

---

48   Quoted in *The American Spectator*, November 2012, p. 40.

49   Douglas Murray, *The Strange Death of Europe*, supra.

rules. Working-class voters, for example, were concerned about the depression of wages as a result of the admission into the EU of Romania and other less-developed Eastern European countries. Many Britons also feared that the trend toward further integration of the European Union could lead to the submersion of the English traditions of liberty, property, and common law into an overtaxed and overregulated continental superstate. The basic issue was sovereignty. Sovereignty is an essential attribute of a nation. In the introductory chapter, we defined a nation as a people associated in a common territory and united by a common history, language, customs, and institutions, and often by a common religion. Its inhabitants are called citizens, and they are held together by common bonds of national solidarity. Were the British people willing to outsource their sovereignty to a separate power like the EU? Faced with the growing political threat of the new UK Independence Party, Prime Minister David Cameron promised an "in-or-out" referendum. The vote took place in June 2016 and resulted in a decision (52 percent to 48 percent) in favor of Britain's withdrawal from the EU, popularly called "Brexit."

Cameron, who had opposed Brexit, resigned as prime minister and was succeeded by Theresa May. Under Article 50 of the European Union Treaty, any EU member state that decides to leave the EU must negotiate its withdrawal within two years. Theresa May triggered the withdrawal process on March 29, 2017, thus, the UK was scheduled to leave on March 29, 2019. A number of trade and financial issues remained to be resolved in the negotiation between Britain and the EU.

Mrs. May had supported the "remain" side in the referendum but appeared to recognize that the people had spoken and initiated the withdrawal process under Article 50 of the EU Treaty. Nevertheless, much of the political establishment (well-represented in Parliament, of course), whose financial interests and cultural sympathies inclined them toward the remain side, resisted withdrawal even though parliament had approved calling the referendum. Theresa May's heart was never in Brexit, and obviously the EU representatives had no interest in facilitating Britain's exit. The result of May's negotiations with the

EU was a very complex withdrawal agreement which, in effect, bound Britain into a customs union with no power to withdraw unilaterally and no representation in Brussels. The deal would have prevented Britain from entering into favorable trade pacts with non-EU countries. This was a genuinely bad deal, which Parliament quite properly rejected.[50] Following an election in December 2019 in which Prime Minister Boris Johnson's Conservative Party won a majority, Britain left the European Union on January 31, 2020.

On balance, I believe that the British people made a wise decision to withdraw from the European Union. The robust common sense of Britons, supported by the unique institutional advantages of the common law; a healthy parliamentary system; and an economy that still respects a tradition of private property, individual freedom, and the rule of law compares favorably with continental Europe's stifling bureaucracy, heavily regulated and taxed economies, and vulnerability to destabilizing immigration. Britain can be strong and prosperous if it opens its economy to the world through the classic liberal model: free trade, flexible labor markets, fiscal responsibility, light regulation, and technological innovation.

CONCLUSION

The character of a civilization is judged by its tangible and intangible accomplishments—buildings and roads; systems of law and religion; the civic spirit of its people; works of literature, art, and philosophy; and domestic furnishings and comforts. The production of these public and private goods requires leisure, imagination, discipline, and an economic system adequate to sustain the activity of priests and artists as well as builders. The society also needs political and military institutions capable of defending it from internal and external enemies and of making sensible decisions on major issues of policy. During the three centuries in

---

50   See Martin Howe, "May's deal, a legal verdict: we will be bound as vassals to the EU indefinitely," *The Spectator*, November 24, 2018.

which Britain created its empire and came to dominate the commercial world, the British people displayed to a remarkable degree the qualities of discipline, endurance, adventurousness, and enterprise that provide the foundations for success. In this short period of time, they turned a small island-state into a major world power whose techniques and political ideas became standards for the entire world to emulate.

The British resembled the Romans in certain important respects. During the period of their initial success, both societies were led by a loyal landowning aristocracy. This aristocracy, rooted in the soil and sustained by a deep sense of public duty, provided stability and aggressive military leadership. In both cases, the decline of the aristocracy coincided with the beginning of national decline. In the case of Rome, the aristocrats acquiesced in a brutal tyranny; in England's case, they failed to ally themselves effectively with the emerging economic forces and eventually were inundated in a wave of egalitarianism and bureaucracy. The British also resembled the Romans in their attachment to law and legal process. In both societies, respect for legal forms provided a solid framework for private property and commercial transactions. Both were outward-looking and self-confident in their foreign policies. The Romans, however, were unable to channel their imperial energies effectively into commercial and industrial development, and they finally sank under the weight of a stifling administrative tyranny. Britain, at its prime, became a worldwide industrial-commercial power, although in the twentieth century it temporarily succumbed to a period of collectivism and economic decline, during which it overtaxed its citizens and strangled its enterprises with excessive government.

Another point of comparison was the virtual collapse of the traditional religion and the accompanying devaluation of values. The established church under Elizabeth II seems scarcely more alive than paganism under Diocletian. A similar observation could be made concerning other Western nations. As Arnold Toynbee argued, no civilization can survive over the long run without genuine religious belief, and religion is not in a healthy condition among the elites who direct the course of Western culture. Religion is more than the private worship of a deity; it is the strongest support for morality and the spiritual bond of society. The visible decay of religion is therefore a manifestation of decline.

The decline of the British educational system was accompanied by a loss of cultural memory and a reduced ability to cope with technological change. While this cultural decline was not as serious as the collapse of classical learning in the late Roman Empire, it remains unclear in the early years of the twenty-first century whether Britain will be able to revive its former intellectual luster.

On the positive side, the British, through their practical genius for government, overcame two of the critical defects of the Roman Empire: the problem of constitutional succession and the absence of civilian control over the military. Britain's most lasting achievement and its greatest gift to the world has been to provide a model for successful governance. The British legal system is a paradigm for reconciling tradition with change. Oppressed people everywhere pay homage to the British example by demanding representative government, civil liberties, protection of private property, due process of law, and other protections that were first conceived and successfully implemented in England. The British willingness to compromise, to respect "the rules of the game," and to adhere to the model of gentlemanly conduct in the face of adversity are ideals of human behavior that commend themselves to all civilized people. The genius of a people is also reflected in its language, and the English language is a success story seldom equaled in history. If any language succeeds in becoming universal, it is virtually certain to be that of Shakespeare and Milton.

In the history of modern Britain, there was, as always, a close interdependence among the various conditions that contributed to national decline. Relative economic decline, imperial overreach, the decay of discipline, egalitarian envy, utopianism, hedonism, relativism, the decline of the family and religion, excessive regulation, and lower educational standards were mutually supporting factors, leading to a temporary decline. The British people, however, have always shown the resilience needed to overcome intermittent setbacks. If it manages successfully to disentangle itself from a lumbering European albatross and remains a free society of independent and self-confident people, Britain will continue to survive and prosper.

3

THE ECONOMIC BASE

WITH THIS HISTORICAL BACKGROUND, we move on to a consideration of the contemporary United States. Its founders did not envisage America as an incipient empire; indeed, they warned against the temptation to undertake foreign adventures. Yet early Americans were an adventurous people, anxious to conquer the continent that seemed to be theirs for the taking, and by the end of the nineteenth century, they had occupied a large part of the North American land mass as well as some foreign territories that had fallen to the United States by war, accident, or entrepreneurial energy. This was the "rising" phase of a new and growing power that took advantage of its opportunities and outmaneuvered or pushed aside those who stood in its way. Like all such powers, America encountered obstacles along the way, which it managed to overcome with varying degrees of success until, in the last part of the twentieth and the early part of the twenty-first century, there were signs that the rising phase had begun to give way to a plateau or even a decline. We will begin our investigation with a look at the economic base that underlies national power.

Civilization requires economic resources. Soldiers, artisans, builders, priests, poets, and philosophers must somehow be sustained. The civilizations of Greece, Rome, Medieval Europe, and Renaissance Italy, to name only a few, were dependent upon trade and commerce as well as agriculture. When a society suffers prolonged economic decline, as in fourth- and fifth-century Rome, the outward signs of civilization and the inner confidence required to sustain it are sure to decay. The shabbiness of Britain and the depressed condition of its culture in the post-World War II period were to a significant extent the result of economic decline. People who lack resources will look to their physical needs first; education, the arts, and other cultural embellishments will be neglected. Economic growth, of course, does not necessarily entail cultural progress. Yet it remains true that a certain degree of economic prosperity is a necessary, though not a sufficient, condition of a vital civilization.

It is hardly necessary to dwell upon the obvious fact that a vigorous national defense requires a strong economic base. This has been true for centuries and is especially true today. The United States prevailed both in World War II and in the Cold War of 1945–1990 for a number of reasons, but one of them was the capacity of the nation to produce advanced weapons of extraordinary quality and power. Recent regional conflicts and outbreaks of terrorism have confirmed that the sophisticated research and development needed to modernize America's arsenal in the face of a wide array of potential challenges will require continued economic and technological productivity. The old Roman motto remains as valid as ever: if you want peace, prepare for war. And modern war (including the unconventional conflicts and terrorist attacks we face today) requires scientific, technological, and economic capacity as well as patriotism, discipline, and self-confidence.

Equally obvious is the common-sense point that economic resources are necessary to the continued well-being of ordinary people. Many around the globe admire and envy the standard of living achieved by the citizens of the industrial democracies. Some of this material abundance is vulgar and distasteful, but most people in poor countries would like to be in a position to make this life-style choice for themselves. The relentless influx of immigrants into Europe and the United States is evidence of this desire. Freedom, in short, means freedom to improve one's material condition as well as freedom to speak, write, and vote.

The most important factor in determining a nation's economic performance is its institutional framework.[1] The historical record shows that the institutions and policies that most effectively promote prosperity are private property rights, limited government, a strong national defense, an educational system that produces capable and patriotic leaders, a sound monetary system, free markets, and the rule of law. Essential support for these foundational institutions is provided by an ethic of individual liberty, hard work, honesty, and responsibility. It is the combination of free markets and competition, based on private property and the rule of law, to which we apply the shorthand term *capitalism*. As Ludwig von Mises has written: "The characteristic feature of modern capitalism is mass production of goods for consumption by the masses. The result is a tendency towards a continuous improvement in the average standard of living of the many. Capitalism deproletarian izes the 'common man' and elevates him to the rank of a 'bourgeois.'"[2] The superiority of free enterprise capitalism in producing wealth was demonstrated by the enormous growth of the British and American economies during the nineteenth century, the recovery of the British economy under Margaret Thatcher in the 1980s after more than three decades of socialism, and the positive response of the US economy after World War II, and later under Ronald Reagan after a decade of "stagflation." Economic strength, of course, is not the only social good,

---

1   For a discussion of the crucial importance of a nation's institutions to its political and economic success, see Daron Acemoglu and James A. Robinson, *Why Nations Fail* (New York: Crown Publishers, 2012).

2   Ludwig von Mises, www.azquotes.com/quote/1522401, accessed June 14, 2018.

but for the average person trying to improve conditions for himself and his family, a healthy economy is a big advantage.

Today we take the industrial revolution and the accompanying system of wealth creation for granted, but this process was not inevitable, as the experience of many other societies has shown. In the long historical period between the foundation of the Roman Empire and the eighteenth century AD, there was basically no growth in real per capita economic output in Europe, but around 1750, economic growth suddenly emerged.[3] Why did this happen? The short answer is that there was a fortuitous combination of scientific discovery, new technology, free markets, capital formation, legally protected property rights, and entrepreneurial energy, which spread outward from England to its colonies and to a handful of other European countries and which provided extraordinary opportunities for motivated individuals and vast new resources for Western societies.

The United States of America was a major beneficiary of the British industrial revolution and its system of limited constitutional government that made freedom and prosperity possible. Through sheer good fortune, opportunism, and politico-military maneuvering (such as the Louisiana Purchase and the Mexican War), a vast continental territory was opened up for expansion. The new nation survived an unnecessary and nearly disastrous Civil War in 1860–65 between blocs of quarrelsome states and went on to consolidate a powerful and, for the most part, united society.

Within a remarkably short time after the Civil War, America became the most powerful nation on earth. The economic rise of the United States during the late nineteenth and twentieth centuries has been skillfully traced by Robert J. Gordon in his book *The Rise and Fall of American Growth* (2016). Gordon describes an unparalleled economic revolution that occurred during the period from 1870 to 1970. This

---

3   Robert J. Gordon, *The Rise and Fall of American Growth* (Princeton: Princeton University Press, 2016), p. 569.

revolution (IR2) carried forward the original industrial revolution (IR1) that had begun in Britain a century earlier with the steam engine and related mechanical devices, followed in the early nineteenth century by the railroad. The principal invention that launched IR2 in the second half of the nineteenth century was electricity, followed early in the next century by the petroleum-powered internal combustion engine. These inventions were primarily made in America, although with scientific input from Europe, and they changed the world forever. Electricity produced rapid and dramatic improvements in lighting, heating, and cooking and spawned innumerable devices that made everyday life more comfortable, convenient, and healthy. The internal combustion engine revolutionized transportation and stimulated rapid urbanization. These developments were accompanied by epochal changes in the production of food, clothing, and shelter. Sewage and water systems, sanitation, refrigeration, farm productivity, nutrition, medical care, and factory conditions were vastly improved. The net result of these changes, as Gordon concludes, was the biggest improvement in standards for ordinary people in the history of the world.

Progress was uneven, of course. Big increases in immigration between 1890 and World War I led to overcrowding and slum conditions in New York and other big cities. The largely rural population in the southern states, especially black people who suffered from discrimination, did not benefit to the same extent from the economic revolution. On the whole, however, American standards of living rose dramatically during this period, even for the least favored. (In later chapters we will discuss some of the accompanying social and cultural changes, many of which were far from benign.)

According to Robert Gordon's analysis, the great inventions of IR2, such as electricity, the internal combustion engine, and the telephone, had their maximum positive effect on US economic productivity in the period 1870–1970. The American standard of living, based on real GDP, tripled between 1870 and 1940—a statistic that ignores important gains that cannot be measured, such as many improvements in the quality and desirability of products.[4] As of 2017, with less than 5 percent of the world's population, the United States produced about 24 percent of global output. By way of contrast, China has 19 percent of the world's population and produced about 15 percent of global output, although it is rapidly advancing and may soon overtake the United States.[5]

IR1 was driven by coal and steam, and IR2 by electricity and the automobile. In the last decade of the twentieth century, the world entered what could be called IR3, powered by the computer and digital technology. We may now be in the early stages of IR4, an economy powered by artificial intelligence (AI), quantum computing, 5G communication, and other revolutionary technology still on the drawing board.[6] IR3 already features an explosion of smartphones, robots, data storage and retrieval facilities, and an enormous increase in internet traffic. All of this will require a great deal of physical infrastructure (e.g., cell towers and fiberoptic cable). America's educational system is currently not capable of teaching the necessary technical skills to enough young people to fill the skill gaps. Our global competitors, particularly China, are advancing rapidly. Chinese spending on research and development is expected to surpass that of the United States within the next few years.[7]

With respect to economic growth, the statistics show that the United States averaged 3.4 percent annual growth in GDP from 1948 through 2008, but thereafter growth slowed to an average of less than 2 percent until 2018 when growth began to pick up again. The slowdown has been attributed to various factors, including an aging population, lower capital formation, high taxes on business and investment, excessive regulation, lower productivity, and disincentives to work such as easier

---

4   Gordon, *op. cit.,* pp. 320–21.

5   www.bloomberg.com/graphics/2017-us-vs-china-economy/

6   Christopher Mims, "Inside the New Industrial Revolution," *Wall Street Journal Technology Report*, November 13, 2018.

7   Wall Street Journal Technology Report, *supra,* p. R2.

eligibility for unemployment and disability, food stamps, and other government welfare benefits.[8]

The 2008–9 recession and the very slow economic recovery thereafter resulted in a drop in the number of job seekers and thus in the labor force participation rate, a sign of subpar economic performance.[9] What occurred during this period was a modest economic slowdown, not a precipitous economic drop, such as the depression of the 1930s. Since the Trump administration took office in early 2017, economic growth has picked up significantly, stimulated by a tax cut, regulatory reform, and a worldwide uptick in growth, but future economic growth, of course, cannot be predicted. IR4 may portend greater productivity, but that depends on the ability of the various competitors to respond to the challenges.[10] The impact of the coronavirus pandemic that struck in early 2020 will certainly have negative effects that cannot be predicted.

One important trend affecting the American economy is the phenomenon usually referred to as *globalization*. Beginning in the 1970s and accelerating after 1990, cheap imports from abroad, especially China, began to replace US-made goods. Lower prices, of course, benefited consumers, and the availability of cheap labor benefited US corporations. But the flood of imports also led to a loss of domestic manufacturing jobs and the outsourcing by US companies of many manufacturing jobs to low-wage locations abroad. A major contributor

---

8   Phil Gramm and Michael Solon, "Finding America's Lost 3% Growth," *The Wall Street Journal*, September 11, 2017, p. A17; Lawrence B. Lindsey, "The Right Cure for What Ails Our Economy," *The Weekly Standard*, February 20, 2017, p. A17. It should be noted that sole reliance on GDP statistics has been criticized because GDP numbers ignore unmeasurable improvements such as the better quality, convenience, and attractiveness of new products.

9   The labor force participation rate (number of people working as a percentage of the total population) dropped from 67.3 percent in 2000 to 62.7 percent in 2018. US Bureau of Labor Statistics, 2018. These percentages vary depending on the ages of workers used in the different surveys, but all of the official studies show a significant drop in the labor force participation rate after the 1990s. Some of this drop is undoubtedly attributable to the aging of the US population.

10   See Peter Morici, "The Indications that 3 percent growth is possible: With a revolution in robotics and artificial intelligence, rising wages and an expanding economy are within grasp. " *Washington Times*, November 14, 2018.

to the explosion of imports was China's export-led expansion in the late twentieth and early twenty-first century, caused by vast overproduction subsidized by the Chinese government, which dumped large quantities of steel and other manufactured goods into the US economy. China continues to gain advantage in global markets by subsidizing domestic industries, limiting imports in certain industries to benefit Chinese producers and forced transfer of technology from foreign companies. The massive spending by the Chinese government on subsidizing its competitive companies as well as on basic scientific research, such as artificial intelligence, 5G wireless systems, and quantum computing is not being matched by the United States.[11]

The loss of jobs and business investment due to globalization and unfair competition resulted in the near-destruction of some older industries and the decline of a number of cities, especially in the Midwestern "rust belt." In addition, a flood of immigrants, many of them illegal, beginning in the 1990s, adversely affected American workers in some industries, especially low-skilled workers. (See the discussion of immigration in Chapter 7.) In addition to foreign trade and immigration, new technology and automation were major factors in the loss of factory jobs. Advanced machinery and robots produced more goods with far less labor, leading to the closing of many factories in industrial areas. The loss of jobs and the adverse impact on industrial regions had political consequences in the United States, manifested in the election of Donald Trump in 2016.[12]

The Trump administration addressed the challenge of China's unfair

---

11   "As the excesses piled up in China over the years, they weighed on global prices, depressing profits for all. However, unlike their international rivals, Chinese firms could carry on expanding, confident of state support." "China's Economy: Created Destruction," *The Economist,* September 9, 2017. See Robert D. Atkinson, Nigel Cory and Stephen J. Ezell, "Stopping China's Mercantilism," Information Technology and Innovation Foundation, March 2017; William A. Galston, "Second Thoughts on Trade with China," *Wall Street Journal,* August 8, 2017.

12   See Salena Zito and Brad Todd, *The Great Revolt: Inside the Populist Coalition Reshaping American Politics* (New York: Crown Forum, 2018).

trade practices by raising tariffs on Chinese goods; in response, China raised tariffs on certain American products. In an attempt to diminish job losses and unfavorable trade balances, the administration also imposed tariffs on steel and aluminum imports from a number of other countries, including Canada, Mexico, and the EU. Serious commercial penalties against China for its unfair practices, such as appropriating intellectual property, massive subsidization of exports, and discriminatory nontariff barriers, are clearly justified.[13] To impose protective tariffs on America's allies, however, is harder to justify, since such tariffs harm the many American consumers of the products in question—such as steel and aluminum—as well as workers in companies that use such products. The history of Britain in the nineteenth century, discussed in the previous chapter, illustrates the benefits of free trade and low tariffs to economic growth over the long run.

The Heritage Foundation in Washington, DC, publishes every year an Index of Economic Freedom based on data including property rights, open markets, extent of government regulation, and other factors influencing the ability of individuals to work, produce, consume and invest. In the 2017 Index, the United States ranked number 17, below Canada, Ireland, Chile, the United Kingdom, the Netherlands, and other countries deemed more competitive than the US. This was the lowest ranking since Heritage started its index. In its report, Heritage called attention to America's large budget deficits, high level of public debt, and increased regulatory and tax burdens. The report noted, however, that the US economy has historically shown considerable resilience and that manufacturing output is strong.[14] As noted above, some of the tax and regulatory burdens have been eased under the Trump administration, and as of the date of this publication, the US economy appears to be relatively healthy. Real challenges persist, however, including

---

13   See White House Fact Sheet, Economy and Jobs, May 29, 2018, "President Donald J. Trump is Confronting China's Unfair Trade Practices," www.whitehouse.gov.

14   See heritage.org/index/country/unitedstates.

fierce global competition, excessive debt, too much government, and an uncertain global economy, making economic prediction impossible.

Some of America's labor and productivity problems could be ameliorated by better vocational education and job training. Secondary education in the United States is of relatively poor quality; and a workforce that is substandard educationally will underperform economically. Research shows a strong correlation between cognitive skills and the growth of per capita GDP. Variations among countries in math and science skills "translate into dramatic differences in economic growth rates."[15] The quality of human capital is fundamental, and this depends on education. Corporate spokesmen say that education has not evolved in accordance with industrial needs, and that colleges and high schools must place more emphasis on technical and vocational education. The topic of education is addressed in more detail in Chapter 5.

America's recent economic difficulties have arisen, in part, from something that is surely a blessing: improvements in medical science, diet, and sanitation have produced a dramatic increase in life expectancy. An American male born in 2015 had a life expectancy of 79 years, compared to 46.8 years for a man born in 1900.[16] These gains in longevity reflect dramatic improvements in medical care, including much lower infant mortality rates, as well as in sanitation and diet. The gain in life expectancy, however, has not been matched by a corresponding gain in the financial ability to support the growing number of elderly people. Americans save too little and spend too much. The cost of Medicare and Medicaid has grown roughly twice as fast as the economy in recent years. The United States is expected to go from 4.8 potential workers per old person (65 or older) to 2.8 in forty years. This means that a rapid

---

15   Eric A. Hanushek, Paul E. Peterson and Ludger Woessman, *Endangering Prosperity: A Global View of the American School,* Brookings Institution, Washington, DC (2013), p. 23 and table p. 24.

16   See Life Expectancy in the USA, www.demog.berkeley.edu; U.S. Centers for Disease Control, www.cdc.gov (2016). It is worth noting that a significant factor in life expectancy is the decline in infant mortality. The number of babies who died within the first year after birth was 150 per thousand in 1912 versus 8 in 2012. www.ahundredyearsago.com; www.data.worldbank.org.

increase in retirement and healthcare costs will place a huge tax burden on younger generations of Americans. Virtually every postwar US administration has expanded benefits under Social Security, Medicare, and Medicaid without asking the public to pay for them.[17] This fiscal irresponsibility is a part of the dilemma of mass democracy that we will encounter repeatedly throughout this book.

To the burdens of an aging population, we must add the other and ever-expanding costs of the modern welfare state, such as food support, low-income housing, tax credits, and other types of welfare spending. (See Chapter 8).

Much of the cost of America's recent explosion of spending has been borrowed. From 1789 until 1971 (except for a brief period during the Civil War), America's bank notes were convertible into silver or gold either directly or, after World War II, under the Bretton Woods System, when only foreign governments were entitled to exchange their dollars for gold. This gold exchange standard continued to provide some degree of discipline on the government's ability to overspend and overborrow. The US government's propensity to spend, however, increased dramatically during the administrations of Lyndon Johnson and Richard Nixon, driven by the Vietnam War and the rise of the welfare state and its accompanying entitlement programs. The political demand for spending overwhelmed the gold exchange standard, and President Nixon abandoned it in 1971.[18] Breaking the last remaining link between the US currency and precious metal removed one more of the original "checks and balances" on excessive government.

Following World War II, the budget of the federal government was generally in or close to balance, except for the periods of the Korean and Vietnam Wars, until the 1970s, when government spending began to outpace revenues by large margins. After a brief period of fiscal probity

---

17   See Laurence J. Kotlikoff and Scott Burns, *The Clash of Generations: Saving Ourselves, Our Kids, and Our Economy* (Cambridge, MA: MIT Press, 2012), Chapter 2.

18   See James Grant, "Time to Worry," *The Weekly Standard*, November 5, 2018, p. 29.

in the 1990s, the spending imbalance worsened. The federal budget deficit grew from $158 billion in 2002 to more than $1 trillion during each of the post-recession years 2009 through 2012, and thereafter the deficit persisted at half a trillion dollars or more per year. There was no politically feasible way to raise tax rates to a level sufficient to cover these imbalances, so the funds had to be borrowed. As of early 2019, the gross federal debt (the sum of debt held by the public and intragovernmental debt) reached $22 trillion, up from $9.9 trillion in 2008. The Office of Management and Budget projects that gross federal debt will rise to roughly $27 trillion by 2023. As a share of the economy, gross federal debt as of February 2019 was 107 percent of GDP and is expected to remain at least at this level or perhaps higher in the future, depending on economic growth.[19] The foregoing figures on government debt do not include consumer debt. As of December 2018, consumer debt (including credit card and installment debt) in the US amounted to $3.898 trillion. Of this amount, student loan debt was $1.524 trillion. If mortgage debt were included, total household debt would exceed $13 trillion. And debt of US corporations reached 46 percent of GDP at the end of 2018, the highest on record.[20]

The official debt figures published by the OMB and other agencies do not reveal the nation's true indebtedness—the "off-balance sheet" debt or the total amount the government will actually have to spend to satisfy its obligations (which is not recognized as a part of the official debt). Economist Laurence Kotlikoff has calculated the "fiscal gap" that faces coming generations: the estimated long-term government spending (including entitlements) net of taxes, discounted at a 3 percent real discount rate. As of 2012, the fiscal gap, according to Kotlikoff, was over $200 trillion. This number probably deserves the over-used

---

19   Office of Management and Budget, Historical Tables, Table 7.1, www.whitehouse.gov/omb/historical-tables.

20   www.lexingtonlaw.com/blog/loans/consumer-debt-statistics-2019-html; "Record Corporate Debt Stirs New Worry," *Wall Street Journal*, January 2, 2019, p. R3.

adjective *unsustainable*. It is difficult to imagine how fast our economy would have to grow and how high our taxes would have to be in order to pay off that kind of indebtedness.[21] Today's politicians, needless to say, are unwilling even to talk about this seemingly inevitable fiscal Armageddon, let alone do anything about it. This is a degree of fiscal irresponsibility never before seen in American history. What seems clear is that, at some point, if the growth of spending and borrowing is not drastically restrained, the bond market will collapse, creating a fiscal and social crisis of unfathomable proportions.

Excessive indebtedness in America is accompanied by an inadequate savings rate. The US personal savings rate (as a percent of disposable personal income) has declined significantly since the 1960s—from over 10 percent in the 1960s and 1970s to under 3 percent in 2018. According to a survey by the Federal Reserve of US households in 2015, 68 percent of households reported that they saved some of their income, but 40 percent reported saving less than 5 percent and two-thirds reported saving 10 percent or less.[22] Since savings provide the resources for investment in growth-producing capital goods and services, a low savings rate holds down long-term economic growth.

There is another solution to America's fiscal gap, a solution that has appealed to rulers throughout history—inflating the money supply. The government could simply print enough money to pay off the debt. But history also teaches that to do so risks causing a drastic inflation similar to what happened in Germany during the 1920s or what has recently happened in Venezuela. Hyperinflation of this kind often leads to economic and political collapse, with dismal consequences.

The most obvious way to reduce government debt, of course, would be to reduce government spending. The fastest-growing portion of federal

21   Kotlikoff and Burns, Chapter 3.

22   www.statista.com/statistics/246234/personal-savings-rate-in-the-united-states; Bureau of Economic Analysis, blog.bea.gov/personal savings rate; federalreserve.gov/econresdata/2016-economic-well-being-of-us-households-in-2015-income-and-savings.

government spending is *entitlements*—Social Security, Medicare, and Medicaid—which collectively account for a majority of federal spending. When other income transfers to individuals, such as food stamps, are added, the category of "payments for individuals" is close to 70 percent of total federal outlays. The growing portion of GDP devoted to entitlements and other welfare benefits deprives taxpayers of resources that would otherwise be available for savings and productive investment.[23] There are simple ways to control entitlement spending, including means testing of benefits, increasing the retirement age for receiving Social Security benefits, and imposing work requirements for able-bodied recipients of Medicaid. And federal spending in general could be cut by simply imposing some modest degree of austerity on politicians and the public. Such common-sense solutions, however, would require the politicians, and those who elect them, to exercise a degree of self-discipline that appears to be impossible in today's mass democracies, which are driven by the political philosophy of satisfying as many demands as possible. Another traditional solution is to raise revenue through higher taxes. But US indebtedness is so high that the taxes needed to reduce the debt significantly would place heavy burdens on households and businesses, crippling commerce and depressing the economy.

Throughout this book, I emphasize the need for fiscal restraint on the part of government. There is one area, however, in which government spending is essential and indeed may have to be substantially increased: this is the field of basic scientific research and technological innovation. Investment by private US companies in scientific research has increased but, as previously noted, private investment is not sufficient to compete with the enormous amounts being spent by the Chinese government on artificial intelligence and related areas of cutting-edge research. Scientific and technological innovation will

---

23   See Center on Budget and Policy Priorities, www.cbpp. org/research/federal-budget/policy-basics-where-do-our-federal- tax-dollars-go. Currently total US government spending, federal, state and local, is estimated to be about 36 percent of GDP, somewhat lower than in Europe's welfare states.

determine which nations gain both economic and military superiority in the future. The United States cannot afford to fall behind in this vital competition.[24]

A novel and creative way to reduce America's debt burden has been proposed: raise money by selling federally owned assets, including valuable land, oil and mineral deposits, and buildings. According to a recent study, if federal energy reserves realized even one-third of their current market prices, the US Treasury would bring in over $23 trillion—more than the $22 trillion national debt. Ownership of these assets by the private sector would increase their productive use and benefit the economy. The chances of Congressional approval of such a program, given the statist/corporatist inclinations of a majority of today's politicians, are close to zero.

Adding to all of the economic burdens described above is the heavy cost of the administrative state. In addition to the direct costs paid by the government, according to the Competitive Enterprise Institute, regulatory compliance costs imposed on business amount to $1.885 trillion annually. Assuming that the regulatory costs ultimately flow down to households, US households incur over $14,000 per household annually on average due to this hidden regulatory tax.[25] The burdens of the administrative state are discussed in greater detail in Chapter 8.

The Economic Crisis of 2007–2008 and Its Aftermath
During the late twentieth and early twenty-first centuries, as previously noted, China and other east Asian countries adopted a policy

---

24 During the Cold War, "[i]nvestments in science surged, peaking in 1965, when 3.6 percent of the federal budget was devoted to basic and applied scientific research." Currently government spending on basic and applied science and technology is only 1 7 percent of all federal spending and only 1.3 percent of US GDP. See Ezekiel Emanuel, Amy Gadsden, and Scott Moore, "How the U.S. Surrendered to China on Scientific Research," *Wall Street Journal*, April 20–21, 2019, p. C3.

25 Clyde Wayne Crews, *Ten Thousand Commandments*, (Washington, DC, 2016). See also Philip Hamburger, *Is Administrative Law Unlawful?* (University of Chicago Press, 2014).

of export-led expansion, resulting in huge trade imbalances as well as capital flows into the US and other Western economies, pushing down interest rates. This trend was exacerbated by the US Federal Reserve Bank's policy after the year 2000 of reducing interest rates in order to stimulate growth following the collapse of the high-tech stock bubble in the late 1990s. Because of high consumption, low savings, and expansive monetary and fiscal policies by Western countries, there was a large increase in public and private debt in these countries. China's export-led expansion also contributed to the overproduction of steel and other basic industrial goods, which plagued the global economy for years.[26]

The easy monetary policy, moreover, was a major factor in accelerating the housing bubble in the United States during the early 2000s, as abnormally low interest rates greatly stimulated the housing market. The housing bubble was further stimulated by amendments to the federal Community Reinvestment Act (CRA) during the 1990s, requiring banks to make mortgage loans to borrowers who were poor credit risks, in the name of "fair housing." The politicians believed that everyone should have the right to a home. Regulators, charged with enforcing the CRA, encouraged the reduction in down payments and even their elimination, as well as the relaxation of income requirements. Under increasing pressure from government agencies, lenders made millions of "subprime" mortgage loans to people who ordinarily would not qualify for loans. The government-sponsored mortgage buyers Fannie Mae and Freddie Mac increased their purchases of subprime loans. The banking industry participated in the bubble-building by packaging the subprime mortgages and selling them to innocent buyers, pocketing large fees in the process. The bank regulators permitted this transparent charade to take place in spite of the obvious risks to investors and the financial system. The process was permitted to continue because of a

---

26   The causes and consequences of the 2008 financial crisis are discussed in an excellent book by Mervyn King, former governor of the Bank of England, *The End of Alchemy: Money, Banking and the Future of the Global Economy,* p. 317 et seq. (New York: Norton, 2016). See also John Taylor, *Getting Off Track* (Stanford, CA: Hoover Institution Press, 2009).

government-sponsored and politically popular policy to promote home ownership by low-income people.

Beginning in 2007, American house prices began to fall, and the housing bubble collapsed. The federal government took over Fannie and Freddie, which placed the US Treasury on the hook for billions of dollars of corporate debt owed or guaranteed by those agencies. American corporations and individuals filed for bankruptcy at an accelerated rate. Many banks around the world had to be bailed out by their governments or be taken over. Issuers of the packaged mortgages, derivative securities, and other exotic investments backed by inflated or overvalued assets defaulted, and investors throughout the financial world suffered. The principal remedy adopted by the US administration—an orgy of trillions of dollars of "stimulus" spending—increased the national debt without generating real economic improvement.[27] The US Federal Reserve Bank and other central banks throughout the developed world implemented expansive monetary policies in an attempt to spur economic growth. These monetary policies resulted in abnormally low interest rates, punishing savers and encouraging investors to reach for higher yields by making riskier investments.

Following the 2007–8 financial crisis, the American economy experienced a slow recovery, with weak GDP growth from 2008 through 2016. Wages were stagnant, and business investment slowed. In 2017–2019, however, the US experienced more rapid growth, stimulated in part by a $1.5 trillion tax cut and a reduction in federal government regulation. The unemployment rate dropped significantly, and real wages increased after years of stagnation. Business confidence rose with the arrival of a pro-business administration.[28] America's economic strength has also been enhanced by improved energy production, due largely to the new technology of "fracking," which makes possible access to significant new reserves of oil and natural gas.

---

27   Mervyn King, *The End of Alchemy,* p. 291.

28   See Jon Hilsenrath, "Signs Point to Sustained Growth," *Wall Street Journal,* April 29, 2019; "Jobless Rate Hits a 50-Year Low," *Wall Street Journal,* May 4–5, 2019.

The Cultural Contradictions of Capitalism
Daniel Bell, in his provocative book *The Cultural Contradictions of Capitalism,* published in 1976, argued that the typical characteristics of late capitalism—easy credit, a high propensity to consume, and purposeless leisure—would eventually destroy the work ethic that made capitalism a success in the first place. This argument is a variant of Ibn Khaldun's thesis that successive generations of a successful dynasty become more luxury-ridden, soft, and somnolent, leading finally to collapse through stagnation, revolution, or defeat by a hardier enemy.

There is no lack of evidence to support Bell's theory. The seductive combination of easy wealth and moral libertinism can hardly be expected to strengthen the national character. Contemporary American society appears to value consumption over savings, leisure over work, and hedonism over discipline. The housing bubble of the decade after 2000, America's weak savings rate, and its government's profligacy are troublesome signs. Yet the combination of economic freedom and entrepreneurial vigor has not yet lost its vitality, in spite of growing government interference. No other nation possesses anything that approaches America's capacity for economic flexibility and productivity. These contradictory signals make predictions difficult.

The long-term demographic prognosis is discouraging. As the population ages, the ratio of nonproductive retirees to active workers is increasing. In order to support the aging population, repay the nation's public and private debt, and pay for the research and development needed to sustain national security and living standards, Americans will have to consume less and save, produce, and export more. This will require what Thomas Jefferson called "a wise and frugal government," instead of today's welfare state that consumes a third or more of the nation's income and reduces large portions of the population to dependence on government. Without a radical change in fiscal policy to encourage savings, investment, and innovation, as well as a restructuring of our educational system to emphasize discipline and excellence, the standard of living of millions of Americans will decline, creating a restless, underemployed, and envious post-industrial proletariat that could become easy prey for a new Caesarian or fascist political movement.

The difficulties described here cannot be blamed on capitalism as such. We must recall the essential philosophical distinction between value-as-means and value-as-end. Economic systems have no intrinsic value. As Robert Conquest has said, an economic system is like plumbing: it has to work, but we don't choose a house for the plumbing.[29] An economic system is valuable only insofar as it fosters social characteristics that have value in themselves. Capitalism encourages desirable social attributes such as personal freedom, creativity, discipline, and choice, and provides resources for charity and art. The testimony in favor of the free enterprise system from those who have lived under other systems is worth heeding.[30] The uniqueness of capitalism is that it brings wealth and economic liberty to so many. History has proved that a capitalist, free market economy is the most successful route to escape poverty and achieve prosperity because capitalism is the only economic system that provides the incentives for innovation and prosperity.[31]

Critics of capitalism often claim that the capitalist economic system is based on an ethic of greed and oppression, but this conclusion is inaccurate. In fact, a successful capitalist system is based on traditional and fundamental moral virtues, such as honesty, trust, and hard work. The Anglo-American legal system emphasizes that businessmen who manage the central institutions of capitalism are subject to legally enforceable fiduciary duties of good faith, loyalty, and prudence that are firmly rooted in the Western moral tradition.[32] And there are many laws and regulations, frequently enforced, that punish fraud and other misconduct

---

29   Robert Conquest, *Reflections on a Ravaged Century* (New York: Norton, 2000), p. 284.

30   See, for example, Balint Vazsonyi, *America on My Mind: Selected Essays* (Vienna, VA: The Potomac Foundation, 2002–3, especially "The Price of Capitalism"), p. 527.

31   Mervyn King, *The End of Alchemy*, p. 17.

32   Joseph F. Johnston, Jr., "Natural Law and the Fiduciary Duty of Business Managers," *Journal of Markets and Morality*, Vol. 8, No. 1 (2005), p. 27.

by corporations and their managers. Of course, moral values as well as laws are often ignored by willful and reckless men, both in economic matters and in every other field of human endeavor. But businessmen are no more intrinsically infected by greed and selfishness than politicians, lawyers, writers, artists, or any other humans.

It is important to emphasize that we must not permit the quest for material gain to distract us from attending to the proper ends of human life. Our adherence to capitalism, while justified by its success in creating prosperity, must be tempered by a recognition that the pursuit of wealth alone is insufficient to achieve the good society. This truth—known by all competent philosophers since Plato—was examined and reaffirmed in *Centesimus Annus,* an astute and persuasive encyclical letter of the late Pope John Paul II, published in 1991. The encyclical strongly supports individual liberty and "the natural character of the right to private property." It concludes that "the free market is the most efficient instrument for utilizing resources and effectively responding to needs." But this is true only for those resources which are marketable and those needs which are realizable through purchasing power. Men also have spiritual and moral needs which cannot be satisfied in the marketplace. For this reason, we cannot understand the human person on the basis of economics alone. "It is not wrong to want to live better," *Centesimus Annus* states. "What is wrong is a style of life which is presumed to be better when it is directed towards 'having' rather than 'being,' and which wants to have more, not in order to be more but in order to spend life in enjoyment as an end in itself."[33] In short, the capitalist economy must take its place within a higher order of values not governed by supply and demand and should be subject to the limitations established by the traditional classical virtues of prudence, courage, temperance, and justice and the Christian virtues of faith, hope, and charity. These virtues are not created by government but are part of the enduring and transcendent moral order proper to free and rational men.

---

33   Encyclical Letter, *Centisimus Annus,* of John Paul II (Boston: St. Paul Books, 1991), p. 27.

The Self-Indulgence of Prosperity

As a byproduct of the unparalleled growth rates experienced by the United States during the twentieth century (interrupted by a major depression and several shorter recessions), Americans have fallen victim to a thoughtless indulgence—a permanent expectation of rising affluence as an entitlement rather than something to be earned. This attitude leads to the indiscipline and hedonism chronicled by the late Roman writers and by the Arab philosopher Ibn Khaldun (see Introduction). In the contemporary world, the trend toward social decadence is shaped by the breakdown of traditional social structures and the emergence of a voting majority unattached to past values. The Spanish philosopher José Ortega y Gasset, in his prescient book *The Revolt of the Masses*, first published in 1937, described the ordinary or mass man who suddenly rose to a position of influence as a result of the social revolution of modernity:

> This leads us to point to two traits in the psychology of the mass man: the free expansion of his desires ... and his radical ingratitude toward all that makes possible the ease of his existence. Both traits constitute the well-known psychology of the spoiled child ... To be spoiled means not limiting one's desires, giving the impression of a being for whom everything is permitted and nothing demanded ... This explains and defines the absurd state of mind that these people reveal: nothing concerns them except their own well-being and, at the same time, they feel no sense of shared responsibility for the causes of this well-being. Since they do not see in the advantages of their civilization a prodigious work and invention, which can be sustained only by great effort and prudence, they believe that their role is reduced to peremptorily demanding these advantages, as if they were natural rights.[34]

---

34   Jose Ortega y Gasset, *La Rebelion de las Masas* (Madrid: Espasa-Calpe, 1972 [1937], pp. 69–70. The translation is mine. I am grateful to Paul Johnston for bringing this passage to my attention. For the authorized translation into English, see *The Revolt of the Masses* (New York: W. W. Norton & Company, 1993), pp. 58–60.

Ortega's "mass men" were not solely the urban proletariat but also the rising, undereducated bourgeoisie who had recklessly neglected their heritage. Today, the category of mass man certainly includes not only uneducated or barely educated citizens but also the semi-educated impostors with little or no knowledge of history, who pose as journalists and "experts."

One of the major themes of the present book is that, despite the resounding successes of the American economy in the past, the financial irresponsibility of voters and politicians in our modern mass democracy has given us a government that is apparently incapable of living within its means. This means that the United States is headed for financial calamity unless its leaders awaken to reality. The financial collapse, when it occurs, is likely to produce a social and political upheaval of drastic proportions. The question is whether the American people are so deeply mired in the soft despotism of self-indulgence and dependency that they cannot rouse themselves to insist upon the rights and duties of free citizens. We will have much more to say on this subject.

As we know, America is vulnerable to attack and will no doubt face foreign adversaries who will continue to test the overall capacity of the nation to respond to challenges. It is to the vital topic of foreign commitments and military defense that we now turn.

4

FOREIGN POLICY AND
NATIONAL DEFENSE

America's Role in the World

The United States is not an empire in the sense that Rome and Britain were empires. The Encyclopedia Britannica defines *empire* as "an aggregate of subject territories ruled over by a sovereign state," citing as an example "Great Britain with its dominions, colonies and dependencies." The word is derived from the Latin *imperium,* signifying the combination of military command and political authority held by the top magistrates in the Roman Republic and subsequently by the emperors. In the course of its expansion across the North American continent, the United States acquired territories, including Alaska and Hawaii, that were later incorporated as integral parts of the nation. They also acquired island territories—such as Puerto Rico, Guam, Midway, and American Samoa—that are under American rule, as well as military bases around the world (with the consent of the countries where they are located). These scattered examples of American power, while important, are hardly consequential enough to constitute an empire in the historical sense.

The geopolitical world order that the United States led after World War II has been described as "a liberal international order that included an institutional commitment to free trade and freedom of the seas. It also included unprecedented assistance to weak nations incapable of fending for themselves through the Marshall Plan, NATO and other alliances."[1] This postwar order turned out to be relatively stable, in spite of a severe challenge by the Soviet Union because it was undergirded by the dominant power of the United States, which resolutely fought a forty-year "Cold War" until the Soviet Union finally collapsed due to the inherent tyranny and inefficiency of its communist system.

Following the disintegration of the Soviet Union in 1990–91, it could properly be said that the United States was the world's only "superpower." This is a shorthand term used to describe a nation that has (1) an array of strategic nuclear weapons capable of being delivered anywhere in the world, (2) powerful conventional forces that can be directed quickly to distant locations and a willingness to use them, and (3) a strong economy that can continue to produce the quantities of technically sophisticated arms needed to conduct modern warfare and to support a high level of domestic well-being. Can America's position in the world be sustained? Can the liberal international "Pax Americana" survive the new challenges posed by rising autocratic governments and emerging terrorist forces?

The United States is a nation that tends to be absorbed largely in its own domestic and business affairs. This quality of self-absorption has been in large part due to America's relative invulnerability; for nearly a century-and-a-half, as a power surrounded by two oceans and relatively peaceful neighbors, we were spared the incessant threats of hostile foreign attack that have plagued most countries around the globe. But

---

1   Herbert London, "The End of Liberal Internationalism," *Washington Times,* January 2, 2017, p. 22.

the hot and cold wars of the twentieth century proved that the United States could not remain isolated; and the terrorist attack of 2001, followed by other terrorist episodes, demonstrated that American society is as vulnerable as any other to the wayward and destructive instincts that have always existed in the irrational heart of man.

The nation's immediate reaction to the September 2001 terror attacks was one of proud and impressive unity. As President George W. Bush said a few days after the September attack, "adversity introduces us to ourselves. This is true of a nation as well." If America can retain this sense of unity and purpose over time, it will succeed in the struggle against sporadic terrorism, which will not prevail against a society that is strong and united. But we already know that national unity over a prolonged period cannot be assumed. The public reaction to the setbacks in the Iraq war that began in 2003 demonstrates the changeableness of contemporary public opinion. In the second decade of the twenty-first century, bitter divisions between America's two major political parties have emerged, affecting both domestic and foreign policy. There are complex forces at work, and it is important to look carefully and objectively at America's strengths and weaknesses to assess the impact of these forces.

There are two strong but opposing geopolitical forces in the world today. The first is the power of "globalization," which breaks down geographical barriers, creates worldwide commercial and financial markets, and provides the same mass-produced culture and media-driven information to every corner of the globe. This force, together with the "information revolution," tends to integrate and homogenize disparate societies. The second force is nationalism and ethnic conflict, which has the opposite effect of dividing people and disrupting peaceful relations. Ironically, the modern technology that supports the integrative information age also enhances the ability of ethnic and religious factions to assert their independence. The disintegrative forces of ethnicity are actively operating today within the boundaries of national states as well as in traditionally fragmented areas, such as the Middle East and Africa. Ethnic fragmentation is evident in the United States, where Hispanic immigration has led to demands for linguistic and cultural separatism, and, in both Europe and the US, where radical Muslim leaders seek to carve out an Islamic culture separate from the traditional Western mainstream. These centrifugal tendencies are supported by a divisive "multiculturalism" that is deeply entrenched in America's universities and political culture.

Before addressing the specific military and foreign policy concerns, a brief historical digression is needed to place America's geopolitical position in perspective. The history of the American role in world affairs in the twentieth century includes splendid triumphs, unnecessary defeats, and a dramatic increase in power and influence. In the first half of the twentieth century, the nineteenth-century world order collapsed. The Ottoman, Austro-Hungarian, and Russian empires were destroyed by World War I; the Second World War eliminated the military power of Germany and Japan; and in its aftermath, Britain and France gave up what remained of their empires. The United States and the Soviet Union emerged from World War II as the two great powers. Having led the successful coalition against the axis powers, the United States felt justifiably proud of its position as the "arsenal of democracy" and defender of freedom.

Meanwhile, however, the Soviet Union by the early 1950s had succeeded in imposing its empire upon the nations of Eastern Europe and in establishing military satellites around the globe. Halting the further spread of Soviet communism was a necessary task that required both economic and military measures. The Marshall Plan for US economic aid to Europe was announced in 1947; its goal was "to permit the emergence of political and social conditions in which free institutions can exist." In the North Atlantic Treaty of April 1949 among the United States, Canada, and ten nations of Western Europe, the allies agreed to resist jointly an armed attack against any member. The American policy became known as "containment," a phrase invented by George Kennan, who predicted in 1947 that, if the Soviet Union were "contained," it would eventually be brought down by its own contradictions. This strategy, in the end, succeeded more or less as Kennan had predicted. The basic contradiction that eventually destroyed the Soviet Union from the inside was the conflict between the Marxist goal of a classless society and the means employed by the communist system to achieve that goal, which involved brutal tyranny, onerous bureaucracy, and the suppression of initiative. The Soviet system and methods gradually undermined the economy and forfeited the support of the Russian people.

The first serious test for America's policy of containing communism was the invasion of South Korea by communist North Korea in June 1950. In spite of the intervention of the Red Chinese army, the US-led forces succeeded in holding the line at the 38th parallel and preserving the independence of South Korea. This result was a victory for the free world and proved that containment would be supported with more than words.

The American public, in general, supported the nation's leaders in conducting the lengthy struggle against Soviet-sponsored communism known as the Cold War. This effort was costly and involved a serious commitment on the part of the public, including a military draft that lasted until the mid-1970s. The decrepit Soviet economy could not compete with the military modernization by the United States and its NATO allies during the 1980s, and the Cold War finally ended with the collapse of the Soviet Union in 1991.

The most damaging setback in America's post-war strategic policy was the war in Vietnam, an unnecessary and costly intervention that exposed a fundamental problem in the conduct of foreign affairs in a modern democracy: the understandable reluctance of the populations of democratic societies to support a military campaign abroad involving heavy casualties over a prolonged period, except where domestic national security is clearly threatened. The Gulf War of 1991 was not particularly controversial because it was the kind of conflict everyone on the victor's side can love: easy, swift, and decisive. The Balkan conflicts of the 1990s scarcely qualified as "wars" at all and presented no serious challenge to US power, although they did give rise to unwise national commitments and established a dangerous precedent for thoughtless interventionism.

The "War on Terror" that began in September 2001 with the terrorist attacks on targets in New York City and Washington, DC, appeared, at first, to have strengthened the resolve of Americans to endure hardship and loss, particularly since the threat seemed to strike directly at the basic values of freedom, security, and the rule of law that undergird our civic and personal lives. The United States properly retaliated against the sponsors of the attack, Al Qaeda and the Taliban in Afghanistan, but then made a mistake in trying to pacify and rehabilitate Afghanistan, a historically fractious and tribal nation that had never experienced democracy or the rule of law—a hopeless endeavor.

In 2003, the United States invaded Iraq, an Arab state governed by Saddam Hussein, a brutal dictator who had killed thousands of Iraq's citizens and had used chemical weapons against Iran in a recent war.[2] One rationale for the invasion was that Saddam's regime possessed "weapons of mass destruction" (WMDs), including chemical weapons. (The existence of such weapons had been credibly alleged by intelligence services of the United States and its allies, but it turned out that the WMDs had been abandoned by Saddam.) On the American side, the war was professionally fought and led, but it had unintended consequences, triggering a radical terrorist uprising that did considerable damage in that part of the world. American forces temporarily occupied Iraq and undertook the fruitless task of rehabilitating this divided country and moving it toward democracy.

Arab-Islamic states have traditionally been governed by theocracies or other forms of authoritarian government. Democracy is not yet practicable in most of these countries. It is theoretically possible that a lengthy military occupation of Iraq, analogous to the British occupation of India, might have eventually have led to some sort of quasi-democracy. However, the American public had neither the British

---

2   For an in-depth insider's view of the origins of the Iraq War, see Douglas J. Feith, *War and Decision: Inside the Pentagon at the Dawn of the War on Terrorism* (New York: Harper, 2000).

instinct for empire nor the patience for a long and costly occupation. Because of the competing and excessive worldwide commitments of US forces, there were insufficient troops available to suppress the unexpectedly strong insurgency encountered by the American military in Iraq. The "surge" strategy devised by Generals David Petraeus and Raymond Odierno and ordered by President George W. Bush in 2007 succeeded in briefly reducing sectarian violence and diminishing the influence of armed insurgents but could not turn Iraq into a stable and united nation.

When the Obama administration took office in 2009, it withdrew most American troops from Iraq, leaving only a small contingent of advisers. The defensive gap was soon occupied by hostile forces, particularly the Islamic State (also known as ISIS or ISIL), and Iraq continued to be wracked by violence. Its largely Shiite government has come under Iranian influence, along with other areas of the Middle East. The Obama administration, together with other American allies, tried to moderate the danger from a rapidly arming Iran through an agreement under which Iran agreed to suspend its attempts to enrich nuclear fuel for a period of years, but this agreement was basically unenforceable and, when the Trump administration entered office, it withdrew from the agreement. As of this writing, Iran has continued its active support for Hezbollah and other terrorist organizations in the Middle East and is suspected of renewing its attempt to develop nuclear weapons.

Other recent US interventions have also been counterproductive. For example, the US was complicit in the overthrow and death of Muammar Gaddafi in Libya in 2011. Today, Libya is a failed state, and its territory is a haven for terrorists and desperate migrants. The full consequences of our military involvement in the Middle East will not be known for many years, but one conclusion is apparent. The United States should be very reluctant to undertake military operations in foreign regions except where our national interests are seriously threatened, the chances for success are reasonably clear, we have or can gain the support of regional allies, and the intervention is likely to produce more good than harm. We should avoid intervening with force merely because the political system of a country does not comport with our notion of republican democracy.

It is important to remember that the US Constitution gives Congress the power to declare war and to raise and support armies. Congress has sometimes given a different name to its approval of using military force—such as "authorization for the use of military force" (AUMF)—but the point is that our constitutional tradition requires Congressional support (and thus public support) for significant military interventions abroad. Without broad and sustained public support, such interventions are unlikely to be sustained. This is a very important point for US leaders to keep in mind.

The Emerging World Order

The geopolitical order has shifted significantly since the fall of the Soviet Union. As has been typical throughout recorded history, the emerging order will involve a changing pattern of alliances and enmities among several major powers. The United States, China, and Russia will almost certainly be at the forefront (in the absence of serious internal disruptions in one or more of these powers). Europe may also be a major participant, although its members are more likely to remain as (relatively weak) allies of the United States. Because of its superior political-legal constitution and the intrinsic common sense of its people, Britain will continue to "punch beyond its weight" in the world arena. Japan and India are also plausible contenders for a leading role in Asia. In the Middle East, Turkey and Iran have the economic strength to become serious geopolitical players (although recent events in both countries cast some doubt upon their long-term stability), and Israel, Saudi Arabia, and Egypt have the potential to become important actors. Efforts to bring about democracy have proved futile in most Muslim countries since democracy is a heresy for Islam. Democracy means that the people are in charge. Under Islam, however, the people cannot be in charge; Allah is in charge, operating through the Koran and the reigning cadres of mullahs, ayatollahs, and sheiks. Workable democracy requires centuries of practice in self-restraint and the rule of law; it cannot be achieved through trying to change tribal and theocratic societies from the outside.

Early in the twenty-first century, the economic power of the United States is unsurpassed. Its command of the technology of modern weaponry puts it militarily ahead of its potential competitors, although China, aided by Western technology, China's predatory economic practices, militaristic leadership, and the industriousness of the Chinese people themselves, is catching up rapidly. But superior power alone does not guarantee peace or stability. In addition to the likelihood of continuing terrorist attacks, threats to American security may include destabilizing changes of regime in major or minor powers, strikes by "rogue states," nuclear blackmail, regional wars, sabotage of information systems, and organized crime. And we know that the US economy may be subject to crises and setbacks, affecting its industrial base.

A major security problem of the twenty-first century will be the proliferation of weapons of mass destruction, including nuclear, biological, and chemical weapons. In addition to Russia and China, there is a strong possibility that a number of rogue states, such as North Korea and Iran, have or soon will have the capacity to direct missile attacks against America and Europe. (North Korea agreed in principle in 2018 to eventually abandon its nuclear weapons, but its long history of noncompliance does not inspire confidence.) If weapons of mass destruction, along with medium- or long-range delivery systems, eventually come into the possession of several nations (some of them with unstable or fanatical governments), any hope of a permanently secure global order would disappear. The "new world order" heralded by some idealists is, in fact, a Hobbesian state of nature, and self-preservation is the ruling principle. Western civilization itself may be at risk, and the freedoms laboriously won by the West are likely to be endangered. As we know from recent terrorist attacks, the enemies of civilization are not limited to nation-states (though some terrorists are supported by nation-states), and their weapons will often be unconventional. If the values and representative institutions of the West are to survive, therefore, a much stronger defensive posture on the part of the civilized nations will be required, including the active participation of countries which for decades have been "free-loading" on America's willingness to act as the defender of freedom and commerce in the world.

Islamic terrorism poses a continuing threat to the United States and its allies. Europe, host to millions of Islamic migrants, is particularly susceptible to terrorist attacks. The attacks of September 11, 2001, on the World Trade Center and the Pentagon have been followed by individual acts of violence committed by terrorists in American cities. Western authorities have used police and counter-terrorist tactics against Islamist extremists, but there has been no serious effort to oppose the radical ideology of jihad. The US should mount a multi-faceted educational information campaign, in partnership with leaders of the nonviolent Muslim community, to counter the ideological indoctrination spread by radical Islamists, while continuing to engage in active counter-measures against militant groups.

There is also a clear potential military threat from China, a country that has been described as a "surveillance state," which stores and uses massive amounts of data to control its people, and conducts espionage on foreigners, steals technology, subsidizes state corporations, persecutes religious believers, and launches cyberattacks against other countries. As noted in Chapter 3, China is devoting enormous resources to scientific research and development in an effort to become the world's foremost economic and military power. Chinese suspicions and belligerence are most likely to break into actual hostility over China's claim to Taiwan, which from China's standpoint is non-negotiable. China is developing increasingly effective missile, naval, and air capabilities, and its militarization of the South China Sea makes its strategic ambitions quite clear. There is no way that the United States acting alone can, with any credibility, guarantee this region of the world against the risk of Chinese aggression. We should therefore encourage responsible Asian countries to form their own alliance for the containment of China, which the United States would support with strategic and technological backup. Japan, South Korea, India, and Australia (together with other ASEAN nations) have the population, technical capacity, and economic clout to make a containment strategy work. India already has nuclear weapons and missile technology, and Japan, a leading economic power, could develop a nuclear retaliatory capacity if it chose to. If the nations most directly affected are not willing to sustain a regional balance of power through their own military efforts (with American and allied help), then they must take their chances with diplomacy. What is *not* acceptable is for the United States to bear the major burden for the defense of wealthy and populous countries that are unwilling to defend themselves. This conclusion also applies to other parts of the world, including Europe. The appropriate strategy for the United States is "regionalization," in which capable nations arm themselves to deter potential aggressors in their own regions, with support from the US where that is feasible. America can take care of itself, with the help of its allies, but it cannot, need not, and should not be the world's peacekeeper.

Globalization and Multilateralism
The globalization of finance and commerce does not eliminate instability and conflict any more than the "Romanization" of commerce in the Mediterranean led to lasting peace in that region. It is a myth that free markets and capital flows will produce a worldwide era of good feelings. To the contrary, by destabilizing settled societies, promoting rapid urbanization and migration, and undermining traditional values, globalization is more likely to foster uncertainty and violent resistance. Human nature remains stubbornly tribal—"us" versus "them"—and the losers in the global development process cannot be expected to retire modestly from the scene. The radicalization of failing Islamic countries provides a clear example. National policies are governed by self-interest and emotion, not by rational economic theories of wealth maximization. Governments and tribes will not give up power easily, and they will protect their institutions, industries, and traditions where possible.

A long period of chaos and confusion is likely, and military force, as always, will be the critical determinant of national power.

Spokesmen for global arrangements often hold out multilateral institutions and peace treaties as the antidote to destructive nationalism. Many internationalists are addicted to the absurd notion that arms control is the solution to aggression. But the history of arms control is largely one of failure. The anti-aggression pacts of the post-World War I period, such as the Kellogg-Briand pact of 1929, were wholly ineffective. More recently, the Nuclear Non-Proliferation Treaty has done little to stop the spread of nuclear arms. Americans are a legalistic people, and legalism encourages the view that a contract-based international system can be made to resemble the American or British legal system. The fallacy of this approach is that in societies like America and Britain, the rule of law and habits of compromise are deeply engrained, so that there is a predisposition for people to conform to legal mandates even when they run contrary to the individual's self-interest. In the international arena, on the other hand, behavior contrary to interest is not only rare but may be disastrous. If, to take an obvious example, the United States were to adhere to a test-ban treaty or an agreement reducing supplies of advanced weapons, but one or more of its major competitors did not, the rapidity of technological change could quickly generate a dangerous imbalance.

The United Nations, founded at the end of World War II, was formed "to save succeeding generations from the scourge of war," as well as to reaffirm human rights, to support international law, and to promote social progress and better standards of living.[3] While the UN has performed some useful services in refugee relief and education, it has not been particularly successful in enforcing peace around the world. The veto power in the Security Council held by a few of the major powers, together with the domination of the General Assembly by weak or irresponsible countries, have limited the organization's effectiveness. The idea of international armies is far-fetched. Efforts by

---

3   Preamble to Charter of the United Nations, www.un.org.

the United Nations to enforce the peace have been less than successful because the motive of patriotism is absent. Soldiers may risk their lives while fighting for their families and their countries in a national army, but few are likely to be ready to die for the UN. Similar problems exist for multinational forces enforcing peace in regions like the Middle East and Africa, which is precisely the reason why national leaders are reluctant to commit ground troops to these kinds of operations. Why should responsible commanders risk severe casualties in support of peripheral and abstract international objectives the average citizen may find hard to understand? This difficulty is based on human nature and the national interest of states.

National armies and alliances among sympathetic nations will therefore continue to fight for the foreseeable future, and the people of each nation will hold its leaders accountable for their national security. This means that (1) military readiness will remain a permanent concern for every nation; and (2) political leaders must assess very carefully the justification for each military intervention and obtain adequate domestic support.

The approach to foreign policy advocated here is a form of geopolitics generally referred to as "realism" or "realpolitik." Realism emphasizes the territorial aspects of power politics, as well as the contributions of economics and technology. Realistic geopolitics claims that "there is an international pecking order, determined by who has power and who does not; . . . . resources and strategic potential, the sources of state power, are unequally distributed worldwide; and power is ephemeral—possession is no guarantee of its permanent retention, and therefore states must take steps to ensure its retention."[4] Power matters more than ideology. Realists believe that we must deal with the world as it is—a world governed by the correlation of forces—and not the world as optimists would like it to be. Successful nations respond to the realities of power rather than relying on the kindness of strangers and

---

4   Mackubin T. Owens, "In Defense of Classic Geopolitics," *Orbis*, Fall 2015, p. 647.

the velleities of international law. International order depends upon a balance of power, within which each nation is expected to advance its own interests, preferably through peaceful means. In the contemporary world, no single nation can preserve this international order alone. This means that the United States must have working relationships with reliable allies that are willing to bear part of the burden of mutual defense.

Overstretch?

There has always been a correlation between economic capacity and military power, inasmuch as a society that has the financial resources to raise large armies and buy expensive weapons will have an obvious advantage over its poorer competitors. Professor Paul Kennedy, in his book, *The Rise and Fall of the Great Powers,* published in 1987, analyzed the economic-military correlation and illustrated how military dominance has fluctuated in accordance with relative economic strength in the modern world. For example, the position of Hapsburg Spain seemed impregnable in the sixteenth century, but Spain's empire was overextended. The Hapsburg emperors were engaged in a continual struggle for solvency and never developed an adequate industrial base. Spain lost most of its European empire by the end of the eighteenth century, and its possessions in South America were lost in the following century. "At the center of the Spanish decline," Kennedy concludes, "was the failure to recognize the importance of preserving the economic underpinnings of a powerful military machine."[5] Similarly, the relative stagnation of the British economy compared to Germany and the United States, discussed in Chapter 2, adversely affected Britain's military position in the twentieth century. By 1940, the United States was far ahead of any other nation in what Kennedy calls "relative war potential," which to a large extent depends on economic productivity. World War II demonstrated the correlation between economic and military power (although other factors such as population, geography, strong political institutions, and

---

5   Paul Kennedy, *The Rise and Fall of the Great Powers* (New York: Random House, 1987), p. 55.

broad popular support obviously played a vital part).

The lesson is clear: a nation's global commitments must be balanced by the ability to defend those commitments. The United States has entered into defense commitments, formal and informal, in Europe, the Middle East, and East Asia, secured by a forward-basing strategy and a global navy. This global posture resembles that of the British Empire in the nineteenth century. America has significant numbers of troops stationed in Europe, Afghanistan, South Korea, Japan, and assorted naval bases, and must be prepared to intervene in these or in other critical areas, such as the Caribbean, when required. A question could be raised as to whether the United States would be able to meet its far-flung commitments successfully if two or more conflicts should break out simultaneously. America's task is made even harder when some of its major allies, such as the European members of NATO, fail to bear their proper share of the alliance's defense burden. Let us briefly review some of the most likely trouble spots.

First, the Middle East, which is notoriously unstable. A number of developments have come together to perpetuate instability, including competition among regional powers, weak or failing states, and religious and tribal conflict. Contributing factors include the endemic corruption, political incapacity, economic backwardness, and weak educational institutions in the Arab countries of this region.[6] Iran actively supports terrorism in the region and has developed a ballistic missile capability. Once it possesses nuclear weapons, which seems likely, this threat could encourage other states in the area to acquire a nuclear capability. (Pakistan and India already have nuclear weapons.) A major conflict in the Middle East, nuclear or nonnuclear, would unleash a flood of refugees into Europe. European nations could do much more to strengthen their own defenses, although continued American support

---

6   See Christopher J. Bolan, "Dealing with Iran Will Not Be enough to Restore Regional Stability," Foreign Policy Research Institute, June 14, 2019; Mehran Kamrava, "Multipolarity and Instability in the Middle East," *Orbis,* Fall 2018, p. 598.

will be required. The US should resist the temptation to engage in nation building in the Middle East and elsewhere. There is nothing to be gained, for example, by keeping US forces in Afghanistan, a region that has been tribal and anarchic for centuries. Following the lengthy and costly interventions in Afghanistan, Iraq, and Syria, US forces worldwide, to use Paul Kennedy's term, may be "overstretched." The United States should seek to preserve a balance of power in the Middle East by working with Saudi Arabia, Israel, Egypt, and other regional states, but without maintaining large, permanent US military bases. Nevertheless, special operations forces, as well as naval and air support to allies, may well be required, and the United States should maintain these capabilities.

A second danger zone is Russia and its "near abroad" in Eastern Europe. Russia in recent years has been augmenting its conventional forces and its undersea, cyber and space capabilities, as well as modernizing its nuclear forces. It has seized the Crimean peninsula by force and supported an insurgency in Eastern Ukraine, in addition to threatening Georgia and other neighbors. It has given active military support to Syrian dictator Bashar al-Assad. It has used disinformation and hostile cyber operations in Europe and the United States. Russia's "near abroad" will continue to be a troubled area, and NATO should strengthen its deterrent capacity in central Europe. This does not mean, however, that Russia will necessarily be a permanent enemy of the United States. We obviously do not approve of Russian violations of international law or invasions of other countries. But over the long run, it is in the interest of America and its European allies to reach an accommodation with Russia, which has historic roots in Western culture and the Christian religion, and, with more cooperative leadership, could be a potential ally in the Middle East and central Asia.

A third region of potential conflict is East Asia. China presents a serious threat to its neighbors and to the international community; it is rapidly militarizing and seems determined to achieve total control of the South China Sea. It is investing heavily in advanced weapon systems such as hypersonic missiles and space technology.[7] China's mercantilist trade policies include subsidies to Chinese companies, below-market financing of exports and theft of intellectual property. Its enormous trade surpluses in recent decades enable it to pay for a great deal of military hardware. China's president, Xi Jinping, has consolidated his power and is moving the country toward totalitarianism. As Gordon Chang has written, Chinese officials are "developing ways to use technology to collect and analyze vast amounts of data for the purpose of controlling behavior.... While Xi is closing down public discussion, he is also walling off China's economy from the world by increasing Beijing's sway over markets, tightening capital controls, creating new state monopolies, enlarging subsidies for favored domestic businesses, and employing an array of tactics to cripple foreign competitors. He has reinvigorated central planning with state-centric initiatives such as the now-notorious Made in China 2025 program, which seeks Chinese dominance in ten crucial industries."[8]

The United States has strategic commitments to Japan, South Korea, and Taiwan. North Korea, a very unstable country with nuclear weapons and an erratic dictator, is a clear menace; it has tested intercontinental ballistic missiles with ranges that can reach the continental US and may soon have full nuclear capability. The preliminary agreement reached in 2018 between the United States and North Korea under

---

7   A recent study by the United States Studies Centre at the University of Sydney concludes that China's advanced counter-intervention systems "have undermined America's ability to project power into the Indo-Pacific, raising the risk that China could use limited force to achieve a *fait accompli* victory before America can respond." "Averting Crisis: American Strategy, Military Spending and Collective Defence in the Indo-Pacific," United States Studies Centre, University of Sydney, August 19, 2019.

8   Gordon Chang, "Xi's Great Leap Backward," *The American Conservative,* July/August 2018, pp. 32 33. China has refused to accept the 2016 ruling of an international court of arbitration which held that China's claim to sovereign rights with respect to the maritime areas of the South China Sea within China's so-called "nine-dash line" (including the Spratly Islands), are unlawful under the UN Convention on the Law of the Sea. PCA Case No. 2013–19, In the Matter of the South China Sea Arbitration, Permanent Court of Arbitration, July 12, 2016.

which the latter agreed in principle to give up its nuclear weapons may or may not bear fruit. As of this writing, North Korea is continuing its development and testing of ballistic missiles. If a serious conflict breaks out in the east Asian region, the United States might not be able to deal with it through diplomacy alone. Again, America will benefit from strong allies in this region.

A fourth major threat is that of terrorism against the US homeland and abroad. The limited wars we have fought in Afghanistan and Iraq did not eliminate this threat, although the more recent campaign against the Islamic State has reduced it. America's borders are, in practice, quite permeable and future domestic terrorist attacks are likely.[9]

To avoid the adverse consequences of overstretch, the United States should limit the extent of its military commitments abroad and avoid intervening militarily except where US interests are clearly threatened. Where we do have troops stationed abroad, we should move, steadily and prudently, in the direction of reducing America's military presence and turning over the principal duties of regional security to those who live there.

One basic point must be kept in mind: *the goal of America's defense policy is deterrence,* which means the credible threat of reprisal sufficient to preclude attacks from adversary powers. It must be made clear to potential aggressors that the United States is prepared to respond to real threats with effective military force, under dedicated leadership and backed by the ability to produce modern, technologically advanced weapons.

Military Readiness
Historically, the US has spent very little on defense in peacetime. Defense spending was about 1 percent of GDP at the beginning of the twentieth century; it spiked to 22 percent during World War I, then dropped back, and rose again to 41 percent of GDP during World

---

9   For an astute analysis of US vulnerability to global crises, see Arthur Waldron, "Four Global Crises," *Orbis,* Spring 2016, p. 162.

War II. During the height of the Cold War, defense spending ran at about 10 percent of GDP and stood at 6.8 percent during the Reagan defense buildup in the 1980s but dropped sharply after the end of the Cold War in 1989, reaching 3.5 percent of GDP in 2001. After the terrorist attacks of 2001, followed by the Afghan and Iraq wars, it jumped to 5.7 percent in 2011 but later declined to under 4 percent. As a share of total federal spending, the percentage devoted to defense has dropped from over 60 percent in the 1950s to a projected 20 percent in 2020.[10] The decline (as a percentage of GDP) in military spending is a byproduct of a significant change in the structure of federal spending toward much greater spending on welfare and entitlement programs. In 2018, about 60 percent of the federal budget was devoted to Social Security, Medicare, Medicaid, and welfare programs, up from only 25 percent in the 1960s.[11] The political shift in favor of welfare spending in most Western democracies has meant a reduction in the resources devoted to the military.

During the 1990s, the US Defense Department conducted a "bottom-up review" of US military forces, which established a benchmark according to which US forces should be able to achieve decisive victory in two nearly simultaneous major regional conflicts or contingencies (MRCs). (An MRC would be a conflict resembling America's twenty-first century military operations in Afghanistan and Iraq.) At the time this benchmark was established, following the collapse of the Soviet Union, this standard appeared to be realistic. The US was more powerful, relative to any likely combination of enemies, than any military force since the Roman Empire. Following the Iraq War of 2003 to 2010, however, military readiness deteriorated. Barrack Obama, who became president in 2009, supported by bipartisan majorities in Congress, made significant cuts in defense spending. The Budget Control Act of 2011 imposed budget caps on both

---

10   See usgovernmentspending.com.

11   www.usgovernmentspending.com/federal_budget_detail; Center on Budget Policy Priorities, www. cbpp. org/research/federal-budget/policy-basics-where-do-our-federal-tax-dollars-go.

defense and nondefense spending. For defense, the budget cap required a substantial reduction in military spending, to be enforced by a process called "sequestration" in case the caps were exceeded.[12] The constraints placed on defense spending seriously impaired readiness, modernization, and capacity for military operations.

Recent studies have revealed serious deficiencies in US military readiness. In 2017, Congress created the National Defense Strategy Commission to make recommendations for the nation's defense strategy. The Commission's report, co-chaired by Eric Edelman and Gary Roughead, was delivered in November 2018. It concluded that "[t]he security and wellbeing of the United States are at greater risk than at any time in decades. America's military superiority—the hard-power backbone of its global influence and national security—has eroded to a dangerous degree." Powerful competitors—especially China and Russia—are pursuing military buildups with advanced weapons (such as hypersonic missiles and artificial intelligence technologies) aimed at neutralizing US strengths. America's weakened defense posture, according to the report, is "due to political dysfunction and decisions made by both political parties—and particularly due to the effects of the Budget Control Act (BCA) of 2011 and years of failing to enact timely appropriations.... Regional military balances in Eastern Europe, the Middle East, and the Western Pacific have shifted in decidedly adverse ways."[13] America's military forces have been strained by extended operations in the Middle East and by inadequate funding to the extent that, according to the Commission's report, "America is very near the point of strategic insolvency, where its 'means' are badly out of line with its 'ends.'"[14] As a result of the Budget Control Act of 2011, defense spending (in constant 2018 dollars) fell

---

12   Congressional Research Service: The Budget Control Act and the Defense Budget, April 28, 2017, p. 9.

13   "Providing for the Common Defense: The Assessment and Recommendations of the National Defense Strategy Commission," November 2018, pp. v–vi.

14   *Id.* p. xii.

from $794 billion in fiscal year (FY) 2010 to $586 billion in FY 2015. Increases in military budgets in the period 2018–20 have helped to remedy these deficiencies but more funding will be required, particularly for the development of advanced weapons systems.

The Heritage Foundation's 2019 Index of Military Strength (a comprehensive report updated annually) contains a detailed summary of the nation's military preparedness.[15] A few of the Heritage Index's findings include the following:

Army. For fiscal year 2019, the Regular Army's authorized end strength was 483,500, down from 566,000 in FY 2011, placing a serious strain on troops under current operational demand for forces. According to Defense Department sources, only about half of the thirty Army Brigade Combat Teams were ready for combat. The Army has more than 170,000 soldiers stationed across 140 countries. Cuts in financing have placed a serious strain on troops and have adversely affected research and development, procurement, and modernization.[16]

Navy. The Navy's "battle force fleet" in 2018 totaled 284 vessels, well below the Navy's fleet goal of 355 ships and insufficient to sustain a conflict involving two major regional conflicts. The shortfall in fleet capacity is due to inadequate funding. The Heritage Index of Military Strength rated the Navy's overall score for capacity, capability and readiness as "marginal," noting that "Navy readiness levels are problematic and will take several years to correct."[17]

---

15   *2019 Index of U.S. Military Strength*, ed. Dakota L Wood (The Heritage Foundation 2019).

16   See Heritage 2019 Index of Military Strength, pp. 327–42.

17   Heritage 2019 Index, p, 361 As an illustrative example, I he Navy maintains at all times one aircraft carrier in each of the three major regions of the world. However. to ensure that ships, aircraft, and crew are in a state of readiness, three additional carriers are needed for each carrier deployed—one returning from deployment, one undergoing maintenance, and one preparing for deployment, in addition to one carrier undergoing an extensive mid-life overhaul, for a total of thirteen carriers. More than one carrier may be needed in a given area in the event of a potential crisis. as recently occurred in the western Pacific near North Korea. As of 2018, the Navy had only eleven carriers. Heritage 2019 Index, p. 348.

Air Force. As in the case of the other services, several years of funding cuts under the Budget Control Act has had a detrimental effect on the readiness and capability of the Air Force, especially on its ability to modernize its aircraft fleets. For example, the average age of a fighter plane in 1990 was 11 years, but by 2018 it was 28 years; and the total number of active-duty aircraft has dropped significantly. The Air Force has shrunk from 70 combat-ready active duty fighter squadrons during operation Desert Storm in 1991 to 55 in 2018.[18]

Marine Corps. The Marine Corps has been required to reduce its active-duty end-strength from 202,000 in FY 2011 to 185,000 in FY 2018, which according to the Marine Corps commandant will leave the Corps with fewer active duty battalions than would be required for two major contingencies. Military officers also worry that the battle tanks used by both the Army and Marines have not been upgraded to remain competitive with new tanks recently introduced by Russia and China. A number of other Marine combat vehicles including amphibious vehicles are outdated and there are serious shortages of Marine combat aircraft.[19]

Nuclear Capability. US nuclear forces are designed primarily to deter nuclear attacks and large-scale conventional attacks that threaten America and its allies. Both Russia and China are engaged in active programs of nuclear buildup. US nuclear deterrence relies on a triad of land, sea and air-based weapons. The nation has a substantial stockpile of nuclear weapons, although experts have cautioned that America's stockpile is in need of modernization. The United States is currently under a self-imposed nuclear testing moratorium, which restricts its ability to develop new and more versatile weapons.[20]

---

18   Heritage gave the Air Force a rating for capacity and capability of "marginal" and "weak" for readiness. Heritage 2019 Index, pp. 385–402.

19   Heritage 2019 Index, pp. 409–28.

20   "The U.S. Nuclear Triad Needs an Upgrade," an open letter signed by a number of former commanders of the U.S. Strategic Command, *Wall Street Journal,* January 12, 2017, p. A17; Heritage 2019 Index, pp. 433–35.

Ballistic Missile Defense. A number of America's military competitors, including Russia, China, North Korea, and undoubtedly others in the future, have or will have the ability to launch ballistic missiles capable of reaching the continental United States. An effective missile defense system is essential to protect the American people and America's economic base, as well as its troops and allies abroad. Unfortunately, this critical aspect of national security has been badly neglected by recent administrations and by Congress. As a result, "the United States does not have in place a comprehensive ballistic missile defense system that would be capable of defending the homeland and allies from robust missile threats."[21]

Outer Space. The importance of satellites to national security has been apparent for decades. Navigation and communication via satellite is vital to military forces as well as to the domestic economy. Space, however, is a notoriously difficult environment for humans and their complex machines. Modern warfare requires vast amounts of information communicated through space. A number of nations are currently developing anti-satellite weapons and, as a result, the protection of our critical space infrastructure will become increasingly difficult and expensive. Defense against ballistic missiles will be increasingly conducted by way of space-based hardware.

Cyberspace. Developments in digital technology have provided potential enemies with opportunities to attack US installations and operating systems. Competition in cyberspace is growing rapidly. As we know, countries use cyberspace to spread propaganda, sow discord, steal secrets and, importantly, disable information systems. It is extremely difficult, as we have learned, to defend against sophisticated cyber attacks. Undoubtedly, the US will have to devote more resources and human effort to protection of the cyber domain.[22]

---

21   Heritage 2019 Index, p. 451.

22   See G. Alexander Crowther, "National Defense and the Cyber Domain," Heritage 2019 Index, p. 83.

In short, at the present time, the US military is probably capable of handling a single major regional conflict but is not adequately prepared to meet a two-MRC-requirement. As former Secretary of Defense Chuck Hagel has said, "We are entering an era where American dominance on the seas, in the skies, and in space—not to mention cyberspace—can no longer be taken for granted."[23]

The US continues to bear heavy military commitments around the world in spite of the deficiencies outlined above. It would appear prudent, therefore, not only to strengthen our military force, but to reduce our commitments to those that are genuinely necessary for our national security. Some of the "overstretch" could be moderated by making it clear to our regional allies that they must do more to defend themselves. The European nations, our Middle Eastern allies, Japan and other developed nations could certainly afford to devote more resources to defense, permitting the US to reduce the number of troops and other assets it now commits to overseas basing. Only a few of NATO's twenty-nine member countries, for example, have reached the alliance's goal of investing 2 percent of GDP on their military. Britain, Poland, and a very few other countries have met the 2 percent requirement, but the others have not. The United States spends more on defense than the twenty-eight other NATO members combined.[24] Unless America's NATO allies can summon the willpower to contribute substantially to their own defense, the future success of the alliance could be questionable.

The United States should insist that our allies do more to meet their own defense needs. The United States has devoted decades of effort

---

23 Who's Afraid of America," *The Economist,* June 13, 2015, p. 57. See Heritage Foundation, 2019 Index of Military Strength, pp. 455–56.

24 "Defence Expenditure of NATO Countries (2010–2017)," June 29, 2017, www.nato.int; "NATO Members Short of Spending Goals," *Wall Street Journal,* February 10–11, 2018. In recent years, some of NATO's European members have increased defense spending, although others, especially Germany, lag far behind. See James Marson, "Nato's Military Spending Edges Up," *Wall Street Journal,* March 15, 2019.

and countless resources in the defense of Europe, the historic source of Western civilization, and the Mediterranean, Europe's vital maritime and commercial crossroads. America has also helped to defend Japan, South Korea, and the Philippines that, along with Australia and New Zealand, remain allies in a region critical to world trade and rich in human and material resources. India is also a friendly power and, along with the nations named above, among the few active and prosperous democracies in Asia. Latin America, because of its proximity and traditional ties to the US, is a region that has a high priority for assistance in the event of a serious threat. We cannot simply walk away from these global relationships. It is possible, even probable, that a major regional contingency would break out in one or more of these regions that would require US military intervention. Thus, the two-major-contingency requirement remains relevant. History teaches us that it is better to be prepared than unprepared. To cite again the Roman motto: if you want peace, prepare for war. A strategy of regionalization that places America in the position of "riding shotgun," with our regional allies bearing the predominant burden of troops and equipment, is the model to be followed.

Donald Trump, who became president in January 2017, had promised during his presidential campaign to improve military readiness. The Trump administration's budget request for fiscal 2020 proposed an increase in defense spending to $718 billion—up about 5 percent from 2019. (The 2020 request amounts to about 4.5 percent of GDP, a significantly lower percentage of GDP than the US spent during the Cold War and the 1980s defense build-up. The increases were deemed necessary to ensure "a more lethal, agile, and innovative Joint Force ... to provide the combat-credible military forces needed for the US to deter or defeat great power adversaries."[25] The budget request focused primarily on four key areas space and cyber domains; modernization of forces; innovation of weapon systems; and increasing operational readiness.

---

25   Department of Defense FY 2020 Budget Request overview.

It is a basic theme of this book that military power is predicated on economic strength. As discussed in Chapter 3, America's economic vitality has been impaired by an enormous increase in the public debt ($22 trillion in gross federal debt in 2019, over 100 percent of GDP, compared to $6 trillion in 2000, about 60 percent of GDP) and constantly rising expenditures for social welfare programs without a corresponding increase in the economic growth needed to pay for them. America's political leaders are paying insufficient attention to this growing fiscal crisis.[26]

Military historians from Thucydides to Clausewitz have always known that military readiness involves much more than money and hardware. As Clausewitz observed, war is in a real sense "the business of the people," not merely of the professionals.[27] Discipline is the essential quality that distinguishes a trained military force from an armed mob. Military discipline stems from months of rigorous physical and mental training under conditions of hardship and leads to a feeling of pride, patriotism, and bonding that is critical to success in combat. There is a growing gap in American culture between civilians and the military. Fewer than 1 percent of US citizens now serve in the military, and only 7 percent of the population are military veterans (a number that is likely to diminish with time).[28] This means that fewer Americans have experienced the discipline of military service or have acquired the skills needed to understand what the military does.

There is also some question as to whether enough young Americans today are physically fit and are willing to undergo the rigors of military

---

26 As discussed in Chapter 3, the real fiscal gap is much larger than the official public debt figure. See Laurence J. Kotlikoff and Scott Burns, *The Clash of Generations* (Cambridge, MA: The MIT Press, 2012); Niall Ferguson and Laurence J. Kotlikoff, "Going Critical: American Power and the Consequences of Fiscal Overstretch," *The National Interest* (Fall 2003), pp. 22, 31.

27 Barry D. Watts, "Clausewitzian Friction and Future War," Institute for National Strategic Studies, McNair Paper 52, 1996, p. 17.

28 "Number of Americans Who've Served in the Military Is Rapidly Declining," www.lifezette.com. (November 10, 2017.)

discipline. An army in a democracy reflects the values of the society. A hedonistic society infatuated with pleasure, entertainment, and government subsidies does not provide fertile soil for an *armée en masse* of patriots. These remarks are not intended to reflect in any way upon the superb skill and professionalism of the American personnel who have served in the Iraq and Afghan campaigns or any other conflict to date. It would be a mistake to underrate the US military. Experience has shown that, when called upon, American soldiers, sailors, marines, and airmen are the finest and fittest warriors in the world. But there must be enough of them, and they must be equipped and supported with what they need to accomplish the missions that they have been given.

A major war, of course, will require moral strength and determination by the entire nation, not just on the part of highly trained and specialized professional forces. At some point, especially if America sees the need to retain its world-wide commitments, the US public and its leaders may have to face up to the need to restore a military draft or some form of broad-based military training to ensure that the nation is ready to meet extraordinary challenges. This issue, of course, is controversial and complex. In a free republic, there are strong arguments in favor of an all-volunteer military. But a strong and secure nation needs a citizenry that has experienced military discipline and understands why it is needed. Congress will no doubt have to face this difficult question in the future.

Prudent Policy for the Twenty-First Century

The history of expansive societies such as Rome, Britain, Spain, and Holland shows that strong and prosperous nations with a sense of dynamism and adventure will intervene abroad to advance what they regard as their commercial and military interests. The United States faces the same pressures to intervene as any other great nation. But excessive foreign undertakings may eventually exceed the nation's willpower and resources, leading to a retraction and then a spiral of withdrawal, defeat, and disillusionment may occur. Every generation of Americans has to deal with this question. Following are some suggestions as to the relevant considerations.

1. Intervene abroad only when necessary to protect America's vital interests.

Vital interests include protection against real and serious threats to the liberty and security of America's citizens, its borders, and its economic well-being, as well as threats to its key allies. The difficulties encountered in some of the recent US military interventions in the Middle East should have disabused knowledgeable observers of any notion that the US, as the world's leading power, should intervene around the world to promote peace, prosperity, and democracy. Our goal has not been to subdue other peoples and should not be to change their ways of life or to restructure their governments or societies. If other countries want democracy and economic development, we can provide advice and assistance if it is in our interest to do so.

The battle against Al Qaeda and the Taliban in Afghanistan is an example of a necessary military intervention since the attacks of September 11, 2001, showed that the national security of the United States was directly affected by those terrorist groups, although it is more difficult to justify the years of attempted nation building that followed. The subsequent invasion of Iraq in 2003 was informed by intelligence estimates indicating that Iraq's ruler Saddam Hussein had developed weapons of mass destruction (although such weapons were not found following the invasion), but the Iraq war resulted in heavy costs that probably exceeded the benefits. The US invasion resulted in further escalation of risk and greater instability in the region. Having intervened in Iraq, the United States felt obligated to help sustain a free and independent Iraq so as to avoid the consequences of a Vietnam-style abandonment. In the absence of WMDs or an equivalent threat, it would be prudent to avoid these kinds of intervention in the future. The military should not be required to undertake quixotic tasks, such as attempting to resolve ancient ethnic hatreds, removing bad rulers, or patching together nonfunctional societies. This has been accurately labeled "foreign policy as social work." There should therefore be a presumption against foreign intervention except where genuinely necessary to protect US security or that of our close strategic allies.

2. Adopt a strategy of regionalization.

For many years, the United States has carried a sizeable burden in defending Europe even though the nations of the European Union, in the aggregate, have population and resources equaling or exceeding America's. For example, the European states (other than Britain) offered little military assistance in NATO's Kosovo campaign of 1999, even though pacification of the Balkans was essentially a regional problem. The United States continues to spend far more as a percentage of GDP than its European allies on defense. This does not suggest that NATO should be dissolved. The defense of Western civilization and its infrastructure is obviously in the mutual interest of all of the allies. For example, NATO should actively pursue the battle against Islamic terrorism. But to do so, our allies need to make a more substantial contribution. Similarly, America should encourage our Asian allies (including Japan, Australia, and India) to make larger contributions toward the containment of China. In the Middle East, Israel too often stands alone, and we should encourage Saudi Arabia, Egypt, Turkey, and Jordan to join in playing a leading role in defending against terrorism and deterring Iranian aggression.

3. Build an effective national missile defense.

As previously noted, the basic goal of US defense policy is the deterrence of war. The potential threat from ballistic missile attacks by Russia, China, or North Korea already exists, and other hostile nations such as Iran are capable of developing a nuclear missile capability. The proliferation of missiles and weapons of mass destruction will pose a growing danger to our Western allies, directly as well as indirectly through blackmail and intimidation. The main obstacle to effective missile defense is political, not scientific or technological. Some ideological opponents of a stronger military argue that arming against ballistic missile attacks is somehow "destabilizing." This is an unfortunate hangover from the obsolete dogma of "mutual assured destruction" and should be set aside. The United States should proceed with the development and implementation of an effective antiballistic missile defense system along with our NATO and Asian allies. Even if an evolving system were initially capable of destroying only a limited number of missiles, it would improve our deterrent and vastly increase the cost to any rogue nation of developing a missile force capable of hitting US targets. As former Secretary of Defense Donald Rumsfeld has said, "History teaches conclusively that weakness is provocative … The way to avoid the threat of weapons of mass destruction is to establish the certain knowledge that such weapons cannot be effectively used against the US. It is irresponsible not to do so promptly."[29]

4. Prepare for high-tech and space warfare.

It is important to establish and maintain US dominance of space, the next frontier for strategic military innovation. Military satellites have been in orbit for decades. China has already shown an inclination to develop anti-satellite weapons, and given that the technology of information-systems sabotage is a real threat, the US military and the defense industry must devote more resources toward the development of an array of "smart weapons," including advanced drones, self-guided sea mines, electromagnetic and "directed energy" weapons, and vastly improved fighter planes. The new technologies will include cyberwarfare, robotics, artificial intelligence, and sophisticated autonomous systems. The successful development of these systems will likely make the difference between victory and defeat in future conflicts. The difficulty is that

---

29   Interview, *Wall Street Journal*, June 20, 1996, p. A18. See Henry F. Cooper and Roland H. Worrell, "Toward a cost-effective ballistic missile defense," *Washington Times,* September 24, 2018.

the research and development effort necessary to produce these weapons is extremely expensive. But there is no real choice. The most important function of the national government is to "provide for the common defense." It is therefore advisable to follow the advice of successful commanders throughout history and "get there first with the most."[30]

5. Public diplomacy and active nonmilitary measures.
The United States must do a better job of employing the weapons of *information warfare*. Islamic terrorism, for example, uses not only bombs and bullets but also ideology, myths, and distorted theology. Russia and China are skilled in the deployment of propaganda and the nonmilitary arts of disinformation and cyber warfare. The United States has done too little to resist these ideological onslaughts. As Dr. John Lenczowski, president of the Institute of World Politics, has written:

> Over the past half century and even longer, America has been assaulted by ideas that denigrate its history and culture, stress group identity, discourage assimilation of immigrants and encourage the Balkanization of the country into different cultural groups. All this amounts to a relentless assault on traditional American values by those who reject the principles of the Declaration of Independence and who would "fundamentally transform," to use President Barrack Obama's term, America as conceived by its founders.[31]

We are, as Lenczowski argues, engaged in a war of ideas, but we are not mounting an adequate counter-strategy, which must be based on a relentless defense of America's founding principles as expressed in the Declaration of Independence and America's other founding documents.

---

30   See Arthur Herman, "The Pentagon's 'Smart' Revolution," *Commentary*, July/August 2016, p. 25; Frank G. Hoffman, "Squaring Clausewitz's Trinity in the Age of Autonomous Weapons," *Orbis*, Winter 2019, p. 44, Jim Sciutto, "The Growing U.S. Vulnerability in the Heavens," *Wall Street Journal*, May 11–12, 2019, p. C3.

31   John Lenczowski, "Integrating Non-Military Arts of Statecraft to Address National Security Threats," *World Affairs*, Summer 2016, p. 48.

And we must confront directly the ideology of our enemies—for example, the doctrines of radical Islamic jihad. This intellectual effort should be combined with the use of other nonmilitary operations such as economic sanctions and cyber techniques. This kind of integrated strategy would follow the classic doctrine of Sun Tzu to attempt to defeat the enemy without resorting to armed force. Lenczowski advocates the creation of a US Public Diplomacy Agency within the State Department, which would be responsible for the development and coordination of such an integrated strategy.[32]

6. Prepare for the kinds of threat the United States is likely to face.
A major war between the United States and either China or Russia is unlikely but is not impossible, and the need for deterrence requires that adequate force must always be available and evident to potential enemies. The possible threats include continued terrorist attacks, regional wars that draw in the United States because of existing commitments, threats to commerce or other vital interests, sabotage of electronic systems, and armed conflicts arising out of economic chaos or internal disintegration in areas of strategic importance, such as Europe. Most responses to rogue-nation or terrorist threats can be met by special operations forces backed as necessary by naval and air power, mobile anti-missile defenses, and reserve forces that could be deployed in a matter of weeks. The army of the future will require a serious reorganization of US military capabilities that is already underway, featuring greatly increased maneuverability, advanced tactical transport, and an emphasis on joint task force warfare and special forces. A critical problem is to keep the reserves in a state of readiness in the face of public apathy and to maintain the capacity to integrate these forces quickly with regular units.

In addition, it is apparent that the United States must pay a great

---

32   The recently disclosed "Global Engagement Center" within the State Department appears to be an attempt to counter foreign propaganda and hostile disinformation efforts by our enemies. Guy Taylor, "Mission to crush Russia's 'fake news,'" *Washington Times,* December 17, 2018.

deal more attention to homeland security, including the improvement of airport and other security measures that may not be popular. Since we know that acts of terrorism have been committed and abetted by aliens admitted to the United States as a result of lax immigration procedures, there should be much stronger controls to prevent illegal immigration, an end to "chain immigration," and more active supervision of those who are in the country under visas. Such restrictions will undoubtedly be resisted by some business groups and others who benefit from less expensive labor. The willingness to control immigration will be a test of national seriousness.

The Protection of Liberty

In implementing the measures necessary to defend against terrorism and other threats, we must remember that the objective is to preserve the freedoms that truly make the United States an exceptional nation. These include rights of free speech, religion, association, and property, protected by a stable legal system based on the rule of law and not the whim of officials.

The requisite security measures will inevitably invade privacy to some extent. The preservation of both security and liberty, therefore, will be a difficult task, involving public understanding and tolerance as well as a sensitivity that few governments have ever exhibited. The limited use of authorized surveillance and similar measures are understandable but should be restricted in time and scope, should follow established procedures, and should be broadly authorized by Congress. The adoption of such practices by the executive branch alone poses a danger to civil liberties. History shows that some of the unusual powers properly accruing to the executive during emergencies may persist and become permanent features of an "administrative state," whose rigidities and bureaucratic excesses can sooner or later erode the trust necessary to a free society.

CONCLUSION

Oswald Spengler, in his great work, *The Decline of the West,* argued that the great art of national survival is to keep one's own nation internally fit for external events. The nation must preserve its internal cohesion and discipline to prevail in the ceaseless struggle for advantage. A related series of these "external events," in the form of savage terrorism, has now materialized out of the amorphous hatreds that coalesce from time to time when civilizations collide. The spread of hedonism, indiscipline, and an extreme attachment to personal autonomy in aspects of American society, as well as the promotion by educational and media elites of an exaggerated form of pluralism or "multiculturalism" that can pull our nation apart rather than uniting it, will inevitably have an adverse impact on national solidarity. The combined result of these social trends will be to impair the "fighting spirit" (Ibn Khaldun's "group feeling") on which armies have always depended.

When the Soviet Union collapsed, there was much celebration and a certain justified triumphalism. From a strategic standpoint, the United States seemed more secure than at any time in its history. The events of the early twenty-first century have placed those events in a more somber perspective. We now understand that we will have to continue to defend our freedom. The battle against terrorism is one that may last for decades, and still other conflicts may break out unexpectedly. The United States has substantial resources, but no nation's human and material resources are inexhaustible, as history has shown. In the light of the conflicts in Vietnam, Afghanistan, and Iraq, we know that technological superiority does not always produce victory; national will is more often the decisive factor. Great nations must use their assets carefully; all too often, wealth and power have been squandered on imprudent commitments and unnecessary adventures. We should resist the temptation to create a "new world order" or to push democracy and capitalism on other countries; let them discover for themselves which economic and political systems best suit their own cultural inclinations.

The principle threat to America's national identity may not be from abroad. "In the broadest sense," as Samuel P. Huntington has written, "American national identity is under challenge from a multiculturalism that subverts it from below and a cosmopolitanism that erodes it from above."[33] According to the multicultural vision held by America's denationalized elites, many of whom hold important positions in our leading educational and cultural institutions, patriotism is merely a relic of a cold war mentality and the nation-state itself is doomed to disappear. National identity is being further eroded by mass immigration, linguistic separation, and the collapse of historical awareness. As history teaches, the internal forces of disintegration can be more important than foreign enemies. Some of the problems of military readiness can be solved by more money. But cultural and moral deterioration cannot. As one of America's great soldiers, General Douglas MacArthur, warned in the 1950s, "History fails to record a single precedent in which nations subject to moral decay have not passed into political and economic decline. There has been either a spiritual awakening to overcome the moral lapse, or a progressive deterioration leading to ultimate national disaster."[34]

In subsequent chapters, we will explore the health of America's educational, cultural, social, civic, and political institutions. It is to the important subject of education that we now turn.

---

33   Samuel P. Huntington, "Robust Nationalism," *The National Interest* (Winter 1999/2000), p. 39.

34   libertytree.ca/quotes/Douglas.MacArthur.Quote.4070.

5

EDUCATION

IT IS A TRUISM that the young are ignorant and will remain so unless they are taught. Children learn the rules of behavior essential to civilized society only through discipline and instruction. From the child's earliest years, it is the parent's job to teach the habits of civilized behavior. In later years, this function is increasingly delegated to professional teachers. If the first function of education is to instill in children the society's rules of conduct, the second is to teach the basic ideas of its culture—its history, legends, heroes, religion, government, and values. These are the common bonds that hold a society together. A civilized society must pass its basic values on to each new generation or it will not survive. Because of the educational deficiencies that we will survey in this chapter, cultural transmission in the United States is declining. As Professor E. D. Hirsch has shown, once "cultural literacy" begins to slip, the process of deterioration accelerates because each subsequent generation of parents and teachers knows less and therefore transmits less.[1] Knowing little or nothing about history or government, Americans have difficulty understanding the meaning of their own institutions and are at the mercy of a debased culture of consumerism, celebrity, and sensationalism. An ignorant population will inevitably be susceptible to demagoguery and deceit. The topic of education, therefore, is highly relevant to the study of decline.

Educational Decline: Statement of the Problem
It has been obvious for many years that something is wrong with education in America. In April 1983, the National Commission on Excellence in Education issued its report, "A Nation at Risk: the Imperative for Educational Reform." The report concluded that "the educational foundations of our society are presently being eroded by a rising tide of mediocrity that threatens our very future as a Nation and a people." The report cited a number of depressing facts:

- Some 23 million American adults, and 13 percent of all 17-year-olds, were functionally illiterate as measured by the simplest tests of everyday reading, writing and comprehension.

- Overall educational levels were falling; the average graduate of American schools and colleges was not as well educated as the average graduate of 25 years previously. "For the first time in the history of our country, the educational skills of one generation will not surpass, will not equal, will not even approach, those of their parents."

- The College Board's Scholastic Aptitude Tests (SAT) showed a virtually unbroken decline from 1963 to 1980. Average verbal scores fell over 50 points and average mathematics scores dropped nearly 40 points.

---

1   E. D. Hirsch, Jr., *Cultural Literacy: What Every American Should Know* (Boston: Houghton Mifflin, 1987).

- Many 17-year-olds did not possess the intellectual skills required for effective participation in modern society. For example, nearly 40 percent could not draw inferences from written material and only one-third could solve an elementary mathematics problem requiring several steps.

The Commission's report identified a number of basic flaws in the education provided by America's public high schools. First, secondary school curricula had been weakened and diffused so that they no longer had a central purpose. High school students wasted much of their time taking physical education, home economics, drivers' education, and other intellectually trivial courses. The time spent in math and science courses even by the most science-oriented American students amounted to only one-third of the time devoted to these subjects in other industrialized nations. Second, the amount of assigned homework had decreased virtually to nothing. Two-thirds of high school seniors reported that they did less than one hour of homework per night. Third, most colleges had lowered their admission standards. Fourth, textbooks had been simplified to ever-lower reading levels in order to accommodate barely literate students. Finally, teachers were poorly paid and inadequately trained. Teachers' training programs emphasized "educational methods" at the expense of real knowledge of the subject. The report concluded that half of the newly employed math, science, and English teachers were not qualified to teach these subjects.

"A Nation at Risk" produced a flurry of front-page news articles and some modest efforts by state legislatures to strengthen academic programs in the public schools. On the whole, though, little progress was made; SAT scores continued to fall, and literacy continued to drop. A 2013 report by the National Assessment of Educational Progress concluded that US seventeen-year-old students had not achieved any significant progress in reading or math since 1971. An updated NAEP study in 2017 showed no significant improvement. Other studies support this conclusion. The Program for International Student Assessment (PISA) tests the reading, math, and science skills of fifteen-year-olds from around the world. According to the PISA results published in December 2016, out of seventy countries, the United States ranked twenty-fifth in science, twenty-fourth in reading, and fortieth in math. In short, the nation is still at risk.[2] Increasing amounts of money have been poured into US education since the 1960s, but student performance has continued to be mediocre. It is noteworthy that, according to OECD data, the United States spends more per student than any other country in the world except Luxembourg, but US student performance among world countries was only slightly above average in reading and science, and below average in math.[3] Some observers have questioned whether US students' mediocre performance on international tests reflects a lack of intellectual aptitude or whether it reflects a lack of motivation, perhaps due to differences in culture and incentives.[4] My conclusion is that it reflects primarily a difference in educational institutions and practices, which of course are strongly affected by the prevailing culture.

By the time American children arrive at college, many of them are educationally crippled. College freshmen write poorly, their analytical skills are feeble, and they are almost entirely ignorant of the history of their own country. Many students find it necessary to take remedial courses in reading, writing, or math. The commonly repeated observation that Americans are "computer literate" is not particularly encouraging since true computer literacy, like any other kind of literacy, requires the ability to manipulate words, numbers, and ideas and to analyze data. These capacities depend upon skills that are *not* being taught in today's schools. Apathy and ignorance are contagious. A study by

---

2   "Performance of U.S. 15-Year-Old Students in Science, Reading and Mathematics Literacy in an International Context," U.S. Department of Education, National Center for Education Statistics, December 2016, Tables 1, 2 and 3; "Nation's Report Card: Achievement Flattens as Gaps Widen Between High and Low Performers," *Education Week,* July 20, 2018.

3   See https://data.oecd.org/education.

4   See "Cash Incentives Lift Test Scores," *Wall Street Journal,* November 28, 2017, citing a study by the National Bureau of Economic Research.

the Pew Research Center found that one in four American adults read no books at all in the past year.[5]

The weakness of American primary and secondary education, particularly in science and mathematics, is troublesome. It is certain that in the twenty-first century, many more workers will be needed in job categories requiring advanced skills. But the American educational system is not designed to teach these skills. Corporate personnel directors have stated repeatedly that as many as 40 percent to 50 percent of their job applicants cannot read at ninth-grade level or even fill out a simple application form. Employers, therefore, have to provide costly training programs just to teach new workers to speak and write correctly. By contrast, secondary school students in Europe and Japan are required to pass rigorous tests demonstrating detailed knowledge of math, history, geography, and government. They spend more time in school than American students, and they do more homework.

The consequences of educational inferiority are potentially severe. A weak educational system has an obvious impact upon America's economic performance. Moreover, a decline in literacy and historical awareness affects the level of political debate. A democratic republic, as Thomas Jefferson pointed out, requires an educated citizenry. The collapse of literacy and the influence of television have reduced the public's capacity to understand complex issues. The childish belligerence and vacuous sloganeering of US political campaigns are sufficient proof of educational and civic debility. The social consequences of educational decline are also serious. More than ever, inferior education increases the growing socioeconomic divide by condemning many people to low-level jobs for the rest of their lives, while wealthier families can afford better schools for their children.

The American educational establishment has devalued the substance of what students learn from grade school all the way through college.

---

5   Andrew Perrin, "Who Doesn't Read Books in America," Pew Research Center, March 23, 2018, www.pewresearchcenter.org.

Over the course of the twentieth century, children read simpler and simpler texts and learned less and less. Why has American education declined? Most studies, reports, and surveys conducted over the past two decades are in agreement on the most obvious causes: standards are low; too little homework is assigned; little or no written work is required; discipline is poor; children spend too little time at school and too much time on the internet or watching television; teachers are underpaid and undereducated; principals lack authority; and parents pay too little attention to their children's education. In short, America's public schools do not teach children what they need to know to become informed citizens.[6]

The fundamental problem is that, in spite of a deluge of political rhetoric, the American public lacks the will to correct the problem. This absence of discipline and willpower on the part of the American people is an advance indicator of social and economic decline. While voters and politicians like to talk about education, there is little evidence that they are seriously interested in doing anything about it.

To understand how we got to this point, some historical perspective is necessary.

How It Happened: A Short History of "Progressive Education"
in the Twentieth Century
At the end of the nineteenth century, an intellectual reform movement linked to the philosophy of pragmatism began to undermine traditional ideas across the intellectual spectrum. Pragmatism was inspired by the extraordinary success of the physical sciences in capturing the scholarly imagination. Since scientific method had worked so well in the natural sciences, pragmatists assumed that the same techniques would work in the social sciences. Just as laboratory scientists experimented without regard to accepted dogma, social scientists (including educators) were

---

6   See E.D. Hirsch, Jr., *Why Knowledge Matters: Rescuing Our Children from Failed Educational Theories* (Cambridge, MA, Harvard Education Press, 2016).

encouraged to abandon academic tradition and seek out the "new" and the "progressive." Pragmatists regarded antecedents as unimportant; only consequences counted. William James, the leader of the pragmatic movement, insisted that reason was goal oriented; the function of thought was to solve problems. Pragmatism's preoccupation with results was apparent in James's famous theory of truth. The truth of an idea, he argued, depends on what difference it makes in anyone's life. Ideas become true insofar as they have "satisfactory" consequences. "'The true,' to put it very briefly, is only the expedient in the way of our thinking, just as 'the right' is only the expedient in the way of our behaving."[7]

Traditional secondary education in America had been based on certain fundamental principles: the importance of teaching specific knowledge about the Western cultural heritage; an emphasis on "basic" subjects (English, Latin and other languages, math, history, science, and civics); an emphasis on discipline and diligence; the use of memorization; competition for grades; and traditional policies of promotion and failure. The educational pragmatists, or "progressives" as they came to be called, questioned all of these principles. The new progressive education stressed "active" learning (working on projects and playing games) over "passive" learning (reading books and memorizing facts). The goals of progressive education were "effective living," "success in daily life," and "how to get along with other people" instead of what the progressives disparagingly called "rote memorization" and "useless knowledge." In line with the aims of pragmatism, the progressives set out to democratize culture by favoring social adjustment over excellence and collectivism over competition.[8]

The best-known proponent of the progressive educational philosophy

---

7   William James, *Pragmatism and Four Essays from the Meaning of Truth* (New York: Meridian, 1955), p. 145

8   See Diane Ravitch, *The Troubled Crusade: American Education 1945–80* (New York: Basic Books, 1983), pp. 44–46, and *Left Back: A Century of Failed School Reforms* (New York: Simon and Schuster, 2000), chapters 2 and 3.

was John Dewey, a leading pragmatic philosopher during the first half of the twentieth century whose theories were immensely influential. In an important essay, "The School and Society," first published in 1899, Dewey argued that the determining factor in the individual learning process is not a fixed human nature or the individual's own capabilities, but rather "the social heredity and social medium." Children were infinitely malleable and could be weaned away from the prejudices of the past by a suitably progressive educational system. This was to be accomplished by a drastic change in the nature of education. Instead of transmitting culture, habits, and character, schools should teach "socialization." The result of this new philosophy of education was to deemphasize the study of history, classics, government, and economics in favor of something called "social studies," consisting of simplified history and easy-to-read lessons about everyday life.

According to Dewey and other progressives, practical social activities—cooking, weaving, shopwork, and the like—should "dominate the school program." Instead of the traditional learning process, the child's own needs must be made the center of the educational effort. In the new child-centered school, the social life of the child becomes the all-controlling aim. The goal should be the development of a spirit of social co-operation and community life, rather than the mere absorption of facts. The children will achieve this goal by "doing things that produce results, and ... doing these in a social and co-operative way." It is significant that practical education, for Dewey and his followers, did not include moral education. Dewey argued that the schools should not attempt to teach what is right. The teacher should not pose as an authority, moral or otherwise, because to do so would suppress the students' potential for self-directed activity and socialization.[9] This viewpoint was directly contrary to centuries of Graeco-Roman and European

---

9   John Dewey, *The School and Society* (Chicago: University of Chicago Press, 1956), pp. 16–17; *Henry T. Edmondson III, John Dewey and the Decline of American Education: How the patron saint of schools has corrupted teaching and learning* (Wilmington, DE: ISI Books, 2008).

educational tradition, which had always emphasized the formation of the student's moral character as well as his rational intellect. The consequences of the demoralization of education are now only too apparent. Teachers report that cheating and plagiarism in school are common, as is disruptive classroom behavior in many urban schools—although, as we will see in a later chapter, there are other social and cultural factors that contribute to behavioral problems.[10]

The educational progressives who followed Dewey's lead, led by the National Education Association (NEA) and its state branches, beginning in the 1920s, developed the new theory of education, which by the 1960s had become dominant in America's public schools. (This progressive theory is explained in detail in Professor E. D. Hirsch's excellent book *Why Knowledge Matters,* published in 2016.) The progressive leaders in education, like their progressive counterparts in politics, rejected longstanding practices and traditional doctrines. They abandoned the old community-centered and knowledge-centered methods of schooling for what they called a child-centered and a skills-centered model. Instead of teaching the common, shared history, literature, and general knowledge that children need to know to become informed citizens (which the progressives ridiculed as "rote memorization" and "useless facts"), the progressives emphasized teaching each child according to his individual abilities and temperament (multiple learning styles) while developing critical thinking skills, such as problem-solving and identifying the main idea of a text. These "skills" are hammered into the young students by a constant barrage of distracting and ineffective tests. The result of the child-centered and skill-centered theories is that they "have produced neither good skills nor good scores on the ever-looming tests." Recent scores on international tests place American students well below those in a number of countries that continue to use traditional

---

10   A study by Dr. Donald McCabe at Rutgers found that an overwhelming majority of high school students surveyed admitted to engaging in some form of cheating. Grace Chen, "Cheating Scandals in Public Schools Grow Exponentially," *Public School Review*, April 30, 2018.

communal knowledge-based curricula in early grades—"a fact which lends support to the idea that broad subject-matter knowledge is the basis of problem-solving abilities."[11]

The educational progressives, led by the National Education Association and its affiliated teachers' unions, achieved their goals by imposing a uniform, monopolistic system of public education on previously autonomous local school districts. State legislatures passed compulsory attendance laws, and state educational bureaucracies mandated uniform curricula. Parents were judged incapable of making the correct decisions about their children's education, and the state occupied the field *in loco parentis.* The public school began to replace the family as the preferred transmitter of social values. The progressive reformers, in education as in government, assumed that centrally planned, bureaucratic organizations were more efficient than independent, locally managed units; therefore, a monopolistic state educational system based on compulsory central planning was the model they aimed for, and eventually achieved. The Deweyite educational theory was consistent with the ideology of egalitarianism, collectivism, and social engineering that came to dominate progressive political circles in the United States in the first half of the twentieth century—an ideology that has never been successfully dislodged.

In keeping with the progressive emphasis on social adjustment in contrast to intellectual excellence, high school curricula were steadily weakened. The progressives believed that one subject was as good as another for teaching mental skills. As a consequence, by the middle of the twentieth century, educators had deemphasized Latin, advanced math, and other subjects that were unpopular as well as intellectually rigorous and difficult to teach. The egalitarian bias of progressivism required that everyone, or nearly everyone, should succeed. (The "all shall have prizes" trend was also reflected in grade inflation at the college level.) Since some

---

11   E. D. Hirsch, *Why Knowledge Matters* (Cambridge, MA: Harvard Education Press, 2016), p. 13
      and fn. 40.

students had trouble dealing with academically difficult material, the solution was to provide a range of brainless courses that anyone could pass, such as "bachelor living," "beautifying the home" and "developing an effective personality." Even basic grammar is neglected, as evidenced by the inability of many recent high school and even college graduates to speak correctly. Since grammar is an inherent part of the architecture of thinking, the failure to teach it has serious consequences for the development of rational thought.[12] Driven by an ideological preference for equality over excellence, many public schools advance children from one grade to the next, whether or not they have learned what they need to know. This process is known as *social promotion*.

By the late 1980s, most state school systems in the US no longer required students to take any course in world history or Western civilization. Most states require one year of American history, but it is not taught well. At the high school level, history has been merged into social studies, which deemphasizes traditional history in favor of topical social issues. Many social science teachers have never taken a history course in college. The history textbooks used in high school have been simplified to the level of the most mediocre students. Public educational specialists no longer consider history important because it is not considered relevant to students' everyday concerns; therefore they are reluctant to include much of it in public school curricula. A 2018 survey by the American Council of Trustees and Alumni (ACTA) found that fewer than 18 percent of US colleges and universities require even a single foundational course in US government or history.[13] The

---

12 See Noam Chomsky, *Reflections on Language,* Chapter 1, "On Cognitive Capacity," in Noam Chomsky, *On Language* (New York: The New Press, 1977). Chomsky argues persuasively that language is based on a "universal grammar" that is an innate property of the human mind.

13 "What Will They Learn? A Survey of Core Requirements at Our Nation's Colleges and Universities," ACTA, 2018. The ACTA study also found that just over 3 percent of the institutions require students to take a basic economics class. See also Karol Markowicz, "Why schools have stopped teaching American history," *New York Post,* January 22, 2017; Diane Ravitch, "Decline and Fall of Teaching History," *New York Times,* November 17, 1985.

result of ignoring history was predictable: today's high school students are unaware of and indifferent to critical facts about the past. A nation that forgets its past, as Churchill said, has no future. This historical ignorance reinforces the modernist view that all experience is subjective, personal, and immediate—a belief that has contributed to the decline of high culture in America.

Education in civics was another victim of progressive education. Traditionally, civics education taught the history of the United States, including its founders, constitutional principles, and basic rights and duties. Today, the traditional model of civics education is largely forgotten. The National Association of Scholars reports that half of the states no longer require civics for high school graduation, and surveys show that the average score for college seniors on a civic literacy exam is barely over 50 percent—in other words, an "F."[14] Today, civic literacy no longer means understanding the bill of rights, the three branches of government, federalism, or the basics of American history, but instead features learning about diversity, environmentalism, inequality, colonialism, and other progressive concerns. Test results from the National Assessment of Educational Progress showed that only 18 percent of eighth-grade students were proficient in history and only 23 percent in civics or government. Scores for twelfth graders were equally poor and in some cases worse. An Annenberg Public Policy Center report in 2017 found that 37 percent of those surveyed cannot name any of the rights guaranteed under the First Amendment, and only 26 percent of Americans can name all three branches of government. A recent national survey by the Woodrow Wilson National Fellowship Foundation found that only 36 percent of Americans could pass a multiple choice test of

---

14 "Making Citizens: How American Universities Teach Civics," National Association of Scholars, January 2017.

items taken from a standard US citizenship test.[15] This gap in civic education could be easily remedied. Every American high school public and private, should teach a basic civics course (perhaps supplemented by a dose of Aristotelian ethics—that is, "civic virtue"). A small group of political science and philosophy professors from any reputable American university could put together such a course in a few weeks.

The attack on authority during the 1960s and 1970s revived the dogmas of progressive education in extreme forms. "Open education," "schools without walls" and other innovations proliferated. Progressive educational theories were recycled under the misleading label of "outcome based education," which opposed the classification of students by ability or achievement and replaced academic standards with vague therapeutic goals, such as self-esteem and social well-being. The progressive doctrine that no particular body of knowledge is important and that children's self-esteem is the proper goal of education is a reflection of a pervasive philosophical subjectivism. This theory is founded on the romantic assumption that if children are taught to be friendly and cooperative, all will turn out for the best. The truth is that specific knowledge—and a great deal of it—is required for effective participation in today's complex, high-tech world.

Increasing Federal Involvement in Education
The word *education* does not appear in the United States Constitution, and for almost 200 years, public education in America was left up to the people of the states, although from time to time the federal government did provide limited financial support through measures such as the Merrill Land Grant Act of 1862 and the 1965 Elementary and Secondary Education Act. A bill establishing a federal department of

---

15   See nationsreportcard.gov, the website for the NAEP; "Americans Are Poorly Informed About Basic Constitutional Provisions," Annenberg Public Policy Center, September 12, 2017; "National Survey Finds Just 1 in 3 Americans Would Pass Citizenship Test," Woodrow Wilson National Fellowship Foundation, October 3, 2018.

education was enacted by Congress in 1867, but this agency was soon reduced to the status of an office within the Department of the Interior, where it had little influence. After World War II, following passage of the GI Bill, the office became part of the Department of Health, Education, and Welfare during the Eisenhower administration. The Progressive Movement, the influence of Dewey's educational theories, and the trend toward centralized government in the twentieth century, as well as persistent lobbying by the powerful National Education Association, led to a growing demand for a cabinet-level Department of Education (DOE), which was finally created during the Carter administration in 1979. (The history of the progressive federalization of American education in the twentieth century is skillfully traced by Vicki E. Alger in *Failure: The Federal Misedukation [sic] of America's Children,* published by The Independent Institute in 2016.) The Purpose of DOE was to improve educational quality by consolidating existing federal educational programs and enhancing education's status as a national activity. Following the creation of DOE, the department's spending on elementary and secondary education grew from $2.7 billion in 1970 to $38.6 billion in 2016, and the federal role in education became more active.[16]

The No Child Left Behind Law (NCLB), passed by Congress in 2001, required states to adopt educational proficiency tests in order to obtain grants from the federal government. Not surprisingly, most states have set the bar quite low so that nearly all children will meet the standards. Subsequently, the states adopted the Common Core State Standards, a joint project of federal and state education administrators, setting forth what students should know at each grade level. The implementation of CCSS has cost billions of dollars with few demonstrable benefits. According to a 2016 national curriculum survey, the CCSS standards

---

16   National Center for Education Statistics, Digest of Education Statistics, Table 401.30 (2016). State and local expenditures on education are far greater, amounting to more than $800 billion. *Id.*, Table 106.40.

do not adequately prepare students for college. A majority of college educators surveyed said most incoming students were not prepared for post-secondary coursework. In short, governments at both the federal and state levels poured money into public schools, but there was no significant improvement in student achievement.[17] The objective observer must question the value of the NCLB act, and the Department of Education that administers it, which together have loaded the educational system with additional layers of bureaucracy, rules, regulations, and incompetence.

Of course, there will always be some children who lack the ability to succeed on a college-bound academic track. As Charles Murray has argued in his book, *Real Education,* by statistical definition a certain percentage of children are below average in natural academic ability, and the poor quality of public schools does not improve their academic achievement.[18] But nearly every student is capable of learning a simple but effective "Core Knowledge" curriculum of the type recommended by E. D. Hirsch's Core Knowledge Foundation.[19] And gifted children are capable of learning a great deal; they could be given a more advanced curriculum, that is, put on a different academic track at an early age. To some extent this is being done today but not on a sufficient or systematic scale.

---

17   Vicki E. Alger, *Failure: The Misedukation (sic) of America's Children* (Oakland, CA: Independent Institute 2016), pp. 154–55; Michael McGrady, "Common Core's Benefits to Students Remain Elusive," *School Reform News* (The Heartland Institute, January 2017), p. 5; "Common Core Does Not Prepare Students for College," *School Reform News* (September 2016), p. 15. See National Assessment of Educational Progress, Long Term Trend Assessments, 17-year-olds (2012), concluding that although the amount spent on the K through 12 education of a student in the United States, adjusted for inflation, has more than doubled since 1970, the academic performance of those leaving high school is flat. And see Peter Copan, "The Common Core Standards: A Utilitarian Straitjacket for Education in America," *Humanitas,* Vol. XXVII, Nos. 1 and 2 (2014), p. 144.

18   Charles Murray, *Real Education: Four Simple Truths for Bringing America's Schools Back to Reality* (New York: Crown Forum, 2008).

19   E. D. Hirsch, Jr., *The Knowledge Deficit: Closing the Shocking Education Gap for American Children* (Boston: Houghton Mifflin, 2006).

Meanwhile, we must give some practical help to those who are not destined for college. Many students and families today question the value of a college degree, along with the rising costs and accompanying heavy indebtedness. Such students should be encouraged to take vocational courses (career and technical education), which are sometimes offered in collaboration with local employers. This may motivate them to stay in school and prepare themselves for productive careers. In Switzerland, 70 percent of young people ages fifteen to nineteen participate in business apprenticeship programs in hundreds of occupations. In Germany and Austria, 55 to 65 percent of youth are in similar programs. About 75 percent of Germany's private economy workforce has taken part in that country's system of vocational and apprenticeship programs. All three countries have youth unemployment rates less than half of America's 16 percent. A working partnership between American schools and businesses could help to produce students better prepared to compete in the global economy.[20]

Monopoly and Bureaucracy
The American public school system is a virtual monopoly, controlled by a vast bureaucracy of government administrators, teachers, unions, and employees.[21] Those parents who cannot afford private schools have no real educational choices for their children unless they are prepared to undertake the demanding and time-consuming task of homeschooling. Monopolies are run for the producers, not the consumers; they tend to harm consumers because they deprive them of choice by eliminating

---

20   Peter Downs, "Can't Find Skilled Workers? Start an Apprentice Program," *Wall Street Journal* (January 17, 2014), p. A13; Edward P. Lazear and Simon Janssen, "Germany Offers a Promising Jobs Model," *Wall Street Journal* (September 9, 2016), p. A11; "Trade School Wins Fans Among Teens," *Wall Street Journal* (March 6, 2018); "DeVos: Apprenticeships, Vocational Education are Top Trump Priority," *Washington Free Beacon* (February 6, 2018).

21   Between 1950 and 2015, the number of students in America's public schools doubled, while nonteaching staffs increased by more than seven times the rate of increase of students. *School Reform News*, The Heartland Institute (September 2017), p. 3.

competition. Those who administer the public school monopoly have a captive clientele, job security, and guaranteed funding regardless of results. There is therefore little incentive for them to innovate.

John Stuart Mill, in his essay "On Liberty," published in 1859, foresaw the danger of a system of public education run by the state. "A general State education," he said, "is a mere contrivance for moulding people to be exactly like one another.... it establishes a despotism over the mind."[22] Those who operate the school system, Mill foresaw, would inevitably communicate their own moral or amoral vision to a captive audience. In the United States, the public school monopoly is commonly justified by two arguments. First, it is said that the system provides to all Americans the training they need to succeed in their chosen occupations. The second argument is that the public schools teach those common principles of history, tradition, and constitutional democracy that give Americans a shared sense of belonging to a national community. The public school system in its present form has failed on both counts. It does not provide the minimum degree of knowledge necessary to operate effectively in a technological world, and it certainly is not teaching the common cultural traditions that bind Americans together. To the contrary, the educational trend has been to replace America's common traditions with cultural and linguistic fragmentation, exemplified by the current obsession with "diversity" and "multiculturalism."

The bureaucratization of education is not an isolated phenomenon but is merely one facet of the vast concentration of power and increase of scale that are characteristic of modern industrial society. In the United States, as in most industrial countries, local communities and local governments have been weakened and largely replaced by centralized power structures operated by a new elite trained to manage and control.[23] Education has not remained immune from this managerial

---

22 John Stuart Mill, "On Liberty," in Mill, *Utilitarianism, Liberty and Representative Government* (New York: E.P. Dutton, 1951), p. 217.

23 See James Burnham, *The Managerial Revolution* (Putnam 1942).

revolution. It is no accident that the dramatic decline in Scholastic Aptitude Test scores beginning in the 1960s coincided with the shift of a large percentage of school funding from local communities to state and federal agencies dominated by the educational establishment. The Department of Education, created in 1979, has about 4,000 employees and an annual budget of $68 billion but has done little or nothing to improve education.

The response by politicians to popular demands for better schools is usually to throw more money at the public schools, but money alone is not the answer. A recent report, for example, shows that while New York City spends more than twice the national average to educate its public school students, recent test results indicate that less than half of students in grades 3 to 8 scored at proficient levels in English and math. Similar results have been reported in other urban school districts.[24]

An important study by John Chubb for the Manhattan Institute concluded that the most significant factor in good educational performance in the past was not money or class size, but local autonomy. "Successful schools were relatively independent of external influence by administrators, superintendents, central office bureaucrats, and union officials."[25] Autonomy brings accountability. In the public school system, teachers and other employees are protected by elaborate job security rules, and no one pays a penalty for poor results. The substantial political power of the teachers' unions has inhibited educational choice alternatives, such as vouchers. A promising alternative is provided in many states by charter schools, which are independently operated public schools, generally union free and run by local boards that are free to hire principals and teachers who can adjust curricula and discipline to

---

24   See *New York Post,* "NYC spends double the national average on education, has little to show for it" (May 21, 2019); *Wall Street Journal,* editorial, "An Education Horror Show" (July 8, 2019), p. A16.

25   John Chubb, "Making Schools Better," Manhattan Paper No. 5, Manhattan Institute (1988), p. 8; James Coleman et al., *High School Achievement: Public, Private and Catholic High Schools Compared* (New York: Basic Books, 1982).

provide a superior education. Charter schools have been successful in some areas, such as New Orleans, where most of the public schools have been converted into charters. The existing evidence indicates that, on average, charter schools outperform public schools.[26] Other alternatives include voucher or tax credit plans, giving parents a choice of either public or private schools. The most common form of school choice is vouchers, which enable parents to direct their children's education funding to private schools.[27] However, voucher and tax credit plans meet with strenuous opposition from teachers' unions and educational bureaucrats, and thus far such plans have had only limited success. Existing school choice programs, including vouchers, tax credits, and charter schools, reach only a small number of American children—probably around 5 percent.[28]

A more promising approach to breaking the educational monopoly and lessening the education gap that exists in American education is to encourage the privatization of elementary and secondary education. Private schools are held accountable through competition and choice. There are already at least 6 million students attending 34,000 private schools in the US, in addition to more than a million being home-schooled and a large number on waiting lists for charter schools. Across the world, there is a rapid growth in low-cost private education serving poor rural and urban communities at lower per-pupil costs than public schools. There are, for example, hundreds of low-cost private schools in Lagos, Nigeria, charging fees averaging $35 per term. These schools are run by charities, churches, or private entrepreneurs. Such schools are

---

26 David Osborne, *Reinventing America's Schools* (New York: Bloomsbury, 2017), p. 6.

27 Greg Foster, "A Win-Win Solution: The Empirical Evidence on School Vouchers," *The Foundation for Educational Choice* (March 2011), p. 4.

28 See James Tooley, "The Role of Government in Education Revisited: The Theory and Practice of Vouchers, With Pointers to Another Solution for American Education," in *Education: Ideals and Practices*, ed. David Schmidtz (Cambridge, UK: Cambridge University Press, 2014), p. 204 and Table 4. Professor Tooley says that "[i]n practical terms, the voucher reform movement appears to have been markedly unsuccessful" (p. 220).

increasingly popular in Africa and India, where they provide instruction that is superior to that provided in the public schools at a much lower cost. The best-known example is Bridge International Academies, backed by Bill Gates and Mark Zuckerberg, a nonprofit that operates hundreds of primary schools in Africa.[29] In the United States, there are already a number of "micro-schools," small private schools with personalized instruction and flexible curricula, reminiscent of the traditional "one-room schoolhouse" approach to education.[30] There is no reason why private, low-cost schools could not be established throughout the US, financed privately or cofounded between parents and entrepreneurs, which could compete effectively with America's inadequate public schools in those areas where students are currently being short-changed. These programs could be supplemented by vouchers or tax credits where needed.

The important point, in addition to local autonomy, is competition: parents need to have more freedom to choose their children's schools. As Vicki Alger states: "A growing body of evidence shows … competition is the critical element for improving student performance."[31]

Discipline, Authority, and the Moral Order

As Aristotle said, "To live temperately and hardily is not pleasant to most people, especially when they are young." To teach children sound

---

29 See James Tooley, "We're not talking Eton: Low-cost schools are changing lives in the third world," *The Spectator* (April 21, 2018); Donald Devine, "Reviving Private Education," newsmax.com insiders (December 10, 2018); "Learning Unleashed: Low Cost Private Schools," *The Economist* (August 1, 2015), www.economist.com.

30 "Micro-Schools Making a Big Splash in Education," *School Reform News* (February 2018), p. 10. Many choices are available online to parents interested in opting out of the public schools. See, for example, www.homeschool.com; www.time4learning.com; and, for a religious alternative, www.exodusmandate.org.

31 Alger, *op. cit.*, p. 179. A study of thirty-nine countries revealed that students in countries with higher private school enrollments performed better, including students from disadvantaged socioeconomic backgrounds. *Id.*, p. 180.

habits requires proper training and constant discipline: "for most people obey necessity rather than argument, and punishments rather than the sense of what is noble."[32] Children must therefore be trained so that good actions become habitual.

The schools, of course, cannot be blamed for family breakdown and other social forces over which teachers have no control. Teachers cannot reverse the low expectations and lack of motivation of students unless parents place greater emphasis on education, turn off the television, and insist that their children perform. But the educational system has surely contributed to social degeneration through its neglect of moral instruction. In all civilized societies, training in virtue has been inseparable from intellectual training. It is hardly surprising, therefore, that the erosion of behavioral standards has accompanied the weakening of academic standards in American schools. While the family is the most important institution for building character, habits taught at school are also critical—doubly so when the family itself is in a state of transition, if not disintegration.

At the heart of the inadequacy of our educational system is the decline in standards of discipline and hard work. Those of us who are aging can remember teachers who were stern disciplinarians and would not tolerate sloppy performance. Today, unfortunately, a kinder and gentler style has taken over American education. We worry that low grades or criticism of children's performance will injure their self-esteem, while memorization is frowned upon, and homework is regarded as cruel and unusual punishment. Actually, the opposite is the case. Overcoming adversity is a necessary condition of character development. The best teachers are those who are strict. Perseverance and effort are the best predictors of success.

During the course of the twentieth century, the moral content of public education in America was virtually destroyed. The nineteenth-century *McGuffey Reader* contained moral tales exhorting students to adhere to sound morality. Stories warned of the consequences of bad behavior and stressed the ethics of self-discipline, self-control,

---

32   Aristotle, *Ethics*, X, Chapter 9, 1179b-1180a.

truthfulness, and obedience. Elementary school readers often featured the story of the indolent grasshopper and the diligent ant. The moral was simple: those who "eat, sing, dance, in the summer, must starve in the winter." The separation of learning from virtue creates a society in which people are rewarded not for their character or probity but for their success in repeating accepted dogmas deemed useful by the educators.

The question of education goes to the heart of what kind of society we want. Millions of Americans have lost confidence in the public schools not merely because their children cannot read and compute, but because the public schools have ignored and even suppressed basic moral and spiritual values. It is absurd to pretend that there is such a thing as "value-neutral" education. Actually, the progressive education-ists have only substituted one set of values for another. The "bourgeois" virtues of thrift, industry, temperance, prudence, respect for authority, and the fear of God have been replaced by self-fulfillment, feminism, multiculturalism, relativism, environmentalism, and pacifism. Today's adolescents grow up in a popular culture that openly encourages promis-cuity and depravity and in a society in which families have abandoned to sex educators the task of teaching sexual morality. It is little wonder that each generation contributes to a vicious cycle of family breakdown and illegitimacy, leading to further educational and moral decline.[33]

The hostility to traditional Judeo-Christian moral values is part of a broader attack on Western culture in general, which we will address in the following chapter. The growing movement for "multicultural" education seeks to eliminate pro-Western bias from texts and teaching. America, of course, has been a multicultural nation from the beginning, in the sense that it has been a "melting pot" of different ethnicities, and no one questions the desirability of learning about other cultures. But the new multicultural movement does not try to encourage people from

---

33   See "2012 Report Card on the Ethics of American Youth," Josephson Institute, Center for Youth Ethics (Los Angeles, 2012); Paul Barnwell, "Students' Broken Moral Compasses," *The Atlantic* (July 25, 2016).

various ethnic groups to live together in the harmony of shared ideals; instead, it emphasizes what separates them by teaching children that the United States is an oppressive society and that the true self-interest of ethnic groups lies in separating themselves from the traditional culture. This is the path of disintegration, not community.

There are some tentative signs that the flight toward moral relativism may have reached its outermost limit. School districts across the country have begun to experiment with "character education" classes, and Catholic private schools are increasingly popular. Through popular demand, religion has begun to creep back into the curriculum. Yet the effort to reverse the trend toward relativism has only scratched the surface. The proponents of "multicultural diversity" are a powerful force in the academy and can be expected to resist vigorously any attempt to restore traditional values.

Mediocrity Enthroned

As the foregoing discussion has shown, the American public school system has enshrined mediocrity, undermined morality, and contributed to cultural illiteracy. Yet the public is quite tolerant of the existing system. This in itself is a sign of an apathetic and decadent society.

Public schools, like other public institutions, reflect the values of society. Among these values, literacy holds a low priority. The average American devotes very little of his leisure time to the printed word, except in the dumbed-down form of *texting* over the internet. Children are overwhelmed from infancy by commercialized TV shows, hypnotized by electronic games and rock music, and raised in homes where reading is rare. Under these conditions, it is not surprising that Americans place more emphasis on entertainment, sports, and popular music than on education. Teachers report that many students expect the process of acquiring knowledge to be as fast and easy as watching television; attention spans are limited.

One major problem is the inadequate training of teachers in US primary and secondary schools. In 2013, the National Council on Teacher

Quality issued a report on the education of teachers, concluding that the vast majority of teacher education programs are mediocre and do not adequately prepare aspiring teachers. Too many graduates of teacher prep programs, according to the report, lack the necessary classroom skills and subject matter knowledge to be effective teachers.[34] It is difficult to replace incompetent teachers due to the practice of tenure, which virtually guarantees teachers permanent jobs after two or three years in the classroom. While tenure at the university level is arguably justifiable to protect academic freedom and independence (although there are also good arguments against it), tenure in primary and secondary schools cannot be justified and should be eliminated. To be sure, good teachers should be paid more, but all teachers should be required to achieve a higher level of professionalism and accountability.

Most Americans are pragmatists at heart. As long as their children obtain a diploma and eventually get a job, they are happy to abdicate responsibility to the schools. Just as they seem to expect government to take care of their old age and healthcare needs, they expect the schools to give their children whatever they need to succeed. The educators, who are public servants, have simply responded to the political pressure to keep the children in school until graduation. While politicians pay lip service to educational reform, they are reluctant to adopt changes that might be unpopular. So long as these attitudes prevail, American children will remain hostages to an ineffective system of education.

The University
Despite the deficiencies in primary and secondary education, discussed above, American universities are reputed to be among the best in the world, as evidenced by the influx of foreign students. It is certainly possible to obtain a good college education in America; and research facilities and postgraduate courses are lavishly funded. On the surface,

---

34 "Teacher Prep Review," National Council on Teacher Quality (December 2013); Stephanie Banchero, "Teacher Training's Low Grade," *Wall Street Journal* (June 18, 2013).

higher education in the United States appears to be boisterously healthy. Yet the wealth and prominence of America's universities conceal some serious weaknesses. To explore these deficiencies, we start with the traditional model of the "liberal arts" university.

"A University," wrote the great nineteenth-century theologian John Henry Newman, "by its very name professes to teach universal knowledge."[35] The university should not be a trade school, designed merely to prepare students for a career. In order to achieve its goal of teaching universal knowledge, the university must teach the facts and principles of the particular branches of knowledge, such as philosophy, history, theology, mathematics, and science. But it must also fit the separate fields of study together into a single interrelated scheme of universal knowledge. If higher education is confined to a single discipline or to the mechanical sciences alone, it will produce semi-educated graduates with only a partial view of the world. Newman, lecturing in 1852, could already see that exclusive concentration on economics (or political economy as it was then called) was dangerous because it promoted the false view that men should seek only to maximize their own self-interest through the acquisition of wealth. The economist, Newman argued, has no right to assert that wealth leads to virtue or happiness; such a conclusion is beyond the scope of his science and intrudes on the sphere of the moralist. It is the function of the university to place these competing considerations in their proper perspective.

In acquiring knowledge, we satisfy an intrinsic need of human nature. Liberal pursuits, involving the acquisition of knowledge and the exercise of reflection, are distinguished from merely useful pursuits. "Liberal Education, viewed in itself, is simply the cultivation of the intellect, as such, and its object is nothing more or less than intellectual excellence." With remarkable foresight, Newman perceived that, even in his day, higher education was being fragmented and weakened by

---

35   John Henry Newman, *The Idea of a University* (Notre Dame: University of Notre Dame Press, 1982), p. 14.

utilitarianism and falling standards. He warned of the degradation of the university by "an unmeaning profusion of subjects ... a smattering in a dozen branches of study." Universities were admitting too many who were unprepared or unmotivated. "Learning is to be without exertion, without attention, without toil; without grounding, without advance, without finishing." When universities pander to popular demand, education becomes mere recreation. "Stuffing birds or playing stringed instruments is an elegant pastime, and a resource to the idle, but it is not education; it does not form or cultivate the intellect."[36]

Newman's observations are perfectly appropriate to the American university of the early twenty-first century, with its "smorgasbord" curriculum designed to appeal to adolescent consumers of education but not to educate them. It is obvious, in fact, that most American universities have abandoned Newman's model altogether. The change in the concept of the university has occurred in part because of the increased size of universities and the vast sums of government and private money available to them. The model of the traditional university required a small-scale institution, separated from the quotidian concerns of the outside world, where a coherent, recognized curriculum could be taught in an atmosphere of fellowship. This model is wholly unsuited to the scale of the modern "multiversity" with tens of thousands of undergraduates and a culture of extravagant leisure interspersed with football.

The decline of the modern university has roots extending back to the seventeenth century. Professor Robert Koons, in a perceptive article, has traced the intellectual history of this decline.[37] Francis Bacon, the seventeenth-century English philosopher and statesman, championed a theory of education based on empiricism and natural science in contrast to the classical tradition based on Plato and Aristotle. The eighteenth-century French philosopher Jean-Jacques Rousseau espoused a theory

---

36   *Id.,* pp. 91–92.

37   Robert C. Koons, "Dark Satanic Mills of Mis-Education: Some Proposals for Reform," *The Imaginative Conservative* (October 31, 2016).

based on the freedom of the individual student to follow his own impulses, liberated from the constraints of religion and custom. These two intellectual trends of scientific and romantic progressivism were synthesized in the research universities of Germany in the nineteenth century, which became the model for higher education in twentieth-century America. The leading apostle of the new model university was Charles William Eliot at Harvard (1869–1909), who developed the elective system, which, as Koons points out, "has been sold to generations of students as a charter of individual autonomy, freeing each student to devise his own education." University professors like this system because it enables them to avoid the constraints of a classical curriculum and teach whatever is convenient for purposes of their own research.

Fortunately, the weakening of the liberal arts curriculum in American universities does not appear to have adversely affected the teaching of engineering and the "hard sciences" (e.g., physics, chemistry, biology, astronomy, and geology), which, in spite of weaknesses at the secondary level, are flourishing at many major universities and private laboratories and must continue to be supported. As discussed in Chapter 2, the neglect of science, technology, and engineering by British universities in the late nineteenth and early twentieth centuries damaged Britain's economic productivity and its military capacity. This is a mistake that the United States can and should avoid. Attaining and preserving high standards in both science and the liberal arts will be expensive but is a necessary condition of America's survival as a civilized and prosperous nation.

The sheer size of some universities is a problem. After World War II, encouraged by the GI Bill, millions of veterans entered American colleges and universities, and higher education became increasingly popular. The ideal of the liberal arts university persisted for a time after World War II but collapsed rapidly in the face of the turbulent events of the 1960s. Under continuing pressure from masses of students, many of them unprepared, the universities eliminated parietal rules, dress codes, and other indicia of civilized behavior. Then they abandoned the last remnant of their moral integrity: academic neutrality. They adopted racial quotas (disguised as "affirmative action" plans); instituted courses in Black Studies, Women's Studies, and other trendy subjects demanded by allegedly victimized groups; and tolerated the disruption by radical students of unpopular speech. University admissions policies were redesigned to reflect the balance, composition, and interests of the entire society, resulting in the admission of many students who lacked the ability to perform at university level. These trends have continued to the present day. A study conducted in 2006 by the National Commission on the Future of Higher Education reported that "only 31 percent of college-educated Americans qualify as 'prose literate,' meaning that they can fully comprehend something as simple as a newspaper story."[38]

As the universities gave way to the political demands for affirmative action, a more "relevant" curriculum, and the admission of more and more students, academic standards began to fall. Colleges introduced "pass-fail" courses, as well as courses in hotel management, parks and outdoor recreation, and other trivialities.[39] The very existence of testing is attacked as discriminatory and elitist. Students have come to expect high grades or have demanded courses with no grades at all. Professors in some schools try to attract students by giving limited reading assignments and inflated grades.[40] Most universities today impose few course requirements. The proportion of the curriculum devoted to general studies required of all students has dropped precipitously. A growing number of colleges no longer require English majors to read Shakespeare,

---

38 Christopher Clausen, "The New Ivory Tower," *Wilson Quarterly* (Autumn 2006), p. 32. About a third of the students who enroll in universities leave without getting a degree. Jeffrey J. Selingo, "Facing the College Dropout Crisis," *New York Post* (June 11, 2018).

39 A recent search revealed that Skidmore College offers a course called "The Sociology of Miley Cyrus," studying "the interplay among race, class and gender, as well as taking a feminist critique of media and sociology of media approach to the Miley 'problem.'" The English Department at the University of Pennsylvania offers "Wasting Time on the Internet," "No textbooks necessary, just laptops and WiFi." The list could go on. www.time.com/4006878/unusual-college-university-courses/.

40 "The Anatomy of Grade Inflation," *Wilson Quarterly* (Autumn 2000), p. 108.

Milton, or Chaucer. A recent survey by the American Council of Trustees and Alumni (ACTA) found that fewer that 18 percent of US colleges and universities require a foundational course in US government or history, only 3 percent require students to take a basic economics class, and only 58 percent require a college-level mathematics class.[41] Another report, by the National Association for Scholars, concluded as follows: "The prevalent unwillingness to set priorities within general education programs, together with the growing disinclination to insist on rigorous standards for completing them, suggest that undergraduate general education has become substantially devalued as an institutional objective. It also indicates that most institutions are no longer seriously committed to ensuring that their students are exposed to broad surveys of basic subject matter."[42]

The dumbing down of higher education has damaged civic literacy. A 2016 study by ACTA showed that "colleges and universities have done a poor job of ensuring the civic literacy on which our nation depends. Too many institutions fail to require courses that ensure civic knowledge and often allow community service projects, well-intentioned as they are, to substitute for deep learning about our nation's institutions of government and their history."[43]

American universities have been inundated with a culture of political correctness, evidenced by the reluctance of faculty and students to allow those holding conservative or other unpopular opinions to speak on campus and the proliferation of courses on race, class, gender, and popular culture. It is not surprising that many students leave college badly educated and unable to communicate intelligibly. As Hunter Rawlings, former president of Cornell University, has said:

---

41 "What Will They Learn? 2017–19: A Survey of Core Requirements at Our Nation's Colleges and Universities," American Council of Trustees and Alumni (2018).

42 National Association of Scholars, "The Dissolution of General Education: 1914–1993" (1996).

43 ACTA, A Crisis in Education (2016).

We have, many of us, relegated undergraduate education to a low place in academia by devaluing undergraduate teaching, and we have broadened and loosened the curriculum to the point where at many universities it is a flabby smorgasbord of courses bearing no relationship to each other, utterly lacking in coherence. It is also true that as enrollments have risen, academic rigor has declined and grades have inflated.[44]

The faculty and administrators in most of America's universities appear to be obsessed with "diversity," which is usually defined in terms of race, ethnicity, and gender. Academia's compulsive focus on diversity and racial balancing has been highlighted in a current lawsuit against Harvard, alleging that it discriminates against people of Asian descent in admissions in order to obtain what university administrators believe to be a proper racial balance.[45] This obsessive concentration on race is divisive and unhealthy in a liberal and tolerant society. We will see more examples of this unfortunate tendency in later chapters.

In recent years, college campuses across America have been disturbed by intolerance and even violent protests against speech deemed objectionable by students on political grounds. Controversial speakers, mostly conservatives, have been shouted down and threatened. This trend is largely due to the growing dominance of leftist ideologues among college faculty and administrators, who capitulate easily to the demands of radicalized students. Name-calling and noisy protests have taken the place of reasoned discussion. As Professor John M. Ellis of the University of California has said, "The campus radical monopoly on political ideas amounts to the shutting down of liberal higher education as we have known it. That, not the increasingly violent flare-ups, is the real

---

44   Speech at Princeton University, February 22, 2014, *Princeton Alumni Weekly* (April 2, 2014), p. 28.

45   See John O. McGinnis, "Discrimination against Asian Americans Reveals the Ugliness of Racial Selection," *Law and Liberty* (June 15, 2018), www.lawliberty.org. And see Heather MacDonald's excellent book, *The Diversity Delusion: How Race and Gender Pandering Corrupt the University and Undermine Our Culture* (New York: St. Martin's Press, 2018).

crisis."[46] Many college students argue that the First Amendment does not protect "hate speech," but this notion is absurd since the only reason for including speech in the First Amendment was to protect speech that some people don't like. As John Stuart Mill taught us nearly two centuries ago, it is only through the free expression of adverse opinions that we can arrive at the truth.

While Western civilization is still studied in universities, it appears that the purpose is not to instill Western culture but to repudiate it because of its alleged sins against the prevailing ideology of egalitarianism.[47] In many universities, students are required to take courses centered around non-European ethnic groups. The effect of these "multicultural" requirements is to deemphasize Western culture and to belittle its role as the core of American civilization. *Diversity* has become a code word for race-conscious admissions and hiring policies, fragmentation of the curriculum, lower academic standards, politicized instruction, and suppression of speech that offends feminists, ethnic minorities, and other activist factions. To attract students, colleges devote vast resources to expensive athletic facilities, lavish dormitories, and high-tech student centers. They hire dozens of administrators at great expense, who do little to improve academic quality. The hordes of entrants, many of them unqualified, are kept coming only by the availability of government-sponsored student loans.

There is nothing wrong, of course, with reading books by authors from different cultural backgrounds. But learning takes place through comparison and analogy. Consequently, it is impossible to understand other cultures until we have first learned something about our own. The difference between our society and other societies is manifested in institutions, ideas, political structures, religion, and art that have evolved

---

46   John M. Ellis, "Higher Education's Deeper Sickness," *Wall Street Journal* (November 14, 2017), p. A21; Warren Treadgold, "The Death of Scholarship: Leftists Are Limiting Academic Work to Demonstrations of Leftist Dogma," *Commentary* (December 2017), p. 29.

47   See Roger Scruton, "The End of the University," *First Thing*, (April 2015), p. 25.

over hundreds of years. Despite the ignorant attacks on "oppressive" Western values, moreover, it is worth remembering that Western civilization, above all others, has addressed the most profound issues affecting human life: freedom, virtue, moral responsibility, the good society, man's relation to God, natural law, civic duty, and the relation of the individual to the state. Plato, Aristotle, Locke, and Kant are not just "Western" writers; they are universal thinkers whose ideas can be used to criticize Western as well as non-Western dogmas. Our Western cultural heritage includes our habits of self-reliance and individualism, the spirit of fair play and compromise, the rule of law, the Ten Commandments, Christian charity, and rationality itself. If these values are destroyed in the name of pluralism and political correctness, American society will be deprived of its only weapons against ignorance and evil.

The decay of Newman's ideal of the university is an integral part of the decline of the Western intellectual tradition. At the center of the Western heritage is a metaphysical concept of order based on religious and philosophical principles. The Judeo-Christian tradition teaches that man is created in the image of God and has an honored place and purpose in the world but is subject to the limitations established by divine transcendence and natural law. The philosophical tradition of the West has explored the problems of metaphysics in an attempt to discover the proper relationship between matter and spirit, contingency and freedom, and being and nothingness. Western literature has explored the heights and depths of the soul through epic, tragedy, and poetry. Higher education today increasingly fails to convey enough of this body of learning. As a result, students are thrown into the world without any sense of the metaphysical order of being, the nature of transcendence, the true limitations inherent in the human condition, or the tragic sense of life. A society without such awareness, having no spiritual anchor, can only drift along in rootless subjectivity, seeking pleasure in degradation or sterile amusement.

As academic standards declined in the late twentieth century, the cost of a college education rose dramatically. Between 1983 and 2014 the cost of tuition and required fees at a public four-year university rose an average of 231 percent after adjusting for inflation. The cost today at a good university typically exceeds $50,000 per year and is often much higher. Recent increases in the cost of college are driven in part by the ready availability of government-sponsored loans that enable students to pay the higher bills, leaving students with heavy debts to repay in the years after graduation. Total student loan debt as of 2018 amounted to nearly $1.5 trillion, a significant percentage of which was in default. The explosion of student debt impairs the financial independence of college graduates, thus delaying their ability to get married, buy homes, and raise families.[48]

As detailed in a recent study by Open the Books, an organization that studies transparency in government, the federal Department of Education spends well over $100 billion annually, including subsidies for such trivial college courses as Game Design, Golf Management, Cosmetology, Bartending, Boat Building, and Fashion. The Department provides lavish funding for very wealthy universities such as Harvard, Yale, and the University of California System, which are able to take care of themselves.[49] The federal government should get out of the business of financing education, except for defense-related matters and basic scientific research that cannot be financed by the states or private sources.

The universities, like many other institutions in American society, have succumbed to the temptations of egalitarianism by applying false notions of "democracy" in the field of higher education, where democracy has little relevance. In the words of Eugene Genovese: "The hard truth is that academic freedom—the real work of scholarship—requires a willingness to set limits to the claims of democracy. It requires a strong dose of hierarchical authority within institutions that must be able to defy a democratic consensus. Sooner or later we shall have to face this fact, or

48 Charles Fain Lehman, "The Student Loan Trap," *The American Conservative* (March/April 2019), p. 49. See "Defaults Rise for Student Loans," *Wall Street Journal* (December 14, 2017).

49 Open The Books Oversight Report, *The U.S. Department of Education* (April 2018), www.openthebooks.com/assets/1/7/ED_Report_Final.pdf.

be defeated by those who seek the total politicization of our campuses."[50]

The *real work* of scholarship requires that universities stop admitting students who are not prepared for college work and start insisting upon serious remedial programs in high school. In addition, tenure should be abolished so that professors who are incompetent or lazy can be removed. Academic standards should be strengthened, and the concept of a real core curriculum—emphasizing history, literature, philosophy, math, and science—should be revived. In addition, the universities could greatly improve their productivity by cutting unnecessary administrative expenses, requiring both students and teachers to work harder and spending less on lavish dormitories and recreational facilities. There are a number of private organizations that are working to restore traditional values in higher education: most notably the Intercollegiate Studies Institute that supports and encourages the teaching of the principles of liberty, the American founding, and Western civilization at American colleges and universities.[51]

As Thomas Jefferson said, a nation cannot be both ignorant and free. The institutions of representative government and the principles of civil liberty require hard work, character, and discipline. That America's parents, teachers, and political leaders are unwilling to insist upon the maintenance of high standards in our nation's schools is a sure sign of decline. The effort that must be made to improve American education will require a significant increase in the threshold of public awareness, which is perhaps unlikely in view of the widespread civic ignorance and apathy that are themselves the products of poor education. Contemporary American culture encourages the opposite of discipline in the form of hedonism, self-indulgence, immediate gratification, rootless mobility, and contempt for authority. The teachers, in short, have given the society what it wants. This moral decay is one of the principal themes of this book.

---

50   Eugene Genovese, "Heresy, Yes—Sensitivity, No," *The New Republic* (April 15, 1991), p. 34.

51   See www.isi.org.

6

THE DECLINE OF
CULTURE

IN THE YEAR 2000, the Modern Museum of Art in New York offered a retrospective exhibit, in three stages, summarizing the art of the twentieth century. This display of hundreds of art works from the museum's massive collection showed an unmistakable deterioration of esthetic standards. By the end of that unfortunate century, every canon of taste—harmony, clarity, balance, dignity, compositional elegance, and art's essential role as the link between the phenomenal world and the noumenal or spiritual world—had been effectively destroyed. The revolution in art was only one aspect of a broader assault on social and cultural norms. Reason, history, and religion were all under relentless attack in the twentieth century by the forces of nihilism.

As Arnold Toynbee noted, cultures operate through mimesis, and the wholesale abandonment of traditional norms by the most prominent and vocal elites was bound to have an effect over time. The "down-market" effects of the mass media, especially television, popular music, tabloid journalism, social media, and pornography added to the cultural fragmentation at all levels of society.

What Is Culture?

Since the principal function of education is to transmit the society's cultural values, it is not surprising that educational decline has been accompanied by a profound change in American culture. It is particularly difficult to separate cause from effect in cultural decline, but it seems clear that educational and cultural trends have been mutually reinforcing.

Matthew Arnold, writing in 1869, defined culture as "a pursuit of our total perfection by means of getting to know, on all the matters which most concern us, the best which has been thought and said in the world."[1] Culture, for Arnold, meant the "sweetness and light" of art, literature, music, and philosophy. It did not include games, eating habits, and other manifestations of "popular culture." Modern anthropology uses a much broader definition of culture than Arnold's. Culture, as defined by anthropologists, is a "set of attributes and products of human societies ... which are extrasomatic and transmissible by mechanisms other than biological heredity."[2] If we accept the broad anthropological definition, culture is simply the sum total of the behavior of a human society. There is no "higher" or "lower" behavior. The anthropological view has given strong support to the modern doctrine of cultural relativism, which holds that the culture of savages is not inferior to that of France in the age of Louis XIV but merely different.

The implications of thoroughgoing anthropological relativism are hard to accept because we know that the culture of seventeenth-century France is superior to that of hunter-gatherers no matter what the anthropologists say. It would be a mistake, nevertheless, to limit our

---

1   Matthew Arnold, *Culture and Anarchy* (New York: Macmillan and Co., 1883), p. xi.

2   Marvin Harris, *The Rise of Anthropological Theory* (New York: Crowell, 1968), p. 9.

understanding of culture to the "higher" pursuits lauded by Matthew Arnold. The reasons for adhering to a broader view of culture were given by T. S. Eliot in his *Notes Towards the Definition of Culture,* published in 1948. Although Eliot was a modernist poet in the sense that stylistically his poetry was modern and unconventional, he approached literature, and culture generally, as embodying the moral and esthetic norms of the Western tradition. Culture, Eliot argued, includes all the characteristic activities and interests of a people, including manners and attitudes of civility as well as appreciation of literature and the arts. As a society develops toward functional complexity and differentiation, multiple cultural patterns emerge. The different aspects of culture are overlapping: the religious sensibility enriches art, while art embellishes manners and material life. Ordinary behavior reflects deep-seated belief. The materialism of the consumer society, for example, shows what we believe by how we behave. Culture, properly conceived, is a way of life, and not merely the sum of certain activities arbitrarily labeled "cultural." Eliot's view of culture, while broader than Arnold's, differs radically from that of the anthropologist. Eliot's goal is not to catalogue human behavior but to provide us with a basis for making those value judgments about culture the anthropologist rigorously avoids and, in particular, to delineate the spiritual component of culture.

The primary channel of transmission for both "high" and "popular" culture is the family; when families disintegrate, culture deteriorates. The family preserves traditions from one generation to the next over long periods of time. "Unless this reverence for past and future is cultivated in the home," Eliot writes, "it can never be more than a verbal convention of the community."[3] Because families occupy different social positions, different social classes will have varying cultural attitudes. In a healthy society, the different levels of culture will not be sharply antagonistic but will reinforce each other; all classes will participate to some significant extent in the common culture. If there is no shared

---

3   T. S. Eliot, *Notes Towards the Definition of Culture,* 4th ed. (Glasgow, 1951), p. 44.

culture, then there is no society. Proponents of "multiculturalism" in its currently fashionable form ignore this basic point. Further, the family itself has been substantially weakened and its role in cultural transmission impaired.

Although there is interaction among cultural levels, it is still important to distinguish between "high" and "popular" culture. Civilizations are judged not by the evanescent frivolities of popular entertainments that soon disappear from view but by the quality of those literary, artistic, and juridical achievements that endure over time. These cultural monuments are produced by a system in which there are social incentives to artistic creativity and appreciation. Cultural excellence presupposes the existence of an elite with the education and leisure to pursue the arts, but it also requires a sufficient degree of social mobility to permit budding artists and connoisseurs from all classes to gain recognition. The function of the guardians of culture is to permit the fine arts to flourish and to remain open to creative change, while preserving the standards from contamination. Art gives us a sense of transcendence, spirit, and essence: a feeling for the permanent things. It is difficult to capture all of the aspects of high culture in a single definition. As a working hypothesis, we will use Samuel Lipman's formulation: "High culture is concerned with, though not strictly limited to, art, literature and learning that is either created to endure or that at some point after its creation is widely recognized to have become a permanent part of the civilization that is transmitted by the settled institutions of society."[4]

It is hard to avoid the conclusion that cultural standards declined during the twentieth century and that the signs of this decline are visible in virtually every department of cultural activity. Or, it may be worse. Ascertainable standards of taste and beauty may no longer exist at all. This chapter will survey the cultural wreckage.

---

4   Samuel Lipman in *The New Criterion* (November 1984), p. 7.

What Is Beauty?
Is it possible to speak objectively about beauty? It is commonly said that "beauty is in the eye of the beholder" (the Latin maxim is *de gustibus non disputandum*) and that matters of taste are entirely subjective. You like Beethoven, and I like Elvis Presley, and that's that. But this conversation-stopping reaction renders meaningless any attempt to communicate intelligibly with others about the most pleasant and inspiring works of the human imagination. As Edmund Burke said in the preface to his *Philosophical Inquiry into the Origin of the Ideas of the Sublime and Beautiful,* "It is probable that the standard both of reason and taste is the same in all human creatures. For if there were not some principles of judgment as well as of sentiment common to all mankind, no hold could possibly be taken either on their reason or their passions, sufficient to maintain the ordinary correspondence of life."[5] There are many people, of course, who exhibit poor taste, just as there are many who make faulty moral judgments. Accordingly, all societies demand that their citizens be educated in matters of common morality, and civilized societies require that at least its elites be given some schooling in the fine arts. A superior civilization admires those who have cultivated the discrimination needed to recognize those works of nature and man that are beautiful and sublime.

THE CULTURE OF MODERNISM

Intellectual and Social Origins of Modernism
I will use the term *modernism* to refer to a movement that began in the late nineteenth century as a revolt against Victorian culture and culminated in the radical alteration of most traditional artistic and literary standards. The Victorian moral synthesis emphasized work, discipline, frugality, and other "respectable" virtues. There were objective moral standards based on the revealed truths of religion and the ascertainable

---

5   *The Works of Edmund Burke* (New York: Harper & Brothers, 1837), Vol. I, p. 37.

principles of ethics. Similarly, there were objective canons of beauty that could be appreciated by educated men and women. Christian and classical traditions, imparted through a rigorous process of education, formed the basis for the high culture of the West.

By the beginning of the twentieth century, the assumptions underlying the Victorian worldview began to break down. Ibsen's heroines openly rebelled against the restraints of family life, while George Bernard Shaw wrote of his dislike for "my duty and my mother." Lytton Strachey ridiculed the lives of eminent Victorians. Freudian psychology undermined confidence in the power of human reason by focusing on unconscious and irrational motivations, while attacking the basis of Victorian morality by urging the liberation of the individual from sexual taboos. Artists and writers began to adopt a variety of experimental techniques tending toward subjectivism, obscurity, and the separation of form from content. Economic and social changes also favored the modernist rebellion. The combination of industrial capitalism and modern technology broke down traditional class barriers and stimulated social mobility. The rise of a large, rootless, urban middle class—badly educated and having few loyalties to past cultural values—provided an inexhaustible market for vacuous cultural novelties. Low-cost printing and lithography permitted the rapid spread of instant ideas and cheap techniques. Progressive education placed socialization ahead of history and scholarship. The rise of egalitarian democracy, accompanied by soak-the-rich tax policies, weakened those classes that had traditionally provided cultural patronage and continuity.

While culture has always evolved over time, modernism tends to be anti-historical. The Victorians preferred linear, historical narrative. History was of fundamental importance to art, architecture, literature, and other aspects of culture. Painting and poems often encompassed historical, religious, or mythical themes that were widely recognized and embodied the common heritage of the West. The modernist view of time, on the other hand, tends to be synchronic rather than diachronic; writers stress structural relationships rather than plot and character.

Since the texture of the work is more important than the substance, artists emphasize surfaces, oblique allusions, hidden meanings, stream of consciousness, and similar techniques, giving their works a discordant and fractured quality. In this respect, art mirrors the dissonance of our society. Modernism, by its nature, implies the rejection of authority and the destruction of limits. Modernist culture was born in rebellion and pursues innovation for its own sake. Its perpetuation requires the achievement of successive thresholds of novelty, based on new sensations and revolutionary techniques. Because it depends on perpetual novelty, modernism seeks to institutionalize the *avant garde*—a logical absurdity but a psychological necessity for the modern mind. What Alexander Solzhenitsyn has called "the relentless cult of novelty" overthrows one restraint after another, while lowering the standards of craftsmanship to the level of crudity.[6] Modern art has no defense against the incursions of deconstruction and nihilism since it has abandoned the protection of order, harmony, reason, and essence.

The Philosophical Destruction of Order
In addition to socioeconomic change, the twentieth century saw the culmination of a philosophical revolution whose foundations had been laid long before. Classical philosophy taught that true knowledge was based on universal forms, essences, and principles rather than sensory and transient perceptions. As Richard Weaver argued in his important book, *Ideas Have Consequences,*[7] the classical tradition of realism was challenged in the fourteenth century by nominalists who asserted that universal principles (redness, justice, etc.) do not have independent existence but are merely names for a collection of individual things. If nominalism is correct, there are no objective values such as the good, the true, the beautiful, or the just. The nominalist position eventually led to

---

6   Solzhenitsyn, "The Relentless Cult of Novelty and How it Wrecked the Century," *New York Times Book Review* (February 7, 1993), p. 3.

7   Richard Weaver, *Ideas Have Consequences* (Chicago: University of Chicago Press, 1948).

phically empty form of radical empiricism or positivism, which ~~replaced~~ the reality apprehended by reason with impressions received by the senses. This philosophical path, Weaver argued, ultimately ends in subjectivism, relativism, and the denial of truth itself. Knowledge is reduced to an endless series of facts without connecting principles; we are trapped in a world of sensation. The transcendental realm is abolished, and man's motivation is reduced to a series of biological urges. Immediate experience becomes an end in itself. Weaver called this attitude "the cult of presentism," which regards forms, essences, and universals as irrelevant to man's desire for immediate gratification. The quest for immediacy puts society on the path to cultural and moral decline. Standards of propriety are abandoned because they might inhibit self-expression. The modern world, Weaver wrote, "has been engulfed by a vast demoralization … its most permanent feature is perhaps materialism, but this has been greatly abetted by that compound of humbug, pretense, and vulgarity which can be labeled 'Hollywood values.'"[8]

The nineteenth-century German philosopher Friedrich Nietzsche set the stage for the final assault upon essence, transcendence, and order. Nietzsche used the term *nihilism* to describe the end result of the ongoing destruction of essence, transcendence, and order. Nihilism implied what Nietzsche called the "devaluation of values"—that is, a radical skepticism that denied the truth of all religious, ethical, and metaphysical values, resulting in a meaningless world. Nietzsche's famous pronouncement that "God is dead" lent support to this dismal theme. In some of his writings, Nietzsche indicated that it might be possible to overcome nihilism through a process of intense self-discipline that was characteristic of what he called the "will to power." (Nietzsche's emphasis on the will to power anticipated a current theme of postmodernism: the values that motivate human conduct arise not from religious or ethical principles but from conflicting relationships of power.)

---

8   *The Southern Essays of Richard M. Weaver,* ed. George M. Curtis III and James J. Thompson, Jr. (Indianapolis: Liberty Press, 1987), p. 27.

Unfortunately, the facts of history seem to prove that humans are seldom capable of the kind of heroic self-control that he hoped for. The implications of Nietzschean nihilism were devastating for philosophy and for culture in general. If there is no authority or principle supporting our decisions, we are governed by no law other than our own will. Without transcendent standards, truth and order are left without any effective support. The history of ideas in the twentieth century bears witness to a long, drawn-out, and agonized attempt to confront the dilemma of nihilism and to fill the void created by the destruction of metaphysical order. In today's society, nihilism takes the form of radical personal autonomy—the attempt to live a life devoted to personal satisfaction, unconstrained by tradition, faith, or reason.

Early in the twentieth century, Western philosophy split into a number of branches, of which two are especially relevant to the English-speaking world: logical positivism and pragmatism. Logical positivism, which held sway principally in English and American universities, taught that the principal task of philosophy was the analysis of language. The positivists believed that statements can have meaning only if they are empirically or scientifically verifiable; metaphysical and moral propositions were empirically unverifiable and therefore meaningless by definition. This conclusion consigned most of traditional philosophy to the ash-heap of history.

A second important philosophical trend of the twentieth century, and the one most identified with the United States, is pragmatism. Pragmatism had its roots in traditional English empiricism but differed from it in important respects. The leading American pragmatists (William James and John Dewey) shifted the focus of empiricism from the analysis of past sensory experience to the practical consequences of experience. James defined pragmatism as "the attitude of looking away from first things, principles, 'categories,' supposed necessities; and of looking towards last things, fruits, consequences, facts."[9] Pragmatists viewed reality not as "given" or as part of the natural order of things but as a vehicle for constant experimentation. They launched a vigorous attack on rules, universals, and standards, emphasizing instead the significance of particular cases and specific results. The truth of an idea, they argued, depends on whether it makes a practical difference in anyone's life. We should believe whatever is useful for us and disbelieve those facts and theories for which we have no use. "'The true,'" James asserted, "is only the expedient in the way of our thinking, just as 'the right' is only the expedient in the way of our behaving."[10]

The identification of the true and the right with the expedient was a fateful step in philosophy. Taking pragmatism seriously meant that no moral or political demand could be rejected as inconsistent with preexisting principles since any such demand might turn out to have "satisfactory" consequences. In the political sphere, the doctrine of satisfactory results meant, as William James argued, that as many demands as possible should be satisfied—a position that provides the conceptual basis for the welfare state. In the domain of morality, it implied that each individual is entitled to seek his own satisfaction regardless of traditional moral rules. In sum, pragmatism provided intellectual support for tendencies—already engrained in American society—favoring experimentation, novelty, short-term results, and "progress" while neglecting historical principles and the moral grounds of action.

Positivism and pragmatism have in common one important feature that is highly relevant to the history of western culture in the twentieth century. Both reject objective, transcendent, and historically based principles in favor of relativism and subjectivity. It is true that some traditional forms of philosophy have survived in the academy and in religious circles, such as Kantian idealism, essentialism, and neo-Thomism,

---

9   William James, *Pragmatism and Four Essays from The Meaning of Truth* (New York: Meridian Books, 1965), p. 47.

10   Id., p. 145.

but the dominance of positivism and pragmatism in society, politics, and general education has left most students without any philosophical basis to resist the fragmentation and dissonance of modern culture. The triumph of relativism has led to the generally held belief that there is no objective standard of right or wrong, true or false, beautiful or ugly. No one wants to be seen as "judgmental." This attitude results in a coarsening of taste in matters of art, literature, entertainment, and ordinary discourse. The damage done to philosophy by these early twentieth-century conceptual trends has never been successfully reversed; indeed, the philosophical flight from essence and reality has continued to the present day.

The Psychology of Gratification and Personal Autonomy

Freudian psychology, which became popular in the early decades of the twentieth century, gave rise to a radically new perception of human nature and further impaired traditional moral authority. The most revolutionary aspect of Freud's teaching was his insistence that the sex drive, or libido, was of fundamental importance in motivating human behavior and, when suppressed, could produce emotionally crippling neuroses. A second influential theory of the Viennese psychiatrist was the doctrine of the unconscious. While the existence of an unconscious aspect of the human personality had long been recognized, Freud elaborated the role of the unconscious and linked it with childhood events and sexuality. Through the use of psychoanalytic techniques, the therapist could help the patient bring his repressed desires to consciousness.

The scientific credentials of Freudian psychology were never solidly based, and many of Freud's conclusions have been exposed as unfounded. Freudianism was, nevertheless, congenial to the modern temperament since it provided a plausible justification for doing what people released from traditional restraints are naturally disposed to do anyway. Sexual liberation was no longer confined to bohemians and wayward aristocrats but could be justified by ordinary people as a requirement of mental health. At a deeper level, psychoanalysis offered a secular substitute for the religious sacrament of confession but without the annoying burden of obedience to transcendent authority. It was a religion of the self, giving hope for personal salvation in this world through the release of sexual instinct. Freudianism also accelerated the twentieth century's retreat from individual responsibility by implying that destructive behavior is attributable to childhood events over which one has no control. This was the worst possible prescription for twentieth-century Western society, which was already moving toward a radical rejection of traditional authority and morality.

Freudian psychology has been largely replaced today, in the popular mind, by an endless variety of "feel good" therapies that teach people to enhance their own pleasure and dominance while avoiding the discomfort of self-discipline. Contemporary psychological theories follow the advice of the behavioral psychologist B. F. Skinner, who said that the secret of life was "to gratify yourself without getting arrested." These popular psychologies teach a so-called *situational morality* that celebrates immediacy, vitality, assertiveness, emancipation from the past, and debunking of authority. What the pop psychologists do *not* teach is how to find new rules to replace those that have been discarded. The breakdown of civil order in many American cities makes it abundantly clear that we need more psychological restraint, not less. But this is not what the public wants to hear. The society is bombarded with therapeutic nostrums of "self-esteem" and other New Age doctrines encouraging worship of the self. The result is a culture devoted to subjective feeling and private experience.

Social psychology in America has recently veered into what seems to be a full-fledged flight from reality. There are now many teachers and others in positions of authority who actively encourage children to "identify" as persons of another sex. A growing menu of sexual identities is celebrated, denoted by an ever-expanding set of initials: LGBTQ (lesbian, gay, bisexual, transgender, queer) and so forth. Personal autonomy is taken quite seriously—you can be whatever you want to be, and whatever that is can change tomorrow.[11] What this kind of psychic disorder might do to a child's development is an interesting question for the therapists to ponder. The "transgender" confusion adds to other symptoms of social breakdown that we will explore in the next chapter.

During the 1960s, the Freudian attack on the alleged repressiveness of religious and moral institutions was united in a bizarre partnership with the Marxist theory of class oppression. The paucity of evidence for either theory did not inhibit the followers of the psycho-Marxist cults who, because of the decline of education, were no longer trained in the demands of logic or the scientific analysis of evidence. Untrammeled by the requirements of objectivity, students were free to seek a rationale for sexual liberation, political revolt, and the rejection of authority generally. This theory has been labeled as "cultural Marxism" and is often linked with the German "Frankfurt School" of neo-Marxist theorists. The cultural Marxists seek to liberate the masses from the traditional cultural and institutional conditions that oppress them, such as capitalism, patriotism, private property, Christianity, paternalism, and the family, all of which they try to undermine.[12]

Cultural Fragmentation

During the first two-thirds of the twentieth century, the United States had what could be regarded as a common culture. The large number of immigrants early in the century were successfully assimilated into America's productive economy, while two world wars and a full recovery from the Great Depression cemented a general sense of patriotism and

---

11   The journal *Nature*, a reputedly authoritative scientific publication, editorialized that determining whether someone is male or female based on objective biological characteristics is erroneous: "The idea that science can make definitive conclusions about a person's sex or gender is fundamentally flawed." Such traditional thinking, the magazine asserted, amounts to "stripping away rights and recognition from those whose identity does not correspond with outdated ideas of sex and gender." *Nature*, www.nature.com/articles/d41586–018–07238–8.

12   See Herbert Marcuse, *One-Dimensional Man* (Boston: Beacon Press, 1964) and *An Essay on Liberation* (Boston: Beacon Press, 1969).

solidarity. Most Americans responded to common cultural stimuli from Hollywood, newspapers, radio, and television. There were writers, leftists, and intellectuals, of course, who deplored babbitry, bourgeois conformity, and chauvinism, but there was a prevailing "Americanism" that nourished a feeling of common identity. In the 1960s, that began to change.

Various social forces that reached critical mass in the United States during the 1960s quickened the pace of cultural change. First, following World War II, there was a remarkable growth in college admissions, supported by the G.I. Bill and other government programs and by a popular belief that many or most high school graduates should go on to college. For the reasons discussed in the previous chapter, the deficiencies in high school education meant that many of those admitted to college were poorly qualified. The basic principles of the American founding were no longer taught. Because of political and financial pressure, public colleges and universities were encouraged to accept and retain academically deficient students. This, in turn, resulted in a reduction in academic standards. The nation's campuses were filled with restless throngs of disinterested adolescents, many of whom were apathetic toward a system that seemed to offer them little of practical value. Second, the culture of rock music, television, and drugs permeated colleges and high schools, dragging down academic standards still further and contributing to a mindless ethos of noise, disruption, and promiscuous sex. Finally, the Vietnam War focused the anger and resentment of students and spawned a generation of disaffected radicals. (The young draftees, quite understandably, resented the fact that upper-class students managed to get deferments, while they were sent to combat in the southeast Asian jungles.) The dissidents, encouraged by university faculties and journalists, attacked the United States as an evil, oppressive power—even though, of all societies in history, America's was the most open to personal freedom and advancement.

An attitude of open hostility toward America and its institutions established itself among an influential segment of America's educated classes. Seldom has a major power been so violently criticized from within by its privileged elites—including students, academics, writers, clerics, and other professionals—who should have supported the society's values and defended its interests. On the political level, prudence gave way to reckless spending and the subsidization of idleness. Sects and subcultures proliferated; many young people rejected traditional religion and turned to cults for spiritual satisfaction, just as they turned to drugs for psychical stimulation. This was the legacy of the 1960s, a decade of social and cultural destructiveness whose noxious effects remain with us today.[13]

At the beginning of the twenty-first century, the fragmentation of American culture was exacerbated by the rise of digital technology, along with social media and the "multiculture." In this atmosphere, any person or small group can create their own identity and social presence and share them immediately with others. As James Poulos has written,

"[D]igital technology's destruction of our monoculture can make us suddenly lose faith in Americanism, with soul-crushing results. Traditional Americanism has been closely associated with the monoculture for a long time. But now that the monoculture has so few ardent public defenders—nobody likes a loser—there is a disheartening pile-on online, where everyone can find their own niche reasons to cast aspersions on Americanism's vision of itself as mainstream."[14]

THE VISUAL ARTS

A philosophical history of modern art would describe the divorce of form from reality through the destruction of subject matter. Medieval and Renaissance art portrayed religion, love, and natural beauty as objective realities—although, of course, these realities were often represented in symbolic or mythical form. The worldview of traditional

---

13   These developments are described by Roger Kimball in *The Long March: How the Cultural Revolution of the 1960s Changed America* (San Francisco: Encounter Books, 2000).

14   James Poulos, "Modern Babel: The Death of the Monoculture and the Crisis of 'Americanism,'" *Washington Examiner* (April 2, 2019), p. 13.

art began to break down during the Enlightenment, when art became wholly secularized, gods and heroes became decorations, and allegory died. Gradually, prominent artists abandoned the effort to illustrate noble and universal truths. The nineteenth-century Romantics began the process of separating the artist from society. Whereas traditional art sought a balance between artistic imagination and objective reality, the romantic artist, immersed in introspection, shifted this balance in the direction of pure imagination. The cult of the artist-as-hero and the doctrine of art for art's sake were products of the romantic movement.

The painterly revolution of the impressionists was an attempt to reduce the observed world to the sensation of light and shadow on surfaces. Cezanne reconstructed reality into geometrical, near-abstract masses. Gauguin carried on the struggle by abandoning Western civilization itself and turning to primitive forms. These were heroic years in the history of art. We must acknowledge the power of the early modernists and the beauty of much of their work. The early modern painters had solid and disciplined training, and they had not yet lost contact with their cultural heritage. Cezanne, the greatest of all the early modern masters, is reported to have said that "the way to nature lies through the Louvre, and the way to the Louvre lies through nature." Yet these artists began a process that could not be controlled. The German expressionists displayed raw emotion and an obsession with self. The cubists broke up and rearranged shapes and colors to produce a multiple, fragmented view of objects. Soon, the link to esthetic sensibility began to dissolve in a haze of subjectivity, childish play, meaningless abstraction, and sheer ugliness. Rationality itself disappeared as artists nailed urinals to the wall, Dadaists read at random the words torn from poems, and surrealists celebrated the fantasies of dreamscapes.

Abstract art took the final step toward the realization of the modernist sensibility by separating the esthetic attributes of style from traditional notions of subject matter. Indeed, style itself became the substitute for subject matter, effectively reducing art to the manipulation of line, color, and shape. The triumph of style over substance placed artists in a trap from which it was difficult to escape. Once the modernists had destroyed the traditional canons, the only path left was the cult of novelty. The history of art in the twentieth century is a paradigm of decadence, which can be defined as the abandonment of a classical ideal or model, leading to a hopelessly disordered condition in which there are no accepted standards for creation or evaluation.

By the 1980s, the dominant tendencies in modern art seemed to have reached a dead end. Galleries were filled with twisted metal and bags of cat food. Contemporary artists immerse themselves in the most mundane, vulgar, and banal aspects of life. By featuring scrap from junkyards, graffiti, and commercial trivia, they hope to concentrate our minds on the superficiality of capitalist culture. Eventually, however, the obsession with surface vulgarity becomes merely tedious. Inevitably, the century-long assault on all previous styles culminated in an assault on art itself. The artist is now free, and even encouraged, to outrage every canon of good taste and to disparage the very idea of artistic sensibility, often with the assistance of public subsidies. Museums, whose original function was to celebrate order and beauty, too often encourage their patrons to wallow in disorder and perversity. A famous example was the exhibit at the Brooklyn Museum of Art in 1999 featuring an obscene painting of the Virgin Mary surrounded by genitalia and covered with elephant dung. This display (which was vigorously defended by the art establishment) represented, as well as anything could, the century-long effort to mock and ultimately demolish the religious and moral heritage of the West.

For readers who have not recently visited a contemporary art gallery, it is virtually impossible to describe in words the displays of degradation and imbecility exhibited in many supposedly respectable museums and galleries. Representative examples include pieces of broken crockery glued together, two basketballs floating in a fish tank, a pile of plastic vomit, walls filled with doodling and scribbling, and lots of aggressive obscenity. A guard at the Whitney Museum in New York commented to this author that people steal the Whitney's garbage cans in the alley because "they think it's art." It was reported in 1995 that critics were "going ape" over paintings by Charles, a 440-pound gorilla who commands up to $585 per painting. Another example, in the Modern Museum's 1999 exhibit "Open Ends," was an entire room filled with empty packing crates and boxes. The curator's explanation was as follows: "Carrying on a dialogue with art history's long tradition of trompe l'oeil, these works re-create and replace the world around us, while visiting the limits of visual description." One spectator, at this point, was heard to remark that he had visited the limits of his patience. Many examples of the nihilistic genre can be found at the Whitney Museum, which specializes in contemporary art works whose bizarre displays have to be explained in the language of "art-speak." The Whitney's 2017 Biennial exhibit, for example, contained a sculpture consisting of a metal pole leaning against a gallery wall with a fragment of a tree trunk that had grown around it hanging from its middle. The title of this art work was "but I sound better since you cut my throat." The Whitney's catalogue explained: "Rather than closing the loop of signification, Mendez's [the artist's] work leaves his objects' meanings indefinite, suspended in a history that continues to unfold."[15] In keeping with the current politicization of every aspect of culture, the Whitney Biennial was filled with works dwelling on issues of race, gender, sexuality, and identity politics. There was a whole room containing exhortations to censor the press, which the artists accused of promoting capitalism, oppression, and imperialism. The market for modern art has become preposterously inflated. Buyers pay tens of millions of dollars for post-modern pieces that anyone with ordinary sensibility would regard as trash. In a few days in November 2014, art auctions at three New York galleries generated $1.66 billion in sales, including an Andy Warhol silkscreen of Elvis Presley that sold for $81.9 million and a Giacometti bronze stick-figure of a goddess on a chariot for $101 million.[16] The

---

15   *Whitney Biennial 2017* (New Haven, CT: Yale University Press, 2017), p. 143.

16   See Don Thompson, *The Orange Balloon Dog: Bubbles, Turmoil and Avarice in the Contemporary Art Market* (Madeira Park, BC: Douglas and McIntyre Ltd., 2017).

absurdly high prices for contemporary works reflect a society of extraordinary affluence in which increasing numbers of very wealthy people are prepared to bid millions for celebrity junk art.

It would be wrong to conclude that all recent art is worthless. There are many artists doing creative work, as well as experimenting with new textures, techniques, and multimedia projects. From this mix of creativity may perhaps emerge works of lasting value. In a society that is so saturated in commercialism and immediacy, however, permanence is only an accidental byproduct. An astute observer has said that there is more beauty in the Saks Fifth Avenue Christmas display than in the entire Whitney Museum of American Art. But neither the Saks windows nor the Whitney's rotating ephemera survive for long. Without recognized standards of taste and judgment—which seem farther away than ever—an art that is "created to endure" is unlikely to be revived. In an age when anything can count as art, what is permanent?

In retrospect, the history of art in the twentieth century has shown some imagination, as well as considerable skill in the manipulation of its materials, yet much of modern art is little more than a hoax imposed upon a gullible public. A similar fraud was perpetrated by the architectural profession, which persuaded the public that it ought to live and work in glass boxes or concrete bunkers because they were "functional." Following World War II, old but perfectly habitable neighborhood houses and lively streets were razed to the ground and replaced by huge public housing projects consisting of stark towers built on empty spaces that swiftly became breeding grounds for crime and degeneracy. As Britain's Prince Charles said, they were "soulless, bureaucratic and inhuman." In the 1980s and 1990s, glass-and-steel rectangular boxes came to dominate the downtowns of American cities (see K Street in Washington, DC), transforming our cities into what architectural critic David Brussat has called "oppressive zones of aesthetic sterility."[17] In some cases, the so-called "postmodernists" have returned to marble,

---

17   David Brussat, "Occupy Le Corbusier," *The American Conservative* (March 30, 2016).

color, decoration, and even to some traditional themes. The popularity of postmodern buildings, in contrast to the glass boxes of modernism, may indicate a latent desire for the reintegration of form, style, and comfort in architecture. Postmodernism, however, has also spawned flamboyant "starchitects" like Frank Gehry, whose buildings feature twisted metal, absurd shapes, and uneven walls. The essential difficulty, as in so many other areas of modern culture, is that the patrons of modern architecture (corporate executives, homebuilders, and government bureaucrats) are untrained in matters of taste and style. The consumers of architecture, therefore, will continue to be dominated by what the architects think they ought to build. This imbalance between the "experts" and the consumers (which runs like a fault line through modern society) is unlikely to produce a golden age of style.[18]

Modernism shattered the unity and continuity of traditional culture. Postmodernists are now attempting to reassemble the pieces into temporarily entertaining forms. This process reflects contemporary American civilization at large: rootless, without permanent ideals, infatuated with technology, and driven by global markets in which capital and people are shifted like electronic bits and local differences are submerged. Under these conditions, it is difficult to adhere to what is culturally permanent because there are no moorings.

LITERATURE AND LITERARY THEORY

One of the traditional functions of literature is to transmit a society's basic values. Literature also satisfies the basic human desire to represent reality in a novel or delightful way—to entertain as well as to instruct. In

---

18   The best account of what happened to architecture in the twentieth century is a book by British philosopher Roger Scruton, *The Aesthetics of Architecture* (Princeton: Princeton University Press, 2013 [1979]). Scruton defends a traditional concept of architecture as a combination of functionality, design, ornament, and style, and urges: "We must try to re-capture what is *central* in the experience of architecture. Like Alberti, Serlio and their followers, we will find that we can do that only if we reinstate aesthetic values at the heart of the builder's enterprise, and allow no question of function to be answered independently of the question of the appropriateness of a building, not just to its function, but to a style of life." *Id.* p. 33.

the nineteenth century, a third view of literature emerged, holding that literature should seek to achieve scientific precision in describing reality. This notion gave birth to various schools of "realism" and "naturalism." In carrying out his project of describing society with scientific precision, however, the realistic novelist is faced with an epistemological dilemma. If he wants to capture "reality," he must try to describe with precision what he knows. The modernist position, however, is based on the subjectivist premise that the novelist cannot know with certainty anything except his own impressions and emotions. Writers who take realism seriously must accordingly deal with inner, hidden, and subjective forces. Plot and subject matter become subordinated to form and impression. The modernist project of reducing or even eliminating subject matter was foreseen in Flaubert's famous statement: "What I should like to write is a book about nothing, a book dependent on nothing external, which would be held together by the internal strength of its style ... a book which would have almost no subject, or at least in which the subject would be almost invisible, if such a thing is possible."[19] The supremacy of style over subject matter became a canon of modernism.

In literature, the prose novel has become a staple of Western culture. It is a flexible art form that permits the display of an infinite number of viewpoints, categories, and attitudes. The significant number of decently written novels and short stories is a sign that the written word has not entirely collapsed under the onslaught of television and the internet. Unfortunately, many of today's "quality" stories and novels, while competently written, are flat, trivial, and boring. With some notable exceptions, contemporary American fiction is largely devoid of ideas, and its characters are lacking in depth. We are treated to an endless succession of dinner parties, vapid conversations, domestic squabbling, and dismal "relationships." One critic has suggested that the short story—and particularly the "minimalist" short story—reflects

---

19 Quoted in James Atlas, review of *The Letters of Gustave Flaubert*, *New York Times* Book Review (October 17, 1982), p. 3.

the society in which we live: "a society, in fact, of aimless transients who are often held together by nothing more than temporary geographical propinquity and who are perhaps most notable for being as migratory emotionally as they are physically."[20]

To be sure, there are more interesting styles of writing, echoing the vivid aspects of American culture. There are well-written novels depicting the ruin, squalor, and desolation of American urban life.[21] There are apocalyptic visions of America as a repressive or ecologically insane society peopled by freaks, proto-fascists, 1960s radicals, and zombies.[22] These novels are sometimes classified as "metafiction," a brand of literary surrealism that uses obscure and bloated language to depict the absurdities of contemporary society. Such views of the world are alternately depressing and exhilarating, though not profound. Themes of sex and violence are common. As the public becomes more accustomed to bloody and raunchy excesses, many writers feel compelled to increase the horror level in order to achieve the desired degree of shock value.

With the possible exception of Saul Bellow and Tom Wolfe, there have been no American writers in recent decades of the stature of Faulkner, Fitzgerald, Hemingway, Dos Passos, or Steinbeck. The books written by these men had a certain tragic dimension because the characters fought against debilitating circumstances on behalf of ideals of courage, endurance, and beauty—ideals associated with belief in the nobility of human feeling. In most post-World War II novels, the permanent ideals have been replaced by chaos, violence, sordidness, or tedium. The protagonists are no longer heroes but psychic misfits, victims, or outsiders. Contemporary American novels are introspective, quirky, often political; but they are seldom tragic because the cornerstones of tragedy are nobility of character and the reality of evil, neither of which can easily exist in the

---

20   John W. Aldridge, *Talents and Technicians* (New York: Scribner's, 1992), p. 57.

21   Madison Smart Bell, *Waiting for the End of the World* (New York: Penguin, 1986).

22   Thomas Pynchon, *Vineland* (Boston: Little, Brown, 1990); T. C. Boyle, *A Friend of the Earth* (New York: Viking, 2000).

introspective, post-Freudian world of the modern novelist. We have been speaking of "serious" American fiction. There is little need to dwell on the rest. Most works of fiction sold today are murder mysteries, science fiction, spy stories, and "romantic" novels. Some of these novels are well written, especially the mystery and spy books. Most are mindless nonsense meant to entertain the barely educated.

It is not surprising that most fiction is shallow since popular books must compete with television, social media, and the popular press for the shortened attention span of a semi-literate public. More troubling is the deterioration of the cultural level among the supposedly educated minority. There are few college graduates today who have sufficient background to deal with Dostoevsky, Joyce, Proust, or Faulkner. In short, our society no longer has an educated community of readers with the shared cultural habits needed to sustain a living tradition of great literature.

There are other signs of the decline of literacy. Most newspapers have been progressively "dumbed down" to appeal to people whose reading comprehension is frozen at junior high school level. Letter writing is a lost art and has largely been replaced by email. Bookstores across the country have been converted into greeting card and gift shops, purveying instant messages for every occasion. Libraries have reduced their hours; many have closed altogether. As a result of the cultural forces described in this chapter, it is likely that we are now witnessing the end of the "print culture" that has dominated Western civilization for 400 years and its replacement by a new "electronic culture." Summarizing this transformation, Professor Alvin Kernan places the death of literature in the broader context of an overall social disorientation that has impaired the effective functioning of traditional institutions and value systems. He points to "a growing narcissism and solipsism in modern life that are making any kind of communication, including the privileged literary kind between authors and readers, increasingly difficult, perhaps ultimately impossible."[23]

---

23   Alvin Kernan, *The Death of Literature* (New Haven, CT: Yale University Press, 1990), p. 206.

Just as modern philosophy forced the natural world to retreat into the mind of the observer, "postmodern" or "deconstructionist" criticism holds that words are merely signs of ideas or links between ideas and sounds, and that the choice of a given bit of sound to name a given idea is not only subjective but arbitrary. The natural effect of the deconstructionist project is to substitute discourse for reality. If language loses its connection with reality, then talking about language is the closest we can come to truth. Talking about language, by happy coincidence, is exactly what critics do for a living. Roland Barthes's famous 1968 essay, "The Death of the Author," signaled the victory of the critic by killing off the author. Once writing has been reduced to "a tissue of signs," the author's "authority" is gone. For Barthes, a text does not convey any intent of the author, but is a multidimensional space in which an infinite variety of meanings conflict. The removal of authority destroys even the possibility of finding the meaning of the text. The implications are revolutionary and ultimately antirational. As Barthes recognized, "to refuse to fix meaning is, in the end, to refuse God and his hypostases—reason, science, law."[24]

Barthes and his followers were not the first to reach this conclusion. Nietzsche made the basic arguments of the deconstructionists in *The Will to Power*, published posthumously in 1901. Here he argued that there are no objective facts but only interpretations. There is no limit to the ways in which the world can be interpreted. "Ultimately," Nietzsche wrote, "man finds in things nothing but what he himself has imported into them."[25] As Nietzsche accurately concluded, the view that there is no meaning or truth, but only interpretation, is a form of nihilism. The modern deconstructionists have not changed the essence of Nietzschean nihilism, but they have repackaged it for academic consumption and elaborated upon its implications for literature. The task of interpretation is to *deconstruct*

---

24   Barthes, "The Death of the Author," in Rice and Waugh, ed., *Modern Literary Theory* (London: E. Arnold, 1989), p. 117.

25   Nietzsche, *The Will to Power*, Book III, Secs. 481–606.

whatever the text may appear to present. There a̶
readings and no standards for resolving conflicting inte̶

Another tendency of modern literary criticism has̶
port the growing politicization of intellectual life. Deconstr̶
argue that every text conceals the hidden ideology of the author̶
intended audience and that books merely echo the narrow interests o̶
dominant class, sex, or race. Culture is reduced to a struggle for power
among competing groups. Literary criticism thus provides another
vehicle for the perpetual chorus of whining by the alleged victims of
a cruel society. In an attempt to appease the Jacobins, educators have
adopted a form of literary affirmative action, in which books by blacks,
women, and Third-World writers have been introduced into college
courses largely because of the color or sex of the authors or because
of their radical political views. All of this is part of the relentless quest
for diversity. Criticism has become a principal tool for the assault on
Western culture and values. Deconstructionist analysis makes it possible
to portray Goneril and Regan as oppressed victims of phallocracy or
Caliban as a courageous opponent of white racism.

A principal consequence of postmodern theory is the destruction
of essences, structures, and certainties. There can be no obligation to
speak the truth if truth is a byproduct of power and discourse is only
the infinite play of arbitrary signifiers. Concepts and social structures
are contingent and temporary. Marriage, for example, is not a sanctified
union of a man and a woman but an arbitrary act of will that can easily
be dissolved by a second act of will. In the end, culture itself becomes
meaningless. If the world is constituted solely by subjective appearances,
it is useless to build anything lasting. Piety toward the past and concern
for the future give way to an eternal present of consumption, amusement, and the struggle for power.

Modern literary theory follows modern philosophy in its central
premise: "the orders of the world are not 'natural' but constructed."[26]

---

26   Rice and Waugh, *Modern Literary Theory*, p. ix.

LTURE

e no right or wrong
pretations.
been to sup-
ctionists
r the
f a

)f the superstructure of modernity,
.d are interpreted by the minds of
from the permanent features of the
is of the human condition. These
ucted. Once literary analysis aban-
ind the natural orders of the world,
ied with the surface texture of words.
nnection between words and things,

undermined a literary culture already eroded by television and a second-rate educational system. To reverse this trend, we must restore the centrality of literary tradition. In his *Preface to Shakespeare,* Samuel Johnson explained the persistence of literary fame over generations:

> What mankind have long possessed they have often examined and compared; and if they persist to value the possession, it is because frequent comparisons have confirmed opinion in its favour ... The reverence due to writings that have long subsisted arises therefore not from any credulous confidence in the superior wisdom of past ages, or gloomy persuasion of the degeneracy of mankind, but is the consequence of acknowledged and indubitable positions, that what has been longest known has been most considered, and what is most considered is best understood.[27]

Although it is fashionable to dismiss the major texts of Western culture as products of a power structure dominated by white males, these books form the basis of our literary culture and, in a real sense, make us what we are. It would be impossible to imagine our culture without the Bible, Homer, the Greek philosophers, Virgil, Dante, Aquinas, Shakespeare, and Milton. Yet these and other classic texts are

---

27 Samuel Johnson, *Selected Poetry and Prose* (Berkeley: University of California Press, 1977), pp. 299–300.

increasingly ignored in education today. A new generation may be fated to discover the meaning (if any) of a culture constituted without serious books or ideas, other than those works of science and economics needed to grease the machinery of production and consumption.

Amid the bleak literary landscape, there are positive signs. Every year, American publishers issue dozens of volumes of history and biography. New collections of the papers of well-known and lesser-known figures are regularly published. Scholarly books on subjects from physics to religion pour from the presses. Science, in particular, is well covered by accessible books and journals. Internet publishing offers the promise of public access for many authors whose books might not meet the profit-oriented criteria of commercial publishers. Numerous literary journals exist, and the art of political commentary is highly developed. The question that remains is whether a serious revival of literature and philosophy is possible under the pressures of consumerism and the electronic age. The daunting nature of this task requires us to explore the wasteland of contemporary popular culture.

TELEVISION, THE INTERNET, AND POPULAR CULTURE
Television and the internet have changed our society, and perhaps even our thought processes, in fundamental ways. Children are raised on them. Adults live by them. TV and smartphones transmit the images that shorten the attention span of each successive generation. Sight (visual reaction) becomes dominant in place of thoughtfulness and literacy. Television and the omnipresent cellphone strengthen the craving for immediate, ever-shifting experience that is a central feature of contemporary society. "The Internet rapidly accelerates the political, social and cultural fragmentation process that has been under way since the mid-twentieth century and profoundly compromises our ability to pay attention.... At the neurological level, the Internet's constant distractions alter the physiological structure of our brain.... The result of this

is a gradual inability to pay attention, to focus and to think deeply."[28]

The average American watches three to five hours of television per day. In contrast to reading, which demands thought and imagination, TV and other electronic viewing is passive behavior requiring little or no mental activity. Millions of people pass their afternoons and evenings watching soap operas, mindless game shows, and violent crime thrillers. News programs on commercial TV are aimed at the barely literate and consist of a few sentences accompanied by vivid camera shots. Electronic media are damaging for young children because they replace storytelling, conversing, sports, and other active recreation; they are also bad for adults because the "digital deluge" brings constant distractions, leading to incessant interruption of thought and adversely affecting productivity.[29] America, in short, is no longer a nation of pioneers, adventurers, or entrepreneurs; it is a nation of TV viewers and cellphone addicts. As Joseph Epstein has written, "The acquisition of culture requires repose, sitting quietly in a room with a book, or alone with one's thoughts even at a crowded concert or art museum. Ours is distinctly not an age of repose ... Information not culture is the great desideratum of our day, distraction our chief theme."[30]

While it is true that there are some good public affairs programs on television and an occasional drama or opera, only a very small percentage of viewers watch these programs. Commercial TV is geared to the mass audience. Its programs therefore tend to become progressively more violent and more vulgar because advertisers have found that these

---

28   Rod Dreher, *The Benedict Option* (New York: Sentinel, 2017), pp. 224–25.

29   "Paying No Mind: Digital Distractions," *The Economist* (December 9, 2017), p. 77. The World Health Organization has classified compulsive video gaming as "gaming disorder," a form of addiction which, for a small percentage of gamers, can result in "significant impairment in personal, family, social, educational or other important areas of functioning." www.who.int/features/qa/gaming_disorder/en (2018). For a more positive view of video games, see Ian Bogost, *Persuasive Games: The Expressive Power of Videogames* (Cambridge, MA: MIT Press, 2007).

30   Joseph Epstein, "Whatever Happened to High Culture?" *The Weekly Standard* (November 9, 2015), p. 26.

qualities appeal to the mass taste. In the presence of the magical screen, intelligent conversation and rational thought are impossible. Television has no durability or continuity. It is a continuous present, without a past or future. It has a hypnotic and deadening effect that radio does not have. The electronic medium reinforces the tendency of Americans to think and live for the short term.

Television has also changed the nature of the civic dialogue. Political campaigns are reduced to thirty-second "sound bites" that convey emotional messages rather than reasoned argument. Television debates are not real debates but a series of polemical assertions and *ad hominem* attacks. The new media technologies have transformed politics. Elections today are driven by "pseudo-events" manufactured by media and public relations specialists, such as photo-ops, staged rallies, and presidential "debates" that are not real debates but televised press conferences. Television also corrupts politics by raising exponentially the cost of political campaigns. No candidate can hope to enter any race without obtaining millions of dollars and, in the process, incurring obligations to the special interests that provide the funding.

The general thrust of TV programming is to distort and ridicule conventional behavior and traditional institutions, and to undermine authority. Television shows portray businessmen as criminals and parents as money-grubbing, vulgar barbarians. TV talk shows feature sex-obsessed exhibitionists revealing to the public the grubby details of their unappetizing private lives. Game programs promise instant riches with no effort, exalting the something-for-nothing psychology of the consumer society. The dialogue on most television programs is insipid beyond belief. Of more serious concern, television's constant emphasis on sex and violence is bound to make an impression on young viewers. The average sixteen-year-old has witnessed thousands of dramatized killings, assaults, and seductions. Pornography is easily available and has a malignant influence on adolescent minds. Since television is addictive, especially to the young, it is hardly surprising that steady exposure of children to violence on television increases the likelihood of aggressive behavior.[31]

There are, of course, many creditable uses for TV and video media, which can be effective educational tools for historical, geographical, and environmental awareness; military training; business presentations; crime control; health advice; and many other useful applications. Moreover, apologists for television argue that, in the pre-TV era, few of today's video junkies would have spent their time reading books or singing in the church choir. It is true that most people throughout recorded history have devoted themselves to mindless entertainment when not working or fighting. Television is no more vapid or brutalizing than gladiatorial contests or bear baiting. But constant TV watching is different because it erodes the sense of community by isolating people from normal social contact, and it occupies the time of many men and women who might have occasionally read a book or attended a lecture. The degraded state of the educational system in America provides little prospect of a more demanding television audience. The trends are mutually reinforcing: lower educational standards mean fewer readers and more viewers, and too much television lowers educational standards still further. Here again, the causes of decline are interlocking.

The TV anchormen and soap queens are not alone in competing for the hearts and minds of Americans. Most Hollywood movies give us the same tasteless sludge as television. Many are reboots of superhero comic strip movies, while others are packed from beginning to end with sex, violence, and obscenity. Popular magazines are devoted to encouraging promiscuity, featuring advice to young women on how to develop the skills of prostitutes. Classical music is available on a few public radio stations in major markets, but contemporary popular music is, for the

---

31   See David G. Myers, *The American Paradox: Spiritual Hunger in an Age of Plenty* (New Haven: Yale University Press, 2000), pp. 197–212: "The irrefutable conclusion is that viewing violence increases violence." Robert Kubey and Mihaly Czikszentmahalyi, "Television Addiction," *Scientific American* (February 2002); "Media Bombardment Is Linked to Ill Effects During Childhood," *Washington Post* (December 2, 2008), p. C7; Patrick F. Fagan, "The Effects of Pornography on Individuals, Marriage, Family and Community," Marriage and Religion Institute (December 2009).

most part, dreadful. While television and movies have done their part to soften our brains, rock music assaults both the senses and the mind like a sledge hammer. High volume and hard beats are accompanied by vocal shouting and screeching. (Some rock music is more appealing, of course—welcome strains of rhythm and blues have survived.) The words of today's popular songs seldom rise above adolescent romanticism or verbal violence. In rap music, melody is abolished entirely; the lyrics exalt belligerent behavior, aggressive sexuality, obscenity, misogyny, and lawlessness. Soft rock and pop songs also flood the airwaves. Most of this music is excruciatingly tedious, consisting of simplistic melody, drumbeats, and childish, repetitive lyrics. Popular music, like television, must appeal to the mass audience in order to succeed economically. Music becomes merely another prepackaged product for targeted groups: a technical problem to be solved by the ad-men and computers of the business-entertainment complex. Less taste equals more profits. Music, of course, is a reflection of the cultural world we inhabit, and changes in music evidence significant shifts in social life. As Plato noted, "When modes of music change, the fundamental mores of the state always change with them."[32] Plato argued that disordered, Dionysian music impairs social harmony. While the lines of causation may not be as obvious as Plato believed, it seems clear that today's world of popular music reinforces our society's infatuation with overt displays of sexuality, aggression, and rebellion and provides additional proof of the general deterioration of taste.

Posterity will judge the value of a civilization not by its everyday entertainment but by its highest and best cultural achievements. The inanities of television and pop music would therefore be tolerable if there were evidence of a flourishing high culture. On the surface, many cultural institutions seem to be healthy. Millions of dollars annually are poured into local symphony orchestras and theater and opera companies. There are journals of culture, such as *The New Criterion*, which

---

32   Plato, *Republic,* IV, 424c.

are well-edited and contain informative, well-written criticism. America has a number of excellent art museums that adequately perform their function of preserving and displaying the art of the past. Yet museums are not well suited to the encouragement of new works. Today there is a great deal of money chasing a vast quantity of objects, but the artists have little talent and the buyers have little taste. The elite class of connoisseurs who knew high culture and could afford it has shrunk.[33]

The technology of modern communication is a double-edged sword. On the one hand, cell phones are extremely useful in enabling people to communicate easily and frequently. This promotes safety and convenience and permits instant access to massive quantities of information. On the other hand, cell phones and related media, such as Twitter, do not advance our ability to communicate in depth, intelligibly, and with real exchange of ideas. (As we know, some public officeholders make public policy via Twitter, which obviously minimizes the substantive content of messages.) On street corners and in restaurants, it is common to see many, if not most, young people staring fixedly at handheld devices or with their heads buried in earphones, cut off from ordinary interaction.

The explosive growth of the internet is often cited as an indicator of progress, but it does not seem likely to improve the condition of popular culture. Indeed, the internet is a particularly convenient medium for the purveyance of obscenity and fraud, with the added feature of being virtually impossible to regulate.[34] The internet also exposes its users to serious invasions of privacy, as evidenced by recent data-collection episodes involving social media. While the internet has certainly become a useful research tool, its ultimate utility will depend on what

---

33 To some extent, the shrinkage in the demand for high culture has been adversely affected by the political redistribution of wealth in Western societies. When income is taken away from the natural buyers of fine art, there will be less of it produced. See Betrand de Jouvenel, *The Ethics of Redistribution* (Indianapolis: Liberty Press, 1990), pp. 40–42.

34 It has been reported that an estimated 35 percent of all internet downloads are related to pornography and that 40 million Americans regularly visit porn sites. See webroot.com/us/in/home/resources/tips/digital-family-life/internet-pornography-by-the-numbers.

sort of research is valued by the society. The internet in many respects complements and supports the immediacy of television, and the two media, in many respects, are merging. The TV/web culture, no matter how sophisticated it becomes, is bound to be vastly different from literary culture. It is likely, in fact, as Alvin Kernan argues, that literary culture has begun to disappear as an active social force. While popular entertainment in all ages has appealed to the grosser instincts, previous civilized societies encouraged the development of an intellectual elite that pursued a literary culture superior to the entertainment of the mob. The danger today is that we have spawned a popular culture that can debase the public taste at all levels. Caliban urged his accomplices to eliminate Prospero by first possessing his books. In our age, barbarism's way is not to destroy civilization's books directly but simply to debase and overwhelm them with worthless trivia so that they no longer pose a threat to the party of ignorance.

The omnipresence of social media, smartphones, and digital entertainment have led to an explosion of content from a vast multitude of sources—much of it trivial, discordant and distasteful—so that a common American culture is fast disappearing. As one cultural critic has recently expressed it, "Digital technology's destruction of our monoculture can make us suddenly lose faith in Americanism, with soul-crushing results."[35] The failure of our educational system to teach America's history and common civic values, discussed in the previous chapter, as well as the rise of "identity politics" and a heavy influx of immigrants, have contributed to the growing tribalism and discordance of our culture.

Who is responsible for the calamitous state of popular culture? There is blame enough to go around. Executives in the movie, TV, and music industries certainly contribute to the problem through their relentless pursuit of profits through debauching young viewers. More to blame are parents, most of whom impose few if any limits on their children's

---

35 James Poulos, "Modern Babel: The death of the monoculture and the crisis of 'Americanism'" *Washington Examiner* (April 2, 2019), p. 13.

addiction to TV and the internet. This is a part of the overall trend toward self-indulgent narcissism and neglect of duty that is a principal theme of this study.

Finally, we must reemphasize the long, slow deterioration of intellectual, moral, and civic discipline under the seductive appeal of philosophies of expedience and hedonism. This betrayal by the semi-educated elites, as Arnold Toynbee argued, destroys the positive effects of "mimesis" (the imitation of superiors) and encourages a race to the bottom.

The Media

The invention of the printing press by Johannes Gutenberg in the fifteenth century revolutionized human communication and helped to create the modern world, including the Renaissance, the Reformation, and the scientific and technological revolutions. Among the offsprings of printing were books and newspapers, which had enormous consequences in social, cultural, and political life. Printing had a decentralizing and empowering effect, giving individuals and groups the ability to develop and spread their ideas in opposition to dominant power centers. The first newspaper in America, *Publick Occurrences* (Boston 1690), was suppressed by the colonial governor.[36] Freedom of the press was protected by the First Amendment to the US Constitution (1791), and American politics has always been accompanied by an open and robust press.

In the twentieth century, the new technologies of radio and television provided to the public additional media outlets for the communication of news, opinion, entertainment, and other content that could be alternatively informative, entertaining, or appalling. In the late twentieth century and into the twenty-first century, the development of the internet spawned various forms of digital communication by way of smartphones, tablets, and other devices. These internet-based applications include the social media, which enable hundreds of millions of people to interact and share information online. It is no exaggeration to say that the media now dominate American culture. Traditionally,

---

36 www.britannica.com/topic/newspaper.

journalistic ethics supposedly required that newspapers should separate news from opinion so that the news pages objectively reported the facts (who, what, where, when, and how) while opinion was confined to the editorial pages. This traditional practice has now been almost entirely abandoned by the mainstream media (both print and TV). Today's major news outlets have, for the most part, given up even the pretense of neutrality in the interest of furthering the prevailing progressive agenda, which includes redistribution of wealth through progressive taxation, expanding the welfare state, increased government regulation of business, feminism, and multiculturalism.

The mainstream media did not invent these ideas; they acquired them from the commanding heights of academia, the home of the new intelligentsia. Academe itself is dominated today, as discussed in Chapter 5, by a progressive (i.e., left-wing) bias. In that chapter, we discussed the decline of the university. We noted that American universities were increasingly dominated by progressives who sought ideological approaches to social problems. These progressive attitudes eventually filtered down to the journalists, who looked to the professors for inspiration and in turn sought to instruct the untutored public in the politically correct attitudes.

While journalists aspire to be professionals (and some are), the methods employed by the media are not always professional, inasmuch as they frequently rely on gossip and on anonymous sources (news articles often cite "a senior administration official" or "an observer who did not want to be identified"). A scientist or a historian who refused to identify his sources would not survive for long in his profession. Shoddy and biased journalism is all too common today. The media search out scurrilous material relating to alleged events that occurred years ago and publicize them in a form designed to defame and destroy whomever they dislike, or stage events, or make them up in order to report on them. This practice has come to be called "fake news," and the events are what Daniel Boorstin has called "pseudo-events."[37]

---

37   See Daniel J. Boorstin, *The Image: A Guide to Pseudo-Events in America* (New York: Vintage Books, 1992) [1961].

The Supreme Court, in *New York Times v. Sullivan,* 376 US 254 (1964), and later cases gave the media virtual *carte blanche* to defame public figures (defined broadly to include persons who voluntarily and prominently participate in a public controversy or are recognized celebrities). Under the *Sullivan* doctrine, all such defamed persons must prove "actual malice" by showing that the statement by the journalist was made with knowledge that it was false or reckless disregard of whether it was false or not. It is all too easy for the press to turn ordinary people into public figures by constantly exposing them to publicity and then slandering them with impunity.

James Bowman has summarized the cultural consequences of the degeneration of the American media:

> What both the fake news, such as it is, and the outcry against it mask is a breakdown in the trust that our political culture—and any democratic polity—depends on. And that breakdown comes from the moralization of politics by the Left with the assistance of the media. Their practice of identity politics is ultimately based on a Marxist-Leninist inspired division of the country into the exploited and the exploiters which allows for no common ground between them and depends on the assumption that what is good for one must be bad for the other. This tendency is exacerbated by the media's obsession with scandal, which has contributed mightily to the moralization of politics and, therefore, to the anti-democratic assumption that political divisions are between good and evil—evil in contemporary terms being racism, sexism, xenophobia, Islamophobia, homophobia (even though Islam is itself homophobic), and, increasingly, capitalism.[38]

A final blow to the credibility of the American mainstream media was delivered by the completion in March 2019 of the report by special counsel Robert Mueller on his investigation of alleged coordination or collusion by Donald Trump and members of his presidential campaign

---

38   James Bowman, "The Media: Faking it and Making it," *The New Criterion* (January 2017), p. 78.

with the Russian government in its efforts to interfere with the 2016 US presidential election. The special counsel's investigation did not find that Trump or any of his team conspired or coordinated with the Russian government. With respect to allegations that President Trump obstructed justice, the Mueller report did not recommend any action against the President, and the Attorney General concluded that the evidence presented was not sufficient to establish that the president obstructed justice.[39] Mueller was appointed as special counsel in May 2017. During the two years of his investigation, major newspapers and most television networks provided nonstop coverage based on the assumption that the president and his campaign team and eventual members of his administration were collaborating with the Russian government. The *New York Times* and the *Washington Post* were given a Pulitzer Prize based on their coverage of the Trump campaign's collusion with Russia. All of this was unsubstantiated. There was no collusion. It was, in short, "a catastrophic media failure."[40]

The breakdown in public trust of the media is part of the general disintegration and demoralization that is occurring throughout American society—a development that we will explore further in the following chapter.

PROSPECTS FOR AMERICAN CULTURE

Hollywood, as someone has said, is only the piano player in the whorehouse. A democratic society produces the kind of culture that its citizens want. The American people want the mass culture of consumerism, and that is what the system generates. This culture, with its television, mind-numbing music, video games, degraded manners, drugs, and

---

39   Attorney General William Barr's summary of Special Counsel Robert Mueller's report of his Russian investigation, March 24, 2019.

40   Sean Davis, "A Catastrophic Media Failure," *The Wall Street Journal"* (March 26, 2019), p. A17. For an informed analysis of the sorry state of America's "mainstreet media," see Mark R. Levin, *Unfreedom of the Press* (New York: Threshold Editions, 2019).

promiscuity, has become a murky Dionysian swamp of immediate sensation that is unlikely to provide a favorable environment for cultural excellence. As Dean Inge foresaw in 1920, "Ancient civilizations were destroyed by imported barbarians; we breed our own."[41]

To see why this deterioration has occurred, let us return to Samuel Lipman's admirably succinct definition of high culture: those aspects of art, literature, and learning that are created to endure or have become a permanent part of the civilization that is transmitted by the settled institutions of society. But culture cannot be transmitted by people who do not know what has endured and cannot understand what is permanent. The average level of cultural literacy, as we have seen, is declining. The literary traditions formerly accepted as the common currency of educated persons are not taught and consequently are not preserved. Even in supposedly educated circles, a common background in art, music, and literature can no longer be assumed. A pseudo-sophisticated elite increasingly dominates what passes for high culture in America. The goals of this group are to undermine Western culture, to discredit the United States as a political and economic model, and to promote "politically correct" art to the same rank as genuine art. The critics of western civilization have adopted the slogans of "diversity" and "pluralism"—an ironic choice of terms since the ideas of diversity, pluralism, and toleration are products of Western civilization and are seldom found in other cultures. The real victim of this process is reason itself.[42]

The assault on Western culture has a direct bearing upon the issue of national decline since the values of Western civilization underlie what is most characteristic and admirable about our society. It was Western civilization that abolished serfdom and slavery, substituted astronomy for astrology, replaced magic with technology, created modern medicine,

---

41   Quoted in Anthony Harrigan, "W. R. Inge: His Vision of a New Barbarian Age," *Modern Age* (Summer 1996), p. 253.

42   See Peter Shaw, *The War against the Intellect: Episodes in the Decline of Discourse* (Iowa City: University of Iowa Press, 1989).

fostered Christian charity, emancipated wo[men,]
asserted the rights of the individual against t[he]
permanent institutions for the protection of priv[ate]
this in addition to producing the glories of Western [art.]
The cultural traditions of the West (in particular, Chris[tian,]
classical heritage of Greece and Rome) are not mere ethnic [or]
curiosities. They are based on universal principles that transce[nd eth-]
nicity—principles that have been used by genuinely oppressed gr[oups]
around the world to support their own claims to freedom and to inspi[re]
the search for truth. During the 1980s, the victims of real oppression
from China to Eastern Europe took to the streets to demand freedom
from totalitarian governments, relying upon the Western tradition for
inspiration. It is pungently ironic that Western intellectuals, speaking
in the name of mythical victims, were busy repudiating these ideals at
the very moment that the wretched of the earth embraced them.

The recent attacks on capitalism, Christianity, and the humanities
have been mounted in the name of "multiculturalism." To observe the
destructive consequences of true multiculturalism, it is useful to consider
countries like Lebanon, Iraq, Pakistan, Libya, the former Yugoslavia,
and parts of Africa, where ethnic and religious minorities do not need
encouragement from Western radicals to slaughter each other. The
very concept of a "multicultural nation" is self-contradictory. There
can be no real nation without a common culture. A feeling of national
solidarity, which is the necessary condition of being a nation, rests upon
the shared sentiment of cultural belonging. Once this shared feeling is
eroded, there is nothing left to hold the nation together. The United
States no longer promotes the basic values of Western culture: Judeo-
Christian values, ordered liberty, individual responsibility, constitution-
alism, private property, the work ethic, and free markets. Instead, we
promote multiculturalism, diversity, collectivism, and the divisiveness
of race, class, and gender.

At the present time, the United States is being pulled apart by a
struggle among factions led by demagogues urging special "victim"

en, invented civil liberties,
e state, and developed
te property—all of
rt and literature.
anity and the
or regional
nd eth-
ups

igration, much of it illegal,
me of the new immigrants
n their own languages and
o be torn by irreconcilable
n, the nation will split into
her than mutual animosity.
ted to the rise of what is
t apparently came into use
le, your statement is factu-
correct.") Political correct-
a form of cultural warfare,
signed to achieve cultural
hegemony for the progressive elite by denigrating and delegitimizing America's Judeo-Christian civilization as racist, sexist, and oppressive.[43] This is part of the growing tendency to subordinate culture to politics—especially the "identity politics" of affirmative action, feminism, class warfare, egalitarianism, and Third-World globalism. The search for truth has been downgraded by the incessant politicization of everything. Ideological partisans determine the truth of statements depending on their political allegiance, not according to the evidence. This tendency if furthered by the efforts of the media to exaggerate every ideological and political dispute.

We should pause at this point in our analysis to contemplate a final irony: American popular culture exercises a powerful influence on other cultures, most of them much older than ours. This influence signifies a strange kind of vitality, although it is certainly not a sign of cultural excellence. The reason for the world's fascination with American popular culture lies in the awakening of latent psychological impulses in all human societies caused by the explosive combination of mass democracy and consumerism. America is the first country that has managed to evade its past and to live for a sensory present and a utopian future.

---

43   Angelo Codevilla, "The Rise of Political Correctness," *Claremont Review of Books* (Fall 2016), p. 37.

People everywhere see the realization of their dreams in the popular images of luxurious homes, fast cars, beautiful clothes, robust health, plentiful food, and constant novelty. While we should certainly not be scornful of the desire for material comfort, we (and those who imitate us) should nevertheless recognize that there is a price to be paid for the immoderate pursuit of material possessions and sensory gratification. Ibn Khaldun warned that when a society adopts "ever newer forms of luxury and sedentary culture and of peace, tranquility and softness," it loses the virtues born of discipline and sacrifice and becomes an easy target for more robust military or commercial enemies.[44]

There are three plausible prospects for American culture in the twenty-first century. Under the first, literary culture will gradually disappear among the public at large and will be celebrated, if at all, by small and dedicated groups performing the same preservative function as the monasteries of the early Middle Ages.[45] Scientific education, however, will retain its vitality because of its obvious importance to production and communication in a technological world. The result will be a two-tiered society, dominated by highly trained technocrats. The organizations that supply the hardware and software for the electronic age will become increasingly powerful. The public will demand that these organizations be regulated by government, resulting in a new version of the corporate state, managed by the technocratic elite and possessing vast powers to manipulate an ignorant and therefore subservient electorate.

Under the second scenario, increasing immigration and balkanization will produce a society of ethnic groups fighting over official "victim" status and government preferences. The destructive combination of interest group politics, immigration, and demagoguery will render the federal government incapable of controlling its budget or performing other essential functions, and the country will split apart into ethnic or regional factions.

---

44   Ibn Khaldun, *The Muqaddimah* (Princeton: Princeton University Press, 1974), p. 135.

45   See Rod Dreher, *The Benedict Option* (New York: Sentinel, 2017).

There is, however, a third and more hopeful prospect. The central defect of the postmodern consciousness is the failure to recognize that there is an order of being—a harmonious order in which essences and events, the individual and the universe, are ineluctably tied together. The renewal of culture begins with a recognition of this conceptual failure and a determination to preserve and build upon the cultural achievements of the past, including our religious roots. A culture that is linked to metaphysical principles of limitation and order protects the realm of the spirit against the corrosive forces that threaten life and society. The religious and secular institutions of cultural transmission—though weakened by relativism and the erosion of authority—still exist. Religion, in particular, remains an important part of life for many Americans. The achievements of Western culture would not have been possible without Christianity: the Bible (now translated into nearly every language), St. Augustine, St. Thomas Aquinas, Gothic cathedrals, medieval liturgical music, Dante, Giotto, the sacred art of the Renaissance, Luther, Bach, Milton, the Book of Common Prayer, the Catholic counter-reformation, the great religious revivals in America— the list could go on. None of this would have happened without the inspiration of the Christian legacy. It seems possible that America will experience another great religious revival in the future; or, at the very least, that a hardy remnant of believers will be able to survive the current spiritual drought and eventually nurture something better, as Rod Dreher has suggested.[46]

Culture enables man to live a life that is more than blind survival, mindless drudgery, or meaningless consumption; it encompasses all that saves human life from degradation. In Eliot's words, "Culture is that which makes life worth living."[47] Culture also performs the essential social function of binding a people together, particularly in difficult

---

46   *The Benedict Option*, op. cit.

47   T. S. Eliot, *Notes Towards the Definition of Culture*, op. cit., p. 27.

times. The ability of Western culture to perform these functions will be severely tested in the near future. We can only hope that enough of its substance is left so that America at the end of the present century will be remembered for something other than its shopping malls, soap operas, and high-tech Disneylands. We must constantly keep in mind that civilization is fragile and that barbarism and ignorance are never finally defeated. To preserve the cultural achievements gained by our ancestors is a task that will require unremitting diligence on the part of those who still remember.

7

THE CONDITION OF
AMERICAN SOCIETY

NO AMERICAN LIVING IN 1900 could have predicted the remarkable changes that occurred in the twentieth century. The US population increased from 76 million to 275 million. Real per capita gross
domestic product grew eightfold. Virtually every income group has
achieved substantial growth in real incomes since the beginning of
the twentieth century. In 1900, per capita income (in 1999 dollars) for
workers was $4,200; it was $33,700 in 1999. The average hourly wage
(in 1999 dollars) rose from $3.80 to $13.90. Employee benefits rose from
near zero to 27.5 percent of total compensation. The average workweek
dropped from fifty-three hours to forty-two hours, and workplace safety
improved dramatically.[1] In 1900 only a small minority of homes had

---

1   Donald M. Fisk, "American Labor in the 20th Century," Bureau of Labor Statistics 2001. www.bls.
     gov. See Stephen Moore and Lincoln Anderson, "Great American Dream Machine," *Wall Street
     Journal,* (December 21, 2005).

running water and electricity, while virtually all Americans had these and countless other material benefits in 2000. Refrigeration, telephones, cars, dishwashers, TV sets, computers, and cellphones are among the luxuries we now take for granted. The progress in medicine has been astonishing. Average life expectancy during the past century rose from forty-seven years to seventy-seven years. In general, and with exceptions that we will discuss, Americans are much healthier and wealthier and certainly more technologically advanced than ever before. The strength of America's economy and the power of its military are unrivaled. Freedom of speech and religion continue to be well protected (in comparison to other countries) by the rule of law. Millions of emigrants from countries across the globe are willing to risk their lives to get into the United States and share in its bounty.

Yet the recitation of positive statistics does not by itself fully reflect the condition of American society. Data on crime, divorce, illegitimacy, child abuse, drug use, educational malpractice, and cultural decline show that material prosperity has not necessarily improved our lives in a profound sense. This chapter will review the state of what has been called "social capital"—those intangible characteristics that hold a society together.

The Decline of the Old Elite and the Rise of the New Class

Every society throughout recorded history has been led by a dominant element in the population, often called an "elite" or an "establishment." The majority of the population generally follows the lead of the elite in critical aspects of behavior and manners. A century ago, the Italian sociologist Vilfredo Pareto showed, in four volumes of exhaustive documentation, the universality in civilized societies of a dominant elite and the qualities that help the elite survive.[2] Foremost among these qualities, Pareto identified what he called "group persistence," a

---

2   Vilfredo Pareto, *The Mind and Society* (New York: Harcourt Brace and Co., 1935) [Tratto di Sociologia Generale, 1916].

characteristic similar to Ibn Khaldun's "group feeling"—an emotional bond of identification, loyalty, and discipline that binds the dominant group together and gives it strength and cohesion. Examples of successful dominant groups are the Roman aristocracy prior to the first century BC, the British aristocracy of the seventeenth to late nineteenth centuries, and (although Pareto does not use this example) the American Protestant bourgeois elite of the nineteenth and early twentieth centuries. Successful elites are rooted, attached to their families, proud of their heritage, disciplined, and capable of self-sacrifice. The discipline of dominant groups is eroded, according to Pareto, by skepticism, hedonism, luxury, pacifism, sentimentality, excessive concern with commercial success, and other disintegrative social forces.

The historian Arnold Toynbee confirmed that all societies are led by an elite or "creative minority," whose leadership is recognized and followed by the majority through a process of mimesis. The authority of the elite is reinforced by qualities of loyalty, courage, discipline, and creativity—character traits that enable the society to respond effectively to internal and external challenges. The weakening of the elite is associated with a deterioration of morale and other indicia of social malfunction. Eventually, the society either spawns a new elite to act as an effective dominant minority or is overcome by hostile internal or external forces.[3]

The form of social decay most pertinent to modern Western societies was summarized by the Spanish philosopher José Ortega y Gasset in *The Revolt of the Masses,* first published in Spanish in 1930 and in English in 1932, which described the consequences of the emerging rebellion against prevailing social and cultural traditions. Ortega's "masses" were not the working classes of Marxist mythology. The mass man, of whatever social origin, was the mediocre man who demands nothing of himself but conforms to the easiest path and follows the popular fashion. Released from traditional restraints, the mass man

---

3   Toynbee's massive work, *A Study of History,* was published by Oxford University Press in ten volumes which appeared between 1934 and 1954.

demands the right to enjoy political and social privileges even though he lacks the discipline and skill to earn them on his own merits. While insisting upon his "rights" (including the right to government subsidies), he is reluctant to acknowledge any obligations. The vulgarity of the mass consumer proudly affirms itself as worthy of respect; and the style of mediocrity proclaims itself through the "mass media"—an appropriate name for the carrier of mass culture. Ortega saw the rise of mass man as an invasion of internal barbarians that threatened the very foundations of European civilization. "The direction of society," Ortega wrote, "has been taken over by a type of man who is not interested in the principles of civilization."[4]

Both Toynbee and Ortega concluded that social and cultural transmission depended upon the success of the leading class in educating the majority and instilling a sense of responsibility. In the last half of the twentieth century, however, precisely the opposite occurred. Instead of the upper classes transmitting the principles of duty and civilization to the masses, American society succumbed to a process of reverse mimesis in which educational standards decayed and the children of the elite began to ape the dress and manners of felons and the lifestyle of tramps. Disaffected individuals and groups adopted the rhetoric of "rights," often accompanied by disruptive and aggressive behavior, without recognizing that rights imply duties. In part, these trends reflected the leveling effect of the ideology of equality that we have observed in American education and culture.

The old elites, unsure of their own principles, lacked the courage to resist. The old families and patrons of the bourgeois elite did not disappear, but they lost their economic and social dominance. By the end of the 1960s, the old bourgeois establishment had effectively abdicated, and social leadership had been assumed by people who disliked the traditional obligations of honor and self-restraint because they interfered with the radical personal autonomy the new elites demanded.

---

4   Jose Ortega y Gasset, *The Revolt of the Masses* (New York: W. W. Norton Co., 1993 [1932], p. 81).

These were the "baby boomers" and their spokesmen in the media and academia. Since a social establishment, open to new blood but able to command respect, is essential to the production of responsible leaders in a democratic society, the collapse of the old bourgeois elite is a matter that deserves careful attention. How did it happen?

The classic treatise on the decline of the American bourgeois establishment (often called the white Anglo-Saxon Protestant or WASP establishment) is Digby Baltzell's *The Protestant Establishment Revisited,* published in 1991. The ethos of a true establishment emphasizes duty, civility, decency, and the rules of fair play. The nineteenth- and early twentieth-century elites had a sense of stewardship and obligation to their communities. Because an establishment carries the authority and nurtures the values that give a society order and coherence, the decline of the establishment is associated with a decline in social order. As authority weakens, communal harmony declines. The revolt against authority in the 1960s impaired all forms of authority in the name of equality. "As all values are now equal," Baltzell wrote, "no values have any real authority. Thus, social conflict and disorder reign."[5]

The bourgeois elite that governed America from the end of the Civil War until the 1960s was not a closed caste; it was always open to new members, yet it was firmly anchored in family, community, and educational background, and it operated in accordance with a strict social and business code (admittedly subject to periodic invasions by greedy predators). In the last decades of the twentieth century, this "rootedness" broke down under the pressures of restless mobility, self-seeking individualism, cultural decay, and the demands of ethnic and immigrant groups too diverse to be assimilated into any establishment. The turmoil of the 1960s showed that the moral code of the old WASP establishment was no longer able to withstand serious challenges. When the pace of the Vietnam war accelerated, the children of the elite avoided the draft

---

5   Digby Baltzell, *The Protestant Establishment Revisited* (New Brunswick, NJ: Transaction Publishers, 1991), p. 35.

by educational deferments and other devices, while boys from working-class families were shipped out to risk their lives. This was a catastrophic abdication of leadership by America's political establishment.

Prestigious universities quickly caved in to the outrageous demands of hoodlums posing as social revolutionaries. Standards of dress and manners deteriorated in a perverse race for the cultural bottom. The family itself entered into a period of steep decline. The destruction of traditional education by the virtual abandonment of moral and civic instruction (as well as the trivialization of history, literature, and the classics) accelerated the collapse of authority. By the end of the twentieth century, customary social authority had been replaced by naked economic and political power. "When class authority declines," Baltzell observes, "money talks, echoing in a moral vacuum."[6]

At the core of the old bourgeois code were values of civility, honor, self-denial, civic duty, and a liberal education. Our present dominant values are self-indulgence, wealth-seeking, radical egalitarianism, and "multicultural diversity." This new and corrosive combination, as Baltzell argues, fosters moral relativism and atomism: qualities that cannot possibly produce social assimilation or harmony. The first function of an elite is to transmit the culture, and the point of cultural transmission is to "cultivate" the lasting values of truth and beauty that make the culture something more than Circe's pig sty. But the society's values cannot be transmitted if its elders abdicate their duty to teach in order to pursue their own pleasure or ambition. Among contemporary elites—the professional classes that constitute the "urban haute bourgeoisie"—it has become common for both parents to work, abandoning their children to day-care facilities and indulgent schools. It is little wonder that upper-class children, like the lost generation in Whit Stillman's films, grow up in a moral and behavioral wasteland, pervaded by peer-induced vulgarity, self-centeredness, and promiscuity.

---

6   Id., p. 79. On the difference between power and authority, see Bertrand de Jouvenel, *Sovereignty* (Indianapolis: Liberty Fund 1997 [1957]), p. 39.

In decline, the elite loses control over the critical institutions that sustained its power. This failure is apparent, for example, in the WASP establishment's abdication of control over the universities, which are crucial carriers of social and moral values. During the twentieth century, the old elite supinely acquiesced in its own destruction by permitting the best colleges and universities to be taken over and administered by people who openly sought to weaken or destroy parietal rules, military training, religious practice, and other traditional social structures and ideals.

Since no society can survive without a governing elite, the vacuum created by the abdication of the old bourgeois elite is now in the process of being filled by a new leading class that embodies a different set of values. The new class has two distinguishable subsets. Robert Reich has coined the term "symbolic analysts" to describe the first subset. (Another term sometimes used is "new class professionals.") As these labels imply, the influence of this group is based on verbal dexterity, technical skills, and professional training. The professional elite includes lawyers, economists, bureaucrats, college professors, consultants, and technical specialists. The second subset comprises an influential category of people whose power is based not on analytic or intellectual ability but on celebrity, money, and political power. This subset of the new elite includes TV producers, media owners, journalists, political and entertainment celebrities, and high-tech billionaires. Of course, the members of what we might call the "professional elites" and the "celebrity elites" overlap to a considerable extent: for example, in the fields of media, law, and politics.

The professional elites and the celebrity elites (together, the "new class") share a set of values that is quite different from the value system of the defunct bourgeois establishment. Generally speaking, the new class tends to distrust religion, except in bland, nondoctrinal forms. It is far more tolerant than the old elite of abortion, promiscuity, illegitimacy, pornography, and other manifestations of what the WASPs regarded as plain, old-fashioned immorality and vulgarity. It devalues patriotism and tends to favor unlimited immigration. The new class is much more willing to use government power to "solve problems" through sweeping programs featuring egalitarian and redistributive measures. As Angelo Codevilla, an astute chronicler of today's ruling class, has written, "Ever since Woodrow Wilson nearly a century and a half ago at Princeton, colleges have taught that ordinary Americans are rightly ruled by experts because they are incapable of governing themselves. Millions of graduates have identified themselves as the personifiers of expertise and believe themselves entitled to rule."[7]

The sense of place and the local loyalties that were features of the old bourgeois ethos mean nothing to the new elites, who are highly mobile, syncretic, and globalist by temperament. Their leaders are not chosen for character or accomplishment but rather for personality, celebrity, and skill at manipulating the media. In order to enhance its own power, the new class has undermined, in the name of equality and diversity, those traditional institutions that previously supported the hegemony of the old bourgeois establishment, such as the family, the military, the church, and the classical humanist curriculum. The new class in America can be identified by its favored location (the coasts and the big urban centers) and its ideological preferences (secular, liberal, and statist).

The above analysis is not intended to suggest that the new elite class is monolithic or firmly established. It is, in fact, fluid, and its boundaries shift in keeping with the mobility and instability that pervade today's society. Fortunately, American society still contains "residues" (to use Pareto's term) of patriotism, individual responsibility, localism, religion, and other traditional moral and social norms. The groups embodying these traditional residues can occasionally be politically mobilized, as was the case in the 2000 and 2016 presidential elections. Neither has the Protestant establishment entirely disappeared as an effective social force. It still operates in a few selected areas, such as fundraising for charities, where WASP allegiances and social skills are particularly useful. Once the receptions at the art museums and symphony halls are over, however,

---

7   Angelo M. Codevilla, "The Cold Civil War," *Claremont Review of Books* (Spring 2017), p. 24.

the aging denizens of the fading WASP culture generally retreat to their country clubs and leave the driving to others. The management of important social issues is increasingly left to government, which, beginning in the early twentieth century, has been managed primarily by the progressive new elites, who have the will to gain and maintain power.

In large part, the decline of the old WASP establishment is attributable to the decline of its religious and metaphysical foundations. As its name implies, the largely Protestant establishment owed its moral vigor to deeply held convictions of faith and mission. Beginning in the late nineteenth century, the conceptual bases of the Protestant elite's worldview were gradually eroded by positivistic and utilitarian systems that reduced the understanding of human experience to the methods of empirical science and emphasized the individuals' pursuit of their own self-interest, with the goal of achieving the greatest possible satisfaction of wants rather than the fulfillment of obligations. The result was to replace social bonds of duty, loyalty, and civic virtue with goals of self-fulfillment, egalitarianism, and relativism. This philosophical shift was disastrous for the old elite because its entire *raison d'être* was based on traditional norms of stoicism and self-restraint that no longer commanded acceptance among the opinion-makers. The WASP consensus was also undermined by the rise of liberal Protestantism in the twentieth century. Activists in the major denominations, especially the socially prominent Episcopal Church, moved toward the political left, replacing traditional dogma with issues of social justice. Once the spiritual foundations of the old elite's hegemony had been eroded, it was easy for the new, articulate class to subvert the authority of the WASPs through ridicule and appeal to impulses of equality and self-indulgence. This appeal was aided by the breakdown of traditional humanist education. By the end of the twentieth century, this intellectual disintegration threatened the very structure of society. As sociologist Talcott Parsons observed in the 1930s, any social structure is "formed mainly by a common system of normative rules which ... rest upon a system of ultimate common value attitudes."[8] If the prevailing attitude is "every man for himself and all values are relative," there is not much commonality left other than a demand for more material satisfaction—a demand that has no assignable limits.

Individualism and Community

Americans have always valued individualism, an attitude that favors personal freedom and recognizes the moral worth of the individual. Individualism is nurtured in the family and in strong communities, whose members support self-reliant people and individual rights; it is found only in societies with well-developed habits of individual responsibility. A society is not a mere abstraction but is based on particular relationships and communities existing over long periods of time. These relationships are maintained through families, clubs, churches, universities, commercial organizations, sports, and other institutions and rituals. A community enforces its values through socially imposed limits to deviance. Children in healthy societies do not regularly disobey the rules because their misconduct brings their parents into disrepute. Strong social networks encourage respectful and disciplined behavior. Recent social trends, however, have undermined the communal behavior that is critical to an effective civil society.

In the last year of the twentieth century, the Harvard sociologist Robert Putnam published an important book, titled *Bowling Alone: The Collapse and Revival of American Community,* in which he set forth a theory of social capital, emphasizing the value of social networks based on norms of reciprocity, trustworthiness, and community bonding. After an exhaustive review of the available evidence, Putnam concluded that, for the first two-thirds of the century, Americans were deeply engaged in community life, but that community engagement and social capital fell noticeably in the last one-third of the century. The years 1960–2000 saw a sharp drop in civic activity, including a decline

---

8   Talcott Parsons, *The Structure of Social Action,* I (New York: Free Press, 1968 [1937]), p. 464.

in the percentage of citizens who voted, declining knowledge of public affairs, and lower participation in public activities. In the private sphere, numerous studies showed a decline in family activities (such as family dining), socializing with neighbors, and traditional community activities, such as league bowling and bridge. The evidence suggests, Putnam writes, that "the last several decades have witnessed a striking diminution of regular contacts with our friends and neighbors."[9] While it is true that charitable giving in the United States remains strong, Putnam argues that many nonprofit organizations are simply vehicles for fundraising rather than community organizations with real social ties. In sum, what he calls "social connectedness" (analogous to Ibn Khaldun's "group feeling") is deteriorating. Putnam's subtitle indicates the possibility of a revival of community, but his hopes for revival are relegated to a wish list in the last few pages of the book, with little evidence to support a real probability of improvement.

What circumstances in the late twentieth century contributed to social disengagement? A fundamental factor, already considered in a previous chapter, is the omnipresence of television and more recently the smartphone, which allow people to consume entertainment, in private and alone, for a large part of their lives. More TV watching and smartphone absorption means less time for community participation and social involvement. A second fundamental factor is the movement of women out of the home into the workplace, which Putnam describes as "the most portentous social change of the last half century."[10] It is obvious that the absence of wives and mothers at home cuts down on home-centered social activities. A less-tangible factor is the decline of the bourgeois elite, previously discussed, and the accompanying decline

---

9   Robert D. Putnam, *Bowling Alone: The Collapse and Revival of American Community* (New York: Simon & Schuster, 2000), p. 115. For a compelling defense of strong communities, see Robert A. Nisbet, *The Quest for Community: A Study in the Ethics of Order and Freedom* (Wilmington, DE: ISI Books, 2010 [1953]).

10   Id., p. 194.

in respect for authority and tradition among the young.

The weakening of communities has been exacerbated by the social effects of deindustrialization and job loss due to automation and foreign competition, discussed in Chapter 3. Economic prosperity is concentrated in the elite ZIP codes, while communities outside of the prosperous urban zones are deteriorating. "The result," according to Timothy Carney in a recent book, *Alienated America,* "is a sort of geographic determinism."[11] Many people in these less-fortunate communities are so busy trying to maintain their standard of living that they have little time for their own families, let alone their neighbors. These communities, therefore, lack the solidly based local institutions and relationships necessary for effective social control. Many cities are more prosperous, although murder, robbery, drug abuse, and vandalism are ordinary daily occurrences in some major cities. Shame and guilt, the traditional internal regulators, no longer operate successfully because the family and social structures necessary to communicate moral judgments have weakened.

A further recognizable trend is the expansion of government to provide a whole range of services that families and private organizations used to provide, including income support and healthcare for the elderly and for lower and moderate income groups. As we will discuss in more detail in the next chapter, these welfare programs have the effect of making more of the population dependent on government; but the state is remote, amoral, and incapable of taking the place of families and organic communities in the complex process of socialization.

---

11   Timothy P. Carney, *Alienated America: While Some Places Thrive While Others Collapse* (New York: Harper Collins, 2019), p. 61; see also J. D. Vance, *Hillbilly Elegy: A Memoir of a Family and Culture in Crisis* (New York: Harper, 2016).

Inequality

Observers often criticize the United States for the rising inequality of its citizens' incomes. President Obama, for example, warned of "a dangerous and growing inequality." Congressional Budget Office figures show that in 2014, household income was $19,000 for the lowest quintile of earners and $281,000 for the highest quintile. Thus, the highest quintile earned 14.8 times more than the lowest quintile. However, these income figures do not account for government means–tested transfer payments (such as Medicaid, food stamps, and Supplemental Security Income) and federal taxes. After government transfers and taxes, these averages were $31,000 and $207,000, a difference of only 6.7 times. Poverty in America is relative and fluid; the predominant pattern is that individuals are likely to experience poverty for a few years, especially when they are young, but then rise out of poverty later in their careers.[12]

It is true that there continues to be a significant gap between the richest Americans and the poorest. But this is largely because the United States is one of the freest societies in the world, and free societies allow the creators of wealth to keep it. People are not equal in abilities or motivation, and those who are more productive acquire more wealth. (An additional reason for the poor performance of many of those at the lower level of the income scale is America's flawed system of public education, discussed in Chapter 5.) Traditional Anglo-American institutions such as free-market capitalism, private property rights, and the rule of law also contribute to economic prosperity, which is necessarily unevenly distributed. In short, inequality is simply a byproduct of human capability and institutions. The attempts by government to reduce inequality by coercively redistributing wealth can be counterproductive if they reduce

---

12 Mark R. Rank and Thomas A. Hirschl, "The Likelihood of Experiencing Relative Poverty over the Life Course," https://journals.plos.org/plosone/articles?id=10.1371/journal.pone.0133513; Congressional Budget Office, "Average Income, Means-Tested Transfers, and Federal Taxes per Household, by Income Group, 2014," www.cbo.gov/topics/income-distribution. See Donald Devine, "Puncturing the Inequality Fact Balloon," Newsmax.com Insiders (July 17, 2018).

economic growth, thereby harming everyone, including those at the bottom of the income scale who are trying to improve circumstances for themselves and their families.

The Family

In human societies, the family is the most universal of all associations and is the basic guardian of morals and manners. The social function of the family is to raise children and acculturate them as members of the community. As human history evolved, the family proved to be an essential device for the transmission of behavioral rules and cultural values. Family members also have traditionally provided mutual comfort and support in times of need and in old age. The family also provides the training ground for the larger political community.

The family, in turn, is based upon the institution of marriage. The US founders understood that marriage was fundamental to a stable society. As James Wilson, a participant in the Constitutional Convention of 1787, wrote, "To that institution (marriage), more than to any other, have mankind been indebted for the share of peace and harmony which has been distributed among them."[13] Charles Murray, in his influential book *Coming Apart: The State of White America, 1960–2010,* has shown that marriage among the white population in the United States began to decline around 1970. By 2010, it had become clear that the decline in marriage was much more severe for lower-income and less-educated whites than for better-off and better-educated whites. The marriage decline for the former was steep: in 2010 only 48 percent of prime-age whites in the lower income group were married, compared to 84 percent in 1960; while the marriage decline among the upper middle class was scarcely noticeable. This is a dramatic difference and one that reflects a real crisis for an important segment

---

13   James Wilson, "Of the Natural Rights of Individuals," *Collected Works of James Wilson*, vol. 2, Chapter XII, ed. Mark David Hall and Kermit L. Hall (Indianapolis: Liberty Fund, 2007), Online Library of Liberty.

of American society.[14] Murray attributes this steep decline in marriage in the lower-income group to rising divorce rates as well as to a large increase in the population of those who never married at all. A review of the extensive literature on this subject will lead the objective observer to agree with Charles Murray's conclusion that "the traditional family plays a special, indispensable role in human flourishing and that social policy must be based on this truth."[15]

Social developments beginning in the second half of the twentieth century have subjected the family to enormous pressures. The rate of divorce in the United States more than doubled between 1960 and 1990 and declined slightly thereafter.[16] Mounting evidence shows that divorce has damaging and long-lasting financial, emotional, and behavioral effects on children. "Divorce damages society. It consumes social and human capital. It substantially increases cost to the taxpayer, while diminishing the taxpaying portion of society. It diminishes children's future competence in all five of society's major tasks or institutions: family, school, religion, marketplace and government.... Divorce also permanently weakens the family and the relationship of children and parents."[17] Of equal or greater significance, beginning in the 1960s, there was an explosive rise in illegitimate births. By the end of the twentieth century, the out-of-wedlock birthrate for the country as a whole was one-third (compared with 5 percent in 1960) with a far higher illegitimacy rate for blacks. By the year 2014, the proportion of

---

14   Charles Murray, *Coming Apart: The State of White America, 1960–2010* (New York: Crown Forum, 2012), pp. 158–59. Murray's study focused on white people. It should be noted that the decline of marriage was even more severe among blacks. See Timothy P. Carney, *Alienated America, op. cit.,* p. 70, for similar findings.

15   *Id.* p. 304.

16   U.S. Census Bureau, Statistical Abstract of the United States, 2011, Table 78.

17   Patrick F. Fagan and Aaron Churchill, "The Effects of Divorce on Children," Marri Research (January 11, 2012), p. 1. See also Judith S. Wallerstein, Julia M. Lewis, and Sandra Blakeslee, *The Unexpected Legacy of Divorce: a 25-year Landmark Study* (New York: Hyperion, 2000).

out-of-wedlock births climbed to more than 40 percent (the percentage for blacks was over two-thirds). The evidence shows that the children of single-parent families are far more likely to be poor and unhealthy, to abuse drugs, to drop out of school, to be unemployed, to commit crimes, and to become parents of one-parent families in their turn. The extensive research that has been done in this area confirms Timothy Carney's conclusion: "the single most important factor in the upward mobility of a child is the strength of families in the community." The trend toward fatherless families is a harbinger of social decline.[18]

Some have argued that many people who used to marry now cohabit so that their children are still being raised in two-parent families. The evidence, however, indicates that the outcomes for these children are no better than for children living with a single parent or in a "cohabiting stepparent" family.[19]

Another important change in the family occurred as a result of the flood of women into the workplace. Between 1960 and 2000, the rate of participation in the workforce by married women nearly doubled, from 32 percent to more than 61 percent. By 2008, 62 percent of married women with children under six (and an even higher percentage of unmarried women with children) worked outside of the home. Most of these women worked full time. For more than half of married families with children, *both* parents were employed. In the 1950s, less than

---

18   Timothy P. Carney, *Alienated America, op. cit.,* p. 85; Pew Research Center: Social and Demographic Trends, www.pewsocialtrends.org/2015. There is also a class aspect to the marriage issue: see Charles Murray, *Coming Apart,* Chapter 8, and "Special Report: Marriage," *The Economist* (November 25, 2017), reporting that marriage is more popular among affluent, educated people while lower income groups are less likely to marry and stay married. A study by the Witherspoon Institute reported that only 10 percent of US children raised in a two-parent family live below the poverty line, while more than 60 percent of children from single-parent families live below the poverty line. "The Two-Biological-Parent Family and Economic Prosperity: What's Gone Wrong," The Witherspoon Institute, Public Discourse (July 20, 2011), thepublicdiscourse.com/2011/07/3532.

19   Murray, *Coming Apart,* pp. 168–69.

one-third of married women were employed.[20] The goals of women in the workplace are directed toward self-fulfillment and money making. These goals are different from family goals, which are essentially communitarian: procreation, nurturing the young, caring for the old, and maintaining permanent bonds of affection, support, and commitment. The increasing number of working mothers thus reinforces the trend, already quite pronounced in American society, toward the culture of personal autonomy, featuring hyper-individualism and self-gratification at the expense of community and "bonding" institutions. These attitudes tend to weaken the "group feeling" that sustains a society. The fact that many children grow up in homes where both parents are absent much of the time may contribute, along with the distractions of the digital age, to the sense of loneliness, isolation, and resentment that is often observed among youth in America.

Marriage in America is a troubled institution. The decline in marriage may be partly a result of deindustrialization; in regions where well-paid male working-class jobs have declined due to technology or globalization, couples are reluctant to marry. It may also be influenced by a welfare state that enables lower-income women to support children without a working husband. What does this trend mean for our society? Marriage is the key to social harmony and therefore to civilization because it controls and channels the aggression and sexual impulses of young males. In the late twentieth century, Western societies decided to free men from a sense of responsibility through easy divorce and a new moral code that placed little or no stigma on sexual promiscuity. Why, then, would a man display the qualities of loyalty and restraint that underlie what we call "civilized" behavior? It is hardly accidental that antisocial impulses are most destructive in those urban communities in which married families are rarest.

Whether other institutions can take over the role of families remains

---

20   U.S. Bureau of Labor Statistics: Women in the Labor Force (2014); Statistical Abstract of the United States, Table 598 (Census Bureau 2010); Putnam, op. cit., p. 194.

to be seen. The most likely such institution is government. As the economic and social roles of the family weaken under the impact of the social forces outlined above, the caregiving function of the family is slowly but relentlessly passing from families to government and organizations financed and controlled by government, through such programs as Social Security, Medicare, Medicaid, state-provided housing, state-sponsored day care, public schools, and other government-supported organizations. The vacuum left by the debility of the family will soon be filled by the only remaining source of effective authority—the state and its managing elites. Political economist Nicholas Eberstadt has made the point succinctly: "as the past century of social policy has demonstrated, government is a highly imperfect substitute for the family—and a very expensive one."[21]

Are there political measures that will help to restore the position of the family as the keystone of the natural social order? Two proposals that have been advanced and should be encouraged are, first, large tax benefits tied to marriage and children that would encourage the nurturing of new generations; and, second, the support of homeschooling and private, as opposed to public schools. The family is a necessary foundation of our children's future, and we should do whatever we can to defend it. At present, however, the forces that are pulling the family apart appear to be stronger than those holding it together. This is not a good omen for social cohesion.

Population and Immigration

A few decades ago, the phrase "demography is destiny" was popular, especially among those who worried about overpopulation. Today, the concern of those who study the dynamics of population change is different. The key demographic statistic is the "total fertility rate" (TFR), which is the number of babies the average woman would bear if she

---

21   Nicholas Eberstadt, "The Global Flight from the Family," *Wall Street Journal* (February 21–22, 2015), p. A11.

survives until the end of her reproductive years. In order for a country to maintain a steady population, it needs a TFR of 2.1. America's TFR as of 2014 was 1.87, rather close to the key number and higher than the TFR in most industrial countries. The TFR rates for all European countries are below 2.1 and, for some countries, far below, but America's rate is not altogether reassuring. America's TFR is kept at this level by the large number of Hispanic women who live here, whose fertility rate is significantly above 2.1 but may not remain at that level. Non-Hispanic middle-class women are reproducing at rates well below the key number. Already, the American population is aging, and it is predictable that it will age more rapidly. An aging population is likely to express a preference for security and comfort over adventure, risk, and innovation, and elderly voters will demand more healthcare and other services, placing a heavier burden on taxpayers. There are many reasons for the declining rate of reproduction, including modern methods of birth control, the delay of marriage, and the growing popularity of college, graduate school, and careers for women. Unless we admit many more female immigrants with high fertility rates, the US population will shrink. Throughout the history of civilization, declining populations have been accompanied by economic stagnation, military weakness, and other social ills.[22]

The demographic threat to Europe should serve as a warning. The population of Europe is about 741 million. The native European population is rich, aging, and shrinking; Europe's overall numbers are sustained by immigration, largely from the Middle East and Africa. The population of Africa is approximately 1.2 billion. This population

---

22   Central Intelligence Agency, The World Factbook, "Total Fertility Rate"; "Why American Women Are Having Fewer Babies Than Ever," Washington Post (August 6, 2016). See Jonathan V. Last, What To Expect when No One's Expecting: America's Coming Demographic Disaster (New York: Encounter Books, 2014). The Center for Disease Control reported that the US birthrate continued to fall in 2018 to less than 3.8 million births—the lowest number of births in 32 years. The general fertility rate was 59 births per 1,000 women, a record low for the US. www.cdc.gov/nchs/data/vsrr/vsrr007–508.pdf.

is young, growing, poor, hungry, and desperate for a better life. Many people in Africa and the Middle East are eager to improve conditions for themselves and their families by migrating into Europe and taking advantage of its wealth, opportunities, and welfare benefits. The short journey to Europe can be dangerous but is irresistible to many. More and more people will make the effort to reach Europe in the coming decades, and as the numbers grow larger and more desperate, there will be no practical way of stopping them. (See Jean Raspail's prophetic novel, *The Camp of the Saints,* published in 1973.) Some areas of European cities have already been effectively occupied by Islamic refugees, and this trend will continue. By the end of this century, European civilization as we have known it may no longer exist in its original heartland. Whether it can be kept alive in some parts of North and South America, in Australia, or elsewhere remains to be seen.[23]

The demographic decline will also have an adverse effect on the West's welfare states. For example, the number or retirees in the US Social Security system is now rising more rapidly than the number of contributors into the system. The solvency of the Medicare system is similarly imperiled. To preserve these entitlements for future generations will require much higher taxes, a drastic cut in benefits, or a massive increase in government spending (with an accompanying increase in the already-elephantine public debt). At the present time, it is hard to find politicians willing to face up to this dilemma. This in itself is a sign of loss of nerve by American political leaders.

The argument is often made that the problems arising from a shrinking or aging population can be solved by bringing in large numbers of immigrants. Immigration into the United States has in fact, increased significantly since the Immigration and Naturalization Act of 1965, which abolished an earlier quota system based on national origin

---

23   See Christopher Caldwell, *Reflections on the Revolution in Europe: Immigration, Islam, and the West* (New York: Doubleday, 2009); Douglas Murray, *The Strange Death of Europe: Immigration, Identity, Islam* (London: Bloomsbury, 2017).

and established a new immigration policy permitting each immigrant to bring in other family members ("chain migration"). This change resulted in a surge of immigration, especially from Mexico and Central America, but recently has included many from other regions. Much of this immigration is illegal, and many of the migrants are lacking in basic skills and less likely to assimilate than previous migrants. The total number of immigrants, legal and illegal (including their American-born children), has been variously estimated at between 40 and 60 million as of December 31, 2015. Official figures from the Office of Immigration Statistics (OIS) indicate that there were about 44 million immigrants living in the United States in 2016, of whom 11.4 were estimated to be "unauthorized." The caravans of migrants are aided and abetted by smugglers, traffickers, and nongovernmental organizations. Most of the unauthorized immigrants come from Mexico and Central America. Many of the migrants are accompanied by children because the migrants have been told that arriving with young children increases their chances of successful entry. The migrants also bring diseases with them, including pneumonia, tuberculosis, and other serious illnesses.[24] The flood of immigrants has been stimulated by the widespread availability of false documentation and a lack of interest by politicians in the enforcement of the law. Many of the migrants take advantage of the social benefits that America generously gives and which politicians are willing to bestow on future voters.

A further contributing factor in the increase of illegal immigration is the demand by American business and agricultural employers for cheap, low-skilled workers. "As long as there are gains to be had, by both the

---

24   See "The Caravan to Nowhere: the March from Honduras Echoes the Mariel Boatlift," *Wall Street Journal* (October 22, 2018); Michael Barone, "We've Been Here Before: America and the Dynamics of Immigration," *Modern Age* (Summer 2016), p. 9; Steven A. Camarota and Karen Ziegler, "Record 44.5 Million Immigrants in 2017," Center for Immigration Studies (September 15, 2018); Migration Policy Institute (February 8, 2018), "Frequently Requested Statistics on Immigrants and Immigration in the United States," www.migrationpolicy.org; "50 Crossers Every Day Need Urgent Medical Care," *Washington Times* (January 1, 2019), p. 1. The official figures on the number of illegal immigrants are probably understated.

employers and the potential migrants, and few penalties to pay, by both the employers and the potential migrants, the incentives remain and illegal immigration continues."[25]

Businesses and the wealthy benefit from illegal immigration because they want to hire low-wage workers, but this harms native workers who compete with undocumented immigrants for jobs. Those who favor large-scale immigration argue that the masses of immigrants entering the United States in the early twentieth century were readily hired and clearly benefited the economy. This was true because there was a booming manufacturing sector eager for low-skilled labor, and the demand continued until the new workers were absorbed. In the 1920s, Congress sharply reduced the number of immigrants, leading to a period of only moderate immigration, but, as noted, immigration increased after the 1965 immigration act. The cultural pressure for assimilation is far less intense in today's climate of multicultural diversity and lax immigration enforcement.

Illegal immigration has imposed serious costs on the United States. The Federation for American Immigration Reform estimates that illegal immigration costs American taxpayers more than $130 billion annually, most of which is borne by state and local governments. A 2017 study estimated that 23 percent of public school students (and even more in border states such as Texas) came from immigrant households, compared to 7 percent in 1980.[26] The fiscal impact on the welfare system (for example, food stamps, cash benefits, and Medicaid) is serious. As Milton Friedman once said, "It's just obvious you can't have free immigration and a welfare state." The reason why this is so is that large-scale immigration brings in many poor people who are entitled to welfare

---

25 George J. Borjas, *We Wanted Workers: Unraveling the Immigration Narrative* (New York: W. W. Norton & Company, 2016), p. 59.

26 Federation for American Immigration Reform, "The Fiscal Burden of Illegal Immigration on United States Taxpayers" (September 27, 2017), www.fairus.org. See Steven A. Camarota, "How Large-Scale Immigration Has Impacted American Schools," Center for Immigration Studies (March 2017).

benefits, such as food stamps and Medicaid. The evidence shows that immigrant households are far more likely to receive welfare assistance than native households. Forty-six percent of immigrant households receive some type of public assistance.[27]

Immigration advocates argue that immigrants are needed to do "jobs that Americans won't do." But this is economically absurd. If the wages paid for these jobs were higher, Americans would do them, but the wages are depressed by the continual influx of immigrants willing to work for low wages. Simple common sense tells us that the availability of large numbers of immigrants working for low pay will depress wage levels in those industries to which the immigrants are attracted. Employers are happy to take advantage of this situation, but American wage earners bear the burden.

As shown by the debates during the run-up to the presidential election of 2020, many political progressives apparently want no restrictions at all on illegal immigration—that is to say, they favor open borders and are willing to grant health, education, welfare, and even voting rights to all immigrants, legal and illegal. If this view should prevail, there would be little point to US citizenship, and the very concept of nationhood would be called into question.

The citizens of a country, like the members of a family, will make sacrifices and bear burdens so long as they feel bound by a common bond (group feeling) that encompasses the tangible and intangible factors of history, institutions, religion, and ideas. The proponents of mass immigration and cultural diversity, however, are more concerned with protecting the particular characteristics of minority groups than with advancing the good of the community as a whole. Moderate numbers of skilled and motivated immigrants can and should be admitted, but mass migrations pose a threat to social cohesion and national identity. The United States already has too many people who cannot or will not work; adding new waves of unskilled aliens is irresponsible. No one

---

27   George Borjas, *We Wanted Workers*, pp. 172–82.

knows what the cultural or political impact of additional millions of Hispanic and non-Western immigrants will be, but when that impact becomes apparent, it may be too late. The hard truth is that a nation can only tolerate a certain amount of immigration without destroying the sense of national solidarity that is at the center of a society's common identity. The Roman Empire was destroyed, in part, by a massive migration of peoples whom it could not assimilate. This is a historical lesson that we should not forget.[28] As a matter of prudent policy, in addition to strengthening border enforcement, we should move away from the system of "chain migration" established by the immigration act of 1965 and adopt a system favoring immigrants meeting certain levels of education and skill—in other words, people with high-earning potential who are less likely to end up on welfare. The need for farm workers can be met by issuing temporary work visas.

Crime

In the 1960s, rates of violent crime and drug use in the United States began to rise rapidly, especially among juveniles. Crime rates in American cities soared from the late 1960s through the early 1990s. Then, in the late 1990s, the violent crime rate began to drop significantly. The violent crime rate, according to FBI data, was 611 per 100,000 people in 1997, 472 per 100,000 people in 2007, and 386 per 100,000 people in 2016.[29] While no one is sure exactly why this happened, possible explanations include the aging of the population, increases in the size of urban police forces, better police administration, more aggressive patrols based on the "broken windows" (or "community disorder") theory of policing, and the "abandonment of hard drugs by

---

28   See Scott McConnell, "The Path to Ethnic Strife: Mass Immigration and the Future of the West," *The American Conservative* (March/April 2018), p. 23.

29   FBI Uniform Crime Reporting Program, www.ucr.fbi.gov/crime-in-the-u.s.-2016. "Violent crimes" are murder, manslaughter, rape, robbery, and aggravated assault.

a new generation of African-Americans."[30] Nevertheless, violent crime is still more than double what it was in 1960 and is especially severe in the poorest neighborhoods of America's major cities.[31]

It seems intuitively obvious that the rise in violent crime in the last half of the twentieth century (about 250 percent according to Department of Justice statistics) must have some correlation with the disintegration of family structures and the breakdown of community and authority, and this conclusion is supported by research.[32] Every major city in the country contains one or more central districts inhabited by a so-called "underclass" that appears to be trapped in a cycle of crime, drugs, illegitimacy, and violence. Murders in the United States are very concentrated: 54 percent of US counties in 2014 had zero murders, while 2 percent of counties had 51 percent of murders. Violent crime is concentrated in certain identifiable urban areas. The worst 5 percent of counties—urban areas containing 47 percent of the US population—account for 68 percent of murders.[33] These crime-ridden centers are dominated by hordes of young males unattached to family or other structural restraints, who join together in competing gangs and thrive on selling drugs and other criminal behavior.

The problem of crime is complex, and there is no easy solution. It is evident that locking up hardened criminals will reduce violent crime. Criminal justice data show that most violent crimes are committed by repeat offenders: 77 percent of prison inmates are rearrested

---

30   Barry Latzer, "The Last Black Hope," *Claremont Review of Books* (Winter 2008–9), pp. 32, 35; William J. Stuntz, "Law and Disorder: The Case for a Police Surge," *The Weekly Standard* (February 23, 2009), p. 19; "The Curious Case of the Fall in Crime," *The Economist* (July 20, 2013), p. 9.

31   See FBI Uniform Crime Reports: Offenses per 100,000 Population.

32   John P. Hoffmann and Mikaela J. Dufur, "Family and School Capital Effects on Delinquency: Substitutes or Complements," *Sociological Perspectives*, Vol. 51 (2008), pp. 29–62; Putnam, *Bowling Alone*, pp. 310 et seq; John J. DiIulio, Jr., "Young and Deadly," *National Review* (April 3, 2000), p. 28.

33   Crime Prevention Research Center, www.crimeresearch.org.

within five years.[34] These violent recidivists should be convicted and locked up. Available law enforcement resources should be devoted to dealing with dangerous criminals, not petty offenders, many of whom are capable of changing. Imprisoning young malefactors during the most potentially productive period of their lives does not seem to be a particularly constructive solution. Imprisonment contributes to the impoverishment not only of the prisoner but also of his family, reducing their potential economic contribution to society. We should pay more attention to rehabilitation, education, training, and social reintegration programs, although, as noted above, incarceration for hardcore incorrigibles is essential.

To restore cohesion and discipline over the long run, we will have to bring back strong communities that exercise effective control over our children's behavior. This will require the public, among other things, to "just say no" to the decadent culture of promiscuity, violence, and degraded entertainment that pervades American life. The present climate of permissiveness and relativism provides little evidence that such a cultural reversal is likely. In the absence of a restoration of civilized moral standards, harsher deterrence seems unavoidable. As Edmund Burke observed in 1791, "Society cannot exist unless a controlling power upon will and appetite be placed somewhere, and the less of it there is within, the more there must be without. It is ordained in the eternal constitution of things, that men of intemperate minds cannot be free. Their passions forge their fetters."[35]

Work, Poverty, and Welfare

The United States has always been a society in which work was a recognized value as well as a contributor to economic productivity. The

---

34 Bureau of Justice Statistics, www.bjs.gov; National Institute of Justice, Office of Justice Programs, www.nji.gov.

35 Edmund Burke, "To a Member of the National Assembly," *Works,* Vol. I (New York: Harper & Brothers, 1837), p. 583.

employment-to-population ratio ("work rate") for Americans sixteen and older was around 67 percent in 1990 but declined to 63 percent by 2017. Beginning in the 1970s, work rates for men over twenty dropped sharply—from over 80 percent in 1970 to 68 percent in 2015. By 2015, nearly 22 percent of US men between the ages of twenty and sixty-five were not engaged in paid work of any kind.[36] The statistics issued by public officials and the news media stating that the United States is at or near "full employment" are misleading because this number does not include those millions who have dropped out of the workforce.

The trend of male detachment from the workforce may, to some extent, be attributable to the extraordinary prosperity of the United States, which can afford to support millions of people who do not work. This is consistent with Ibn Khaldun's observation that affluent societies indulge themselves with leisure and luxuries that hungrier, rising societies cannot afford. In the case of contemporary America, automation has reduced the demand for low-skilled and middle-skilled labor. In addition, beginning around the turn of the twenty-first century, a flood of imports from low-wage countries (particularly China) poured into American markets, and US companies began to shift production abroad. The combination of automation and low-wage competition from abroad (accompanied by a big increase in immigrant labor, much of it illegal) destroyed many factories and jobs in the industrial heartland of the country, although a demand for other jobs has been created, often requiring different skills. (See the discussion in Chapter 3.)

Also, the growing welfare state provides many more benefits for men not in the labor force than were available a generation ago. In 2013, 63 percent of homes with nonworking men received one or more means-tested benefits (such as food stamps and Medicaid) versus 43.6 percent

---

36 See "The Long-Term Decline in Prime-Age Male Labor Force Participation," Executive Office of the President (June 2016), https://obamawhitehouse.archives.gov; Bureau of Labor Statistics, data. bls.gov; Nicholas Eberstadt, *Men Without Work* (West Conshohocken, PA: Templeton Press, 2016), pp. 20–22; Edward Lazear, "The Incredible Shrinking Workforce," *Wall Street Journal* (December 8, 2017), p. A17.

in 1965.[37] A report by the White House Council of Economic Advisors issued in July 2018 found that the majority of nondisabled working age recipients of food stamps, Medicaid, and rental housing assistance worked few if any hours per week while receiving benefits.[38]

In addition, disability benefits—government payments such as Social Security Disability Insurance (SSDI) and other government programs for those officially declared incapable of working to support themselves—have been growing rapidly. The exact amounts are difficult to determine, but Nicholas Eberstadt estimates that "the United States is currently spending hundreds of billions of dollars a year on disability payments and the bureaucracies that administer them," and that 57 percent of prime-age nonworking men lived in homes reporting disability benefits, nearly 20 percentage points higher than in 1985. It is likely that much of the "disability" is feigned, not real. Whatever the cause, there is a growing dependence by working-age males on government welfare and disability programs (and on spouses and families who also provide support), reflecting, in Nicholas Eberstadt's words, "an almost revolutionary change in male attitudes toward work and dependence in postwar America."[39] Some of the rise in disability may be attributable to the growing incidence of obesity among both poor and nonpoor Americans. The United Health Foundation reported that in 2017, one in three adults was obese and that obesity is a leading cause of cardiovascular disease.[40]

In sum, the presence in American society of large numbers of unemployed men is not a good sign. A certain amount of leisure, of course, is a necessary condition of culture. Some people must have the

---

37   Eberstadt, *Men Without Work,* pp. 114–15.

38   Council of Economic Advisors, "Expanding Work Requirements in Non-Cash Welfare Programs" (July 2018), www.whitehouse.gov.

39   Eberstadt, *Men Without Work,* p. 127. See Charles Murray, "The Unbelievable Rise in Physical Disability," in *Coming Apart, op. cit.,* pp. 174–75.

40   www.americashealthrankings.org.

time to contemplate, study, and create. But leisure, if wasted, becomes a vice. Sloth, after all, is one of the seven deadly sins. It degrades men and injures their families. A healthy society would reverse the disengagement from work.

The American economy has experienced a revival in the period 2017–2020, due in part to a significant reduction in taxes and government regulation and to a worldwide economic upturn. This economic improvement has significantly reduced unemployment. Whether these favorable conditions will continue, of course, cannot be predicted.

Civilized societies throughout history have been confronted with relative degrees of poverty. Because of the prosperity generated by America's productive economy over the past two centuries, it has fewer poor people as a percentage of its population than all but a handful of other nations. The United States and other Western societies have sought to reduce the remaining poverty through government welfare programs. In the United States, government spending on the poor increased rapidly beginning in 1965. By 2016, the federal government was spending on "human services" (principally Social Security, Medicare, Medicaid, food stamps, and other income security, education, and veterans benefits) about 15 percent of GDP, more than three times what it spent on such welfare benefits in 1962.[41] But these programs, while they have reduced poverty to some extent, have not succeeded in eliminating it. The existing welfare system, in fact, may exacerbate the problem it was meant to solve by subsidizing idleness, illegitimacy, and family breakup. In an unusual act of political courage, Congress and President Clinton in 1996 replaced the old Aid to Families with Dependent Children program with a new program designed to increase self-sufficiency by imposing work requirements and time limits on recipients. The result was a significant cut in the welfare rolls. Yet the reform legislation failed to address the underlying social ills of dependency, family breakup, and illegitimacy that brought about the welfare

---

41 Pew Research Center, www.pewresearch.org/fact-tank/2017.

problem in the first place. Millions of families (most of them headed by unmarried women) remain dependent on government programs and are no closer to self-sufficiency than they were before welfare was reformed. While the number of families receiving direct cash benefits from Aid to Families with Dependent Children has been greatly reduced, other programs for the poor, including the Earned Income Tax Credit, Medicaid, food stamps, and disability benefits, have been expanded. The increasing dependency on welfare programs, not surprisingly, is accompanied by a decline in work effort on the part of those who receive the benefits. Based on the political realities of the welfare state, it is predictable that these and similar programs will continue to grow, as political parties engage in bidding wars to grant ever-increasing subsidies both to the lower and middle classes. Modern antipoverty programs should, instead, promote self-sufficiency through work requirements and improving America's poor system of public education, which leaves too many young people without the skills they need to succeed.

From the vast literature on this subject, three conclusions emerge. First, many, if not most, long-term dependent individuals have such poor education and skill levels that they are virtually unemployable. This suggests, as we have repeatedly stated, that America's weak system of public education is particularly damaging to the least-favored members of society and that a successful program of vocational training is urgently needed (see the discussion in Chapter 5). Second, since unemployment in the inner cities is a major problem and since many low-skill jobs are taken by immigrants, government could help by reducing immigration. Third, welfare reform measures have not addressed the disastrous increase in out-of-wedlock births and the culture of violence in urban neighborhoods, which are among the principal factors contributing to long-term dependence.

Drugs
Drug addiction in the United States is common among the poor (and increasingly among the nonpoor). The Centers for Disease Control

reported that over 70,000 drug overdose deaths occurred in the United States in 2017, mainly from opioids, including highly addictive and dangerous synthetic opioids, such as fentanyl, that are brought by drug cartels illegally across the US–Mexican border. The flood of opioids into the country is so serious that President Trump declared a National Health Emergency in October 2017. While the opioid crisis is often attributed to overprescription by physicians, the dramatic influx of synthetic opioids smuggled into the United States is a significant factor, emphasizing the urgent need for better security on the country's frontiers. Deaths from methamphetamine overdose are also rising—a serious problem because there are apparently no effective pharmacological treatments for meth addiction.[42]

While poverty is often associated with addiction, the remedy lies in controlling this kind of self-destructive behavior. The roots of poverty are more cultural than economic. We must reject the reigning myths of social welfare liberalism: that the poor are victims of an oppressive, racist society and cannot be held responsible for their own behavior and that poverty can be cured only by government programs. These assumptions are inconsistent with the basic truths that individual responsibility is a necessary condition of individual progress and that excessive dependence on government is incompatible with a free and prosperous society. We will discuss issues related to excessive government in more detail in Chapter 8.

Morals and Manners

In the history of the Western world, as in all other civilizations, religion and morality have been inseparable. The moral values taught to Europeans were those of the Old and New Testament, in addition

---

42 See Andrew Kolodny *et al.* "The Prescription Opioid and Heroin Crisis: A Public Health Approach to an Epidemic of Addiction," *Annual Review of Public Health*, Vol. 30 (March 2015); "Briefing Opioids: The Death Curve," *The Economist* (February 23, 2019); and Michael Patrick Flanagan, "Tracing the Real Root of America's Opioid Crisis," *Washington Times* (February 25, 2019). On Methamphetamine, see "Meth Deaths: Sscourge Upon Scourge," *The Economist* (March 9, 2019).

to the classical virtues taught by the Greek and Roman philosophers and natural lawyers. In the eighteenth century, the doctrinal basis of Christianity began to be questioned. This process was accelerated by Darwin's theory of evolution, and nineteenth century positivist philosophers asserted that no proposition was true unless empirically proven. Moral statements were cast into philosophical disrepute as unprovable and thus unknowable. The radical philosophical split between fact and value led skeptical modern thinkers to the deadly paradox formulated in its starkest terms by Friedrich Nietzsche: that which is valuable (moral and religious doctrine) cannot be true; and that which is true (science) has no value. In this bleak vision, which rejected the essential core of Western philosophy since Plato, truthfulness had turned against morality. In Nietzsche's words: "Insofar as we believe in morality we pass sentence on existence." The supposed contradiction between morality and truth is the foundation of nihilism, defined by Nietzsche as "the radical repudiation of value, meaning, and desirability."[43] It is not entirely clear whether Nietzsche himself shared this pessimistic view or whether he was simply outlining the growth of a modern skeptical attitude. In either case, the shadow of nihilism has fallen on the modern age, with real consequences.

The devaluation of values heralded by Nietzsche has led to a thoroughgoing relativism, which holds that all moral truths are relative to a particular person or group. Relativism is reflected in the public schools, where ethical teaching is based on "values clarification," in which children are not told what is right but instead are taught to distinguish their values from alternative values. It is no surprise, given the absence of moral guidance, that children are confused about morals and that cheating, corruption, and crime pervade all segments of society.

The demoralization of America moved into high gear during the 1960s, a decade that featured a general loosening of sexual restraints as well as outbreaks of civil disobedience and political violence. The sexual

---

43   Nietzsche, *The Will to Power* (New York: Vintage Books, 1968), pp. 7, 10.

revolution was furthered by the discovery of the birth control pill and the widespread availability of abortion, which received judicial approval in *Roe v. Wade* (1973). (The Centers for Disease Control reported that there were more than 45 million abortions in America between 1970 and 2015, lending credence to Pope John Paul II's reference to Western society as a "culture of death.") Social attitudes in America gradually shifted toward greater tolerance of what previous generations had quaintly called "free love." Feminists demanded that women should be liberated from traditional sexual restraints, which was, of course, fine with men. The revolution culminated in the so-called "summer of love" during 1967, when as many as 100,000 "hippies" converged in San Francisco's Haight Ashbury district for a festival of sex, drugs, and rock music. Similar events took place across the country; in general, they were regarded by the press and the public as episodes of youthful exuberance that should not be judged harshly. As the age-old rules of sexual behavior were weakened, women became more vulnerable to predators, as we have recently learned from the widespread revelations of sexual harassment.

Moral relativism is based intellectually upon the assumption that because a moral proposition cannot be verified by empirical proof, it cannot be true or false. But the concept of moral truth is different from that of empirical truth. Empirical or scientific propositions are established by means of a certain method of proof: sensory or scientific verification. Moral propositions, on the other hand, are true because they follow from the nature of man as a rational being capable of choice. (In this discussion, I follow the reasoning of Hadley Arkes in *First Things* [Princeton: Princeton University Press, 1986]). Men have the capacity to reason about alternative actions and to justify the choices they make. Even the radical moral skeptic, when he asserts that others are wrong to impose their values on him, necessarily invokes the logic of morality. The notions of justification and obligation are fundamental to all human societies and are inherent in the very idea of human freedom and respon-sibility. The meaning of responsibility is that one's acts may be judged by others. The process of reasoning that leads to moral judgment derives from the logic of moral reasoning and not from empirical observation, although, of course, empirical proof may be needed to establish relevant facts about the actor's conduct. Our entire legal system is based on the principle that men can choose to do right or wrong; otherwise, why are we justified in punishing some and not others?

Until recently, "good character" was the attribute of the moral person—the result of disciplined habituation to right conduct. Good character was based on the Victorian virtue of self-control and featured such moral values as thrift, hard work, temperance, loyalty, and prudence. In the twentieth century, character was replaced by "personality," which can be defined as "the style or form of a person's presentation of himself, typically in more or less short-lived encounters."[44] Unlike character, personality can be turned on or off, shaped and reshaped. Similarly, self-restraint—the essence of character—has been replaced by permissiveness, self-indulgence, and conspicuous consumption. The destruction of character, the erosion of objective moral standards, and the undermining of authority constitute related aspects of what has been called the "metaphysical platform of modernity," which in recent times has sought to destroy the classical conception of the nature or essence of man and to replace it with the idea that the individual is the product of social convention and personal choice.[45] If the idea of human nature is demolished, it follows that individuals are entirely malleable. Having no determinate form, they may either transform themselves at will or be molded by the state, depending on one's political outlook. This conclusion is congenial to egalitarianism, socialism, feminism, and the other reigning doctrines of the Western intelligentsia. It is hardly necessary to add that this point of view leads to the elimination of a moral order since good and evil are metaphysically nonexistent. And the absence of moral order is moral chaos.

---

44 Anthony Quinton, "Character and Culture," *The New Republic* (October 17, 1983), p. 26.

45 James Patrick, "Modernity as Gnosis," *Modern Age* (Summer/Fall 1987), p. 222.

Moral chaos means tolerance of pornography, sexual license, abortion, drug use, and other forms of conduct which, while always present, were formerly subject to forceful social sanctions. Under the influence of moral relativism, people hesitate to condemn such conduct because to do so might be deemed judgmental or intolerant. The disappearance of enforceable moral standards has put the population of our cities at risk from illegitimacy, crime, and disease. Newsstands and video screens issue a constant barrage of violence, brutality, and sex. The lyrics of popular songs celebrate sadomasochism and perversion. The climate of public debate is increasingly poisonous. All efforts to mobilize the public against pornography and slander are met with scorn by the liberal elites and resistance from the news media and the federal courts. Journalists destroy reputations by making scurrilous allegations based on anonymous sources that are difficult or impossible to verify. Lawsuits against the media for defamation are expensive and uncertain under the US legal system. No one is willing to fight for higher standards; therefore, the standards slip progressively lower. A society in which people cannot defend themselves against depravity and falsehood is in trouble.

The values that define the American character seem to be changing. Surveys two or three decades ago showed that Americans rated hard work, patriotism, commitment to religion, and having children as very important values. A recent survey showed that the proportion of those surveyed choosing these values has fallen, particularly among the young.[46] While public opinion polls are not always reliable, these findings do seem to be consistent with recent manifestations of public sentiment.

The decline of manners has accompanied the erosion of moral standards. Manners in America began to deteriorate rapidly during the 1960s, when many sons and daughters of the upper middle classes decided to look, act, and talk like proletarian revolutionaries. The barbarization of manners was an integral part of the cultural revolution of

---

46   "Old and Young Diverge on Values: Poll Shows Patriotism, Religion, Having Children Rate Lower for More Recent Generations," *Wall Street Journal* (August 26, 2019), p. A4.

that era, which featured aggressive feminism, the frenzy of rock music, and the attack on every form of hierarchy and authority. All of this evidenced a perverse egalitarianism, a *nostalgie de la boue* that could not tolerate the discipline implied by canons of taste and mannered behavior. "Democracy" came to mean a reduction of standards to the lowest common denominator. Parents were increasingly reluctant to discipline their children. Ideals of sportsmanship and dress codes began to disappear, while extravagant public displays of emotion and incivility became widely acceptable. A recent example: "Researchers say the bad sportsmanship, rude behavior and outright violence adults display at youth sporting events has become a national epidemic that sends the wrong message to child athletes and drives referees from playing fields in droves."[47] Shameful conduct no longer shocks anyone. The culture of shamelessness reflects a society that elevates self-esteem over honor and exhibitionism over restraint.

Following the presidential election of 2016, a deepening political conflict brought with it a further decline in manners and civility. Democrats and Republicans, Liberals and Conservatives, attacked each other with increasing hostility. Extremists on both sides, but particularly on the left, initiated bitter confrontations. Radical groups on college campuses and elsewhere tried to prevent those with whom they disagreed from speaking. Editorial commentary in the press and on television became increasingly partisan and unbalanced. These are signs of a society slipping into excess.

Religion and Society

The United States was founded by people who believed that religion is necessary to the survival of republican principles. As George Washington said in his farewell address, "Of all the dispositions and habits which lead to political prosperity, Religion and morality are indispensable

---

47   Adam Zielonka, "'Rabid' Parents Spoil Sports for Youth Leagues," *Washington Times* (July 26, 2019), p. A1.

supports." Common sense tells us that traditional moral values will be affected by the decay of religion. The reason for this is not so much the popular fear of divine judgment after death (although that may play a part) as the capacity of religion to invest customary rules with a legitimate aura of sanctity. While moral philosophers may be able to regulate their conduct in accordance with the principles of utilitarianism, ordinary people need support from a source that rises above the calculus of pleasure and pain. Religion contributes to the formation of moral character and to civic consciousness because it motivates the faithful to act for reasons that transcend their own self-interest. This motivation stimulates an above-average spirit of sacrifice.

The Christian religion, in particular, advances a doctrine of human nature that recognizes the value of the human person. As Pope John Paul II said in 1996:

> Precisely by reflecting on the union of the two natures, human and divine, in the person of the Incarnate Word, Christian thinkers have come to explain the concept of person as the unique and unrepeatable center of freedom and responsibility, whose inalienable dignity must be recognized. This concept of the person has proved to be the cornerstone of any genuinely human civilization.[48]

In the twentieth century, the outward profession of religious belief appeared to decline. Religious practices, to a significant extent, have been watered down and demystified in order to make them more acceptable to a secularized society. America's major institutions, attitudes, and activities are scarcely touched by religious values. The Supreme Court has issued a series of decisions greatly reducing the influence of religion on public life. The public schools have become radically secularized; even the basic facts about the role of religion in history are not adequately taught. Secularization is most advanced among the articulate and influential "new class" of journalists, editors, teachers, lawyers, and

---

48   John Paul II, address to the Pontifical Academies, November 28, 1996.

other professionals who derive their livelihood from the distribution and manipulation of information and opinion. The new class generally regards religion with indifference or skepticism, if not outright hostility, an attitude that is part of the damaging legacy of multiculturalism that seeks to undermine the intellectual formation of the West. The modern secular state attempts to confine religion to private life and thus to marginalize religion and neutralize its effectiveness.[49]

In contemporary society, religion tends to be banished to the realm of the purely subjective and treated as a matter of private whim; those who make public policy generally disregard it in practice, although they may pay lip service to it during election years. The Supreme Court's "wall of separation" between church and state and the decline of the Protestant establishment have combined to produce a state of society described by Richard John Neuhaus as the "naked public square," in which public life is purged of its religious underpinning. When the traditional religion is no longer respected, support for the old institutions is weakened, and the society becomes vulnerable to challenge by other ideological forces.

In spite of these secularizing trends, particularly among what I have referred to as the new elite, I believe that the United States remains fundamentally a religious nation. A Pew Research Center study issued in 2018 found that 53 percent of the US adults surveyed said that religion is very important in their lives, 50 percent said that they attend religious services at least monthly, and 63 percent said that they believe in God with "absolute certainty." Europeans tend to be less religiously observant. While surveys must be read with some skepticism, I believe

---

49   See Frederick M. Gedicks, "Public Life and Hostility to Religion," 78 *Virginia Law Review* 671, 679 (1992); "Religion May Become Extinct in Nine Nations, Study Says," BBC News (March 22, 2011) (study based on census data showing a steady rise in those claiming no religious affiliation; the countries named were Australia, Austria, Canada, The Czech Republic, Finland, Ireland, the Netherlands, New Zealand, and Switzerland), www.bbc.co.uk/news/science-environment-12811197. See also Rod Dreher, *The Benedict Option: A Strategy for Christians in a Post-Christian Nation* (New York: Sentinel, 2017), an eloquent appeal for a rejection of radical secularism and a return to traditional faith.

that this survey correctly reflects the religious inclinations of a majority of the American people.[50] Nevertheless, the decline in church attendance is troubling because church has always been one of the key institutions that brings people together. Religious practice has been linked to better health and well-being. A 2018 study by Harvard's T.H Chan School of Public Health found that people who attended religious services regularly or practiced daily prayer or meditation in their youth reported greater satisfaction and better health in later life.[51]

Present-day American society is intoxicated with personal self-fulfillment and with the enhancement of those spheres of activity open to the sovereign individual. Yet the achievement of unlimited self-realization is impossible. There must be something beyond the individual, a stopping point at which he comes up against some principle of limitation that he himself has not created; otherwise, every form of evil can be justified. This "something beyond," whatever it may be called, is in essence religious. In the absence of a principle of limitation based upon a transcendent order of being, adherence to the rules of civilized conduct will increasingly depend upon the guns of the state and nothing else. This is a dangerous ground on which to rest the future of civil society.

We must acknowledge, of course, that past societies, even very religious societies, were not exempt from immorality and corruption. But the vulgarity, degradation, and outright depravity in American culture today are warning signals that should not be ignored. Religious practice does make a practical difference in social behavior. The regular practice of religion appears to have a beneficial effect on family stability and helps to mitigate a range of social ills including suicide, illegitimacy,

50   See Neha Segal, "10 Key Findings About Religion in Western Europe," Pew Research Center (May 29, 2018); Donald Devine, "Is God Dead … or Is It Nietzsche?" *The Imaginative Conservative* (August 10, 2018).

51   Harvard T.H. Chan School of Public Health, "Religious upbringing linked to better health and well-being during adulthood" (September 13, 2018).

drug abuse, and crime.[52] Since the beginning of recorded history, religious beliefs have provided support for moral rules. Many if not most of our moral principles are of scriptural origin or have received their authoritative formulation in scripture. The laws against perjury, for example, are supported by the biblical injunction against bearing false witness; and the prohibitions against adultery and covetousness, though frequently disregarded, have contributed in some measure to the preservation of social harmony. The religious history of America gives us grounds to hope that, sooner or later, the nation will experience another "Great Awakening" that will renew its spiritual roots.

CONCLUSION

In this chapter, we have described some indicators of social decline: the rise of a new elite that values self-indulgence, celebrity, novelty, and multicultural diversity over the old bourgeois values of self-discipline, civic responsibility, and patriotism; the weakening of marriage, families, and local communities; fatherless and abused children; an influx of immigrants who resist assimilation; a deepening of social and political divisions; the persistence of crime and drug addiction; falling work rates among men; increased dependence on welfare; and an erosion of moral and religious values. Against these indicia of decline, however, we can cite the facts set forth in the first paragraph of this chapter, which provide evidence for the proposition that, comparatively speaking, America remains an exceptional and productive nation. If the United States can continue to be a society of free and responsible individuals, and if its citizens can renew their sense of self-reliance, innovation, entrepreneurialism, religious faith, and national solidarity, the nation can revive its founding principles and flourish, even in an increasingly troubled environment.

---

52 "Why Religion Matters: The Impact of Religious Practice on Social Stability," Heritage Foundation Report (January 25, 1996). See also Timothy P. Carney, *Alienated America, op. cit.*, Chapter 7, "It's about Church."

8

GOVERNMENT[1]

THE TWENTIETH CENTURY witnessed some of history's most terrifying examples of tyranny and official brutality, including Hitler's Third Reich, Stalin's *gulag* society, the Cambodian killing fields, Mao's cultural revolution, the Rwandan genocide, and many other examples of man's relentless inhumanity to man. A full factual recitation of these tyrannical horrors would require several volumes. With the collapse of Nazi and Soviet communist totalitarianism, the worst of these excesses were at least temporarily expunged. Yet some of the social forces that produced that century's monsters are still alive and present a continuing danger to liberty. Modern technology gives governments—including our own—the tools that sustain effective systems of espionage, invasion of privacy, tax collection, and propaganda, while mass mobility of people

1   Portions of this chapter are taken from *The Limits of Government*, by Joseph F. Johnston, Jr. (Chicago: Regnery Gateway, 1984), Chapter 2, with permission of the publisher.

and mass communications raise new possibilities for manipulation, demagoguery, and terrorism.

Concentrated power, moreover, is inherently dangerous to freedom. This is true whether the power is in private hands, as in the case of a corporate monopoly, or wielded by government officials. But government power is always more to be feared because governments have at their disposal armies, police forces, tax authorities, and prisons. Even with a democratic or constitutional form of government, the practical concentration of power in the hands of a few hundred people raises the possibility of incremental invasions of liberty and property that may, over time, erode the freedoms that sustain civilization. The danger is multiplied when government joins with large corporations, which it controls, or with labor unions and other sympathetic sources of power, to manage the private sector—thus creating the social force often called "fascism," reflecting the corporate state developed by Mussolini and copied by other political strongmen.

The Expansion of Government

For the founders of the United States in the late eighteenth century, the principal purposes of the new unified government they created were to defend its people and to protect individual liberty and private property. In the words of Thomas Jefferson, the national government was to be "a wise and frugal government, which shall restrain men from injuring one another and shall leave them otherwise free to regulate their own pursuits of industry and improvement, and shall not take from the mouth of labor the bread it has earned. This is the sum of good government."[2] The founders had learned from their own experience and from the study of history that a government that became too powerful was dangerous. Accordingly, they established a federal government with strictly limited powers. As James Madison stated in Federalist 45, "The powers delegated by the proposed constitution to the federal government, are few

---

2   Thomas Jefferson, First Inaugural Address, 1801.

and defined. Those which are to remain in the state governments are numerous and indefinite." As the Federalist Papers and other contemporary sources make clear, none of the powers delegated to the federal government, severally or jointly, grant any general jurisdiction over the welfare of citizens of the sort that is today regularly exercised by the federal government. As the Tenth Amendment explicitly states, except for the limited powers granted to the federal government, all powers were to remain with the states or the people.

The Civil War, not surprisingly, resulted in some increase in the power of the central government at the expense of the states, but the basic constitutional structure was not changed. The late nineteenth century, however, saw the beginning of a political reform movement that changed the American federal government from a constitutional republic of limited functions, spending no more than three percent of the nation's GDP, into a centralized administrative state that spends more than 20 percent of GDP and intervenes in every corner of the society. When state and local governments are included, government takes and spends more than one-third of GDP, not including the heavy cost that regulation imposes on the economy. How did this happen?

The Populist and Progressive Movements
The Populist movement in America arose in the 1890s in response to a serious agricultural depression in the South and Middle West, which stirred up anger among farmers and small businessmen over railroad rates, interest rates, and high tariffs imposed for the benefit of northern manufacturers. The growing discontent among farmers led to the formation of the People's Party (better known as the Populist Party) in 1892, whose platform demanded a number of new government programs, including increased coinage of silver, a graduated income tax, and shorter hours for labor. Grover Cleveland, a Democrat, won the presidential election in 1892, but as the agricultural and industrial recession continued, strikes and labor disturbances proliferated. In 1896 the Democratic Party borrowed from the Populists the silver issue

and other radical ideas and nominated the Populist William Jennings Bryan as its presidential candidate. William McKinley, the Republican candidate, won the 1896 election, running on a "sound money" (gold standard) and high-tariff platform. McKinley was reelected in 1900 with Theodore Roosevelt as his running mate. McKinley was assassinated in 1901, and Roosevelt became president. Roosevelt had a reputation as a reformer, and his administration moved decisively to use the power of the federal government to curb the growing power of corporate monopolies through vigorous enforcement of the Sherman Antitrust Act of 1890. The momentum for reform was actively stimulated by President Roosevelt, as well as by Woodrow Wilson, who became president in 1912, and reform was actively promoted by the "muckraker" media and through socialist ideas imported from Europe. The nationwide zeal for reform resulted in constitutional changes such as the Sixteenth Amendment, authorizing the progressive income tax, and the Seventeenth Amendment, mandating the popular election of senators in place of their appointment by state legislators. These two measures, along with other progressive measures such as increased power for the Interstate Commerce Commission as well as the creation of the Federal Trade Commission and the Federal Reserve System under Woodrow Wilson, contributed significantly to shifting government in the United States away from the federal republicanism of the founding fathers and toward the centralized welfare state.

The philosopher John Dewey provided important intellectual support for the Progressive Movement. Dewey had a fervent belief in the efficacy of scientific method. Science, for Dewey, provided a "technique of social and moral engineering" that should be used as a means of "directing our thoughts and efforts to a planned control of social forces."[3] According to Dewey, American individualism had become reactionary and destructive; there must be a change from "individualistic to

---

3   John Dewey, *Reconstruction in Philosophy* (Boston: Beacon Press, 1964 [1920]), p. 173; and *Philosophy and Civilization* (New York: Capricorn, 1963 [1931]), p. 321.

collectivistic liberalism" through "collective social planning."[4] Dewey's philosophical views, which were enormously influential during the early twentieth century, were, of course, radically different from those of the US founders.

The principal political and intellectual architect of the attack on the original understanding of the Constitution was Woodrow Wilson, whose book *Constitutional Government in the United States,* published in 1908, criticized the constitutional doctrine of separation of powers as inefficient and obsolete. Wilson believed that the Constitution was "organic" and subject to evolution and that this evolution must be guided by scientific planning—"a machinery of constant adaptation."[5] The industrial revolution, Wilson argued, has united the nation in ways that render state boundaries meaningless, but we have not altered the constitutional structure accordingly. The president, for Wilson, is the political leader of the nation, which has chosen him as the representative of the whole people, and "his is the vital place of action in the system."[6] Wilson's view turned out to be prophetic of the shift toward presidential power in subsequent years.

The New Deal and the Welfare State

Following the financial crisis of 1929–30 and the beginning of the Great Depression, Franklin D. Roosevelt assumed the presidency of the United States and initiated what he called the New Deal, a political program that drastically altered the American political economy by introducing federal government intervention to an extent never before attempted in this country in peacetime. A national agricultural policy was established, including production and price controls. Public works were created to provide employment. New federal agencies were created

---

4   John Dewey, *Liberalism and Social Action* (New York: Capricorn, 1963 [1935]), pp. 20, 43.

5   Woodrow Wilson, *Constitutional Government in the United States* (New Orleans: Quid Quo Books, 2011), p. 3.

6   *Id.,* p. 41.

to regulate the banking, securities, and communications industries. The federal government entered the electric power business through the establishment of the Tennessee Valley Authority. A compulsory social security system was adopted requiring private employees to buy government annuities. A federal minimum wage law was passed. Steep progressive taxes were enacted for the purposes of paying for these programs and to redistribute the nation's wealth. The effect of this vast array of legislative and administrative measures was to invest the federal government with the authority to solve those social and economic problems identified by the ruling Progressives as in need of solution. As FDR stated in his second inaugural address in 1937, "Instinctively we recognized a deeper need—the need to find through government the instrument of our united purpose to solve for the individual the ever-rising problems of a complex civilization." Roosevelt's statement is the very essence of Progressive political theory: the use of government planning to "solve" for the individual the problems of a complex civilization. The two unstated assumptions of this theory are that, first, individuals are incapable of solving these problems for themselves, and second, that government officials are somehow capable of gathering, mastering, and effectively using the vast amounts of information necessary to solve the problems of hundreds of millions of individual citizens. There is no empirical support for either of these assumptions.

Near the end of FDR's presidency, just a year prior to his death, he summarized the philosophy of the New Deal in his State of the Union message in 1944. This remarkable statement shows how far the nation had moved toward a collectivist approach to social policy. The president began by enumerating the traditional rights protected by the US Constitution: freedom of speech, press, and religions, and other enumerated rights. He noted, however, that as our industrial system has grown more burdensome, "these political rights proved inadequate to assure us equality in the pursuit of happiness." A new "economic bill of rights" is needed. It must include the following:

The right to a useful and remunerative job...;

The right to earn enough to provide adequate food and clothing and recreation;

The right of every farmer to raise and sell his products at a return which will give him and his family a decent living;

The right of every businessman, large and small, to trade in an atmosphere of freedom from unfair competition and domination by monopolies at home or abroad;

The right of every family to a decent home;

The right to adequate medical care and the opportunity to achieve and enjoy good health;

The right to adequate protection from the economic fears of old age, sickness, accident, and unemployment;

The right to a good education;

All of these rights spell security. And after this war is won we must be prepared to move forward, in the implementation of these rights, to new goals of human happiness and well-being.[7]

If these hopes and desires are deemed to be "rights," then someone has an obligation to provide them. That could only mean the US government, supported by the taxpayers. The taxpaying public, in other words, has a duty to provide, as a matter of right, economic security for every man, woman, and child in the country. Any serious attempt to accomplish this utopian objective was bound to require a drastic expansion in the size of government—an expansion that is well under way and is probably irreversible.

The New Deal created what is now called the "welfare state," a form

---

7   www.ushistory.org/documents/economic-bill-of-rights.htm.

of government in which the state plays the central role in promoting the economic and social well-being of its citizens. As John F. Cogan has written in his comprehensive book on US federal entitlement programs:

> The New Deal produced a fundamental pivot in the evolution of the US government. The gradual expansion of the federal government's reach that had taken place during the twentieth century's first three decades gave way to a sharp acceleration. The New Deal also permanently altered the balance in the federalist system that the founding fathers had carefully constructed by profoundly changing the relationship between the federal government and the individual, the allocation of authority between federal and state governments, and the role of the federal courts in making public policy.[8]

Prior to the New Deal, families, state and local governments, and private charities provided assistance to the poor, elderly, unemployed, and disabled. The New Dealers believed, however, that these traditional sources lacked the resources and ability to cope with the economic difficulties arising out of the Great Depression.

The first step toward the modern entitlement state was the Social Security Act of 1933, which enacted a compulsory social insurance program providing cash assistance to all participants age sixty-five or older. Program benefits were financed by a new federal payroll tax levied equally on workers and employers. The fact that employees paid payroll taxes supported the claim that they were entitled to the benefits and that Social Security was different from welfare. This helped to make the program politically invulnerable.

From the beginning, the surplus funds raised by the Social Security payroll tax were used to finance the federal government's general operations rather than to reduce the government's publicly held debt. This meant there was never a real trust fund to finance future benefits, so that future benefit increases (which were frequent) had to be financed

8   John F. Cogan, *The High Cost of Good Intentions: A History of U.S. Federal Entitlement Programs* (Stanford: Stanford University Press, 2017), p. 79.

by payroll tax increases, general taxation, or borrowing. The welfare state game of spend, tax, and borrow had begun in earnest. The Social Security Act also included an unemployment insurance program financed by a federal tax on payrolls of business firms. In 1956, Congress adopted a Social Security Disability law providing benefits for disabled workers, financed according to the same model as Social Security. In future decades, this program was greatly expanded and would prove difficult to control.

The constitutionality of the Social Security Act was promptly challenged on the ground that the spending power of Congress was limited to expenditures necessary to carry out the specific powers enumerated in Article I, Section 8 of the Constitution. In two crucially important Supreme Court decisions, the Court held that not only is Congress empowered by the Constitution to levy taxes "to promote the general welfare" but that Congress, not the Supreme Court, is the body having the discretion to determine whether a given expenditure promotes the general welfare.[9] These decisions, and other decisions upholding the New Deal's expansive enactments, drastically altered the original constitutional framework that had established a central government of limited powers. There was thereafter no effective constitutional limit on the spending and taxing power of Congress other than the political process itself, including the veto power of the president and periodic elections. These features, of course, were vitally important political limitations, but when both Congress and the Presidency were in Progressive hands, there was little resistance to the entitlement steamroller. The Supreme Court decisions in the New Deal years and subsequently also changed the federal system by permitting the federal government to intervene in areas previously entrusted to the states. By the 1960s, the central government had moved into education, housing, healthcare, and various other social welfare fields. By this time, there was little point in talking about "limited government" in the United States.

---

9   *United States v. Butler*, 297 U.S. 1, 65 (1936); *Helvering v. Davis*, 301 U.S. 619, 640 (1937).

Lyndon Johnson became president in 1963 following the assassination of John F. Kennedy. Shortly after taking office, Johnson declared "unconditional war on poverty in America."[10] The Aid to Families with Dependent Children (AFDC) program was greatly expanded. A federal food stamp program was enacted in 1964 as a part of what was now called Johnson's "Great Society" program. The food stamp program was a political deal in which urban members of Congress voted for farm price supports while rural legislators voted for the food stamp program. This kind of "logrolling" is what made the welfare state possible and what makes its growth politically unstoppable. Under astute political leadership, a majority can almost always be cobbled together for more spending. The Great Society bonanza moved forward with overwhelming Congressional support, based on an expanding economy. Congress adopted vast new healthcare programs. The first was Medicare, which covered hospital expenses, outpatient care, physician, and related services. Medicare bills were to be paid by health insurers and reimbursed by the federal government. This cost reimbursement system gave hospitals and doctors no incentive to restrain costs and led to a substantial and continuing rise in government spending on healthcare.

Medicare was quickly followed by Medicaid, which covered medical care to "medically needy" people. This program was administered by the states with most of the costs paid for by the federal government. Medicare and Medicaid together created a large increase in demand for healthcare services, which in turn led to a dramatic rise in healthcare costs.

Other government programs enacted in the 1960s included agricultural subsidies, housing allowances for low- and moderate-income earners, loans for small businessmen, highways for the middle classes, educational assistance for the young, tax rebates for business, and higher minimum wages for labor. All of this was done while fighting a costly war in Vietnam (this combined national exercise in fiscal excess was known as "guns and butter"). Little attention was given to the taxpayers,

---

10   Lyndon B. Johnson, Annual Message to Congress on the State of the Union, January 8, 1964.

present and future, who will have to pay the bills.

The various welfare programs continued to grow rapidly. The number of food stamp (SNAP) recipients increased from 3 million in 1969 to 17 million by the end of the 1970s. By 2017 the number had reached 42 million at a total cost to the federal government of $68 billion per year.[11] The AFDC program also expanded rapidly. By 1980, 49 percent of all US households received cash or in-kind assistance from at least one federal entitlement program.

Most of the growth in government spending has been driven by the entitlement programs, especially Social Security, Medicare, and Medicaid. Some of the many entitlement programs overlap, so that millions of households collect benefits from two or more programs. As John Cogan has observed, "The blistering growth in entitlements from the War on Poverty's launch in 1964 to 1980 is without parallel in US history.... Entitlement spending had transformed the federal government into a massive check-writing machine to support the lifestyles of middle-class households."[12] The War on Poverty went far beyond poor people. By 1980, according to Cogan, 71 percent of federal entitlements went to groups above the lowest income quintile. And, of course, the size of the federal bureaucracy grew along with the costs; Americans are all too familiar with the vast amount of paperwork that comes with the entitlement state.

The Reagan administration (1981–89) induced Congress to make modest reductions in entitlement spending and nondefense discretionary programs. These reductions did little more than hold the increase in federal spending to the rate of inflation.[13] Attempts to eliminate abuses in the major entitlement programs, such as unqualified people receiving Social Security disability benefits, were largely unsuccessful. A permanent

---

11   U.S. Department of Agriculture, Food and Nutrition Service, www.fns.usda.gov/pd-supplemental-nutrition-assistance-program.

12   Cogan, *op. cit.,* pp. 288–89.

13   Cogan, *op. cit.,* p. 304.

feature of the welfare state is that it is extremely difficult to take away an entitlement. An exception was the welfare reform legislation enacted by a Republican Congress and signed by President Bill Clinton, a Democrat, in 1996, which replaced the federal AFDC program with a Temporary Assistance to Needy Families program that placed time limits on welfare assistance and imposed work requirements.

As the welfare rolls grew during the 1960s and 1970s, critics argued that existing welfare programs were discouraging low-income people from working. In response, Congress in 1975 created the Earned Income Tax Credit (EITC), a refundable tax credit for low- and moderate-income people designed to encourage and reward work. Despite this modestly successful program, the US welfare system as a whole increases dependency on government and weakens America's traditional culture of self-reliance and individual responsibility. In 2017, 42 million Americans received supplemental nutritional food benefits (SNAP or food stamps) from the federal government. Assistance is of course justifiable for those who are elderly or disabled, but not for the able-bodied.[14] Imposing work requirements on those able to work would put these families back on the path to self-sufficiency. On the positive side, it appears that government dependency has dropped somewhat since the Trump administration took office. Enrollment in SNAP has dropped significantly, the number of workers in the Social Security Disability program has declined, and the number of those on other welfare programs has also dropped.[15]

The entry of the federal government into healthcare took a major leap forward in 2010 under the Obama administration with the passage of the Affordable Care Act (the ACA, often called "Obamacare"). This

---

14 See "Most Working-Age SNAP Participants Work, But Often in Unstable Jobs," Center on Budget and Policy Priorities (March 15, 2018), www.cbpp.org; "The Food Stamp Farce," *Wall Street Journal* (August 23, 2018).

15 See John Merline, "Government Dependency Plunges under Trump," *Issues and Insights* (July 8, 2019).

legislation was a far-reaching and highly partisan bill supported entirely by Democrats without a single Republican vote in either chamber of Congress. The ACA was the largest new entitlement since the New Deal. The law contained a mandate that individuals must buy health insurance, with a penalty for noncompliance, and that employers must provide insurance to their employees; the policies were required to meet certain "essential benefits" standards. It provided subsidies to individuals below certain income levels and prohibited insurers from charging higher premiums based on preexisting conditions. The ACA also expanded Medicaid benefits to prime-age adults well above the poverty line. The mandate to purchase compliant health insurance was challenged in court but was upheld by the Supreme Court, which held in an opinion by Chief Justice Roberts that, even though the requirement could not be supported under the commerce clause, the penalty was a "tax" and therefore constitutional (even though in the law itself the noncompliance payment was consistently referred to as a "penalty" and not a "tax"). Republicans in Congress have attempted on a number of occasions to repeal the ACA, so far (as of this writing) without success, although the mandate that individuals must buy insurance has been repealed.

To summarize the fiscal burden, since the early twentieth century, total federal spending as a share of the nation's GDP has increased from 3 percent to over 20 percent. The growth in entitlement spending accounts for most of this increase. At current spending levels, entitlement programs and interest on federal debt will consume more than 90 percent of federal revenue by 2030. The cost of entitlement programs is the principal reason why the national debt has risen to over $23 trillion and continues to rise. Federal debt held by the public rose from 36 percent of GDP in 2000 to 78 percent in 2018 and, if current laws and spending patterns remain unchanged, would reach 152 percent of GDP by 2048, the highest in the nation's history.[16]

The Trustees of the Social Security and Medicare programs reported

---

16   CBO, "The Long-Term Budget Outlook" (June 2018), www.cbo.gov/publication/53919.

in June 2018 that the programs' assets will be depleted by 2034, which will require very substantial benefit cuts or tax increases.[17] America's politicians are currently unwilling to face up to the large tax increases and spending decreases that would be necessary to reduce this debt to manageable proportions. In the absence of serious reforms of the entitlement programs, a fiscal crisis is inevitable. Some obvious reforms would include extending the retirement age, raising taxes, and reducing benefits. Another, more creative reform would enable participants to set up their own retirement and health savings programs, which would be offered by for-profit and nonprofit companies in a competitive market, giving beneficiaries more choices and better returns.

The United States is not alone in expanding its welfare state. Spending on social welfare programs in the OECD group of countries increased from 5 percent of GDP in the 1950s to 15 percent in 1980 to 21 percent in 2016.[18] There is, apparently, an inherent characteristic of modern mass democracy that leads governors and governed alike to bestow benefits on themselves without regard to fiscal responsibility.

Government welfare expenditures are often justified as "compassionate." But compassion with other people's money is not really compassion. Government expenditures must be financed through compulsory taxes, levied upon present and future taxpayers under penalty of fines and imprisonment. Massive borrowing by government does not create free money; it merely passes the burden to future taxpayers.

The Administrative State

A name commonly given to the modern welfare state is the "administrative state," which describes the administrative bureaucracy created as a result of the Progressive Movement, staffed by "experts" and designed to promote social and economic reform. The founders of the

---

17   www.home.treasury.gov/news/press-releases/sm0405.

18   *The Economist* (July 14, 2018), p. 53.

administrative state—in particular, Woodrow Wilson—believed that the US Constitution, which placed serious limitations on the power of the federal government, was obsolete and inefficient, especially in its separation of governmental functions between executive, legislative, and judicial powers. The Progressives sought to cut through these legal restraints by creating administrative agencies within the executive branch of the national government combining all three governmental functions in order to "solve problems" more efficiently and to get socially desirable results. The resulting administrative state that developed during the twentieth century has played a major role in transforming the United States from a constitutional republic into a centralized leviathan that grows more powerful and less accountable with almost every electoral change.

The most thorough account of the rise of the administrative state is Philip Hamburger's book titled *Is Administrative Law Unlawful?* published in 2014. Hamburger traces the evolution of the administrative state back to the centuries-old struggle between the English monarchs who sought to exercise unrestrained power, on the one hand, and the powerful nobility and rising commons, on the other hand. The English kings and their supporters, in the sixteenth and seventeenth centuries, used the doctrine of the "king's prerogative" to justify executive action by the Crown, including arbitrary taxation, which under the developing tradition of the common law should have fallen within the jurisdiction of Parliament. The Tudor and Stuart monarchs set up bodies of trusted servants, such as the infamous "Star Chamber," to issue arbitrary, discretionary decrees binding on the subjects.

During the course of the seventeenth century, the English people rebelled against this and other aspects of royal overreach, leading to a civil war in the 1640s, the execution of Charles I in 1649, and eventually the expulsion of James II in 1688 and his replacement by William and Mary. The Declaration of Rights of 1689 declared that taxation without grant by Parliament is illegal and specified that various "ancient rights and liberties" of the English people, including rights of speech and petition and the right to bear arms, were to be preserved. The "Glorious Revolution" of the seventeenth century settled the question of where political power in England resided: in Parliament and ultimately in the people, who granted to the government whatever power it possessed. This constitutional settlement, as Hamburger states, established the principle that "a government could not bind its people except through laws made with their consent—meaning the people's ancient legal customs or the acts of their legislature."[19]

The members of the Constitutional convention of 1787 in Philadelphia, of course, were intimately familiar with the history of the English revolution a century earlier, and they crafted a Constitution designed to protect against the dangers of arbitrary power through the separation of powers, the careful enumeration of the powers granted to Congress, the establishment of a federal system preserving the essential integrity of the states (including a requirement that US senators be chosen by state legislators, subsequently and unfortunately repealed), and the addition of a Bill of Rights protecting such fundamental rights as freedom of speech, assembly, and religion; the right to bear arms; and the right not to be deprived of life, liberty, and property without due process of law. Of particular importance was the separation of legislative, executive, and judicial powers, which the founders learned from their study of Roman and British history, the writings of Locke and Montesquieu, and other available sources. As James Madison wrote in Federalist 47, "The accumulation of all powers, legislative, executive, and judiciary, in the same hands, whether of one, a few, or many, and whether hereditary, self-appointed, or elective, may justly be pronounced the very definition of tyranny."

This admonition of Madison's was explicitly rejected by Woodrow Wilson and his Progressive followers because they believed that the power of the national government, and in particular its executive branch,

---

19   Philip Hamburger, *Is Administrative Law Unlawful?* (Chicago: University of Chicago Press, 2014), pp. 48–49.

should be expanded, not limited, in order to regulate the economy and improve social welfare. The Progressives called for new administrative bodies, staffed with "experts," to manage the complexities of the modern economy. For the sake of efficiency, these agencies should combine legislative, executive, and judicial functions without regard to what Progressives regarded as obsolete legal and institutional restraints. This could be done readily without worrying about the Constitution, Wilson argued, because the Constitution is an "evolutionary" document that changes in response to new circumstances. During the twentieth century, this view came to be widely accepted by America's political elites because it gave them the leeway they needed to make sweeping political change.

The New Deal during the 1930s produced a proliferation of federal commissions, including the Federal Communications Commission, the Securities and Exchange Commission, the Federal Power Commission, and many others. Congress gave these agencies sweeping powers to issue regulations binding on the public. This delegation of power to administrative agencies, as Peter Wallison has argued in a recent book, "has created a powerful and unaccountable bureaucracy, which is gradually supplanting Congress as a policy-making body."[20]

The modern administrative agency operates through the delegation by Congress to the agency of extremely wide powers to enact regulations limited only by broad and essentially meaningless standards. For example, the Federal Communications Act of 1934 requires that broadcast licensees operate in the "public interest, convenience and necessity." Congress has never defined what is meant by this phrase. Thus, the Act implicitly delegates to the Federal Communications Commission (FCC) authority to interpret this vague standard as it chooses, and the courts have upheld this delegation to the FCC of virtually unlimited

---

20   Peter Wallison, *Judicial Fortitude: The Last Chance to Reign in the Administrative State* (New
      York: Encounter Books, 2018), p. 38. Wallison's book contains a fine treatment of the malign
      consequences of the delegation of vast powers to unelected bureaucracies and the need for renewed
      judicial oversight.

discretion.[21] The use by Congress of vague and amorphous standards in its delegations to agencies is quite common. This kind of delegation violates the principle of separation of powers because there is no separation of powers if one branch of government can grant its powers to another branch.[22] Until the 1930s, the Supreme Court had traditionally held that Congress is not constitutionally permitted to transfer to others the legislative functions with which it is vested. The last such case was *Schechter Poultry v. United States,* 295 US 495, 529 (1935). Since then, the nondelegation doctrine has been abandoned.[23] The Court has thus far acquiesced in the Progressive consensus that government cannot operate effectively without administrative agencies that combine all three governmental functions in the same body. Since the heads of the agencies are appointed by the president (usually with the consent of the Senate), the administrative state reflects the concentration of power in the executive branch of the government.

A typical federal administrative agency issues regulations having the force of law, then conducts an investigation to determine whether the rule has been violated, issues a complaint, prosecutes the complaint, and adjudicates the alleged violation before an administrative law judge employed by the agency, and the verdict is then ratified by the agency itself. The defendant can ultimately appeal to an Article III constitutional court, but the courts are reluctant to upset agency findings and conclusions because of the so-called "doctrine of deference" set forth by the Supreme Court in *Chevron v. Natural Resources Defense Council* (1984). In this case the Court held that where Congress has given authority to an agency to pass regulations pursuant to a statute, the agency's regulations must be given controlling weight "unless they are

---

21   See Stuart N. Brotman, "Revisiting the Broadcast Public Interest Standard in Communications Law and Regulation," Brookings (March 23, 2017), www.brookings.edu.

22   Federalist No. 48.

23   See Wallison, *op. cit.,* Chapter 6, "The Nondelegation Doctrine;" Gary Lawson, *The Rise and Rise of the Administrative State,* 107 Harv. L. Rev. 1231 (1994).

arbitrary, capricious, or manifestly contrary to the statute." This is a very difficult burden for a complainant to meet. The Court also said that if the regulation requires interpretation, judges are not experts in the field and should therefore defer to the agency's interpretation (in this case, the Environmental Protection Agency). The doctrine of deference as formulated by the Supreme Court amounts to an abandonment of the duty of judges to exercise their independent judgment to interpret the law. As Philip Hamburger states, this kind of deference gives the administrators a power above the law, while denying to litigants their rights to have their cases decided by real courts with real judges and juries.[24]

The net result of the administrative state, as Hamburger says, is to create an "extralegal system of governance" that consolidates the previously separated powers of government into executive branch agencies. This, as Madison said, is the very definition of tyranny. Defenders of the administrative state argue that its consolidation of powers is justifiable because administrative agencies are ultimately accountable to the people through Congress and the president, who are elected. But this is fiction. Congress and the president happily transfer their responsibilities to agencies precisely so that there will be someone else to hold responsible. In the administrative state, legislative power has largely shifted to unelected administrators. These are people who gain influence through their specialized knowledge and training and are part of the elite "new class," described in Chapter 7, that today dominates American society. (The quasi-permanent bureaucracy that runs the administrative state is popularly referred to as the "deep state.") The shift of power toward the executive branch is also evidenced by the increased use of executive orders by recent presidents to avoid seeking Congressional approval.

The administrative state produces, over time, more regulation and more bureaucracy. In the United States, hundreds of federal laws and tens of thousands of regulations are issued every year. It is impossible for public officials and lawyers, let alone the voters, to understand this complex mass

---

24   Hamburger, *op. cit.*, p. 317.

of hyperlegalism. Federal regulation imposes nearly $2 trillion in costs on American consumers and investors, in addition to the government spending included in the federal budget. Donald Trump, who became president in 2017, has moved aggressively to reduce regulation. The federal government in 2017 adopted fewer new regulations than in any year since the 1970s, and the Trump administration has repealed a substantial number of existing regulations. But this attempt at deregulation, while significant, has merely scratched the surface.[25] In addition to publishing regulations, federal agencies issue uncountable numbers of guidance letters, no-action letters, alerts, and similar documents that do not have the force of law but are clearly intended to, and do, influence behavior. All of this administrative outpouring amounts to an unaccountable, arbitrary, and uncontrollable body of unlawful governance.

The characteristic features of excessive government are high taxation, increasing levels of public debt, burdensome regulation, inflation, an imperious bureaucracy, suppression of individual freedom, and a temptation toward foreign imperialism. All of these conditions contributed to the decline and fall of the Roman state. While the governments of most modern industrialized nations have not reached the same level of rigidification and fiscal irresponsibility as Rome under the late Caesars, clear danger signs exist. An overcentralized state makes too many laws, and legal overload then opens the door for crime and corruption, which sooner or later destroy respect for the law and the trust of the citizens.[26]

When the state dominates the lives of its citizens, they become increasingly dependent on government. This is a slippery slope that, if not checked, can lead to the worst kind of repression. In socialist

---

25 The Competitive Enterprise Institute concluded that the cost of federal regulations in 2016 imposed an estimated $1.9 trillion burden on the economy. The Federal Register, which publishes federal regulations annually, grew from 50,501 pages in 1989 to 95,894 pages in 2016, the last year of the Obama administration. www.cei.org. The cumulative number of final rules published in the Federal Register rose from 4,369 in 1993 to 101,380 in 2017. Wallison, *op. cit.,* p. 94.

26 See F. H. Buckley, *The Republic of Virtue: How We Tried to Ban Corruption, Failed and What We Can Do About It* (New York: Encounter Books, 2017).

Venezuela, for example, much of the public has been reduced to penury. The government controls the food supply, and elections are subject to surveillance. Since most people, especially the poor, depend on government rations, they vote for the elected officials for fear of losing access to essential supplies.[27] I am not suggesting that the United States is approaching Venezuelan levels of tyranny or deprivation, but I am merely pointing out that, as our founders knew, excessive dependence on government is dangerous to liberty and prosperity.

The Burden of the Administrative/Welfare State

The goal of the civil service reforms of the 1880s was to replace the political "spoils system" with nonpolitical civil servants who supposedly would be chosen based on objective exams rather than political affiliation As the bureaucracy increased in size in the twentieth century under the impetus of the Progressive movement, it became clear that the nonpartisan nature of the civil service was largely mythical. The top echelons of the administrative agencies were chosen by the party in power based on their political loyalty. As "public choice" economists have frequently pointed out, most public officials, like most actors in the private marketplace, are motivated by self-interest, and it is usually in the interest of government officials to act in accordance with the wishes of those who put them in office.[28] In recent years, many political appointees have become bureaucratic civil servants who are said to constitute the "deep state" that is entrenched, difficult to remove, and interested in advancing the appointees' own political goals.

When considering the burdens of excessive government, we begin with two simple propositions. *First,* history has shown that free markets are superior to governments in distributing goods and services. The inefficiencies of socialist central planning have been plainly demonstrated.

---

27 See Mary Anastasia O'Grady, "Venezuela's Sham Election," *Wall Street Journal* (May 21, 2018).

28 See Jane S. Shaw, "Public Choice Theory," *The Concise Encyclopedia of Economics*, Library of Economics and Liberty, www.econlib.org.

Governments, as monopolistic suppliers, lack the incentives to efficiency provided by competitive markets, and the high taxes required to finance government welfare programs act as a "deadweight cost" on the economy. It is always in the interest of government officials as well as recipients of government largesse to expand these programs at the expense of those who produce the wealth to pay for them.

Second, government cannot operate without compulsion, and compulsion by definition interferes with individual freedom. (To take obvious examples, taxing away a third or more of someone's income, forcing him to buy a government Social Security annuity or a health insurance policy whether or not he wants one, or forcing him to pay his employees more than a competitively determined wage, deprives him of a considerable amount of choice.) Therefore, in principle, government intervention should be avoided except where necessary to perform essential functions, such as national defense and law enforcement, that cannot effectively be performed by individuals and private groups themselves.[29]

In spite of these considerations, voters in most democratic countries continue to demand more services and subsidies from government. Why? The answer lies not in economics but in human nature and the political dynamics of mass democracy. The managers of the caregiver state know that most people obtain psychological comfort from turning over their major problems to someone else, and government is an obvious choice. Citizens can thus avoid at least some of the pain of saving for their retirement, paying for their children's education, and taking care of sick and aging relatives. The quest for security, of course, has a price: the inexorable rise of taxes and the loss of large chunks of individual freedom. To the extent that government subsidizes your various life choices, it will compel you to pay your taxes and to follow its instructions.

Modern political systems, including the growing social welfare states of the twentieth and twenty-first centuries, have increasingly pandered

---

29   The classic text is F. A. Hayek, *The Constitution of Liberty* (Chicago: University of Chicago Press, 1960).

to this psychological desire for security. Political parties compete to win the support of poor as well as median or "swing" voters. Consequently, politicians will always promise to provide additional transfer payments or services to these voters at the expense of the taxpayers. As a prominent US senator is alleged to have said in the 1980s, "Everyone loves free money." Because the programs are paid for largely by broad-based income taxes that are automatically withheld and thus scarcely noticed by most voters, recipients of welfare believe that they are receiving a net benefit at little or no cost to themselves. More than 40 percent of households do not pay any federal income taxes, while about half of Americans receive significant income from government programs. This explains the popularity of such massive federal programs as Social Security, Medicare, Medicaid, supplemental security income, student loans, agricultural subsidies, food stamps, and many others. Welfare state programs come with a great deal of burdensome regulation attached. The cost of federal regulation for 2019 has been estimated at nearly $2 trillion annually, or 9 percent of US GDP.[30]

The costs of the ever-expanding welfare state are severe. In fiscal year 2017, the federal government spent a total of $3.98 trillion, amounting to 21 percent of the nation's GDP. Of this amount, $1.59 trillion, or 40 percent, was spent on Social Security and Medicare; while $729 billion, or 19 percent, was spent on what can be categorized as "welfare." (Welfare includes Medicaid [the biggest], SNAP [food stamps], disability payments, child nutrition, earned income tax credits, housing assistance, Pell Grants for college, and various other cash payments to low-income individuals.)[31] The costs of the welfare state always go up, never down, until, as Margaret Thatcher said, the government runs out of other peoples' money.

---

30   Competitive Enterprise Institute: Ten Thousand Commandments 2019, p. 4 . Cei.org/10KC2019/
      executive-summary. For statistics on welfare benefits, see US Census Bureau, Survey of Income
      and Program Participation.

31   federalsafetynet.com/welfare-budget.html.

Neither of the major political parties can be relied upon to control spending. The Democratic Party has retained its New Deal enthusiasm for "tax and tax, spend and spend, elect and elect."[32] The Republican Party, during the administration of George W. Bush, set new records for government spending. Under Democratic President Obama, government spending rose even faster. Neither the Trump administration nor the Congress seems inclined to reduce government spending significantly, although Congress did cut income taxes in 2017 and the Trump administration has reduced the number of burdensome government regulations. The Congressional Budget Office has estimated that anticipated spending will rise from $4 trillion (20.8 percent of GDP) in 2018 to $7 trillion (23.6 percent of GDP) in 2028, increasing America's publicly held debt from 76 percent of GDP to 96 percent of GDP. The number of federal workers has reached a record high under President Trump.[33]

The public debt of the United States government (over $23 trillion as of 2019) is only a small fraction of its true indebtedness, including future obligations, such as Social Security and Medicare, which we are passing on to future generations. This fiscal gap has been estimated at more than $200 trillion, a truly staggering sum. In short, because of decades of profligate and irresponsible spending, the United States is effectively bankrupt.[34] Today's politicians refuse to address the reckless growth of the major entitlement and welfare programs, which account for about two-thirds of federal government spending and more than 20 percent of GDP.[35]

---

32 This quote was attributed to prominent New Dealer Harry Hopkins, although Hopkins denied that he said it. See en.wikiquote.org/wiki/harryhopkins. Whether or not he said it, this remark accurately reflects the New Deal political program.

33 "Federal workforce hits record high under Trump," *Washington Times,* March 19, 2019. See CBO: The Budget and Economic Outlook, 2018 to 2028, April 2018, www.cbo.gov/publication 53651. On the regulatory reductions, see American Action Forum, "The Trump Administration's Deregulatory Progress and Forecast," May 21, 2018, www.americanactionforum.org.

34 Laurence J. Kotlikoff and Scott Burns, *The Clash of Generations: Saving Ourselves, Our Kids and Our Economy* (Cambridge, MA: The MIT Press, 2012), Chapter 3.

35 www.pewresearch.org/fact-tank2017/04/04.

The US experience is similar to that of other Western welfare states; in the US, about half of entitlement benefits go to the middle classes (who vote and make political contributions) and not to the poor.[36] This alone puts into question the basic justification for the welfare state. The various interests involved are represented by lavishly funded lobbying organizations. Because of this potent political support, the major subsidy programs cannot be reduced but always grow larger. While minor welfare programs, such as cash subsidies to the unemployed poor, have occasionally been reduced, this is possible only because the recipients of these programs, for the most part, do not vote and are not represented by influential lobbies. It is virtually impossible, on the other hand, to reduce subsidies to the middle classes, such as retirement and health programs—for example, as we have seen, it has thus far proved to be politically impossible to eliminate the vastly expensive Obamacare health insurance program.

The process of government subsidization of demanding groups (in Roman terms, "bread and circuses") suffers from declining marginal returns.[37] Each level of benefits becomes a fixed entitlement, requiring heavier taxes, and more must be distributed just to keep the population in a state of nonrevolt. This process places the productive sector in a tightening vise and eventually leads to economic stagnation or collapse.[38] If present trends continue, the major entitlement programs, together with interest on the national debt, will eventually devour every dollar that the present tax system produces, leaving the nation facing a major economic and social crisis. The large rise in fiscal obligations due to

---

36   Cogan, *op. cit.*, p. 381.

37   The term "bread and circuses" (*panem et circenses*) was used by the poet Juvenal (c. AD 100) to describe the practice of Roman political leaders in buying the allegiance of the masses by giving them cheap food and entertainment.

38   See Joseph A. Tainter, *The Collapse of Complex Societies* (New York: Cambridge University Press, 1989), pp. 116–17. See also Jonathan Rauch, *Demosclerosis: The Silent Killer of American Government* (New York: Times Books, 1994).

an aging and increasingly subsidized population can be paid for only if the economy grows. But the economy cannot grow rapidly enough to support the bourgeoning entitlement programs when the fiscal and regulatory burdens of government continue to rise. This is the painful paradox of welfare politics that threatens to push America into economic decline. In the absence of a serious reduction in the fiscal burdens of the welfare state, there is no room for maneuver: either a costly war or another financial crisis would place the nation in a dangerously unstable position. The Trump administration that took office in 2017 has implemented policies, including a significant reduction in taxes and some reduction in the regulation of business, that have stimulated economic growth, but these efforts have encountered serious political opposition and the fiscal prospects remain uncertain.

The federal government today is so large and complex that it consistently fails to deliver effective results. In contrast to the operation of a market economy, government operations lack the incentives and price signals provided by competition and free markets. Instead, government is burdened by top-down coercion, overstaffing, arcane rules, and politically driven and often conflicting goals. As F. A. Hayek argued, government officials cannot assemble the vast amounts of knowledge that would be needed to manage a complex economy. The result is that the costs of many government programs exceed the benefits.[39] Congress should impose more effective spending restraints, and better management is always possible. But the fundamental problem is structural. The only really effective way to obtain better governance is to reduce the size and scope of the federal government and give most ordinary governmental functions back to the states and the people. Under present political circumstances, this course of action is unlikely, to say the least.

---

39   For a detailed analysis of government failure, see Chris Edwards, "Why the Federal Government Fails," CATO Institute, Policy Analysis Number 777 (July 27, 2015).

Government and Politics in the Twenty-First Century
In this chapter, we have briefly reviewed various significant political shifts in the United States that occurred during the twentieth century, including the Progressive Movement that culminated in Franklin Roosevelt's New Deal in the 1930s and Lyndon Johnson's Great Society in the 1960s, and a modest political counter-revolution under Ronald Reagan in the 1980s. The twenty-first century saw a revival of the Progressive tendency under Barrack Obama from 2009 through 2016, followed by what Salena Zito has called "The Great Revolt" that brought Donald Trump to the White House in January of 2017.

The Obama administration, in an effort to stimulate the economy after the recession of 2007–8, brought about a significant increase in government spending and made a bold move toward government-mandated healthcare in the form of the Affordable Care Act. President Obama also enhanced the administrative state by making extensive and questionable use of executive orders to avoid the need for Congressional approval. Nearly all political observers expected the Progressive trend to continue under Hillary Rodham Clinton, the Democratic candidate for president in 2016. To the surprise of the pundits, however (and of this writer), Mrs. Clinton was defeated in November 2016 by the Republican candidate and businessman, Donald Trump. This unex-pected development was greeted with general (though far from universal) relief by Republicans but with undisguised anguish, often amounting to fury, by Democrats and their allies in the news media, many of whom contended that something improper or even illegal must have happened.

What actually happened, in political reality, has been carefully docu-mented and explained in an excellent book by Salena Zito and Brad Todd, titled *The Great Revolt: Inside the Populist Coalition Reshaping American Politics* (New York: Crown Forum, 2018). Traveling through several Midwestern states, including western Pennsylvania, Ohio, Michigan, Wisconsin, and Iowa, and with the aid of a team of experi-enced pollsters, Zito and Todd have provided a notable work of "shoe-leather" journalism, interviewing hundreds of voters in Midwestern counties that were key to Trump's victory. These voters and their communities had suffered serious economic damage in the early years of the present century from automation and from a flood of cheap imported goods, primarily from China, which badly damaged America's industrial base. Many factories and jobs were moved overseas, and once-thriving manufacturing towns were devastated.

> These are the voters who have gone through the most traumatic economic and cultural change in America in the past thirty years; technology, global wage competition, and a nationalizing, secularizing culture have upended the way of life of the American blue-collar manufacturing worker more than they have for any other subgroup. In their eyes, they have lived by the rules and done everything they were supposed to: they worked hard, prayed hard, raised their kids to do the right thing, coached their kids' softball games, served as ushers at their churches, were civically engaged, and asked only to watch their favorite team play football on Sundays and to have a chance to give their offspring a slightly better economic situation in their hometowns when they were done.
>
> But the world did not return the favor. Big companies did not cater to them to earn their business anymore, big media did not share their values, big Hollywood made them the butt of their jokes, and big business and big government showed them the door when technology replaced their job skills.[40]

And these are the voters that Hillary Clinton referred to during the 2016 campaign as "deplorables." One of the causes of the massive influx of subsidized Chinese exports that decimated America's manufacturing towns was the US government's decision in 2000 to grant China favorable access to the American market (see the discussion in Chapter 3). But no one in government did anything to help the workers who lost

---

40 Salena Zito and Brad Todd, *The Great Revolt: Inside the Populist Coalition Reshaping American Politics* (New York: Crown Forum, 2018), p. 45.

their jobs as a result. So the voters spoke their minds in the voting booth, contributing to the election of Donald Trump.

Trump's victory in 2016 reflected not only the economic plight of the neglected industrial working class but also the revival of the latent patriotism within this class ("make America great again") and a growing skepticism among the voting public about immigration, welfare, globalism, and the political/cultural establishment in general, including the mainstream media. The new class elites ridiculed the Trump followers as "populist-nationalists," a term they also applied to similar popular, anti-establishment manifestations in European countries. Whether this populist impulse produces a lasting change in American politics remains to be seen.

The political atmosphere in the United States became increasingly bitter following the 2016 presidential election. The conduct of public discussion today demonstrates a troubling level of intolerance and even outright hostility toward opposing opinions. Democrats routinely attack President Trump and other Republicans as racists and bigots, while Republicans charge Democrats with promoting extremism and division. There is little common ground in this debate. Agitators on both sides (but particularly on the left) have used tactics such as disrupting lawful meetings, shouting down speakers, harassing officeholders in public places, and other forms of open intimidation. All of this is reminiscent of the "politics in the streets" that helped to bring about fascism in 1930s Europe. Politics today has become further embittered by the loud and immoderate voices of social media, which are not subject to the ordinary restraints of polite discourse. In this cultural climate, governing becomes a zero-sum game of irreconcilable hostility in which compromise, the mother's milk of politics, becomes increasingly difficult. A constitutional republic that cannot take constructive political action is in trouble.

The vicious political hostility that emerged following the nomination of Donald Trump for president in 2016 was manifested in the open efforts of anti-Trump partisans, including top officials of the Obama administration, to elect Trump's opponent, Hillary Clinton and, failing that, to mount a government investigation against Trump that would cripple his presidency by implicating Trump and his associates in a "Russian collusion" narrative that had no basis in fact. This dismal episode in American history has been exposed in a carefully researched and well-written book by Andrew McCarthy, who describes it as "a scandalous abuse of power."[41]

Civic Virtue and Public Corruption

Democracy, as political philosophers from Plato and Aristotle to the present have known, poses a fundamental challenge: the virtually irresistible temptation on the part of irresponsible voters to vote themselves a living and to lower standards of conduct and taste to a level that suits their own inclinations. This tendency is a part of human nature and can only be constrained by the preservation of civic virtue and constitutional limitations in an ordered society.

Classical political philosophy taught that disorder in the state reflects disorder in the souls of the citizens, and especially the rulers. Aristotle observed that just conduct presupposes a virtuous moral condition. For the ruler to act unjustly (e.g., to be a coward or to violate an oath) is not merely to do certain acts but to do them as the result of a certain state of character. Neither an individual or a state can do right actions without virtue and wisdom. "Thus the courage, justice, and wisdom of a state have the same form and nature as the qualities which give the individual who possesses them the name of just, wise, or temperate."[42] To be virtuous, Aristotle argued, one must have been trained in the right habits. When education lacks moral principle and people are taught that political or financial success is all that matters, corruption is inevitable. In democracies, the most potent cause of revolution is the unprincipled

---

41   Andrew C. McCarthy, *Ball of Collusion: The Plot to Rig an Election and Destroy a Presidency* (New York: Encounter Books, 2019), p. xvi.

42   Aristotle, *Politics,* Chap. VII, 1323b, *The Basic Works of Aristotle,* ed. Richard McKeon (New York: Random House, 1941), p. 1278.]

character of popular demagogues who stir up the multitude to rebel, impose heavy taxes on the rich, and slander those who oppose them. (Aristotle's examples are fully applicable to today's politics.) He concluded that the most important safeguard for the state is education in civic virtue—as he put it, "the best laws, though sanctioned by every citizen of the state, will be of no avail unless the young are trained by habit and education in the spirit of the constitution."[43] As discussed in Chapter 5 on education, America's public school system no longer seriously tries to teach civic virtue or constitutional principles.

Cicero, a student of philosophy who was also a Roman senator, restated the classical view that adherence to the classical virtues (prudence, courage, temperance, and justice) was not possible for men who believed that pleasure is the sovereign good. The excessive pursuit of pleasure leads to self-indulgence. And "where self-indulgence reigns, decent behavior is excluded."[44] The vice of self-indulgence has a debilitating effect upon both the leaders and the people. Centuries later, the Arab philosopher Ibn Khaldun would affirm Cicero's insight (see the discussion of Ibn Khaldun's ideas in the Introduction to this book). The point of the classical philosophers is simple and profound: we cannot have self-government if we cannot govern ourselves.

The lessons of classical political philosophy were thoroughly absorbed by the founding fathers of the United States. The founders derived from their study of the classics the principles of civic virtue, which (with exceptions) they tried to follow in their public lives. George Mason summarized the founders' attitude in the Virginia Declaration of Rights (1776) as follows:

---

43   *Id.*, V, 1310a.

44   Cicero, *On Old Age*, Chap. IV (Penguin Classics 1975), p. 229.

XV. No free government, or the blessing of liberty, can be preserved to any people but by a firm adherence to justice, moderation, temperance, frugality, and virtue, and by frequent recurrence to fundamental principles.[45]

To these men, it was obvious that civic virtue required discipline, hard work and a sense of responsibility. Self-indulgence and licentious behavior must be restrained; otherwise, liberty would become license. The founders chose a mixed or republican form of government over democracy because they knew that unrestrained popular will can lead to demagoguery and tyranny.

The founders assumed that public virtue must be grounded in religion and natural law. The letters and speeches of the revolutionary period were pervaded with a sense of divine providence. Washington's farewell address spoke to the religious foundation of civil society: "Of all the dispositions and habits which lead to political prosperity, religion and morality are indispensable." And, in particular, "let it simply be asked where is the security for property, for reputation, for life, if the sense of religious obligation desert the oaths, which are the instruments of investigation in Courts of Justice?" Even Jefferson, one of the least religious of the founders, understood that the rights of man came from "Nature and Nature's God." The "higher law" principles embodied in the American founding are consistent with the lessons of classical philosophy.[46] These traditions teach that men who are the slaves of passion or self-interest are not free; therefore law, which is the political manifestation of right reason, must rule over the baser inclinations of both governors and governed. As the Federalist Papers made clear, "a mere demarkation on parchment" of the limits of government was not sufficient; the ultimate guarantee of liberty lies in the virtue and

---

45   Virginia Declaration of Rights, drafted by George Mason, June 12, 1776, and adopted by the Virginia Convention of Delegates.

46   For a summary of this foundational view see Edward S. Corwin, *The "Higher Law" Background of American Constitutional Law* (Indianapolis: Liberty Fund, 2008).

intelligence of the people. (See Nos. 46, 48, 49 and 51.) The virtual absence of religious and ethical instruction in American schools and colleges deprives the citizens of their moral anchor.

Calvin Coolidge was the last US president whose public pronouncements fully embodied the old ideal of civic virtue:

> In a free republic a great government is the product of a great people. They will look to themselves rather than government for success. The destiny, the greatness of America lies around the hearthstone. If thrift and industry are taught there, and the example of self-sacrifice oft appears, if honor abide there, and high ideals, if there the building of fortune be subordinated to the building of character, America will live in security, rejoicing in an abundant prosperity and good government at home and in peace, respect, and confidence abroad. If these virtues be absent, there is no power that can supply these blessings.[47]

As in many other aspects of American life, the New Deal represented a decisive break with the past. Quite abruptly, the civic dialogue was transformed. The public philosophy expounded by America's new leaders was no longer based on civic virtue and character, but instead on government subsidies, redistribution, social engineering, and "compassion" (with other people's money). The federal government was now deemed by many to be responsible for the happiness as well as the security of the entire populace.

With each successive decade, this system was progressively entrenched and is now in practice irreversible. An incestuous relationship of mutual dependency between active government and passive recipients guarantees its continuance. A symbol of this political degeneracy was the 1992 debate in which someone asked the presidential candidates, "What are you going to do to meet our needs?" Coolidge would have asked him what he was doing to meet his own needs. In our demotic age, the feckless and neutered candidates responded, like the cowed parents of

---

47   Quoted in Robert Sobel, *Coolidge: An American Enigma* (Washington, DC: Regnery, 1998), p. 202.

spoiled children, by making more promises. Large blocks of voters are now dependent on Social Security, Medicare, education grants, housing allowances, food stamps, tax benefits for business, and other subsidies too numerous to list. The result is a form of mutual corruption. As Jefferson observed in his Notes on the State of Virginia, "Dependency begets subservience and venality, suffocates the germ of virtue, and prepares fit tools for the designs of ambition."[48]

The reigning political philosophy of today is centered not on duties but on a concept of rights and entitlements. The function of politics is no longer to promote a good society but to satisfy as many wants as possible, at the taxpayers' expense. As William James (one of the most influential of modern American philosophers) wrote, the guiding principle for ethical and political philosophy must be "to satisfy at all times as many demands as we can."[49] In short, what classical and Christian thinkers considered to be defects—selfishness and self-indulgence—became the basis for a positive moral principle of demand satisfaction. This was a disastrous turn in political philosophy. Political decisions now depend on the whims of public opinion, which has taken the place of constitutional principle and the common good as the guiding authority for public policy.

A significant segment of the public seems to believe that economic prosperity cures all ills and that this cure can be achieved by government. Economic prosperity, however, is not self-sustaining but is based upon such elementary principles of civic morality as honesty, thrift, hard work, and obedience to law. Once these values are eroded, a free economy cannot survive for long. The "democratic capitalism" celebrated by today's optimists is vulnerable to the collapse of its moral substructure. John Adams wrote to Thomas Jefferson in 1819 that "without Virtue,

---

48   Thomas Jefferson, *Notes on the State of Virginia,* Jefferson Writings, Query xix (New York: The Library of America, 1984), p. 290–91.

49   William James, "The Moral Philosopher and the Moral Life" (1891) in *Essays on Faith and Morals* (Cleveland: Meridian Books, 1968), p. 205.

there can be no political liberty," and he added that prosperity tends to produce luxury, which in turn produces "effeminacy intoxication extravagance Vice and folly."[50] This raises the question of whether a democratic society, founded on the pursuit of happiness, can prevent what Jefferson called a "licentious commerce" from undermining the prudence and self-control on which responsible self-government depends.

The seemingly inexorable growth of the welfare-administrative state points to an inherent problem with democracy. As Professor Nicholas Capaldi has said: "There are no objective limits and no procedural restraints on what a democracy can do... the only such restraint to have emerged historically is the 'rule of law' in a civil association as exemplified in the Anglo-American legal inheritance."[51] America's founders did, in fact, try to put in place a constitutional structure that would support ordered liberty based on the rule of law. In the next chapter we will explore this structure in more detail.

---

50   To Thomas Jefferson from John Adams, December 21, 1819, rotunda.upress.virginia.edu/founders.

51   Email to the author, May 6, 2019.

9

FEDERALISM, LAW, AND LIBERTY

Federalism

The political structure of the United States as set forth in the Constitution, adopted in Philadelphia in 1787 and subsequently ratified by the original states, has been generally characterized as a *federal system*. Federalism is a form of government consisting of two or more states under one central body, united for a common cause, such as defense against a common enemy or enemies. The preamble to the US Constitution states that its purpose is "to form a more perfect Union, establish Justice, insure domestic Tranquility, provide for the common defence, promote the general Welfare, and secure the Blessings of Liberty to ourselves and our Posterity." In a federal system, the several states grant to the central government certain powers, such as the conduct of war and foreign policy and the regulation of certain inherently national concerns, while the states retain their sovereignty over other matters. Among the early examples of federal political structures were various leagues of city-states in ancient Greece. Other examples of more or less federal structures from European history include the Holy Roman Empire, the Swiss Confederation, the confederation of the Netherlands Provinces and the contemporary Federal Republic of Germany.

The principle of federalism resembles the doctrine of "subsidiarity," a principle of political philosophy according to which political and social matters should be handled by the lowest (most local) responsible authority. In other words, political and social activity should be decentralized to the maximum extent possible. The gradual growth of liberty and prosperity in Western civilization from the sixteenth to the twentieth century—manifested, *inter alia,* in the Protestant Reformation, the Glorious Revolution in England, and the American Revolution—was a history of decentralized power and limited government. The ideal of subsidiarity supports a society of free and responsible individuals, and it conflicts with the tendency toward centralization of power characteristic of the modern administrative/welfare state, which we discussed in the previous chapter.

Most of the delegates of the American states assembled at Philadelphia in 1787 were no doubt familiar with the early examples of federalism. Delegates from the larger states, including Virginia's James Madison, wanted power to be centralized in the federal government to avoid the problems created by fiscally irresponsible states under the Articles of Confederation, but the small-state delegates were determined to preserve the sovereignty of their states to prevent undue domination by the larger states. The result of the Philadelphia convention was a compromise in which the federal Congress was granted certain specified powers: chiefly, the power to borrow and coin money, regulate commerce, declare war, raise and support armies, and lay and collect taxes (subject to restrictions). The president was given executive power, command of the military, veto power over bills passed by Congress (subject to a super-majority override), and power (with consent of the Senate) to make treaties and appoint ambassadors. The president was to be chosen by electors appointed under state law, except that if no candidate won a majority of the electors, the president would be chosen by the House of Representatives, voting by states. The judicial power was vested in a Supreme Court and such inferior courts as Congress established. The states retained broad powers over their internal affairs and were to be represented by two Senators from each state, chosen by the state legislatures (changed in 1913 to popular election). The House of Representatives was to be chosen by the people of the states.

The principle of federalism was firmly established in the Tenth Amendment to the Constitution: "The powers not delegated to the United States by the Constitution, nor prohibited by it to the States, are reserved to the States respectively, or to the people."

An important advantage of federalism is to keep decision-making close to the people who are affected by it. It is easier for local citizens to communicate with local officials than with distant officeholders in the national capital. A voter can contact a city councilman or a state representative rather easily, but for the average citizen to exercise any influence on the central government in Washington is extremely difficult. Another advantage of federalism is that it helps to localize and contain bad decisions and local disturbances. If one state suffers from an unwise policy, others can avoid it, and similarly, a successful policy in one state can serve as a model for others. As Justice Louis Brandeis observed: "It is one of the happy incidents of the federal system that a single courageous State may, if its citizens choose, serve as a laboratory; and try novel social and economic experiments without risk to the rest of the country."[1] Federalism gives the individual citizen a choice: if there is bad government in his state, he can move to another. Jurisdictional competition and the "right of exit" promote good and honest government.[2]

The original federal structure of the US Constitution has been badly damaged over the course of American history, as more and more power has accrued to the federal government at the expense of the states and

---

1   *New York Ice Co. v. Liebmann*, 285 U.S. 262, 311 (1932).

2   See F. H. Buckley, *The Republic of Virtue* (New York: Encounter Books, 2017), p. 99.

the people. Part of this centralization was the result of the Civil War and the Fourteenth Amendment that followed it, which, among other restrictions on the states, prohibited the states from depriving any person of life, liberty, or property without due process of law or denying to any person the equal protection of the laws. This sweeping provision enabled the Supreme Court in the twentieth century to nationalize many issues previously left to the states, such as abortion, school prayer, key aspects of criminal procedure, regulation of pornography, reapportionment of state legislative districts, and the operation of schools and prisons. Further, there are today few restrictions on the power of the national government to legislate on subjects formerly seen as local matters. The original and plain meaning of the Constitution was that Congress exercises only those powers delegated to it, while the remainder are reserved to the states or the people. This understanding is now a dead letter. "The Constitution, according to the Supreme Court, no longer places any significant federalism-based obstacle to congressional action."[3]

Political power today is largely centralized in the federal government. The history of how this took place is described in the previous chapter. The centralization of power in Washington has not promoted political harmony; on the contrary, the nation is more deeply divided than at any time since the Civil War. Recent polls show that a majority of Americans are dissatisfied with the national government but are satisfied with their local communities. This suggests that it might be helpful "to repair the US political divisions by allowing people to live as they want in their own local communities without Washington forcing one set of policies and moralities on all."[4]

Because so many Americans are now dependent on subsidies provided by the federal government, it is probably impossible, as a

---

3   Lino A. Graglia, "In Defense of 'Federalism,'" *Harvard Journal of Law and Public Policy*, Vol. 6 (1982), p. 27.

4   Donald Devine, "Division and Repair of American Politics: For Dissatisfied Americans, the More Local Their Orientation the Less Unhappy They Are," *The American Spectator* (December 18, 2017).

political matter, to return to anything close to the federalist model of the Constitution as originally adopted. However, real federalism is still a desirable goal, and therefore, we should try to move in the direction of returning as many governmental functions as possible to states and localities so that citizens can more effectively control their own destinies.

Law

When America's founders adopted the Declaration of Independence in 1776, they based their action on certain "self-evident" truths, namely that men are endowed by God with inalienable rights, including the right to life, liberty, and the pursuit of happiness, and that governments are instituted to secure these rights. From the very outset of the nation, therefore, its independence was based upon the ancient tradition of natural law, which holds that there are objective rights and that these rights rest upon a higher moral law.[5] The natural law is in sharp contrast to the opposing theory of legal positivism, which asserts that law is merely the will of the sovereign, implying that power-holding governments have a floating charter to enact anything in the name of the law.

In the decade following the American Revolution, when the founders drafted a constitution for the new nation, they followed the natural law principles outlined in the Declaration by instituting a government that would protect the natural rights of the people. The ideals of a "higher law" are embodied in the Constitution, but this does not mean that the Constitution is somehow subject to, or may be overridden by, doctrines of natural law or the principles set forth in the Declaration of Independence. The Constitution is the governing legal document of the United States, as the text itself makes clear in Article VI: "This Constitution, and the Laws of the United States which shall be made in Pursuance thereof; and all Treaties made, or which shall be made, under the Authority of the United States, shall be the supreme

---

5   See Edward S. Corwin, *The Higher Law Background of American Constitutional Law* (Indianapolis: Liberty Fund, 2008 [1928]).

Law of the Land; and the Judges in every State shall be bound thereby, any Thing in the Constitution or Laws of any State to the Contrary notwithstanding."

The economic strength and political health of any nation depends upon adherence to the rule of law, which can be defined as a set of institutionalized principles designed to defend the individual against invasions of his person and property and to provide a mechanism for the fair adjudication of disputes. An effective and lasting system of liberty under law is extremely rare in the history of the world. The rights established by the seventeenth-century Glorious Revolution in England and the American Revolution were not simply invented; they were achieved after centuries of hard-fought struggle.

Under the Anglo-American system, impartial judges are supposed to decide cases according to known rules. In the United States, these rules are established by the Constitution and the laws adopted pursuant to it, and by the common law and statutory laws of the several states consistent with the Constitution. Because the rules are known, people can regulate their conduct and plan their transactions with assurance. In the absence of known rules protecting persons and property, the future is uncertain, and society dissolves into conflict. Properly conceived, the law does not tell the citizens what their goals ought to be but merely establishes basic rules of conduct: penalizing violence, theft, and fraud; providing restitution for injury; and enforcing contracts. These legal rules are based on permanent principles of the moral order and on long-standing custom. So long as they respect the basic rules, citizens are free to pursue their own goals and projects. Because of the obvious importance of certainty, stability, and predictability, judge-made law should change only gradually, and legislatures should normally be reluctant to make radical changes.

In the twentieth century, the traditional view of the law changed. The new Progressive political and legal elites, who came to dominate the universities and the political establishment, argued that central government planning was the most efficient way to resolve social and economic problems and that sweeping change was needed. In the New Deal and thereafter, as we have seen, this viewpoint became politically dominant, resulting in an avalanche of legislation and administrative regulation. This outpouring of federal and state rulemaking has been accompanied by a similar increase in judicial activity. One objective of the legal reform movement that began early in the twentieth century was to simplify and encourage litigation. This trend was accelerated in the 1960s by the liberalization of the rules permitting "class actions" on behalf of large groups of claimants and the adoption of numerous procedural rules that, either on their face or by judicial interpretation, gave private individuals and groups expanded rights to enforce federal statutes and regulations through court actions. The courts, meanwhile, began to make exceptions to traditional doctrines of judicial restraint. Judges and regulators now took upon themselves the authority to operate schools and prisons, to tell landladies whom they could and could not exclude, to order municipal officials to build housing projects that local residents had rejected, and to force state legislatures to reapportion their legislatures. The rise of public interest advocacy groups devoted to the pursuit of political and ideological causes in the courts, as well as the growing practice of awarding attorneys' fees to successful plaintiffs, further encouraged lawyers to file lawsuits. The courts promoted the litigation explosion by becoming more "activist," reaching decisions based on preferences of social policy rather than on adherence to existing law.

The excesses and impenetrability of our legal system bring the law into disrespect and, in the end, impair individual freedom. More legislation and regulation produce more coercion and less freedom of choice. The Roman example provides us with a warning: legal overload, like imperial overstretch, is both a symptom and a cause of economic, social, and political decline.[6]

---

6   See Bruno Leoni, *Freedom and the Law* (Indianapolis: Liberty Fund 1991 [1961]) for a discussion of the adverse impact of excessive legislation on individual freedom.

The Constitution and the Courts

Chapters 5 and 6 discussed the rise of relativism, the systematic lowering of educational standards, and the debasement of language, resulting in a denial of the validity of objective truth and the deconstruction of the ordinary meaning of words. A similar process has taken place in law, and its effects can be seen in the changing interpretation of the US Constitution.

The original function of the Constitution, as Alexander Hamilton argued in the first Federalist paper, was to preserve the Union and to secure the blessings of liberty, property and the republican form of government. A constitution performs its function by limiting the constituent elements of government to their proper spheres. For nearly 200 years, lawyers and judges assumed that the words of the Constitution should be interpreted in accordance with the text of the document and, in the case of ambiguity, with reference to the intention of those who wrote and ratified it. This assumption had the merit of common sense. If a document contains an ambiguity, the first reaction of any normal person is to seek evidence of the author's intent, and this has been an established canon of legal construction since time immemorial. The doctrine of "original intent" was self-evident to jurists until quite recently. Chief Justice John Marshall, for example, assumed it in some of his most famous opinions.[7]

The doctrine of originalism is an important part of the justification for a judiciary endowed with the extraordinary power to declare legislation unconstitutional. If unelected justices can nullify laws by reinterpreting the Constitution in line with their own preferences, they possess political power that cannot be reconciled with a republic of laws. Hamilton's view that the judiciary was the "least dangerous" branch of

---

7   See, for example, *McCulloch v. Maryland,* 4 Wheat. 316, 415, 420 (the word *necessary* as used in the "necessary and proper" clause, is to be construed according to the intention of the framers); and *Barron v. Baltimore,* 32 U.S. (7 Pet.) 243, 250 (refusing to apply Bill of Rights to the states because "these amendments contain no expression indicating an intention to apply them to the state governments"—an interpretation changed by subsequent Supreme Court decisions).

government was based on the assumption that the court would decide cases in accordance with the Constitution as written. The existence of a specific constitutional amendment procedure set forth in Article V presupposed that changes in the Constitution were to be made by the people in the prescribed manner and not by judges who want to reach a given result by changing the meaning of the text. If judges can change the meaning of words, they are imposing on the people something they never agreed to. This was the view of constitutional interpretation favored by the late Justice Antonin Scalia, who preferred the term "original meaning" to "original intent." Justice Scalia argued that it is impossible to determine the subjective intent of those who voted for a constitutional or legislative enactment but that it *is* possible to determine "what is the most probable meaning of the *words* of the enactment, in the context of the whole body of public law with which they must be reconciled.... This does not mean, of course, that the expressions of the Framers are irrelevant. To the contrary, they are strong indications of what the most knowledgeable people of the time understood the words to mean."[8] Whatever label may be applied to it, the doctrine of originalism was a bulwark of constitutional stability.

In the years after World War I, however, the doctrine of original intent (or original meaning) began to be seriously weakened, first by the law schools and then by the federal courts, in favor of a jurisprudence of results derived from a doctrine sometimes called "legal realism" but more properly called "legal pragmatism" since it derives its premises from the philosophy of pragmatism that dominated American thought throughout the twentieth century. Legal pragmatism holds that judicial decisions, like other actions, should be judged solely by their consequences.[9] But how do the judges decide what consequences are desirable?

---

8   *Scalia Speaks,* ed. Christopher J. Scalia and Edward Whelan (New York: Crown Forum, 2017), pp. 182–83.

9   As Albert Alschuler points out, this instrumentalist perspective disregards the most basic principles of justice recognized by Western juristic thought from Aristotle to the twentieth century. Alschuler, *Law Without Values* (Chicago: Chicago University Press, 2000), p. 101.

In practice, legal pragmatism permits them to decide in accordance with their political inclinations or, as some spokesmen for legal realism openly admitted, based on their "hunches," and then rationalize the result by clothing it in the form of a reasoned opinion. Pragmatic doctrine thus gives federal judges free rein to make political decisions of sweeping scope even though they have not been elected and, as lifetime appointees, are unaccountable. The American people have tolerated this extraordinary judicial power because they instinctively respect the courts and because they do not fully understand what is really happening. The public education system does not convey much useful information about the judicial system or indeed about any other aspect of our constitutional structure. Those who manage the news media share the public's ignorance of the legal system and, in any event, are unlikely to protest because the judges have appeased the editors by making it extremely difficult to sue the media for defamation.[10] Newspapers, therefore, tend to be docile supporters of judicial activism. It is also likely that most journalists and newspaper editors are ideologically predisposed in favor of the Supreme Court's "liberal" decisions.

Beginning in the 1950s, under the leadership of Earl Warren (Chief Justice from 1953 to 1969), the Supreme Court initiated what has been called the "rights revolution," in which the Court moved aggressively to protect the rights of disadvantaged minorities. (The Court had previously indicated the transition toward a rights-based jurisprudence in a 1938 decision, which stated that the courts should be especially protective of the rights of "discrete and insular minorities."[11] The Warren Court proceeded to incorporate, selectively, most of the federal Bill of Rights provisions into the Constitution via the Fourteenth Amendment so that they became applicable to the states. This paved the way for a series of decisions extending the equal protection clause of

---

10   *New York Times v. Sullivan,* 376 U.S. 254 (1964).

11   *United States v. Carolene Products,* 304 U.S. 144,152, n.4 (1938).

the amendment to a number of allegedly disadvantaged constituencies. "Encouraged by the Supreme Court, federal district courts embarked on ambitious, long-standing ventures to reform school districts, prisons, mental institutions, and other state and local agencies by means of consent decrees and broad 'structural' injunctions."[12] Congress joined in the expansion of benefits to minorities through numerous civil rights and entitlement bills. (See Chapter 8.)

A few examples will serve to illustrate the manner in which the federal judiciary has altered the constitutional structure of government in America without the consent of any legislative body or the people.

Reapportionment

In *Reynolds v. Sims* (1964), the Court held that the Equal Protection Clause of the Fourteenth Amendment required that the seats in both houses of a state legislature be apportioned substantially on a population basis, even though the US Senate itself is not so apportioned.[13] Even where the majority of the voters in every county of the state approved the retention of an upper house not represented in accordance with population, the Court held that the apportionment was unconstitutional.[14] There was no precedent for either of these decisions. Chief Justice Warren simply invented a new constitutional principle: the "fundamental principle of representative government in this country is one of equal representation for equal numbers of people, without regard to race, sex, economic status, or place of residence within a State ... Legislators represent people, not trees or acres."[15] There is nothing in the history of representative institutions that supports this alleged principle,

---

12   Michael S. Greve, *The Upside-Down Constitution* (Cambridge, MA: Harvard University Press, 2012), p. 267.

13   377 U.S. 533 (1964).

14   *Lucas v. Forty-Fourth Gen. Assembly*, 377 U.S. 713, 737 (1964).

15   *Reynolds v. Sims*, supra.

and it was decisively rejected by the founders when they designed the constitutional framework in 1787. The idea of a second legislative body based on a principle other than population is designed to be a check on the tendency of temporary majorities to act impulsively and irresponsibly, thus injecting an element of stability and prudence into the political system at both the federal and state level. Now the states have been deprived by the Supreme Court of a useful tool for promoting responsible republican government. The Warren Court, in defiance of history and common sense, simply decided that the abstract dogma of numerical egalitarian democracy must be forced upon the people of the several states whether they wanted it or not.

Affirmative Action
In *Brown v. Board of Education*,[16] decided in 1954, the Supreme Court held that state laws requiring segregation in public schools according to race violated the Fourteenth Amendment to the Constitution, which forbids a state to deny to any person within its jurisdiction the equal protection of the laws. The Court's decision was based on its finding that segregation deprived Negro children of "equal educational opportunities." This decision was controversial in those states in which racial segregation had long been mandated; nevertheless, it has been widely accepted by the American public. Virtually everyone now agrees that mandatory racial segregation is bad social policy. Early opponents of the *Brown* decision argued that such a significant change should have been made by Congress because the Fourteenth Amendment specifically gives to Congress (rather than to the courts) the function of enforcing the amendment by "appropriate legislation." In 1964, Congress did, in fact, pass such legislation in the Civil Rights Act of 1964, which prohibited segregation in public schools and other public facilities on account of race, color, religion, or national origin. Accordingly, the issue of mandatory school segregation was appropriately settled as a matter of law.

---

16   347 U.S. 483 (1954).

The *Brown* decision, however, left open the question of whether integration of schools to achieve racial balance should be mandated by the courts or left to the states. The federal Civil Rights Act of 1964 addressed this very point by specifically providing that "nothing [in the Act] shall empower any official or court of the United States to issue any order seeking to achieve a racial balance in any school by requiring the transportation of pupils from one school to another or one school district to another." The sponsors of the Civil Rights Act stated unequivocally that the legislation was designed to achieve equal opportunity, not to mandate racial balance.[17] In spite of the clear language of the Civil Rights Act, the federal courts proceeded to do exactly what the statute seemed to forbid: they required school districts to transport pupils in order to achieve racial balance. The Supreme Court upheld the use of busing to achieve racial desegregation in schools, stating that Congress did not intend to withdraw from the federal courts their historic equitable remedial powers in such cases—in other words, the Act did not mean what it said.[18] Subsequent federal cases required extensive busing of students and even ordered detailed restructuring of school operations, including remedial education, testing, and counseling, which imposed heavy costs on school districts and states.[19]

Far from forbidding racial classifications in public education (which is what the *Brown* decision seemed to mean), compulsory integration *required* that pupils be assigned according to race. Compulsory school integration was a social and educational disaster in many cities, resulting in "white flight" that in many cases left inner city schools in worse condition than before. The Supreme Court was not alone to blame. Some state legislatures and federal agencies, supported by the elite press, joined in the pressure for racial categorization by passing numerous

---

17   Civil Rights Act of 1964, Section 407(a). See Nicholas Capaldi, "Twisting the Law," *Policy Review* (Spring 1980).

18   *Swann v. Charlotte-Mecklenburg Board of Education*, 402 U.S. 1, 17–18 (1971).

19   See *Milliken v. Bradley*, 433 U.S. 267 (1977).

laws and regulations requiring racial preferences in hiring, housing, and other areas. The net effect of "affirmative action" programs has been to encourage an ongoing struggle among racial groups over the allocation of jobs and other benefits, and to divide the society rather than unite it.

A review of preferential racial programs in societies around the world by Thomas Sowell showed that such programs almost always produce polarization, political backlash, and corruption.[20] In the United States, federal affirmative action policies were implemented beginning in the 1970s. Sowell's research shows that affirmative action programs may have benefited some black earners who were already relatively well-off but did little for low-income blacks.[21] Aid to minority businesses went overwhelmingly to a small fraction of mostly Hispanic and Asian-American firms. In the field of education, the admission of less-qualified minority students often resulted in lowering standards of performance in order to get better numerical results.[22] Although affirmative action was designed primarily to help poor black people, as Sowell concludes, "[a]ffirmative action does little for the poor in America, as elsewhere. The poverty rate among blacks was cut in half before there was affirmative action and has changed very little since then."[23] Volunteer programs, under which employers seek out qualified members of minority groups, can be beneficial. When commanded by edict of the state, however, preferential selection by race or sex will produce confrontation and tension rather than tolerance. Group preferences are also politically dangerous because preferences to one group lead to demands by other groups for similar preferential treatment. Affirmative action for blacks was followed by demands for special treatment for Hispanics, women,

---

20   Thomas Sowell, *Affirmative Action Around the World: an Empirical Study* (New Haven: Yale University Press, 2004).

21   *Ibid.,* p. 120.

22   *Ibid.,* p. 163.

23   *Ibid.,* p. 166.

and other groups. While some people in these groups have no doubt been helped, it is doubtful whether there have been overall social benefits from group preferences mandated by government.

There is a common thread running through the proliferating demands for group preferences: whatever problems any demanding group may encounter are always blamed on someone else. This is a conclusion that many politicians, courting the support of bloc voters, are eager to endorse. America has become a nation of would-be victims and complainants. All the unavoidable difficulties of life in a diverse society, instead of being resolved by individuals and communities, end up before the legislatures and the courts. In America today, group grievances tend to be politicized and turned into a form of mass resentment, accompanied by expressions of outrage and protest, that can sometimes generate serious social unrest.[24]

Religion and the Law

Previous chapters have emphasized the crucial importance of religion to social and cultural cohesion. From a historical perspective, legal systems have generally supported the basic religious and moral tenets that underlie the society's core beliefs. This was certainly true in the period of America's founding, when jurisprudential principles were based on the objective truths of an acknowledged moral order. This fundamental relationship between law and morality, however, was decisively altered in the twentieth century, when America's legal and policy elites fell under the influence of an increasingly secular and materialistic culture.

The First Amendment to the US Constitution provides that the federal Congress shall make no law respecting an establishment of religion or prohibiting the free exercise thereof. On its face, the establishment clause applies only to action by Congress and does not bind

---

24   For an interesting treatment of the phenomenon of mass resentment, see Max Scheler, *Ressentiment,* trans. Lewis B. Coser and William W. Holdheim (Milwaukee, WI: Marquette University Press, 2007 [1912]).

the states. One of the curiosities of contemporary jurisprudence is the Supreme Court's post–World War II interpretation of this clause, which on its face applies only to the "establishment of religion" by the federal Congress, to prohibit menorahs in public parks, public displays of religious symbols, and prayers before high school football games. The seminal case for the Supreme Court's current interpretation of the establishment clause is *Everson v. Board of Education,* decided in 1947, in which the Court took the occasion to declare what has now become accepted dogma:

> No tax in any amount, large or small, can be levied to support any religious activities or institutions, whatever they may be called, or whatever form they may adopt to teach or practice religion … In the words of Jefferson, the clause against establishment of religion was intended to erect a "wall of separation between church and State."[25]

Subsequent to *Everson,* the federal courts have struck down as unconstitutional the following practices, which any observer other than an antireligious zealot should regard as either harmless or trivial: the voluntary recitation of a nondenominational prayer in public schools, a one-minute period of silence for "meditation or voluntary prayer" in public schools, and the furnishing of maps and other secular instructional materials by a state for use in parochial schools.[26]

These establishment clause cases represent bad history as well as bad law. The establishment clause, as written, does not bind the states, and this was the unchallenged view of the federal courts for 150 years following the adoption of the Constitution. The 1789 debates make it clear that Congress did not want to interfere with the jurisdiction of the states in matters of religion: the states could, and did, continue

---

25   330 U.S. 1, 15–16 (1947).

26   *Engel v. Vitale,* 370 U.S. 421 (1962); *Wallace v. Jaffree,* 472 U.S. 38 (1985); *Meek v. Pittenger,* 421 U.S. 349 (1975); *Wolman v. Walter,* 433 U.S. 229 (1977); *Illinois ex rel. McCollum v. Board of Education,* 333 U.S. 203 (1948).

actively to promote religion. Bible reading in the public schools, for example, was a common practice throughout the nineteenth century and well into the twentieth.[27] There was never the slightest manifestation, either in Congress or in the state ratifying conventions, of an intention to erect a "wall of separation" between government and religion. The same Congress that wrote the First Amendment also appointed Congressional and military chaplains to be paid by the federal government. This alone makes nonsense of the Supreme Court's *dictum* in the *Everson* case that "[n]o tax in any amount, large or small, can be levied to support any religious activities or institutions, whatever they may be called." In the light of this history, the Supreme Court's conclusion that a statute permitting a minute of silent meditation or prayer is a step toward an established church "borders on, if it does not trespass into, the ridiculous."[28]

It is difficult in the best of societies to uphold moral order without the aid of religion. In contemporary urban civilization, it is all but impossible. The Supreme Court's "wall of separation" jurisprudence, by drastically weakening the capacity of the states to sustain the traditional link between public policy, morality, and religion, has contributed to the deterioration of the moral fabric that holds our society together.

In the recent case of *American Legion v. American Humanist Assn.,* the Supreme Court, including two recently appointed justices, indicated a willingness to reconsider some of its sweepingly secular interpretations of the establishment clause. The case involved a World War I memorial in the shape of a Latin cross erected on public land in Bladensburg, Maryland. The American Humanist Association sued the state commission that owned the land. The lower federal appellate court ruled that

---

27   Justice Rehnquist, dissenting, in *Wallace v. Jaffree,* 472 U.S. 38, 99 (1985) When I was a buy in the Virginia public schools during the 1940s, my teacher used to say a prayer every morning before beginning class.

28   Burger, C. J., dissenting, in *Wallace v. Jaffree,* 472 U.S. 38, 89 (1985). See David Upham, "The Court Should Tear Down Everson, Not the Maryland Cross," Law & Liberty (February 14, 2019), www.lawliberty.org.

the state commission's ownership and maintenance of the monument was an endorsement of Christianity in violation of the establishment clause. The Supreme Court reversed, holding that the establishment clause was not violated. The justices gave different reasons for their opinions, but the result was seven to two in favor of defending the monument. Justice Alito, writing for the majority, emphasized the symbolism of the cross as a memorial to the sacrifice of American lives during the war. He noted that "[a] government that roams the land, tearing down monuments with religious symbolism and scrubbing away the divine will strike many as aggressively hostile to religion" (citing the violent dechristianization during the French Revolution).[29]

Abortion

In 1973, the Supreme Court delivered an opinion that was perhaps the boldest act of extra-constitutional adjudication in its entire history. In *Roe v. Wade,* a pregnant single woman (Roe) brought an action challenging the constitutionality of the Texas criminal abortion laws, which prohibited procuring or attempting an abortion except on medical advice for the purpose of saving the mother's life. The Supreme Court held that the Texas law violated Roe's constitutional right to privacy, which the Court held to be implicit in the "due process" clause of the Fourteenth Amendment.[30] As in the case of the reapportionment decisions, this was pure judicial legislation. The Court disregarded the historical fact that a majority of the states had imposed restrictions on abortion for over a century; all such laws were struck down by the Court's edict. Moreover, in order to reach this result, the Court had to invent a right to privacy under the Fourteenth Amendment that could not have been contemplated when that amendment was adopted since no such legal right then existed.

---

29   *American Legion v. American Humanist Assn.,* 588 U.S.—(2019), No. 17–1717 (slip op. at 20).

30   *Roe v. Wade,* 410 U.S. 113 (1973).

In *Roe*, the Court unilaterally affirmed the constitutional right to destroy the lives of unborn children, a quintessentially unprotected and vulnerable class of persons. In *Planned Parenthood v. Casey*, which reaffirmed *Roe*, the Court opined that the right to abortion was based on a newly invented "right to define one's own concept of existence, of meaning, of the universe, and of the mystery of human life," a right that apparently included the privilege to take some innocent human lives at will.[31] This statement is profoundly wrong because it assumes that each individual can actually define his own concept of existence, meaning, and so forth without regard to social and moral obligations to others. It exemplifies the flawed doctrine of unlimited personal autonomy that is a major aspect of the modern temperament.[32] By the end of the twentieth century, over one million unborn children per year were being killed by abortion. This result is a startling instance of the worship of self that has taken the place of religion. If everyone can define the "mystery of life" in this wholly subjective and brutal fashion, the society has truly succumbed, as Christopher Lasch predicted, to the culture of narcissism.[33]

The precise constitutional issue was whether states have a right to prohibit the killing of unborn children, just as they have a right to prohibit the willful killing of dogs, cats, and postnatal humans. There are certainly some plausible arguments in favor of a woman's "right to choose." But such questions of life and death ought to be decided by a legislature, after open and public debate, rather than by an unelected court. Many state legislatures did, in fact, permit abortions at various stages of pregnancy, but the subject was at least open to democratic choice. All of this was foreclosed by *Roe*. The decision created a climate of bitter hostility and recrimination that has only worsened over the

---

31 *Planned Parenthood v. Casey*, 505 U.S. 833, 851 (1992).

32 The politics of personal autonomy is linked to the currently fashionable politics of identity. See Richard Reinsch, "Autonomy on the Road to Tyranny," *Modern Age* (Winter 2018), Vol. 60, No. 1.

33 Christopher Lasch, *The Culture of Narcissism* (New York: Warner Books, 1979).

years.[34] It seems clear that the constitutional privilege to abort is related to the right to consume pornography and other aspects of sexual liberation that have recently been elevated by the courts to the status of constitutionally protected rights. It is a wonderful irony, as Professor Gerard Bradley has pointed out, that sexual choice has been elevated to sacred status as part of the "mystery of existence" at the same time that the sacredness of religion has been diminished by the judicial secularization of the public realm.[35] This cultural anomaly reveals the real priorities of the society or at least those of its governing elites. The hedonism of rights-without-obligations has prevailed.

The legacy of *Roe* is a continuing trend toward the devaluation of human life. Prestigious universities have hired professors who defend the unlimited right of abortion and, in certain cases, even justify infanticide. There is a widespread demand for experimentation on live, fertilized human embryos. This is a slippery slope leading toward dehumanization and a culture of death.

Sex and Equal Protection

Virginia Military Institute (VMI), founded in 1839, was one of the nation's first military colleges. The Commonwealth of Virginia has always given it financial support. VMI's mission was to train men for leadership in military and civilian life through a rigorous system of physical and mental discipline and a traditional Code of Honor ("The Code of a Gentleman"). VMI has been extremely successful in accomplishing its mission, having graduated many distinguished military officers as well as business and political leaders. It was to be expected, therefore, that VMI would become a principal target of the radical feminists who seek to destroy every institution that retains any vestige of traditional male exclusiveness. In 1996, the feminists succeeded: the

---

34   The cultural war over abortion has been dramatically portrayed in Joyce Carol Oates's novel, *A Book of American Martyrs* (New York: HarperCollins 2017).

35   Gerard Bradley, "The Fantasy Life of Justices," *National Review* (December 31, 1999), p. 26.

United States Supreme Court held that Virginia's support of VMI violated the equal protection clause of the Fourteenth Amendment because it did not admit women.[36] Any government action based on sex, the Court said, must be based upon an "exceedingly persuasive justification." But it is obvious from the opinion that *no* justification would ever have satisfied the Court since it cursorily dismissed a century-and-a-half of proud tradition, the overwhelming support of VMI's alumni body, the consistently held views of Virginia's executive and legislative branches, and the existence of an alternative women's leadership program created by the Virginia legislature. The decision is especially questionable in view of the historical fact that when the Fourteenth Amendment was ratified in 1868, VMI and other all-male state-supported schools had long existed, and no one could possibly have contemplated that the amendment was intended to force them to admit women.

Marriage

Throughout the recorded history of the human race, marriage has been recognized as "a physical, legal and moral union between man and woman in complete community of life for the establishment of a family."[37] Marriage developed out of a primeval habit for a man and a woman to live together and to raise their offspring in common. As civilization developed, marriage between man and woman was sanctioned by custom and law, and became an established social institution.[38]

Marriage as a union between a man and a woman was recognized under Roman law, canon law, English law, and until recently, under the laws of the United States. When the Fourteenth Amendment was ratified in 1868, every state in the United States limited marriage to one man and one woman. This universal principle was challenged in the

---

36   United States v. Virginia, 518 U.S. 515 (1996).

37   *Encyclopedia Britannica,* Eleventh Ed., Vol. 17. (1911).

38   Edward Westermark, *The History of Human Marriage,* Vol. I, pp. 27–28 (Nabu Public Domain Reprints, undated, originally published in London in 1891).

case of *Obergefell v. Hodges* (2015) by several same-sex couples in various states whose laws defined marriage as a union between one man and one woman. Plaintiffs claimed that the officials of these states violated the due process and equal protection clauses of the Fourteenth Amendment to the Constitution. The United States Supreme Court held that the right to marry is a fundamental right inherent in the liberty of the person and that under the Fourteenth Amendment couples of the same sex may not be deprived of that right. Justice Kennedy, speaking for the majority, said, "Under the Constitution, same-sex couples seek in marriage the same legal treatment as opposite-sex couples, and it would disparage their choices and diminish their personhood to deny them this right."[39] This decision is another example of the doctrine of personal autonomy that has replaced traditional community values. Kennedy wrote at length about the history of traditional marriage, but he noted that marriage "has evolved over time." This process of evolution is in accordance with the Progressive doctrine that the Constitution itself has evolved and must continue to evolve based on the Justices' changing views of public policy. In a telling phrase, Kennedy stated that the people who wrote the Bill of Rights and the Fourteenth Amendment could not know all of the possible future dimensions of freedom, "so they entrusted to future generations a charter protecting the right of all persons to enjoy liberty as we learn its meaning."[40] Liberty, in other words, means whatever five of the current Justices want it to mean.

If the legal aspects of a social custom as longstanding and basic as marriage are altered overnight in such a fundamental way, one would think that the people or their elected representatives should have some choice in the matter. The majority brushes off this objection with the conclusory statement that "when the rights of persons are violated, the Constitution requires redress by the courts, notwithstanding the more

---

39   *Obergefell v. Hodges*, 576 U.S.—-,—-(2015), slip op. at 19.

40   576 U.S. at—-, slip op. at 11.

general value of democratic decisionmaking."[41] But in the case of a social change as drastic and controversial as this, prudence and common sense, as well as ordinary notions of judicial restraint, should have led the Court to proceed with more caution, at the very least giving the state legislatures time to consider the question. As Chief Justice Roberts stated in his dissent: "the Court invalidates the marriage laws of more than half the States and orders the transformation of a social institution that has formed the basis of human society for millennia, for the Kalahari Bushmen and the Han Chinese, the Carthaginians and the Aztecs. Just who do we think we are?"[42] The real question at issue is who decides what constitutes marriage—the people acting through their elected representatives or five unelected judges?

This case represents another step in the accumulation of power by the Supreme Court at the expense of the states and the people. Justice Scalia, in his separate dissent, called the Court's opinion a "threat to American democracy." Scalia continued, in a memorable passage:

> Today's decree says that my Ruler, and the Ruler of 320 million Americans coast-to-coast, is a majority of the nine lawyers on the Supreme Court. The opinion in these cases is the furthest extension in fact—and the furthest extension one can even imagine—of the Court's claimed power to create "liberties" that the Constitution and its Amendments neglect to mention. This practice of constitutional revision by an unelected committee of nine, always accompanied (as it is today) by extravagant praise of liberty, robs the People of the most important liberty they asserted in the Declaration of Independence and won in the Revolution of 1776: the freedom to govern themselves.[43]

---

41   576 U.S.—-, slip op. at 24.

42   576 U.S. at—-, slip op. diss. at 3.

43   576 U.S.—- at—-, slip op. diss. at 2.

The decisions discussed in this section manifest several major themes of this book: the egalitarian impulse toward breaking down local particularities and customary social distinctions; the centralization of power at the expense of local institutions; the change in the rule of law from a system founded on objective legal principles to a jurisprudence of results based on currently popular notions of social policy; the assumption by the courts of an openly legislative role; and the weakening of traditional values of marriage, family, and discipline and their replacement by diversity and personal autonomy, the values favored by today's new elites.

The Politicization of the Courts

The role of the courts under the traditional Anglo-American system of justice was to apply the existing common and statutory law to the facts pursuant to neutral and established constitutional principles. In the twentieth century, as we have seen, this traditional view of the law changed as the courts began to reach decisions based on considerations of social policy, which had previously been deemed to be within the purview of the legislature. The US Congress has encouraged this "progressive" policy by delegating more and more of its policy-making responsibility to federal agencies. By doing so, Congress may hope to avoid accountability for difficult and controversial decisions. Those adversely affected have found that the only practical way to hold the bureaucrats accountable is to bring them before the courts, with the result that the courts are pushed even further into the political arena. Accordingly, as Senator Ben Sasse has said, "the Supreme Court becomes a substitute political battleground."[44]

The politicization of the Supreme Court has been evident since the advent of the Warren Court in the 1950s and has become plainly visible in recent Congressional hearings for the confirmation of judicial nominees. The confirmation hearings for Judge Brett Kavanaugh in

---

44   Ben Sasse, "Blame Congress for Politicizing the Court," *Wall Street Journal* (September 6, 2018), p. A19.

2018 turned into a political circus, with Democratic Senators constantly interrupting the chairman of the Senate Judiciary Committee, while protestors screamed vulgarities in an attempt to disrupt the hearings. (Dozens of them were arrested.) This travesty of senatorial process was followed by a barrage of unsupported accusations of personal misconduct on the part of the nominee. As Judge Kavanagh himself expressed it during the confirmation hearings, "advise and consent has become search and destroy." The flagrant effort to intimidate Kavanaugh and his supporters reflected the high political and philosophical stakes of the battle, as well as the degree of open hostility on the part of the American left to constitutional conservatism. Judge Kavanaugh represented the judicial philosophy of constitutional originalism, discussed earlier in this chapter. Originalism means deciding cases in accordance with the Constitution and laws as written, a process which makes the law reasonably predictable. The opposing philosophy held by the activist progressives who opposed Kavanaugh holds that the Constitution is a "living document" that can be revised and adjusted in accordance with the changing policy views of the judges. This view makes the legal process unpredictable and leads to the arbitrary exercise of government power. These two opposing judicial philosophies cannot easily be reconciled.

Senator Ben Sasse has provided the responsible answer:

> The solution is not to try to find judges who will be policy makers or to turn the Supreme Court into an election battle. The solution is to restore a proper constitutional order with the balance of powers. We need a Congress that writes laws then stands before the people and faces the consequences. We need an executive branch that has a humble view of its job as enforcing the law, not trying to write laws in Congress's absence. And we need a judiciary that applies written laws to facts in cases that are actually before it.
>
> This is the elegant, fair process the Founders created.... This is why we say justice is blind. This is why we give judges lifetime tenure.[45]

---

45   Ibid.

Law and the Quest for a Risk-Free Society

A vital and creative society is characterized by bold self-confidence; but a declining nation is preoccupied with failure rather than success. In contemporary America, the evidence is mixed. US technology is the most innovative in the world, and America's system of financial capitalism, in spite of periodic setbacks, has produced more prosperity than could possibly have been imagined two centuries ago. Nevertheless, contemporary American society is beset by hypochondria, complaining, and anxiety. Medical advertisements and commentary fill the airwaves. The news media regularly stimulate popular anxiety about depletion of the earth's resources, global warming, the population explosion, pollution, and a thousand other purported perils to civilization, most of them exaggerated or unproven. In America's litigious society, virtually any accident will be followed by lawsuits seeking to shift the cost to someone else. Freedom from risk has become an obsession, shackling the American economy with unworkable regulations and suppressing innovation.

Americans have always been litigious. We have not been subject to the same social restraints that inhibit more traditional peoples, and the customary European reluctance to bring lawsuits has never existed in the United States. Foreigners have often cited with amazement the extraordinary number of lawyers in the United States; relative to population, the United States has many more lawyers than any other country in the world.[46] John Maynard Keynes commented that the *Mayflower,* when she sailed from Plymouth, must have been filled entirely with attorneys.

Social forces more profound than simple litigiousness and self-interested lawyers are at work. American society has experienced a significant shift away from the traditional values of individual responsibility, thrift, and self-discipline. In the age of instant gratification, everyone demands and expects a certain life style as a matter of right. Television, one of the most powerful social forces in America today, fosters the twin illusions

---

46 Mary Ann Glendon, *A Nation Under Lawyers* (New York: Farrar Straus & Giroux, 1994), pp. 3, 53.

that wealth is instantly accessible and that most evils are the fault of rich malefactors or conspirators. No one can be expected, under contemporary conditions, to suffer injury without demanding liberal recompense. Multimillion-dollar jury verdicts simply reflect these social expectations. In the political sphere, many social functions have been shifted from individuals and families to government. The expansion of liability is only one part of this larger movement toward the collectivization of risk.

In the legal arena, these trends were reflected in what is called the "tort law revolution." Beginning in the 1920s and accelerating after World War II, the tort liability system in the United States shifted from a traditional system in which liability was predicated on individual fault to a system based largely on the social goal of compensation. Under the new liability regime, fault as a prerequisite to liability has been eroded or even eliminated, and traditional defenses have been weakened. Jury awards and settlements have risen dramatically. The tort law revolution occurred because courts and legislatures accepted the policy argument that losses from injuries should be shifted from injured persons to manufacturers or service providers, no matter who was at fault. The rationale for this doctrine was to redistribute the burden of risk from individuals to corporations and, via the insurance mechanism, to society at large. This was a radical change from traditional legal rules under which a defendant was not liable unless the plaintiff could show that the defendant had done something wrong.[47]

Legal scholars and proponents of "legal realism" in the 1930s initiated a reform movement designed to make it easier for complainants to start lawsuits, leading to major changes in the Federal Rules of Civil Procedure in 1938, followed by similar changes in state procedural law. The courts began to tolerate vague and uninformative complaints, often copied almost verbatim from lawyers' formbooks. Complaints

---

47 George Priest, "The Invention of Enterprise Liability: A Critical History of the Intellectual Foundations of Modern Tort Law," 14 *Journal of Legal Studies* 461 (1985); Glendon, *supra*, p. 53 et seq.

giving minimal information about the actual charges were sufficient to get the plaintiff into court, requiring the defendant to hire a lawyer and respond. Once a complaint survived a motion for summary judgment (which was relatively easy under the new rules and the tolerance of sympathetic judges), the case had real settlement value—that is, defendants were faced with the heavy costs of "discovery" (a process through which lawyers can require opponents to produce voluminous documents and give deposition testimony prior to trial), forcing them to incur substantial legal fees. Discovery in complex litigation can involve hundreds of thousands of pages of documents, depositions of corporate officers lasting for weeks, and legal costs of many millions of dollars. If the case goes to trial, defendants face the additional risk of a potentially ruinous verdict. Under these circumstances, defendants usually decide to settle the case for an amount large enough to provide the plaintiff's attorney with a healthy contingent fee. The threat of major litigation thus, all too often, becomes a tool of legalized extortion.[48]

Under the American legal system, damage recoveries can be enormous, frequently amounting to millions or even billions of dollars. In the 1990s, for example, tobacco companies agreed to pay more than $200 billion to settle cases involving a product known by its users to be dangerous.[49] According to the US Chamber of Commerce's Institute for Legal Reform, the US tort system imposed on the American economy costs totaling $429 billion in 2016, or 2.3 percent of the nation's GDP (up from 1 percent of GDP in 1960). Of the $429 billion total, only 57 percent went to compensate injured plaintiffs, while 31 percent went to lawyers for plaintiffs and defendants and 12 percent

---

48 See Walter K. Olson, *The Litigation Explosion: What Happened When America Unleashed the Lawsuit* (New York: Truman Talley Dutton, 1991), Chapter 6. Olson's book provides useful information on America's burdensome legal system.

49 Greve, *op. cit.,* p. 295.

for insurance costs.[50] Litigation is encouraged in the United States by the practice of awarding contingent fees to successful plaintiffs' lawyers, often amounting to as much as one-third of the recovery, and by the availability of "punitive damages" (intended to punish the defendant for his conduct) sometimes awarded in amounts far exceeding compensatory damages. Some American law firms accept money from third parties to finance cases in exchange for a percentage of the recovery.[51] These practices do not exist in most other advanced countries. In view of these incentives, it is not surprising that suing for damages is a growth industry in America.

Eddie Rickenbacker was once quoted as having said that "accidents are the price we pay for motion." We are all aware that nothing is free, and the quest for the risk-free society through shifting the costs of accidents has imposed a heavy cost on American consumers and taxpayers. The costs of the tort system are far higher in the United States than in any other major industrialized country. Between 1950 and the end of the century, US tort costs grew far more rapidly than the US economy, imposing a "deadweight cost" on the economy. Liability insurance has become extremely expensive, especially for small businesses, doctors, and others who are particularly exposed to lawsuits. Many day care centers and playgrounds have closed because they cannot obtain insurance. Some products—vaccines for example—have been withdrawn from the market altogether for fear of legal liability.

The American legal system imposes heavy costs on business and on the public generally. These costs could be substantially reduced by a few simple reforms; for example, adopting the European rule of assessing legal costs (including attorneys' fees) against the losing party; assessing

---

50 "Costs and Compensation of the US Tort System," US Chamber of Commerce Institute for Legal Reform (2018); Towers Watson, 2011 Update on US Tort Cost Trends. www.casact.org/library/studynotes/Towers-Watson-Tort-Costs-Trends.pdf.

51 See "Appealing Returns: Third-Party Funding for Lawsuits Attracts Investors and Lawyers Alike," *The Economist* (August 18, 2018), p. 63.

stiffer penalties for frivolous claims; limiting class actions by requiring members of the class to affirmatively opt in to the class; placing stricter limits on punitive damages; and encouraging arbitration and other forms of alternate dispute resolution. Some of these reforms have been adopted at the state level. But they are usually resisted by lawyers, who thrive on the existing system, and by the self-appointed spokesmen for consumers, who favor punishing corporations regardless of the impact on the economy. Congress and state legislatures also resist such reforms because they are dominated by lawyers. Not surprisingly, many ordinary people also resist reform of the tort system on the expectation that someday they, too, may be the beneficiary of a large recovery. This is a part of the "lottery syndrome" that is a feature of American society. The costly tort system and the public's aversion to risk are signs that we are in the process of abandoning the spirit of adventure and risk-taking that made America the most creative nation on earth.

In addition to private litigation, federal and state governments have been increasingly active in investigating and prosecuting individuals and businesses, especially financial institutions. Dozens of government agencies are empowered to enforce thousands of laws and regulations. Aiding the assault on business, as noted above, are armies of private lawyers. All of this regulation and litigation is time-consuming and very costly. As *The Economist* put it, "The upshot is a deluge of paperwork. If banks once did banking, now they practice law."[52] There are hundreds of crimes set forth in Title 18 of the United States Code and additional thousands of regulations in the Code of Federal Regulations involving potential penalties. A determined prosecutor with enough time and money can find some violation of law by virtually anyone he chooses to investigate, and few people can afford to pay the heavy costs of defending against a serious criminal prosecution. We read regularly in the news media about people accused of crimes who plead guilty to lesser offenses in order to avoid being financially ruined by a hostile

---

52   "America's Financial System: Law and Disorder," *The Economist* (October 13, 2012), p. 83.

prosecutor. The rule of law has been overburdened with deadly snares and costly obstacles. It is time for a good house cleaning.

Liberty

Any meaningful discussion of liberty assumes two basic principles. *First,* human liberty cannot survive without lawful constraint. If every person is free to threaten the life or property of others, then no one is free. An excess of liberty produces anarchy, which in turn leads to tyranny when the strongest person or faction eventually asserts control by force. True liberty, as Edmund Burke argued, requires placing chains on human appetites. This, indeed, is what civilization is all about.

Second, political liberty means freedom from arbitrary and capricious power; this implies that the rulers themselves must be restrained by law. If, as democratic theory assumes, the real rulers are the people, then the will of the people, as well as the actions of their appointed agents, must be limited by law. In Goethe's words, "He who seeks great things must practice self-control;/In limitation reveals himself the master,/And law alone can give us freedom."[53] These lines by Goethe aptly summarize one of the main themes of this book: great men and great nations seek ordered liberty, not license, in governance as in art.

In the twenty-first century, the American experiment of "ordered liberty" is undergoing significant strains as a result of the social infirmities previously described, including family breakup, deterioration of some urban areas, drug abuse, pornography, violent crime, uncontrolled immigration, poor education, irresponsible government, and moral anarchy. We have also seen an increase in violent demonstrations by extreme left-wing and right-wing agitators. These disorders have been accompanied by the emergence of an erroneous belief that liberty means

---

53   My translation. The poem is "Natur und Kunst" ("Nature and Art"), 1800. These lines in the original German are "Wer Grosses will, muss sich Zusammenruffen;/In der Beschrankung zeigt sich erst der Meister,/Und das Gesetz nur kann uns Freiheit geben." See Goethe's *Selected Poetry* (Libris), Trans. David Luke.

the absence of restraints on personal conduct. Beginning in the 1960s, it became fashionable to interpret many ordinary behavioral restrictions as infringements on individual liberty. This attitude encourages the belief that the individual is entitled to gratify himself according to his own inclinations and that most conventional moral rules are oppressive. The traditional psychological and social mechanisms of restraint—guilt, shame, and stigma—are regarded as insignia of repression that ought to be eliminated, either by therapy or simply by desuetude. The prevailing doctrine of relativism has added to the confusion by teaching that one moral view is as good as another. Honor, respect, manners, filial piety, patriotism, and similar traditional values that held families and communities together have largely been abandoned in favor of "self-realization" and personal autonomy.

Liberty must be limited by law in order to secure the benefits of civic order. It seems plain enough that the construction of a public philosophy of limits is a necessary condition for the return to a sense of community. But "community" does not mean the centralized power of a remote and bureaucratic government. The reconciliation of liberty and individual responsibility should be left to the genuine, rooted institutions of family, churches, private associations, and local government, in which each person may fulfill himself not as a solitary individual but as a member of a true community. Such communities, founded upon mutual respect for the integrity of life and property, would not tolerate those forms of conduct that, by destroying civility, create an atmosphere ultimately destructive of freedom itself.

The activity of volunteer nonprofit organizations shows that Americans are still willing to commit time and money to helping others. On the other hand, care for the elderly, education, health, welfare, and many other vital aspects of everyday life are increasingly concentrated in the hands of a permanently entrenched bureaucratic elite that is impervious to family or community control. The society is managed by the administrative state to the extent necessary to provide a docile electorate, while at the same time people are induced to believe that they are "free" because they have been released from the traditional moral authority of the community. We have, therefore, the peculiar paradox of administrative tyranny and personal irresponsibility (a condition which the late political theorist Samuel Francis called "anarcho-tyranny"). This was precisely the situation in the late Roman Empire. The only way out of this trap is a political, cultural, and religious counter-revolution that will restore the United States to its republican roots. Fortunately, there are signs that at least a portion of the electorate has recognized that a movement back toward individual and local responsibility is needed. Such a revolution faces serious obstacles, however, because a majority of the population is functionally dependent on the services provided by the administrative state, yet psychologically dependent on virtually unlimited autonomy in matters of personal conduct. This contradiction will be difficult to resolve.

There are some structural changes that might alleviate the worst excesses of political ignorance and dependency. A sweeping reform of education is needed, beginning with rediscovery of the kind of civic education that links rights with responsibilities. Central government should be restructured by returning most governmental functions to the local and state level so that the citizens can more effectively guard the guardians. That will require convincing Americans of the moral value of limited government and the importance of character in political leaders. In the absence of a moral and religious revival, such a change of heart is unlikely. Historically, a thoroughgoing social reformation has often required a serious crisis induced by war, civil upheaval, or economic calamity. In the meantime, the shallow optimism of today, based on faith in a provident government and lasting material comfort, is likely to prove fragile.

10

CONCLUSION

IN THE LIGHT OF OUR HISTORICAL REVIEW, we must ask: Is the United States going the way of Rome? Of course, we do not yet know the answer to this question. As Hegel observed, "The owl of Minerva spreads its wings only when the dusk has fallen," and the day is not yet over. There are some aspects of America's recent history that resemble conditions in the late Roman Empire, including threats from external enemies, excessive strategic commitments, fiscal irresponsibility, oppressive bureaucracy, burdensome regulation, centralization of power, bitter internal dissension, and educational and moral decline. But there are also strengths in twenty-first century America, including considerable military power, a comparatively free and flourishing economy, a high standard of living, and freedom of speech and religion. Reflecting upon the themes we have discussed, what conclusions can we draw?

National Commitments and Military Strength

The historical record shows that every nation must be prepared to defend its territory and its people unless it is willing to submit to the protection of a stronger power. As a nation expands its political and commercial commitments, its defense requirements increase. The decline of Rome, Britain, and other historical empires was due in large part to their diminished ability to deliver sufficient military force to defend their extended interests. The terrorist war that began with the attack on the United States in September 2001 showed that America is vulnerable to threats from irregular and hostile forces. The terrorist attack on the American homeland was premeditated and savage, and the United States was wholly justified in responding with lethal force. Although the United States and its allies have achieved significant success in defeating the Islamic State on the ground in the Middle East, the threat from Islamic terrorism is a continuing one. Other nations, particularly China and Russia, have increased their military strength and have opposed US interests abroad. It is clear, therefore, that US defense capabilities will have to be greatly strengthened.

If the ability to project military power were the sole criterion of national strength, it would appear on the surface that the United States need not be concerned. As the Persian Gulf conflict of 1991 and the Afghan and Iraq wars that followed September 2001 demonstrated, the United States is capable of projecting a devastating array of air, ground, and naval forces virtually anywhere in the world. At the present time, the United States stands unrivaled as the most powerful military state on earth. But the same was said of Rome and Britain at the height of their prestige. In retrospect, it is clear that both were vastly overextended, and once it became obvious that their military forces and economic power were insufficient to sustain their far-flung commitments, their empires began to unravel. During the twentieth century, America's power was a force that supported Western civilization and a stable world order, and the United States should be given credit for that accomplishment. Today, however, America's commitments are extraordinarily diverse and burdensome. The United States has troops stationed across the world in Europe, the Middle East, Korea, Japan, and elsewhere and has made serious formal and informal commitments to NATO members and other vulnerable countries. Meanwhile, our European allies, who could afford to defend themselves, spend a pittance on defense and often indulge in the luxury of criticizing America while counting on our military support. The United States cannot be expected to underwrite the defense of the entire free world. American leaders will not for long risk the destruction of American cities to protect countries that are unwilling to protect themselves.

Nevertheless, sometimes we have no choice but to fight. The United States is now engaged in a struggle that is the latest chapter in a lengthy battle to preserve Western civilization. Our radical Islamic enemies believe that they are permitted, and even compelled by a belligerent and implacable version of their faith, to destroy what they regard as our decadent and corrupt Western societies. Western views favoring individual freedom, tolerance, and democracy are not part of the Islamic creed. While most Muslims are not terrorists, some are, and some have infiltrated into Western Europe, have done serious damage there, and have also attacked our country. This conflict is not over.

Since the end of the Cold War, the United States has dismantled a significant part of its military capability. It is particularly dismaying that Congress for many years has been unwilling to finance an adequate strategic defense system against incoming missiles. Some potentially hostile nations already have access to nuclear-armed ballistic missiles capable of reaching our cities. The failure to construct a solid defense against this threat is a conspicuous sign of weakness. The challenges of cyberwarfare and combat in outer space will require substantial resources. China poses a growing military threat, and other threats may emerge unexpectedly. Over time, an adequate national defense may require serious sacrifices, including higher taxes and cutbacks in many popular domestic programs. Whether the American public, accustomed to half a century of easy living and increasing dependency on government subsidies, will be prepared to make real sacrifices will be a crucial test of the nation's discipline and stamina.

The Economic Base

The US economy remains the strongest in the world, and Americans enjoy a remarkably high standard of living. A combination of individual freedom, a relatively free market, property and contract rights, access to capital, and the rule of law have helped to make Americans productive and wealthy. American science has produced a long series of dramatic accomplishments that have changed the course of history, including the harnessing of electricity, the internal combustion engine, aeronautics, nuclear power, the exploration of space, the computer revolution, and the internet. Yet there are some disturbing signs. American education in science and math is inferior to that of many of its competitors. The nation's slow rate of domestic savings in recent decades has stifled capital formation. The Federal Reserve's decade-long low interest rate policy has been politically popular, but it has punished savers and the elderly. Our industrial leaders have emphasized short-term profits at the expense of long-term growth while excessive consumption and inadequate investment erode the nation's infrastructure. The economy is burdened with a mountain of debt and unfunded entitlements, while an increased proportion of America's wealth goes to nonproductive government programs. In the near future, Social Security, Medicare, and other government programs will place a crushing tax burden on the productive middle classes unless these programs can be sharply limited. With this governmental overload, along with inadequate savings rates and excessive reliance on debt, the nation faces frightening fiscal risks.

Capitalism is the most successful system for the creation of wealth that the world has known. As Pope John Paul II observed, "It would appear that, on the level of individual nations and of international relations the free market is the most efficient instrument for utilizing resources and effectively responding to needs."[1] Pope John Paul went on to emphasize, however, that there are many human needs that do not find satisfaction in an economic market. Moreover, we know that capitalism is subject to periodic phases of "bubbles" and "slumps," resulting in what has been called the "creative destruction" of enterprises, a historical process in which some firms fail and others arise. The process of creative destruction is often sudden and brutal, in that weak firms quickly go to the wall, while the strong survive. An example of this economic volatility is the 2007–8 recession, which resulted from a combination of excessively expansionist monetary policy by the US Federal Reserve and aggressive government promotion of mortgage lending to unqualified borrowers together with reckless lending by banks and widespread use of credit swaps and other derivative securities that were poorly understood by those who issued them, all of which was fueled by a combination of greed and negligence, which we have come to expect from these periodic lapses of discipline. This crisis, like many others in modern times, led to widespread demands for government action. The Bush and Obama administrations responded to these demands by spending trillions of dollars on "stimulus" programs that imposed heavy debt and tax burdens on the public.

Why do these economic difficulties matter? One reason is that the military forces needed to defend a nation's interests require a strong economy and a productive population. A second and equally important reason for worrying about economics is that a strong economy provides an opportunity for people with energy or talent to achieve a better material life for themselves and their families. Without this safety valve, social frustrations among a rootless population would quickly reach explosive levels. Economic opportunity, moreover, channels man's aggressive drives into benign or at least relatively harmless undertakings. As Dr. Samuel Johnson said, "There are few ways in which a man can be more

---

1   John Paul II, *Centisimus Annus*, (Boston: St. Paul Books, 1998), p. 49.

innocently employed than in getting money."[2] In all great civilizations, commercial undertakings give rise to adventures, energies, and ideas that expand the mind and stimulate the imagination. Art, music, and literature are among the beneficiaries of this process.

Whatever its form of economic organization, the consequences to any nation of permitting its economy to deteriorate are serious. Britain was able to extend Western civilization and constitutional government to the far reaches of the globe because of the technology and wealth generated by the industrial revolution. As a result of overstretch, together with a lapse in technological education and industrial innovation (along with the misfortune of World War I), Britain's economy could no longer support its role in the world. Britain's economic decline, in turn, contributed to the political climate that produced the stagnation of post-World War II socialism. Other examples are abundant. The economic weakness of other empires from ancient Rome and early modern Spain to the Soviet Union was a critical factor leading to their disintegration. Furthermore, as we have argued throughout this book, economic, political, and moral factors are closely interrelated. The absence of economic opportunity deprives people of a useful outlet for their energies and leads them to engage in less desirable forms of aggression and manipulation in a struggle over shrinking resources. A weak economy, social unrest, corruption, bureaucratic inertia, and cultural stagnation are likely to be mutually reinforcing, as can be seen in the case of many less developed countries today.

For all of these reasons, it is important that the productivity of the American economy and America's entrepreneurial culture be maintained and strengthened. The best way to achieve this goal is to return to the principles of political economy that have traditionally sustained America's economic vitality. These principles include low rates of taxation, limited government, free markets, encouragement of private enterprise, fiscal responsibility, sound money, and the rule of law. America's

---

2   James Boswell, *The Life of Samuel Johnson* (London: Penguin Books, 2008), p. 435.

economic revival of 2017–19, stimulated by a reduction in taxation and regulation as well as by a global economic recovery, showed that economic growth is still possible for nations willing to adopt responsible economic policies.

Education and Culture

A vigorous economy also depends upon sound educational institutions. By almost any measure American educational standards have declined in recent decades. American public school students are far from the top of the industrial world's scholastic curve in history, geography, languages, mathematics, and science. Popular ignorance is so vast that literate communication with the average high school graduate, and even many college graduates, is next to impossible. The educational debacle can be traced to a combination of misguided egalitarianism, lower standards, and weakened discipline. There is no better evidence of the decadence of American society than the acquiescence of the public in the perpetuation of a monopolistic system of public education that has clearly failed. The passivity of a majority of parents in the face of the dismal inadequacy of so many of our public schools is a clear sign of cultural and social decline. Fortunately, there are signs that some Americans are becoming aware of the need for restoration of excellence in education, and educational choice plans have been implemented in a few places. But there is strong political opposition to the steps that would have to be taken to achieve genuinely higher standards, which would mean providing parents with a real alternative to public schooling.

A further source of disorder is the startling fact that a powerful and vocal faction within the "progressive" elite that manages American education has turned against American values and even against Western culture itself. This trend raises the interesting question of whether the process of mimesis, described by Arnold Toynbee, in which the high standards of the dominant elite spread down gradually to elevate the rest, is now operating in reverse, as it did in the late Roman Empire, so that the habits of the "mass man" destroy the dominant culture rather than preserving it. That result will follow if the countercultural elites of today succeed in turning the educated classes (or what is left of them) against the classical-Christian synthesis that constitutes the intellectual structure of Western culture. As it happens, the countercultural advocates do not offer anything in the place of Western culture other than a syrupy amalgam of third-world folklore and socialist nostalgia. If they succeed in the nihilistic enterprise of undermining the existing culture, whatever takes its place is likely to be much weaker than what we have.

The cultural breakdown has recently become more widespread and alarming. Mobs of illiterate students have prevented speakers whose views are unwelcome from speaking on college campuses. Other mobs of (mostly left-wing) agitators have disrupted lawful gatherings on campuses and elsewhere. Historically ignorant politicians and activists have torn down monuments to decent and honorable soldiers who fought in America's Civil War and are renaming old streets and buildings in an Orwellian effort to rewrite history. These are our internal barbarians at work.

The degradation of art is a further symptom of cultural decline. Oswald Spengler, in his powerful book *The Decline of the West,* predicted that the decline of objective standards of judgment would adversely affect art as well as philosophy, and he has surely been proven correct. While the early modernists brought novel and exciting ways of representing reality, these efforts were eventually replaced by the cultivation of novelty for its own sake, resulting in a deluge of junk art. Once all standards had been abandoned, anything was permitted. As in Gibbon's Roman empire, we see everywhere freakishness masquerading as originality. The fragmented quality and inherent subjectivity of modern art undermine the foundation for a widely shared view of its significance. Since the signs are uncertain or undecipherable, art's role in cultural transmission is critically impaired.

The model of decline discussed in this book predicts that spiritual decline is likely to be associated with cultural and social decline. In America, the breadth of religious practice still seems impressive in comparison to other Western industrialized countries. Public opinion polls continue to show relatively high levels of church attendance and belief in God. But the depth of religious commitment is open to question. The leadership of the mainline Christian denominations seems more interested in feminism, pacifism, social equality, and other trendy political causes than in interpreting the spiritual meaning of Scripture. There are signs that Buddhism and Islam are on the rise, in addition to a number of Wiccan and other bizarre cults. (Spengler argued that such cults tend to proliferate in the last stages of a dying civilization.) In the alternative, the secularized masses will seek consolation through socialism, fascism, or some other form of secular utopia. When the utopian dream collapses, they will be thrown back to tribalism and self-aggrandizement ("the will to power").

The real choice for the citizens of Western nations is either to return to their traditions, including recovery of their religious and intellectual sources, or to acquiesce in the continuing dissolution of Western culture and to look for something else. What that "something else" might be is, of course, unknown. It is likely to involve some mixture of oriental and "New Age" beliefs, stimulated by immigration from the south and east and by the ideology of multiculturalism. Political balkanization is also likely since there will no longer be a common culture to hold the society together. America is already seriously divided by a seemingly unbridgeable ideological gap between traditional "Middle Americans," who cling to religious faith, property rights, hard work, family values, patriotism, and a stubborn distrust of government, and the influential "progressive" elites who dominate the national political and cultural agenda and favor secularism, moral relativism, pacifism, globalism, and the omni-competent administrative welfare state. If we give up the culture that created and sustained our country, there is nothing of value to replace it. We will simply fail and slip back into the receding tide of historical decline.

Social Cohesion and Leadership

In a declining society, the forces that tie people together are weakened. Early Roman society, led by a vigorous and duty-conscious aristocracy, was characterized by a close relationship between social and military forms of organization, tight links between religion and the family (*pietas*), and the development over several centuries of an ingrained respect for tradition and law. When these social forces began to unravel, social cohesion was impaired, and the underlying contradictions of a rigidly class-based society came to the surface, resulting in a vicious civil war in the first century BC, followed by the establishment of imperial tyranny. Roman society was later undermined by a flood of immigration and a weakening agricultural economy, which together produced a vast and unassimilable urban proletariat. The decline of the pagan religion was another serious blow. Without a living religion to support the code of *pietas*, Roman society could be held together only by inertia and brute force. Once religion and customary restraints have eroded, respect for community standards gives way to the pursuit of momentary pleasure, which in turn accelerates the decline both of the family and of the values of loyalty and solidarity that families reinforce. The hard civic values of honor and courage are succeeded by pacifism, skepticism, and cynicism. Ordinary citizens are unwilling to make sacrifices in support of corrupt and self-seeking governors. Fortunately for those who survived the collapse of Rome, the advent of Christianity brought new hope and real spiritual comfort.

The worth of a society depends on its leadership. Every civilization is identified with its elite (or "creative minority," as Arnold Toynbee called it), and the failure of the elite is invariably associated with decline. Both Rome and Britain were originally aristocracies, and the decline of the leading classes contributed to the diminished vitality of their societies. In both cases, when the creative minority lost its vigor, the state came to be managed by bureaucrats and functionaries, who lacked the sense of *noblesse oblige* that separates a true leading class from a group of more or less competent nonentities. The United States has never had a hereditary aristocracy. It once had a leading landowning and commercial class that held values similar to those of the English establishment, but (as was the case in England) political, economic, and cultural change have reduced this group to social insignificance. In the late nineteenth and early twentieth centuries, America's elites were drawn from the business, financial, and professional middle classes. The nineteenth and early twentieth century bourgeois establishment, which was successful in sustaining a robust and patriotic nation, has now been largely superseded by a diffuse, mobile, pseudo-intellectual, rootless, media-driven elite that seeks wealth and power while undermining the traditional structures of order that constrain and civilize power. The present system encourages ambitious people to seek wealth without civic responsibility. Corporate leadership is passing from owners and entrepreneurs to experts in finance or law and techno-bureaucrats. The politically correct print and television news and entertainment media disparage such traditional values as individualism, self-reliance, and religion. Political leadership, with a few notable exceptions, has devolved upon professional politicians who spend their lives running for office and have a vested interest in big and expensive government. There is, in fact, no longer a civic establishment worthy of the name. In the absence of such an establishment, there is no social force left to promote honor, patriotism, manners, culture, discipline, thrift, and other traditional civic virtues. If enough of America's so-called leaders turn against its culture and principles, the country will not survive.

The key to more effective leadership is a sound humanistic education which teaches the basic arts and sciences as well as the rudiments of honor, duty, and civic pride. Secondary schools, colleges, and professional schools must play a central part in teaching the history, philosophy, and ethics needed to broaden the perspective of future leaders beyond the profit motive. This will require a more selective educational system that separates students based on ability at various stages in their careers, while giving everyone the basic education needed to cope with modern life. The aim would be to create a relatively accessible leadership class, open to people from every economic and social group, whose members would be expected to rise above narrow material interests.

Political and Legal Institutions

Aristotle argued that freedom is a principle feature of democracy, but this does not mean that everyone does whatever he pleases. Men are the beneficiaries of rights but also the bearers of duties and are subject to restraints under the rule of law.[3] Political institutions should protect individual rights but must also enforce obligations. A nation's worth is reflected in the legal and political institutions it chooses, and observation of the body politic often reveals the strengths or weaknesses of the society as a whole. In their emerging period as great powers, Rome and Britain were cohesive societies in which government power was limited and balanced by other social forces. The essential purpose of government was to fight wars, keep order, protect property, maintain commerce, and promote the traditional religion. As it turned out, constitutional arrangements in Britain were favorable to individual liberty; and the British people and their American successors developed constitutional structures that protected liberty. As we saw in Chapter 8 on government, Thomas Jefferson captured the philosophy of limited government when he called for "a wise and frugal government, which shall restrain men from injuring one another, shall leave them otherwise free to regulate their own pursuits of industry and improvement, and shall not take from the mouth of labor the bread it has earned."

The American republic as presently constituted bears a formal resemblance to Jefferson's United States, but in substance, it is radically different. During the course of more than two centuries, Americans have permitted the federal government to appropriate many of the rights originally reserved to the states and to the people, resulting in a massive, overcentralized political structure whose salient features are uncontrollable spending, enormous debt, a tyrannical and opaque tax

---

3   Aristotle, *Politics,* Book V, Ch. 9, 1310a.

structure, diminishing civil liberties, and intrusive federal intervention in education, health, welfare, crime control, and other areas previously left to states and local communities. Much of what government does has been handed over to administrative agencies and thus removed from any real and effective control by the citizens. The independence of the citizenry has been further subverted by reducing a large portion of the population to dependence on government programs. Mass democracy, liberated from constitutional limitations, enables voters to demand ever-increasing subsidies, which are willingly supplied by a class of permanent politicians.

It is characteristic of our age that the rapid growth of government has been accompanied by the prevalence of an extreme form of hedonistic individualism. This is an apparent paradox, but in fact the two trends are not only consistent but mutually reinforcing. Government subsidies encourage people to abandon thrift because the government will supposedly take care of them in the end. Modern governments deprive the citizens of their economic liberty through taxation and regulation, while appeasing them with subsidies and permitting and even encouraging promiscuity, license, and pornography in the name of "personal autonomy." This trade-off appears to satisfy the populace, but it is not true liberty, which requires, as Edmund Burke argued, placing chains on the appetite. The citizen's principal goal, too often, is material gratification, and his principal civic duty becomes the negative one of paying taxes to a remote entity over which he has little or no influence.

The picture is familiar to students of the Roman Empire. A giant and cumbersome governmental structure employs a growing army of bureaucrats and lawyers to interpret a mass of unintelligible regulations but has limited ability to control the restless internal dependents, whom it pacifies temporarily with handouts and entertainment. The decline and fall of the former Soviet Union and the corruption of its Russian successor also may serve as a warning: more government does not mean more stability. When government ceases to fulfill its first priority of protecting liberty and property and instead becomes a burden rather than a benefit to the citizens, the constitutional structure is in danger. While the United States has not yet reached the condition of fourth-century Rome or the Soviet Union of the 1980s, the signs of government overload are clearly present.

The fact that the present political arrangement apparently represents the choice of the majority will not save the system from decay. As Polybius warned, a wealthy commonwealth that prides itself on its democracy is in danger of internal decay when the citizens adopt an increasingly extravagant and undisciplined manner of life, demand greater benefits for themselves, and abandon the strictures of duty and honor. While such a constitution may have the name of democracy, there is a risk that "it will become that worst of all governments, mob rule."[4] The price of liberty, as always, is eternal vigilance. Americans should, from their earliest years, be taught civic virtue and the principles of the American founding. This should not be difficult since these principles are readily accessible. All that is needed is self-discipline and persistence. Our founders had these qualities, and we can recover them.

Unity, Patriotism, and National Confidence

Confidence is based on unity, loyalty and trust; it grows along with sound institutions and effective leadership. Nations on the rise exhibit an aggressive spirit and a deep patriotism, usually connected with strongly held religious views. Rome and England, in the early centuries of their development, showed all of these characteristics—as did the rising nation-states of early modern Europe. The citizens of a declining society, on the other hand, lack confidence in themselves; they are pulled apart by divisions and distrust, and they value security over risk-taking.

The historical record seems to show that Ibn Khaldun's dialectic of success and failure is difficult to avoid. The rising nation over-expands and takes on excessive commitments. The leaders as well as the followers

---

4   *Polybius on Roman Imperialism* (Washington, DC: Regnery Gateway, 1987), p. 218.

eventually are corrupted by wealth or power and neglect the frugal practices that brought them success. Sooner or later the society forgets its past, lives for the present, and lacks faith in the future. This lack of confidence has been reflected historically in a decline in the birth rate of the leading social classes, a phenomenon that characterizes every Western industrialized nation of the early twenty-first century as well as some advanced non-Western countries like Japan and is perhaps the best evidence we have of objective decadence. Aging populations can be supported only by heavy immigration, whose social and cultural consequences may not be benign. We have emphasized the drastic burden that Social Security, Medicare, and similar subsidies to the nonproductive will place on the productive classes.

The United States has, for the most part, avoided the most damaging effects of declining confidence. Its corporations continue to dominate the global business world (though this dominance is beginning to erode), its military forces have performed more than adequately in recent wars, and its scientific and technological capabilities are superior. Yet there is evidence of serious instability. Rates of divorce, illegitimacy, and abortion are at historically high levels. The most basic of human institutions—the family—is in decline. The use of therapeutic drugs and dangerous illegal substances among all classes of the population indicates a widespread social pathology. Americans are increasingly given to complaining, risk shifting, and blaming others for their problems. The public educational system does not provide an adequate education. Ethnic, linguistic, and political divisions are sharpening as America divides itself into demanding and conflicting groups. While America's population (unlike that of most Western European nations) continues to increase, one-third or more of all births are illegitimate, while a considerable part of the increase is attributable to large-scale immigration, much of it illegal, bringing in large numbers of non-English-speaking laborers to take jobs from American citizens. The financial crisis of 2007–2008 failed to restore a sense of fiscal responsibility to our political leaders. These are not good signs.

The test of America's confidence and its capacities will be the reaction of its affluent and cosseted population to a serious crisis. Such a crisis emerged as a result of the terrorist attacks of 2001, which to some extent stimulated national unity and patriotism. This crisis, together with the results of the recent Afghan and Iraqi wars, may cause the United States to reconsider some of the policies that have led it into excessive and dangerous commitments. Yet the country is seriously divided. The nation's new elites, represented most prominently by the news media and prominent intellectuals, no longer support the virtues of duty, honor, and country. The contrary effects of luxury, indiscipline, and "presentism" are deeply rooted.

Final Observations on National Rise and Decline
The signals early in the twenty-first century are mixed. The United States is the world's greatest military and commercial power. Its relatively free economic system permits people with ambition and skill to improve material life for themselves and their families. The standard of living of our citizens is among the highest in history. Americans are capable of great generosity and expend billions of private and public dollars annually on assistance to other people.

The signs of decay, on the other hand, are present. The great attraction of America historically was that anyone could come here and "make it" on his own; but now, increasingly, people and companies ask to be "bailed out" by government. Dependency on government welfare programs is growing. Divorce, illegitimacy, taxes, and addiction have impaired the basic institution of the family. There is a general decline of authority and discipline in the society: parents and teachers, for example, have lost much of their authority over children. The power of local communities to enforce the shared values of ordinary civility has suffered as a result of weakened standards, mobility, social breakdown, and TV-induced inertia. Large sections of America's cities are terrorized by criminals. Elected "leaders" are in fact followers, responding to political pressures and buying votes through subsidization of favored interest groups. The educational system fails to educate the children entrusted to it by a naive and apathetic public. Many American universities are dominated by teachers who oppose the basic values of the society that sustains them. The mass popular culture has deteriorated to a level of cheapness and vulgarity scarcely imaginable a century ago.

These features of American society reflect a shift of values away from the classic individualism of free citizens, acting with entrepreneurial zeal, thrift, and self-discipline; and toward hedonism and a sense of entitlement. This is a basic moral problem that government intervention only exacerbates by diluting personal responsibility still further. The "culture of narcissism" (identified by Christopher Lasch) is the culmination of a long flight from the classical concepts of reason, order, being, and substance to the evanescent categories of subjectivity and personal authenticity. These psychological and philosophical trends, over time, will erode and finally extinguish the civic values that hold any society together.

This book has set forth certain indicators of decline in American society and culture, as well as some countervailing indicia of continued vitality. I will end by briefly repeating certain practical steps, already suggested in previous chapters, that could be taken to overcome these weaknesses and to reinforce the positive values that still flourish within our nation. These steps include:

- creating a superior educational system, based on the core values of Western civilization, emphasizing character, morality, and knowledge of history, featuring higher standards and tougher discipline, and combined with vocational training that will provide every high school graduate who enters the work force with practical job skills;

- building up the nation's military to defend against a series of likely threats, including terrorism, ballistic missiles, cyberwarfare, and predatory national aggressors;

- a more effective system of crime prevention, including swift and certain punishment for criminals, community-based policing, reeducation for young offenders, and a much higher budgetary priority for criminal justice;

- reduce the tax and regulatory burdens that stifle the energies and talents of the American people;

- free future generations from the crushing national debt that is the product of fiscal irresponsibility; and

- a return of political power to the states and local communities.

We must recognize, however, that these and other practical reforms will not happen in the absence of a return to fundamental principles of civic and moral responsibility. Western man's attachment to technology and material progress has become so strong that Western civilization no longer rests on a spiritual foundation. We have forgotten that man's spirituality is at the heart of his existence and is the source of his freedom. The successes of technology have led us to believe that society and human nature itself are scientifically controllable. But this is an illusion. The health of the spirit depends on its relation to truth and goodness, not upon doctrines of utility or welfare. Having power over nature is not enough. Man, as Romano Guardini says, is a "regent," holding power in trust and acting in fulfillment of his God-given assignment to rule over the earth as part of an order in which he is only a participant.[5]

The essence of the dilemma in the practical realm lies in the difficulty of balancing individualism against community and rights against duties. As a free people, we properly favor individual liberty and self-realization. On the other hand, the society needs cohesive communities with shared values in which civility, honor, and self-discipline can be sustained. The reinvigoration of community will require a rediscovery

---

5   Romano Guardini, *The End of the Modern World* (Intercollegiate Studies Institute, 1998 [1956]), p. 199.

of the sources of the values and intermediate institutions necessary to sustain civic life. The prerequisites for the success of such institutions are political decentralization and a revived sense of civic obligation.

The enforcement of community values also implies the existence of true social leadership. At the same time, to avoid stagnation and dangerous resentment, those at the bottom of the hierarchy must have a real opportunity to advance. This in turn requires much better education and a reduction of economic barriers. Free social mobility, admittedly, tends to work against the traditional values that support stable communities. This is a contradiction that can never be resolved in a free society but can only be adjusted over time in the ebb and flow of social movements. At present, the adjustment has gotten out of balance. We have made the wrong choice by attempting to enforce an artificial and abstract form of community through centralized government, while permitting true communities (which are based on personal responsibility and not on government edict) to disintegrate. Communities can be restored only by the free choice of those who live in them. A minimum condition is that the majority in each community be free to suppress vicious conduct—that is, to make value judgments and enforce them. A further condition of the restoration of community is rediscovery of the spiritual sources of moral order. The extent to which these goals can be achieved before the society is fractured beyond repair will determine the future of the American republic.

INDEX